Memory *and* Mind

Gordon H. Bower Festschrift. May, 2005. Jordan Hall, Stanford University.

FIFTH ROW: John Gabrieli, Irv Biederman, Richard Shiffrin, Brian Ross, Steve Sloman, Larry Barsalou

FOURTH ROW: Claude Steele, Anders Ericsson, Herman Buschke, Perry Thorndike, Arnie Glass, Herb Clark, Gary Olson, Eric Eich, Trey Hedden, Keith Holyoak, Stephen Kosslyn, Anthony Wagner, Anthony Wright

THIRD ROW: John Black, David Spiegal, John Anderson, Michael Conant, Mike Rink, Eni Becker, Judy Olson, Art Graesser, John Clapper, Bob Bjork, Teal Eich, Dan Morrow, George Wolford.

SECOND ROW: David Shanks, Beth Loftus, Barbara Tversky, Chizuko Izawa, Mark Gluck, Ian Gotlib, Roger Shepard, Elizabeth Marsh, Elizabeth Bjork, Laura Carstensen, Bob Zajonc

FRONT ROW: Sharon Bower, Bill Estes, Gordon Bower, Karl Pribram, Lera Boroditsky

Memory *and* Mind

A Festschrift for Gordon H. Bower

Edited by

Mark A. Gluck

John R. Anderson

Stephen M. Kosslyn

Ψ Psychology Press
Taylor & Francis Group

LONDON AND NEW YORK

First published 2008 by
Lawrence Erlbaum Associates, Inc.

Published 2014 by Psychology Press
27 Church Road, Hove, East Sussex, BN3 2FA
and by Psychology Press
711 Third Avenue, New York, NY 10017

First issued in paperback 2014

Psychology Press is an imprint of the Taylor & Francis Group, an informa business

© 2008 by Taylor & Francis Group, LLC

International Standard Book Number-13: 978-0-8058-6344-4 (Hardcover)

Library of Congress Cataloging-in-Publication Data

Memory and mind : a festschrift for Gordon H. Bower / editors, Mark A. Gluck, John R. Anderson, and Steven M. Kosslyn.
    p. cm.
Includes bibliographical references and index.
ISBN 978-0-80586-344-4 (hbk)
ISBN 978-1-13800-429-0 (pbk)
    1. Memory. 2. Cognition. 3. Psychology. I. Bower, Gordon H. II. Gluck, Mark A. III. Anderson, John R. (John Robert), 1947- IV. Kosslyn, Stephen Michael, 1948-

BF371.M44825 2008
153--dc22   2007031289

Contents

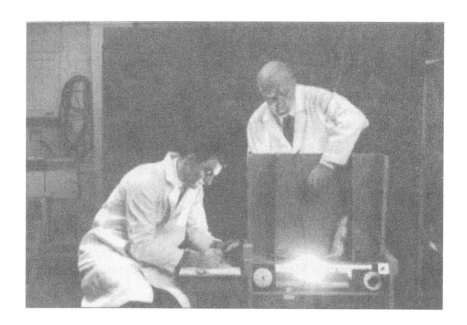

Gordon with his graduate mentor, Neal Miller, testing a rat with a dual reward-punishment electrode: these animals would press a lever (see the left side of the cage) to turn on the brain stimulation, then as it continued, rotate a wheel (right side) to turn it off. They would perform this on-then-off cycle until all concerned (except the rats) wearied of it. Photo taken circa 1956; these experiments were the basis for Gordon's first talk at the APA and his first co-authored publication with Miller: Bower, G. H., & Miller, N. (1958). Rewarding and punishing effects from stimulating the same place in the rat's brain. *Journal of Comparative and Physiological Psychology, 51,* 669–674.

Preface

Gordon H. Bower was born in 1932 in Scio, Ohio, a small Midwestern town of less than 1,000 residents struggling at that time to survive the Great Depression. Inspired by the movie, *The Lou Gehrig Story,* Gordon resolved at the age of 8 to become a professional baseball player. By 11, he was good enough (and big enough) to play on local semiprofessional baseball teams. Although tempted by an offer to enter professional baseball with the Cleveland Indians' farm system, Gordon instead decided to attend Western Reserve University (now Case-Western Reserve) where he played on their varsity baseball team. Considering a possible career in psychiatry, he took a job at the Cleveland State Mental Hospital in the summer of 1951 where he encountered the primitive state of psychiatric medicine, an experience that dissuaded him from pursuing that career. However, his interest in understanding mental disorders was undiminished, and at the end of that summer's experience Gordon returned to college with a new desire to pursue basic psychological research.

Graduating in 1954, Gordon had two career choices: professional baseball or graduate school in psychology. Although tempted by the former, Gordon figured that he had a better chance of long-term success in psychology than in baseball. After a year spent learning mathematics and statistics at the University of Minnesota, Gordon entered the Ph.D. program at Yale in the fall of 1955. There he became caught up in the heady excitement of the early days of mathematical psychology. He was especially captivated by Estes's work on statistical learning theory as well as a recent book by two other leading mathematical psychologists, Robert Bush and Frederick Mosteller, entitled *Stochastic Models for Learning* (1955). While working with his Ph.D. adviser, Neal Miller, on electrical brain stimulation studies in rats, Gordon also studied mathematical psychology with Frank Logan who was, at that time, working on variations and extensions to Clark Hull's mathematical theories of learning.

In the summer of 1957, Gordon won an award to attend a workshop on mathematics in the social sciences at Stanford University. There he met W. K. (Bill) Estes. In the years to follow, Gordon would have a powerful influence on Bill's research (and vice versa). Bill offers a personal memoir of Gordon's research career and its context during the period 1957 to 2006 in chapter 1, "Gordon H. Bower: His Life and Times."

Gordon attended the then-famous summer school in mathematical psychology at Stanford University, where he met most of the luminaries in the field. So impressive was Gordon that he was offered a job at Stanford before even finishing his Ph.D. thesis at Yale, and, in 1959, Gordon moved to the Stanford Psychology Department—never having had to go through a formal interview! He was joined soon thereafter by Bill Estes and other mathematical psychologists. Trained as a behaviorist, Gordon established an extensive animal-conditioning laboratory, including Skinner boxes that he built with elaborate circuits cannibalized from discarded pinball machines acquired from the local junkyard. By the mid 1960s, however, Gordon's animal research was crowded out by his growing interest in mathematical models of human learning.

In 1963, Doug Hintzman was a 1st-year graduate student in the Stanford Psychology Department whose 1st-year project, developed in another lab, was not going well: His adviser unexpectedly decided to take a leave of absence, and a lab assistant plugged his DC circuitry into an AC outlet—thereby destroying the apparatus. Desperate for new start, Doug made an appointment to see Gordon and explained his situation. Gordon glowered at Doug, said he was too busy to hold the hand of a student who didn't know what he was interested in. However, to Doug's relief, Gordon's gruff exterior turned out to mask a sympathetic soul. They worked out a project to study the short-term recall of strings of digits and letters. As Doug's Ph.D. adviser, Gordon continued to provide Doug with a morale-boosting combination of independence, respect, and support. In chapter 2, "Memory From the Outside, Memory From the Inside," Doug speculates that Gordon's research success can be attributed largely to his ability to view cognition from two quite different but complementary perspectives: the reverse-engineering perspective of the formal modeler, and the first-person perspective of a self-aware cognitive system.

In September of 1964, Gordon traveled down the coast of California for a meeting of the *American Psychological Association* in Los Angeles. There, he heard Endel Tulving present the results of two experiments showing that repetition of material can lead to decrements in recall. At the end of the talk, a tall young man whom Endel had never seen before, sitting close to the front in the crowded lecture hall, stood up and in a booming voice announced to the audience that the talk they had just heard was balderdash and the results horsefeathers (or words to that effect). He backed up these assertions with astute observations and carefully considered arguments. After the session ended, the troublemaker trundled to the front of the hall and addressed himself: "I'm Gordon Bower." Endel knew the name, of course. "Everybody knew the name of the boy wonder of experimental psychology at that time," he recalls.

From those inauspicious beginnings, Endel and Gordon's relationship was all uphill. Before his sabbatical at Berkeley in 1964/1965 ended, Endel and his wife Ruth had visited Gordon and Sharon in Palo Alto, broken bread together, and formed the foundation for a friendship that has lasted to this day. As his friend, Tulving learned that behind Gordon's rough exterior and highly honed skill of intimidation lay "a soul as sweet as Mother Theresa's, a soul that he did not wish to reveal to many, for reasons that probably only Sharon and his analyst can fathom." Tulving's chapter 3, "On the Law of Primacy," does not have much to do with Gordon's past work, nor with Tulving's own. Rather, it contains a germ of an idea, whose appearance in this book Tulving hopes may not only honor Gordon but perhaps please him, as well.

A few years later, 1966, Elizabeth (Beth) Fishbein (soon to be Loftus) arrived at Stanford as a new graduate student in psychology. Beth didn't work with Gordon directly, but became closer to him later as their lives converged through professional organizations, and Gordon became a *de facto* mentor to her. In chapter 4, "Gordon and Me," Beth writes about how Gordon's career and hers have been intertwined, with examples of the times and places their paths crossed. Again and again, whenever she was at a difficult spot in her life, Gordon was there to back her up and encourage her. Today, Beth counts Gordon as among the most important influences on her career. The lesson here, she notes, is that a mentor doesn't have to be someone who chaired your thesis committee; others can, and do, play a significant role, as well.

As a new graduate student in 1967, Alan Lesgold first met Gordon following a luncheon for a departing departmental colleague. Walking back from lunch, Gordon spotted Alan, and introduced himself, asking, "Who the hell are you?" Alan soon became Gordon's graduate student, drawn in part by what he recalls as Gordon's "fundamental disposition to dig deeper into phenomena that seem of social importance." In chapter 5, "Toward Valued Human Expertise," Alan describes the forms of cognition that he hopes will distinguish people from machines in the future.

How does one best prepare to be a successful graduate in psychology? In the fall of 1968, Gordon's advice to one entering Stanford student, John Anderson, was straightforward: Take a speed-reading course. While a graduate student with Gordon, the two wrote a book, *Human Associative Memory* (HAM), that served as the intellectual thrust that determined the course of John's scientific life. The ACT theories that John has worked on for 30 years have their foundation in his early work on HAM at Stanford. Gordon, John recalls, was "always concerned with how to bring the rigor of science to applications of importance to society."

John's contribution to this volume, chapter 6, "The Algebraic Brain," describes how one cognitive science method (in particular, neuroimaging) contributes to our understanding of learning algebra.

Stephen Kosslyn will never forget the day he met Gordon Bower. All of the cognitive students and faculty met every Friday afternoon, and a graduate student presented his or her work. "I first saw Gordon at such a Friday seminar," remembers Steve. And continuing:

> Gordon had been overseas my first quarter of graduate school, and this was the first seminar he attended after I had become a student. I was sitting next to the speaker, who seemed unusually nervous. I noticed a line of sweat on his forehead, and he was clearly agitated. I couldn't understand why. Then I noticed that in spite of the fact that people were standing by the walls and sitting on the floor, the seat at the other end of the long table was empty; moreover, we were running late, but everyone was waiting. At that point a very large man, who looked remarkably like John Wayne, entered. He ambled to the empty chair, sat down, and said, "OK, we can begin." I wondered who he was. Within minutes he began asking extraordinarily insightful and blunt questions. He was very quick on the uptake, very confident, and unusually assertive. At one point he interrupted the speaker, and pounded his fist (the size of a ham, in my memory) on the table, creating a sine wave that propagated down to my end. Roberta (then known as Bobby) Klazky came to the rescue, with a trenchant rejoinder to Gordon's broadside. In fact, before Gordon was completely finished, Bobby (who then looked about 17) cut him off, and explained that there was another finding he was ignoring. Gordon listened carefully, head cocked to one side, nodded, and grumbled to a halt. I was in a state of semishock. Not only did I feel totally inadequate, having no idea what either of them were talking about, but I also was impressed by Gordon's ability to extrapolate and search for implications of empirical findings. But more than that, I was amazed that he did not mind being interrupted and corrected. Gordon clearly wanted to "get it right."

Months later, Steve got to experience the Bower Effect firsthand when he gave his own first Friday Seminar, describing his early work on mental imagery. A few days later, Gordon stopped Steve in the fourth-floor lounge of the psychology building, and they talked for over an hour. "I discovered that he wasn't simply critical," recalls Steve, "but very constructive, supportive and helpful." Gordon began showing up at Steve's office from time to time, giving him reprints and chatting. Steve soon realized that Gordon was someone he could count on to be on his side in the deepest sense. Soon thereafter, Steve switched advisors and began working with Gordon, a move he describes as "one of the best decisions I have ever made."

Kosslyn's extensive body of research on mental imagery, some of which is summarized in chapter 7, "Remembering Images," can all be traced back to a single sentence of a paper that Gordon wrote—a sentence that appeared in a preprint manuscript, but, for some unknown reason, was deleted in the published version. As Kosslyn recalls, the sentence said something like, "If visual mental images are like pictures, and can be scanned and so on, then … ." It was the bit on scanning that stuck in Steve's mind, and led to his first experiments on mental imagery.

In 1970, Barbara Tversky arrived at Stanford to do a 1-year postdoctoral fellowship with Gordon. He greeted her warmly, and promptly took off for London for the quarter. Having worked largely on her own during graduate school, Barbara assumed this was the norm for a postdoc–mentor relationship and dug into her own projects while Gordon was away. She returned to Stanford in 1977 as a visiting scholar and stayed on in various faculty roles during which time the two became colleagues, attended each other's lab meetings, shared a few students, co-taught a graduate course in cognition, and served on many dissertation committees together. Barbara says:

> I learned an enormous amount from him, not just psychology, but how to do psychology, how to interact with students and colleagues, how to contribute outside the university. Not that I always emulated him, he had his own style, but thinking about what he was accomplishing and how helped me set mine.

Barbara's chapter 8, "Sharing Landmarks and Paths," describes Gordon's and her comings and goings at Stanford, and ways in which their interests intersected on scientific topics, memory (especially recognition memory and imagery), spatial mental models, and events.

Arriving in 1971 as a new graduate student with Gordon, Arnie Glass soon came to view Gordon as more than just an adviser. When he got married 2 years later, and neither his nor his wife's family could make it to California for the nuptials, it was Gordon and Sharon who gave the young couple a wedding. Arnie remembers Gordon discussing his all-or-none learning model, including the objections that caused him to abandon it. "It seemed to me then that the model wasn't untestable in principle, as others assumed," notes Arnie, "but that no one had yet come up with a good way to test it." Arnie thought about this problem for about 25 years until he came up with a suitable experimental paradigm described here in chapter 9, "Evidence of All-or-None Learning From a Repetition Detection Task."

In 1972, the year after Glass arrived, Keith Holyoak entered the graduate program in psychology at Stanford. In his first quarter, Gordon assigned Keith a project on recognition memory for naturalistic sounds, which resulted in a quick publication in the Journal of Experimental Psychology. Keith recalls that Gordon did all the writing, and that the article was accepted on its first submission, without revision—an event never replicated in Keith's subsequent publishing career. While being mentored by Gordon, Keith worked with Arnie Glass to explore the field of semantic memory; his chapter 10, "Relations in Semantic Memory: Still Puzzling After All These Years," takes a retrospective look at what has been learned since the 1970s.

Also arriving in 1972 as a new graduate student seeking to work with Gordon was Robert (Bob) Sternberg. Bob remembers that "Gordon was a wonderful advisor because he left his students alone to pursue their own dreams, helping them when they wanted, but never interfering." In chapter 11, "Using Cognitive Theory to Reconceptualize College Admissions Testing," Bob describes his work on culture and abilities, an extension and broadening of his dissertation studies with Gordon on the nature of intelligence.

David Rosenbaum began his graduate studies with Gordon in 1973. From his 2nd year of graduate school onward, David chose to focus on the planning and control of physical movements, a topic far removed from Gordon's own interests. Nevertheless, Gordon supported David's foray into a different research domain. In later years, Gordon, the faithful and loyal advisor, always came to David's talks at Psychonomics as well as the talks of all his other former students, no matter how removed from his own interests those talks were. In chapter 12, "Moving Cognition," David summarizes his research on the planning and control of movements, especially hand and arm movements. Gordon's willingness to apply what he knew about cognition to Rosenbaum's nascent ideas about the control of physical action helped Rosenbaum see that cognitive psychological principles could be profitably applied to the problem of translating cognition into overt performance.

As an Army officer, John Black was stationed in 1972 at the now-closed Sacramento Army Depot, a few hours' drive from Stanford University. Having read papers by Gordon and Richard Atkinson (also at Stanford) while an undergraduate, John hoped to leave the Army and study mathematical psychology. As John recalls:

> I thought I wanted to work with Gordon, so I called him on the phone only to have him tell me that he wasn't there—this was my first contact with Gordon. He went on to say he was spending the year at the Center for Advanced Study writing a book with a former student (this turned out to be *Human Associative Memory* with John Anderson), and that I should talk to Dick Atkinson instead. I did talk to Dick and arranged to visit Stanford on a Friday, where I had my next contact with Gordon watching him rip to shreds a presentation by a Post-doc in the Friday Seminar. Perhaps perversely I found this appealing because I wanted to prove I could stand up to such criticism.

John soon became interested in story understanding, which was a hot topic at the time, but Atkinson discouraged his interests in story understanding and encouraged him to do memory-scanning experiments with word lists instead. A few days later, John ran into Gordon in the men's restroom, where Gordon said that he had heard John was interested in story understanding. Gordon was too, he told John, and so the two began a collaboration that produced many studies of story understanding during John's 4 years at Stanford. The research he did with Gordon on story understanding has provided the foundation on which John built his subsequent research on imaginary worlds and its application to technology and learning, work described in his chapter 13, "Imaginary Worlds."

Arriving in June of 1977, eager to get an early start on graduate school, Larry Barsalou asked Gordon for advice on how to be a successful graduate student. "It's 20% ability and 80% motivation," replied Gordon. Barsalou's chapter 14, "Continuing Themes in the Study of Human Knowledge: Associations, Imagery, Propositions, and Situations," demonstrates what Larry describes as a resonance that Gordon and he share, a tolerance and appreciation for multiple conflicting perspectives—as well as evidence of a lot of motivation!

A year later, in 1978, Brian Ross arrived at Stanford to work with Gordon. "Gordon's broad approach to cognition has been an encouragement in my trying to integrate category learning with the many areas of Psychology," notes Brian. In his chapter 15, "Category Learning: Learning to Access and Use Relevant Knowledge," Brian shows why categories are important by considering various types of goal-oriented category learning.

While at a conference in 1979, Eric Eich and a friend were chatting as they made their way across a crowded hotel lobby. Eric brushed by a very tall gentleman, who was speaking to someone else. Not recognizing him, Eric kept on walking and talking with his friend. He got about two or three steps when, behind him, he heard a booming voice say: "Well, so you're Eich? I know what you do. Get over here."

Eric doesn't remember much of what Gordon said: There was a dull ringing in his ears brought on by the realization that the speaker was none other than Gordon H. Bower and that he did indeed know something about Eric (a grad student with Endel Tulving at the University of Toronto at the time) and his work (on drugs and memory). But Eric does recall Gordon's discussing his recent studies of mood and memory, and speculating on how drug and mood effects might be related. These are, in fact, the central issues in Eric's chapter 16, "Revisiting the Idea of Mood Mediation in Drug-Dependent and Place-Dependent Memory."

Joe Forgas spent his first-ever sabbatical leave in 1980 at Stanford with Gordon. As a newcomer to the field, Gordon's theoretical approach guided their research, whereas Joe's interest in perceptual processes influenced what they actually ended up doing together. Joe returned several more times to Stanford on sabbatical visits, and Gordon and Sharon visited Joe in Australia several times as well, allowing Joe and Gordon to continue a collaboration for many years, resulting in several journal papers and review chapters together. Their joint work on the influence of mood on social judgments and behavior combined Gordon's interest in affect, from the point of view of a cognitive psychologist, with Joe's interest in social judgments and person perception, from the point of view of a social psychologist. This work is reviewed in Joe's chapter 17, "Affect, Cognition and Social Behavior: The Effects of Mood on Memory, Social Judgments and Social Interaction."

In 1982, Gordon turned 50 and to mark this occasion, John Anderson and Stephen Kosslyn organized Gordon's students to write chapters for a first Festshrift volume, which appeared as *Tutorials in Learning and Memory: Essays in Honor of Gordon Bower* (Anderson & Kosslyn, 1984). They gave Gordon early copies of the chapters, and soon thereafter, each of contributors received a long handwritten note from Gordon telling them how important it was for each of them to support each other and to attend to the human and social side of life even while they worked hard on their research. Of course, they also all received their drafts back, marked up with the detail and care that had characterized their earlier student relationships with Gordon. As Alan Lesgold recalls, "This combination of being supportive and caring combined with not being afraid to be helpful in both professional and personal ways was characteristic of Gordon."

In the fall of 1982, Mark Gluck arrived at Stanford as a 1st-year graduate student. As an undergraduate at Harvard, Mark had worked with two members of the extended Bower circle: Gordon's former graduate student Steve Kosslyn and his former Stanford colleague, Bill Estes. Not surprisingly, both Kosslyn and Estes encouraged Mark to apply to Stanford to do a Ph.D. with Gordon. Mark and Gordon's first phone conversation got off to a bad start when Mark admitted to Gordon that not only had he never been to a baseball game, but he had no interest in the sport at all.

Gordon was away on sabbatical when Mark arrived at Stanford in the fall of 1982, and Mark began working with Amos Tversky and Roger Shepard. During this year, Mark was frequently regaled by students and faculty with "Gordon Stories" until, in Mark's expectation, Gordon must surely be 10 feet tall, broad as a linebacker, and tough as an ironworker. A year later, Gordon returned from sabbatical and the two met for the first time. "Young man," said Gordon as they passed in the hallway of Jordan Hall, "you're flying at half-mast," as Gordon pointed to Mark's semiopen pant zipper.

With an interest in mathematical models of category learning that had developed during his work with Kosslyn and Estes, Mark continued to pursue this topic at Stanford as well. A chance encounter with another professor in the Psychology Department, Richard Thompson, introduced Mark to neuroscience. Through this side project with Thompson, Mark developed an appreciation and admiration for the elegance, simplicity, and power of Rescorla and Wagner's (1972) mathematical model of animal conditioning. Taking advantage of the new paradigm of connectionist neural-network models that Mark had learned about while working with Estes at Harvard, Mark proposed to Gordon that they use connectionist network models as a framework for applying the Rescorla–Wagner model to human category learning. This work with Gordon, and its influence on Mark's later work in cognitive neuroscience, is described in his chapter 18, "Behavioral and Neural Correlates of Error-Correction in Classical Conditioning and Human Category Learning."

In 1983, Gordon was on sabbatical at Carnegie-Mellon University (CMU) in Pittsburgh where he met John Clapper, a visiting prospective graduate applicant who had already been accepted to both CMU and Stanford. Meeting Gordon convinced John that he wanted to go to Stanford and work with Gordon. John was Gordon's Ph.D. student from 1983 to 1988, and then continued working with Gordon as a research associate (with Air Force funding) until 1993. John then left academia for several years to work in the nonprofit sector but never lost his interest in cognitive psychology. He began to teach on a part-time basis at Humboldt State University in 1997, and soon had a small research program back up and running. He found himself reinfected with the cognitive psychology "bug" and—with Gordon's support and encouragement—decided to return to academia on a full-time basis. John's chapter 19, "Category Learning as Schema Induction," is a summary of some of the early work he carried out with Gordon and a description of the directions he has taken since reentering the field.

Evan Heit arrived at Stanford in 1986 to work with Gordon as a graduate student. His chapter 20, "Categorization, Recognition, and Unsupervised Learning," offers a window into what was happening in Gordon's lab in the late 1980s and early 1990s, as well as how these ideas transmogrified 10 years later and 5,000 miles away in Evan's lab in England.

"So what do you know about connectionism?" asked Gordon (in lieu of any standard form of greeting) when Steven Sloman poked his head into Gordon office for the first time in 1986. Connectionism was then an up-and-coming approach to cognitive theorizing, and Gordon always made sure that he and his students were abreast of the latest movements in the field. Steven's chapter 21, "Updating Beliefs With Causal Models: Violations of Screening Off," investigates the viability of a Markov model of human reasoning, a type of mathematical model that Gordon helped bring to psychology over 40 years ago.

In spite of the fact that Gordon was deeply involved with this students' research (and typically, their lives), he found time to travel widely. While giving a talk at Marburg University, Germany, in 1987, Gordon met Mike Rinck, who later came to work with Gordon as a postdoctoral fellow in 1991. This led to a 10-year collaboration that continued long after Mike had returned to Germany. In the final chapter of this volume, chapter 22, "Spatial Situation Models and Narrative Comprehension," Mike describes one of Gordon's later research interests—mental models and text comprehension.

As the preceding narrative makes clear, Gordon—throughout his career—would identify a critical unsolved problem, make seminal contributions that established a new area of research, attract many other people to this new fertile domain, and then move on to do it all over again in some completely different area of learning and memory research. As noted earlier (and described in more detail in the chapters to follow), some of the vexing problems that Gordon addressed include: How do people reorganize memory during learning? How do mnemonic devices work? How does hypnosis affect memory? What role does mental imagery play in memory? How do we understand and remember simple narratives? How does our mood influence what we learn and remember? How do principles of animal conditioning apply to human category learning?

Gordon's considerable influence on the field of memory research stems not only from his own research but also from his role as a prolific educator and mentor to young psychologists—including the authors of the chapters that follow—many of whom went on after their training with Gordon to play major roles in the growing field of cognitive psychology. The breadth of Gordon's reach can also be seen in the diverse (and almost contradictory) spectrum of journals on whose editorial boards he served, including the leading journals of both Skinnerian behaviorism and the opposing cognitive psychology movement, and ranging from the most applied areas of clinical psychology to the most abstract realms of theory.

Gordon never fulfilled his early dream of pitching a no-hitter at Yankee Stadium; he spent his entire professional career at Stanford University where he retired in 2005. However, in his chosen career of psychology, where he went up to bat time after time against a broad and diverse lineup of the most challenging problems in learning and memory, Gordon hit a string of home runs worthy of his childhood idol, Lou Gehrig.

Gordon H. Bower: His Life and Times

W. K. Estes
Indiana University

My contribution to the celebration of Gordon Bower's 75th birthday by means of this volume is this memoir on his research career and its context. I plan not to dwell on reminiscences (although, see Box), but, rather, to look forward, seeking to detect trends dating from the mid-1900s that will lead to the events of the 2000s. Because of the incredible scope of Gordon Bower's contributions to psychology, the task calls for what is now popularly known as a team approach, and I concentrate on two issues that motivated much of the theoretically oriented research on learning, broadly defined, during the 1900s—

Is a theory of human learning possible?

How many kinds of learning exist?

and the role of Gordon Bower in progressing toward their resolution. I conclude with a characterization of his influence on a large, and still growing, network of investigators.

IS A THEORY OF HUMAN LEARNING POSSIBLE?

The answer to this question may seem obvious to sophisticates of the present era, although the same was far from the case when I was introduced to psychology in the 1940s, as represented (imaginatively) in Figure 1–1. Frequencies of plotted points in the four quadrants of Figure 1–1 index my impressions of the relative sizes of the existing literatures of the four kinds as of 1950 and sizes of the entries reflect the contributions of individual investigators. Awareness of the blank cell in the lower left quadrant of Figure 1–1 by a young investigator with a theoretical bent appeared to confine him to a career of studying rats in mazes or Skinner boxes.

Learning theory was a hot topic, but it was the learning theory of an almost closed aristocracy. The leaders were the senior "classical" systematists: Guthrie (1940, 1942), Hull (1937, 1943), Skinner, 1938, and Tolman (1932, 1951). The empirical basis was entirely derived from research on lower animals.

In sharp contrast, the psychology of human learning was a search for empirical generalizations without reference to classical learning theory. The search was typified by the decades-long series of contributions on conditions of learning and forgetting by L. Postman (Postman, 1962, 1976) and B. J. Underwood (1957, 1964). The spirit of this period was epitomized and the body of accumulated facts

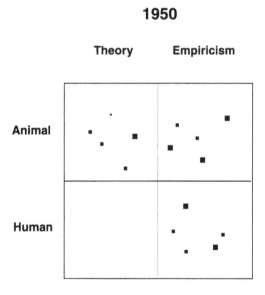

Figure 1–1.   State of human versus animal learning theory in 1950. Cell entries represent investigators, contributions being roughly proportional to magnitudes.

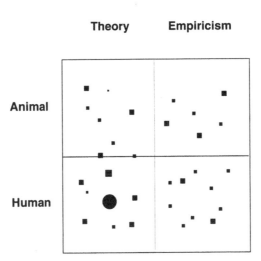

Figure 1–2. State of human versus animal learning theory in 2005, the largest entry representing the contributions of Gordon Bower.

about human learning was summarized in its leading textbook (McGeoch, 1942; McGeoch & Irion, 1952).

The overall theoretical landscape illustrated in Figure 1–1 was drastically changed within a relatively few years to that in Figure 1–2 largely by the efforts of Gordon Bower and his associates.the largest entry representing the contributions of Gordon Bower.

In the mid-1900s, theories of human learning with any semblance of formal structure had yet to appear; hence the vacant lower left-hand quadrant in Figure 1–1. But by the early 2000s, the formerly empty quadrant contained many new entries, revolving around the very large one (representing Gordon Bower, of course) like planets around the sun (Fig. 1–2). One of the larger "planets" signifies the appearance of the first textbook of mathematical learning theory, Atkinson, Bower, and Crothers's An Introduction to Mathematical Learning Theory (1965), henceforth ABC. Among Bower's contributions to ABC, he produced striking examples of mathematical learning theory applied to data obtained from human subjects. One, drawn from work presented in Bower (1961), is a demonstration of the seemingly endless aspects of a set of data that can be predicted by a simple mathematical model with a single free parameter. The experiment was on paired-associate learning with the standard anticipation procedure. Stimuli were common English words and the responses were digits, for example, fox–3. Training was given to a criterion of correct responding. The single parameter c, probability of learning on any precriterion trial, was estimated by the formula

$$\text{mean total errors} = (1 - 1/N)/c,$$

where N denotes number of observations entering into the mean. All of the remaining entries in Table 1–1 (and many more) were predicted by the model.

Table 1–1

Predictions of Performance by a Model
(Shades of ABC; Credit to Gordon Bower)

Statistic	Observed	Predicted
Total errors		
M	1.45	—
SD	1.37	1.74
Errors before 1st success		
M	.78	.75
SD	1.08	.98
Trial of last error		
M	2.33	2.18
SD	2.47	2.40
Number of error runs	.97	.97
Alternations	1.43	1.45

Note.   ABC = Atkinson, Bower, and Crothers (1965)

These findings were amplified and extended by Bower (1961, 1962, 1967) and Trabasso and Bower (1964).

Once the wall between experimental analysis and formal theory of human learning had been breached by Bower and his associates, it appeared that every experimenter was ready to take on also the role of theorist. Thus some of the "planets" in the lower left quadrant of Figure 1–2 represent combinations of experimental research and theory on attention in learning (Kruschke, 1992; Restle, 1955; Trabasso & Bower, 1968), probability learning (Estes 1964; Myers, 1976), and categorization (Estes, 1986; Medin & Schaffer, 1978; Nosofsky, 1984).

Two of the "planets" in the left-hand quadrants of Figure 1–2 deserve closer attention because of a special relationship. The one in the upper left represents the most broadly influential quantitative model of animal conditioning and learning from the early 1970s to the present, that of Rescorla and Wagner (1972). The counterpart in the lower left dropped in out of the blue in the late 1980s; it represents a strikingly successful application of the formal conditioning mechanism of Rescorla and Wagner (1972) to human category learning by Gluck and Bower (1988a, 1998b).

The significance of this development lies in its implications for themes that may play leading roles in the 2000s. The stage was set for these by findings of Knowlton, Squire, and Gluck (1994) that effects of hippocampal damage appear only late in learning of a categorization task by amnesic patients. A follow-up by Gluck, Oliver, and Myers (1996) showed that this late-training deficit is predictable by Gluck and Myers's (1993) interpretation of hippocampal function. Thus it appears that models arising in the work of Gordon Bower and his associates are having continuing and perhaps expanding roles in the research of the 2000s as they are applied with close attention to stages of learning in both animal and human subjects, to differences between patient populations, and to connections of psychological with neural theory.

HOW MANY KINDS OF LEARNING?

This question was first raised in a research context by Edward L. Thorndike in his distinction between "associative shifting" and "trial-and-error learning" (Thorndike, 1913), but interest among psychologists of learning lapsed until revived in a new theoretical framework by Hilgard and Marquis (1940). Cutting across research and theory on animal and human learning, this question was undoubtedly the one most widely debated in the literature of some four decades from the appearance of the first formal single-factor theory (Hull, 1937, 1943) to the sweeping review by Bower and Hilgard (1981).

The preoccupation with kinds of learning appears to have originated as a reaction to Clark L. Hull's strenuous development and defense of what seemed to most of his contemporaries as a radical proposal: Despite almost unlimited variety in empirical "laws" and minitheories of learning, all could, in principle, be derived from a single unified set of axioms, which he explicated in Hull (1943). The modal view of other theorists of learning for a period of some 40 years following Hull's proposal was a consensus on two basic kinds of learning (Bower and Hilgard, 1981).

The two kinds have been defined in different ways, but I limit consideration to grouping by (a) experimental procedures and associated empirical phenomena; (b) underlying cognitive processes; and (c) neural bases or correlates of learning:

1. Grouping by procedures and phenomena was first treated systematically by Hilgard and Marquis (1940), whose review has been successively updated and amplified by Kimble (1961) and Bower and Hilgard (1981). A condensed

summary abstracted from these reviews that illustrates the major prevailing theme is given in Table 1–2. Bower and Hilgard seemed to view choice among these binary categorizations as largely a matter of convenience and, in fact, at the conclusion of their review expressed sympathy for Hull's perspective (see also Perkins, 1955; Terrace, 1973).

Table 1–2
Dichotomies of Learning, "The Standard Theory" after Kimble (1961)

Authors	First Type	Second Type
Hilgard & Marquis, 1940	Classical	Instrumental
Konorski & Miller, 1937	Type I	Type II
Mowrer, 1956	Conditioning	Problem Solving
Schlosberg, 1937	Conditioning	Success learning
Skinner, 1937	Respondent	Operant

2. Grouping of kinds of learning associated with inferred underlying processes is well illustrated by the work of Gordon Bower and his associates in the 1960s. As was detailed in a preceding section, Gordon Bower's first published presentation of a model for paired-associate learning surprised many of his contemporaries with the assumption that such learning proceeds by abrupt all-or-none (henceforth A-O-N) jumps between unlearned and learned states. An assumption with a very long tradition in learning theory was that, in contrast, simple learning should be represented as a growthlike process in which a learner proceeds from an unlearned to a learned state by small, progressive increments (Bush & Mosteller, 1955; Hull, 1943).

In Table 1–3, I compare predictions of paired-associate data by Bower's single-parameter A-O-N model with predictions by a single-parameter incremental model—the "linear model" of Bush and Mosteller (1955), based on analyses presented in ABC, chapter 3. These results, strongly favoring the A-O-N model, are typical of many accumulated by Bower and his associates that point up the fruitfulness of recognizing A-O-N and incremental learning as two basic kinds of learning, defined at the level of underlying processes.

3. Grouping related to neural factors is a tactic initiated by the neuroscientist D. O. Hebb (1949). On the basis of his theory of cell assemblies together with research on both animal and human, infant and adult, and, within the human category, clinical and nonclinical subjects (drawing heavily on the exhaustive review by Senden, 1932), Hebb supported a binary grouping:

Table 1–3
Comparison of Models with A-O-N versus Incremental Learning Processes
(Credit to Gordon Bower)

Statistic	Data	A-O-N	Incremental
Total errors			
M	1.45	—	—
SD	1.37	1.63	1.00
Errors before 1st success			
M	.78	.75	.70
Trial of last error			
M	2.33	2.18	3.08
SD	2.47	2.40	3.39
Number of error runs	.97	.97	1.16
Alternations	1.43	1.45	1.83

Note. A-O-N = All or None

"There are two kinds of learning. One is that of the newborn infant or the visual learning of the adult reared in darkness or with congenital cataract; the other that of the normal adult" (p. 000).

The former kind Hebb conceived as essentially a growth process; the latter a typically abrupt reorganization of cell assemblies produced by earlier learning. Clearly, this categorization corresponds closely to Bower's categorization in terms of A-O-N versus incremental learning.

The story of this correspondence does not end here. In a much more recent study, by Wolford, Miller, and Gazzaniga (2000), split-brain patients were studied in a form of simple associative learning known as "probability learning." The special feature was that each patient was engaged simultaneously in two tasks that differed only with respect to the particular stimuli used, but with stimuli for one task directed to the patient's left cortical hemisphere and the other to the right hemisphere. Results for the left and right brains conformed to the investigators' expectations on the premise that the left brains were engaged in a variant of A-O-N learning whereas the right brains were employing a form of incremental learning. A suggestion (awaiting testing by continuing research) is that A-O-N and incremental learning are not necessarily kinds of learning that characterize different individuals, but that they may occur concurrently in normal, adult humans, competing for control of motor output in a decision process that remains to be explicated.

GORDON BOWER AT THE CENTER
OF A SOCIAL NETWORK

To this point, I have concentrated on Gordon Bower, the research scientist. Now I turn to his sphere of influence in the contemporary realm of human learning and memory, beyond that of a master role model. As a preliminary, however, to lighten the inevitably scholastic tenor of this review, I insert a sketch of "Gordon Bower: the individual" based on my interactions with Gordon over a period of nearly 50 years.

I suppose I am leading off this parade of Gordon Bower's well-wishers because I have known him longer than anyone here—except Sharon, of course. It seems to me that I have always known Gordon, but that's an exaggeration. To the best of my recollection, our paths first intersected in the early summer of 1957. I was participating in a summer workshop on mathematics in the social sciences held at Stanford University and Gordon, then a graduate student at Yale, had won an award to come as a student observer.

Gordon was not cut out for the role of passive observer, however. When first we met at the workshop, I was greeted with "Hello Dr. E., I have a couple of results I'd like to show you." One of these was a demonstration of how elements of my stimulus sampling theory and the "behavior system" of one of his much more famous mentors at Yale, Clark L. Hull, could be combined to give an elegant account of serial learning. The other was a novel but nicely crafted model for decision at a choice point. The latter was a forerunner of the dominant class of information-acquisition models of the 1990's, and both were developed during the summer into chapters of the conference proceedings, published in book form by Stanford University Press under the editorship of Robert R. Bush and myself (Bush and Estes, 1959).

My acquaintance with Gordon grew into a lasting friendship during several succeeding summers. I, with my wife, Kay, plus children, and dog, trekked across country from Indiana to Palo Alto annually for similar summer gatherings and found Gordon and Sharon on hand, Gordon having made the transition from student at Yale to a faculty position in the Department of Psychology at Stanford. On each occasion, Gordon met me with a bundle of yellow scratchpads containing new findings on several fronts of the now flourishing mathematical learning theories that absorbed us both.

In 1962, I joined the faculty of the Stanford Psychology Department, with the effect, curiously, that the pace of my interchanges of ideas with Gordon slackened a bit. The reason was not that either of us was running out of ideas, but that I rarely had patience to wait out the lengthy line of students that queued up outside Gordon's office door waiting for criticism, advice, or inspiration from the master. Another factor was that the Bowers had come to be world travelers. A letter from me to Gordon dated February 1966 was addressed to him at University College, London, where he and Sharon were evidently spending the year. The letter runs,

"I'm glad but not surprised that you're getting a chance at the Rockefeller setup. But, don't get in too deep,—we need you here.... Best to Sharon. I hope she got exposed last year to Bill McGill's tales of the horrors of living in New York. If not, maybe we could arrange to have a record made and shipped over."

April, 1966 found the Bowers still in London, and a note from me to Gordon began,

"I expect you have enough on your mind to keep you occupied, but at least the problem of the supply of graduate assistants for next year needn't be among them. Actually, you may not want your full cadre of assistants at all when you see the incoming mob of NSF fellows, etc., who will be looking for people to work with.... For heaven's sake, come on back and help out.

I might add that the "mob" is well represented at this gathering.

In May, 1972, I had moved to New York and Gordon was back at Stanford. A note from me reads,

"Dear Gordon: This piece by you and Anderson [John R., 1972] in the latest *Psychological Review* strikes me as a very nice bit of work. It's reassuring to find that our ideas have again turned independently into a somewhat similar channel. I seem to remember this happening several times before and on actuarial grounds the prognosis seems pretty good."

The next spring, April, 1973, I had a very pleasant occasion for a note: "Dear Gordon: I expect that by now even Western Union has managed to get a message through to you. I can't claim to be surprised at your election to the Academy [the National Academy of Sciences]. Be assured, you came in as a theoretical-experimentalist,—I think hardly anyone still remembers that you once put an electrode into a midbrain."

The last item in this series of communications, dated February, 1981, runs

"Dear Gordon I recently got a copy of B&H [Bower and Hilgard, *Theories of Learning*], 5th edition from your publisher and had a weekend trip on which to leaf it through. Unfortunately, you and Jack will suffer a financial loss, for I had seen the ad and was about to buy the book. Still, Harvard students will probably make up the deficit.

"You did a nice workup on me."

"I'm currently working on a human-learning chapter for the forthcoming revision of Stevens' *Handbook*. I just hope that I can do as good a job of bringing Hovland down to 1980 as you and Jack have done for the original Hilgard."

I must not conclude this reverie without mention of the powerful influence Gordon has had on my own research. High points are his contribution of the "one-element" model (1961) and the multidimensional memory trace (1967) to the family of statistical learning models, and his development, with Mark Gluck, of an interactive network model of category learning (1988a, 1988b). Each of these has broadened my theoretical perspective in significant ways. Less tangible but at least as important has been Gordon's demonstration of how long-continuing devotion to research can fit into an active and multi-faceted life.

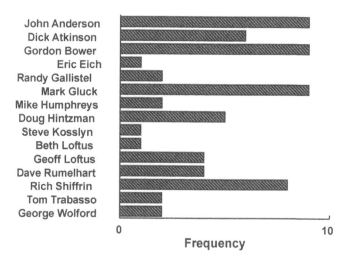

Figure 1–3.   Relative frequencies of citations of publications of other members of the BowerNet by a single representative member.

Bower has been a central figure in the evolution of cognitive science, not only because of his own towering record of research accomplishment, but because of his influence on his students and postdoctoral associates, many of whom have become stars in their own right, and on colleagues of all varieties. One tangible source of evidence on this role is the frequency with which these individuals cite Bower and those he has influenced, collectively the "BowerNet," when writing for readerships outside of their own specialties.

To illustrate the structure of the BowerNet for one member, I have volunteered myself as a subject and show in Figure 1–3 the frequency of my citations of members of the BowerNet in a set of my relevant publications (Estes, 1994, 1998, 2002). Analogous graphs for other members would doubtless vary in particulars but perhaps with much commonality.

I lack the temerity to predict the central issues of the psychology of learning and memory much beyond the date of writing (2006), but I confidently foresee that the BowerNet will play a major role in coping with them for many years to come.

ACKNOWLEDGMENTS

Preparation of this article was supported by National Science Foundation Grants SBR–996206 and BCS–0130512.

REFERENCES

Anderson, J. R., & Bower, G. H. (1972). Recognition and retrieval processes in free recall. *Psychological Review, 79,* 97–123.

Atkinson, R., Bower, G. H., & Crothers, E. J. (1965). *An introduction to mathematical learning theory.* New York: Wiley.

Bower, G. H. (1961). Application of a model to paired-associate learning. *Psychometrika, 26,* 255–280.

Bower, G. H. (1962). An association model for response and training variables in paired-associate learning. *Psychological Review, 69,* 34–53.

Bower, G. H. (1967). A multicomponent theory of the memory trace. In K. W. Spence & J. T. Spence (Ed.), *The psychology of learning and motivation: Advances in research and theory* (pp. 230–327). New York: Academic Press.

Bower, G. H., & Hilgard, E, R. (1981). *Theories of learning.* Englewood Cliffs, NJ: Prentice-Hall.

Bush, R. R., & Estes, W. K. (1959). *Studies in mathematical learning theory.* Stanford, CA: Stanford University Press.

Bush, R. R., & Mosteller, F. (1955). *Stochastic models for learning.* New York: Wiley.

Estes, W. K. (1950). Toward a statistical theory of learning. *Psychological Review, 57,* 94–104.

Estes, W. K. (1964). Probability learning. In A. W. Melton (Ed.) *Categories of human learning.* New York Academic Press.

Estes, W. K. (1986). Array models for category learning. *Cognitive Psychology, 18,* 500–549.

Estes, W. K. (1994). *Classification and cognition.* Oxford, England: Oxford University Press.

Estes, W. K. (1998). Models of human memory and their implications for research on aging and psychopathology. *Development and Psychopathology, 10,* 607–624.

Estes, W. K. (2002). Traps en route to models of memory and decision. *Psychonomic Bulletin & Review, 9,* 3–25.

Gluck, M. A., & Bower, G. H. (1988a). Evaluating an adaptive network model of human learning. *Journal of Memory and Language, 27,* 166–195.

Gluck, M. A., & Bower, G. H. (1988b). From conditioning to category learning: An adaptive network model. *Journal of Experimental Psychology: General, 117,* 227–247.

Gluck, M. A., & Myers, C. E. (1993). Hippocampal mediation of stimulus representation" A computational theory. *Hippocampus, 3,* 491–516.

Gluck, M. A., Oliver, L. M., & Myers, C. E. (1996). Late-training amnesic deficits in probabilistic category learning; A neurocomputational analysis. *Learning & Memory, 3,* 326–340.

Hebb, D. O. (1949). *Organization of behavior.* New York: Wiley.

Hilgard, E. R., & Marquis. D. G. (1940). *Conditioning and learning.* New York: Appleton–Century–Crofts.

Hull, C. L. (1937). Mind, mechanism, and adaptive behavior. *Psychological Review, 44,* 1–32.

Kimble, G. A. (1961). *Hilgard and Marquis' conditioning and learning* (2nd ed.). New York: Appleton–Century–Crofts.

Knowlton, B. J., Squire, L. R., & Gluck, M. A. (1994). Probabilistic category learning in amnesia. *Learning and Memory, 1,* 106–120.

Konorski, J., & Miller, S. (1937). On two types of conditioned reflex. *Journal of General Psychology, 16,* 264–272.

Kruschke, J. K. (1992). ALCOVE: An exemplar-based connectionist model of category learning. *Psychological Review, 99,* 22–44.

McGeoch, J. A. (1942). *The psychology of human learning.* New York: Longmans Green.

McGeoch, J. A., & Irion, A. L. (1952). The psychology of human learning. New York: Longmans Green.

Medin, D. L., & Schaffer, M. M. (1978). Context theory of classification learning. *Psychological Review, 85,* 207–238.

Mowrer, O. H. (1956). Two-factor learning theory reconsidered, with special reference to secondary reinforcement and the concept of habit. *Psychological Review, 63,* 114–128.

Nosofsky, R. N. (1984). Choice, similarity, and the context theory of classification. *Journal of Experimental Psychology: Learning, Memory, and Cognition, 10,* 104–114.

Perkins, C. C. (1955). The stimulus conditions which follow learned responses. *Psychological Review, 62,* 341–348.

Postman, L. (1976). Methodology of human learning. In W. K. Estes (Ed.), *Handbook of learning and cognitive processes* (Vol. 3, pp. 11–70). Hillsdale, NJ: Lawrence Erlbaum Associates.

Rescorla, R. A. , & Wagner, A. R. (1972). A theory of Pavlovian conditioning: Variation in effectiveness of reinforcement and non-reinforcement. In A. H. Black & W. F. Prokasy (Eds.) *Classical conditioning II: Current research and theory* (pp. 64–99). New York: Appleton–Century–Crofts.

Restle, F. (1955). A theory of discrimination learning. *Psychological Review, 62,* 11–19.

Schlosberg, H, (1937). The relationship between success and the laws of conditioning. *Psychological Review, 44,* 379–394.

Senden, M. V. (1932). Raum- und Gestalt Auffassung bei operierten Blindgeboren vor und Nach der Operation. Leipzig, Germany: Barth.

Skinner, B. F. (1937). Two types of conditioned reflex: A reply to Konorski and Miller. *Journal of General Psychology, 16,* 272–279.

Terrace, H. S. (1973). Classical conditioning. In G. S. Reynolds, C. Catania, & B. Schard (Eds.), *Contemporary experimental psychology.* Chicago: Scott, Foresman.

Thorndike, E. L. (1913). *Educational psychology: The psychology of learning* (Vol. 2). New York: Teachers College.

Trabasso, T., & Bower, G. H. (1964). Memory in concept identification, *Psychonomic Science, 1,* 133–134.

Trabasso, T., & Bower, G. H. (1968). *Attention in learning: Theory and research. New* York: Wiley.

Underwood, B. J. (1957). Interference and forgetting. *Psychological Review, 64,* 49–60.

Underwood, B. J. (1964). The representativeness of rote verbal learning. In A. W. Melton (Ed.), *Categories of human learning.* New York: Academic Press.

Wolford, G., Miller, M. B., & Gazzaniga, M. (2000). The left hemisphere's role in hypothesis formation. *Journal of Neuroscience, 20* (RC64), 1–4.

Memory from the Outside, Memory from the Inside

Douglas L. Hintzman
University of Oregon

Gordon Bower has influenced cognitive psychology in many significant ways. Probably no one else possessed the broad mastery of the literature that was needed to repeatedly update Hilgard's classic *Theories of Learning*. The fifth edition of that volume lists more than 1,200 references, on topics ranging from neurophysiology through experimental research on both animals and humans, through mathematical models, to educational applications. Generations of psychology students have profited from Bower's ability to extract the central concepts from that broad literature, and to repackage the concepts in crystal-clear prose. On a more personal level, a remarkable number of graduate students took their first toddling steps in research under Bower's eye, and then raced off in all directions to help shape cognitive psychology as we know it today.

But these indirect influences are overshadowed by the contribution of Bower's own research. In this chapter, I review some of his publications on the topic of memory, and relate it to some of my own research. Along the way, I attempt to partially explain why his papers have had such a broad influence on the field. The main idea I explore is that Bower's writings reveal an ability to look at cognition in two quite different but complementary ways: from the outside, and from the inside. What I mean by this should become clear as we go along.

MEMORY FROM THE OUTSIDE

By looking at memory from the outside, I mean formulating and testing theories about memory as one would study any other object of scientifically inquiry—for example, a photon, an ant colony, or a hurricane. In the philosophy of science, this paradigmatic approach is commonly referred to as the *hypothetico-deductive method*. A more descriptive expression is *reverse engineering,* which implies analyzing the behavior of the system under investigation and trying to infer what processes, functions, or algorithms control the system's behavior. Yet another expression used to characterize this approach is *analysis by synthesis.* If you really understand how a natural system works, you should be able to duplicate its essential characteristics artificially. In most fields of science, this means producing a model that mimics the behavior of the original in certain crucial ways. The goal is an explicit explanation of how this artificial system—and by inference the natural system—works. There is almost always a verbal explanation of the model system, which may be supplemented by diagrams, mathematical arguments, or mechanical simulations, which these days are almost always are done on a digital computer.

In cognitive psychology, this mode of theorizing often takes a form labeled *information processing.* The approach has become so common today that it is often taken for granted, but it was novel enough 40 years ago to merit explicit comment. In introducing one of his modeling efforts, Bower (1967) explained it this way:

> Perhaps it is wise to first expose our theoretical bias so that the reader is fairly warned. We take it that the job for a theory of memory is to specify the structures, organization, and rules of operation of a machine (a model) that will behave in a manner that resembles or simulates memory phenomena in important respects. The machine, of course, need not actually be built if its behavior can be forecast by arguments, either verbal, mathematical, or in computer programs. ... In general, this approach represents the model organism in terms of an array of information-processing mechanisms, each of which carries out certain elementary operations upon information provided to it. These mechanisms moreover, are assumed to be organized and sequenced in a way designed to achieve certain results. (pp. 230–231)

It is often desirable that such models be relatively simple, so they can be used to explore the explanatory power of a small set of interacting concepts or principles. However, a cognitive model may become quite complex, particularly if it is implemented as a computer program. Obviously, a complete model of cognition would have to be enormously complex.

As formal models go, Bower's one-element model occupies the extreme minimalist end of this continuum (Bower, 1961). The model sought to explain paired-associate learning with two discrete memory states and one free parameter. It provided astonishingly good quantitative fits to various aspects of the data from a handful of paired-associate learning experiments, but this set of experiments was extremely limited. As it turned out, the model was more broadly applicable to the concept-identification task (Trabasso & Bower, 1968). The one-element model's impressive but partial success inspired attempts to fit data from associative learning experiments with models having three or more discrete memory states (e.g., Bower & Theios, 1964; Ross & Bower, 1981). Today's multinomial models for analysis of categorical data derive partly from this earlier work.

During my first year as a graduate student at Stanford, Bower suggested that I read a couple of technical reports from the information-processing group at the Carnegie Institute of Technology. These reports described development of a computer model of human learning called EPAM, which was based on a stimulus sorting tree, or *discrimination net* (e.g., Feigenbaum, 1963). This work convinced me that computers could be used to model human cognition while avoiding some of the constraints that purely mathematical models impose on the theorist. However, I felt that EPAM contained several assumptions that were not sufficiently motivated by data, and I was bothered by the deterministic nature of the model. If you had EPAM repeatedly learn the same list (erasing the memory between runs), it would make exactly the same correct responses and errors on each run. This lack of variability made it difficult to compare the model's predictions with experimental data from human subjects.

To sidestep both of these problems, I wrote a paired-associate learning program (dubbed SAL), based on a discrimination net similar to the one in EPAM, but with several of EPAM's additional information-processing assumptions replaced by a couple of stochastic processes. SAL's relative simplicity made it possible to see unambiguously how several phenomena of learning and memory could be explained in terms of processes related to stimulus generalization and discrimination. The program listing for SAL took just three pages of B5500 Algol. With Bower's encouragement, I eventually turned this project into my dissertation (Hintzman, 1968). I believe I was the first student in Bower's lab to develop a simulation model.

At the time that I was working with SAL, Bower was developing a memory model that characterized the memory trace as a vector of components or features. The paper describing this model explored various assumptions concerning how stimulus features might be encoded and lost, and about how the same memory vectors might underlie performance in recall and recognition memory tasks (Bower, 1967). This *multicomponent model* can be seen as a forerunner of several more recent efforts by other theorists—especially in they way it was applied to yes–no, forced-choice, and confidence-rating measures of recognition memory (e.g., Gillund & Shiffrin, 1984; Glanzer & Adams, 1990; Hintzman, 1988; Murdock, 1982).

Over the next several years the multicomponent model apparently evolved into a much more ambitious project, which came to be known as HAM (Anderson & Bower, 1973). In HAM, the earlier model's features were replaced by associations between concept nodes, and the earlier model's vectors were replaced by hierar-chical trees, inspired by linguistic theories of deep structure. The trees represented human knowledge in terms of logic-like propositions. The main test bed of HAM came from experiments on memory for sentences, although it was also applied to other experimental tasks. Because HAM was more complex than the multicom-ponent model, predictions had to be derived by computer simulation.

In the 1980s, there was a surge of interest in connectionist models of learning, which contrasted sharply with the information-processing approach exemplified by the EPAM, SAL, and HAM models. In connectionist models, learning is not accomplished by storing and manipulating symbols, but by gradually adjusting the weights of connections among neuronlike units that represent features of the input and features of the output, possibly mediated by intermediate layers of units. In many ways, this connectionist movement can be seen as a reversion to neobehaviorist attempts to explain human learning with principles derived from the study of simple conditioning in animals. An especially intriguing connection-ist insight was that the "delta rule" of network modeling corresponds to the Rescorla–Wagner equation for associative blocking, which had been applied with great success to phenomena of classical conditioning (Rescorla & Wagner, 1972). Implications of this correspondence were explored in Bower's lab. Predictions of blocking-like phenomena were derived from a simple network model, and applied to experiments on classification learning in humans (Gluck & Bower, 1988). The network model was found to fit the data from these experiments bet-ter than several other classification learning models did. As in Rescorla and Wagner's work on classical conditioning, the general conclusion was that a stim-ulus feature becomes associated with an outcome, not to the extent that it is paired with the outcome—as one might suppose—but to the extent that it uniquely "pre-dicts" the outcome in competition with the other features.

The foregoing brief review should give the general flavor of Bower's broad contributions to the memory-modeling literature. I have more to say about some of these models later, specifically with regard to the effects of repetition on memory.

MEMORY FROM THE INSIDE

The hypothetico-deductive approach to research seen in the preceding examples is sometimes taken by philosophers as defining the very essence of science. To be accorded full respect, a theory's assumptions must be stated explicitly, and pre-dictions must be derived from the assumptions in a rigorous way. As I have argued elsewhere, formal models are useful tools in science because they enforce these requirements of explicitness and rigor (Hintzman, 1991). But cognitive psy-chology differs from most other areas of science in a crucial way: If you are a cognitive psychologist, you are an exemplar of the type of system you are trying to understand. This adds a dimension to cognitive psychology that is notably absent in the "harder" sciences. A good cognitive psychologist will always ask, "What would I do if I were a subject in this experiment?" It would make no sense to ask a similar question about a bacterium, a neutron star, or a neuron.

The "cognitive revolution" that began around 1960 is usually attributed to the use of the digital computer as a metaphor for the mind (e.g., Lachman, Lachman, & Butterfield, 1979), an approach exemplified by the information-processing passage from Bower (1967) that I quoted earlier. But Gestalt psychology provided an equally important stimulus for the emergence of cognitive psychology (Murray, 1995). The Gestaltists' best-known influence on mainstream psychology lay in their principles of perceptual organization, but they applied similar concepts to higher level abilities such as problem solving (Köhler, 1925) and memory (Katona, 1940). The power of the Gestalt concepts did not derive from a clearly articulated scientific theory—for there was none—but from subjectively compelling demonstrations. In present terms, the Gestalt psychologists excelled at taking an inside view of cognition.

One might expect an upcoming young psychologist with a stellar reputation as a formal modeler to simply polish and build upon his previous successes. We students were therefore surprised to watch as Bower's research took on a completely new "insider" focus. The impetus for this work was typically to better understand some phenomenon of memory that made subjective sense, but for which a mechanistic account was lacking. Various of Bower's papers explored the questions of why rhymes are easy to learn (Bower & Bolton, 1969), how hierarchical organization of word lists aids their recall (Bower, Clark, Lesgold, & Winzenz, 1969), how subjects impose their own organization on lists of digits (Winzenz & Bower, 1970), how narrative stories aid recall (Bower & Clark, 1969), and—most famously—why visual imagery is an effective mnemonic device (Bower, 1970a). Some of the techniques explored in this research substantially improved memory performance.

In one article, Bower discussed much of this new work from his lab and those of others (Bower, 1970b). He proclaimed, "A modest revolution is afoot today within the field of human learning, and the rebels are marching under the banner of 'cognitive organization'"(p. 18). The research he described did not derive from the one-element model, the multicomponent model, or some other attempt to reverse-engineer the human memory system. It consisted of demonstrations stimulated by intuitively plausible conjectures about strategies of effective memorization. As a general conclusion, Bower argued that an experimental subject required to learn a word pair might do so in several different ways: by generating a linking sentence, forming a mental picture, finding an intermediate associate, or noting some graphemic, phonological, or semantic similarity between the members of the pair. Moreover:

A preferred strategy of the adult human in learning a large body of material is to ... subdivide the material into smaller groups by some means, and then learn these parts as integrated packets of information. The bases for the groupings can be richly varied depending upon the nature of the material and the person's mental set. (p. 41)

There were—and still are—no models that explain the human learner's flexibility in inventing, selecting among, and implementing such tactics.

A more recent topic of Bower's research has been the comprehension of prose, at a level higher than the individual sentence (which had been HAM's focus). This work demonstrates that memory for narrative material can be distorted by the reader's understanding of a character's motives (Owens, Bower, & Black, 1979), that shifts in the narrator's point of view can disrupt comprehension and memory for the material (Black, Turner, & Bower, 1979), and that access to information about an object named in a narrative decreases with the object's implied distance from the reader's focus of attention (Rinck, Hähnel, Bower, & Glowalla, 1997). The effect of these papers has been to spotlight high-level aspects of language comprehension, imagination, and memory that are well beyond the scope of extant cognitive theories.

Yet another thread running through Bower's research has concerned the effects on memory of change and reinstatement of context. One aspect of context is mood, whose effects were demonstrated by Gilligan and Bower (1983). In an earlier attempt to account for context effects, Bower (1972) developed a mathematical model of encoding that was based partly on the stimulus-fluctuation model of Estes (1955). Following Estes, Bower assumed that contextual elements drift in and out of an active set over time according to an exponential function. Such a specification is explicit and quantitatively precise, but it does not really explain what the term context refers to.

Memory theorists who invoke context usually ignore the reader's need for a more intuitive explication of the term's meaning, but Bower was not so negligent. He explained context as follows:

I think of "context" in terms of background external and interoceptive stimulation prevailing during presentation of the phasic experimental stimuli. Included here would be internal factors like posture, temperature, room and apparatus cues, and stray noises, as well as internal physiological stimuli such as a dry throat, pounding heartbeat, stomach gurgles, nausea, and boredom. But more significant than any of these is what the subject is thinking about, what his mental set is, at the time the experimental stimulus intrudes. I think of this psychological context as being produced by the free flow of the "stream of consciousness," the internal monologue as the subject describes to himself what is going on around him and comments upon or free associates to his descriptions. These descriptions provide his moment-to-moment conception of the structure of the experimental task, his instructions, the nature of the materials he has been encountering, strategies of encoding and learning he thinks have been helpful, and what he thinks the experiment is really about. The free associations contain thoughts about the experimenter's stupidity, the subject's stupidity, what he ate for lunch, what he will do with this earnings, and similar wool-gatherings. (Bower, 1972, pp. 92–93)

Over the years, I have often returned to this evocative, insider's perspective on cognitive context, and I have always found it compelling. At the same time, however, I have never been able to relate the passage to the simple exponential equation for context change that Bower (1972) offered just two pages later. I make this comment not to criticize an article that I have always admired, but to highlight what seems to be a general dilemma of cognitive psychology, which I discuss in the next section.

THE OUTSIDE VERSUS THE INSIDE

By this point I assume that all readers understand what I mean by the outside and inside views of cognition, although they might want to substitute different labels. Instead of outside versus inside, they might prefer objective versus subjective, mechanistic versus mentalistic, or even third-person versus first-person. These all seem like acceptable alternatives. To restate a point that I made earlier, cognitive psychology differs in an important way from most other areas of science. The outsider's reverse-engineering perspective is the only one available to a geneticist, a vulcanologist, or a cosmologist, but the cognitive psychologist, being an exemplar of a cognitive system, is not subject to the same restriction. Taking the inside perspective seems to be a common strategy in cognitive psychology. Surprisingly, however, it is seldom explicitly acknowledged as a strategy. This may be because adult humans reflexively understand the mental states of others by mapping them onto their own mental states (see Malle & Hodges, 2005), and cognitive psychologists are adult humans. If we do this routinely as a matter of course, we may not be fully aware that we are doing so when we employ it as a tool in our research.

If this conjecture is right, a few observations might be worth making about the outside-versus-inside distinction. First, it is obviously related to the debate about whether subjective reports are acceptable as data in psychology (e.g., Ericsson & Crutcher, 1991; Nisbett & Wilson, 1977), but the two issues are not identical. Following Ericsson and Crutcher, I suggest that there are some mental processes that are slow, deliberate, and serial, and that under the right conditions these may be tapped to yield reliable subjective reports. There are many more processes that are fast, automatic, and parallel, and function entirely outside of awareness. But I believe this is a continuum, not a dichotomy. There are also processes that fall in a sort of gray area in between—too fast for reliable observation, but slow enough to allow brief and fragmentary conscious access. In themselves, these fragments (or verbal reports on them) may not be trustworthy as data, but they can provide useful hints of the cognitive processes at work in a range of mental tasks. Some of the processes that are engaged in memory encoding and retrieval happen to lie in this middle region of the continuum. Behaviorism ruled out not only subjective data, but also hypotheses stated in mentalistic terms. A major effect of the overthrow of behaviorism was to reopen this inner perspective to psychologists.

Second, the outside and inside perspectives are not coequal. Your implicit "theory of mind" may be a good source of hunches about experiments, but it is not a scientific theory. Scientific concepts still must be clearly defined, and their rules of interaction must be explicitly stated. In a scientific theory, any scientist—not just the theorist—should be able to apply the rules to the concepts and generate the same predictions. If a machine (a computer) can follow the rules, then you know the theory is free of ambiguity. So in the end, the inside perspective is of scientific use only to the extent that it helps one develop the outside perspective— that is, to reverse-engineer a model of the cognitive system based on reliable data.

Third, in domains where both views can be applied (where not everything is too fast and parallel for conscious access) development of the outside view tends to lag behind that of the inside view. This may be because the early experiments on a topic produce needed grist for the theorist's mill. In cognitive psychology, pioneering experiments are most likely to arise from attempts to establish empirical evidence for a phenomenon that seems likely from a subjective perspective, but is beyond the realm of existing theory. The study of mental imagery provides an obvious example.

Fourth, people may differ in their access to the relatively slow processes that can enlighten the inside perspective. To finally get to the question with which I opened this chapter, I think one reason for Gordon Bower's broad influence on cognitive psychology has been his ability to shift between the outside and inside perspectives, and his willingness to do so. Some cognitive psychologists are known almost exclusively as builders and testers of explicit, mechanistic models; others are known almost exclusively for their intuitively inspired experimental work. Still others (including some of Bower's students) adopt a mix of the two approaches—but few can match Bower's record of path-breaking work deriving from both perspectives. When Stanford hired Gordon Bower fresh out of graduate school, it was in effect hiring two outstanding young psychologists.

My fifth point is this: A person casually scanning his publications might actually suspect that the Stanford Department of Psychology included two Gordon Bowers—one a master of the outside perspective, and the other a master of the inside perspective. Most of Bower's modeling articles say little that resonates with the reader's subjective intuition, and the publications on organization, mnemonics, and narrative comprehension are generally not concerned with models. Both perspectives appear in the book on HAM (Anderson & Bower, 1973), and I say more about this later. Also, both perspectives appear in the chapter on context that

I cited earlier (Bower, 1972)—but as I commented there, it is hard to see a connection between Bower's description of the flow of the stream of consciousness, on the one hand, and his simple equation for context change, on the other. As a general rule, it seems very difficult to bring the outside and inside perspectives into alignment. This may be why laypeople are naturally inclined to grow up as commonsense Cartesian dualists (Bloom, 2004), and why philosophy has made little progress in bridging the "explanatory gap" between physical brain states and the *qualia* of subjective experience (e.g., Levine, 1983). It may also be why some cognitive psychologists have grown to doubt the value of formal models (e.g., Glenberg, 2001), and why some computer scientists have become disenchanted with the prospects for artificial intelligence (e.g., Hawkins, 2004).

Without completely discounting such concerns, I doubt that the outside and inside views of cognition are completely incommensurable. For one thing, it seems indisputable that information-processing theories have helped to bring mentalistic and mechanistic concepts together in cognitive science. Indeed, a very respectable mechanistic model of human memory was developed more than 300 years ago by the scientist Robert Hooke, seemingly based on nothing more than engineering genius and subjective observations (Hintzman, 2003). Another reason for optimism lies in the rapid development of cognitive neuroscience, which may yield theories that link mechanistic and mentalistic concepts. A third reason, which I turn to next, is that the outside and inside views can be used in combination, by placing their experimental predictions in opposition.

The historic rivalry of Clark Hull and Edwin Tolman in the field of animal learning shows how an opposition strategy can work. Hull attempted to reverse-engineer a mechanistic, stimulus–response (S–R) theory of learning, by emulating the hypothetico-deductive method of Newtonian physics. Tolman, by contrast, once stated that he made experimental predictions by first "imagining how, *if I were a rat,* I would behave," in an experimental situation, and then turning those insights into theoretical constructs such as *cognitive map* and *expectancy* (Tolman, 1938). Experiments on several different issues showed that Tolman's theory predicted the behavior of rats in runways and mazes better than Hull's theory did—outcomes that forced Hull and others to make fundamental changes to the mechanistic S–R theory (see, e.g., Bower & Hilgard, 1981). Such changes notwithstanding, the concepts of cognitive map and expectancy seem more prominent in psychology today than is the concept of the S–R association.

If this works with rats, it ought to work with people—but there is no guarantee that the inside perspective will come out on top. In their early work on sentence memory, Anderson and Bower (1973, chap. 11) contrasted predictions of an associative tree model, in which associations were encoded or lost independently of each other, with a "gestalt theory" prediction that a sentence would be retained or lost as a whole. Anderson and Bower reported that the gestalt predictions seemed most consistent with their own intuitions and with those of most of their colleagues. Contrary to the gestalt hypothesis, however, experiments showed that sentence memory was fragmented rather than holistic, and that sentences with overlapping concepts interfered with each other in ways consistent with the associative structure hypothesized in their model. These early experimental results encouraged the researchers to develop their more elaborate HAM model.

The preceding two examples suggest that placing the outside and inside views in opposition can be a fruitful research strategy. The two views are commensurable if they make predictions about the same experimental data. More than once, in my own research, I have found myself using this strategy of opposition. I give a recent example in the next section.

REPETITION FROM THE OUTSIDE AND THE INSIDE

Repetition is one of the most powerful variables affecting memory, but there is little theoretical agreement on how its effects are produced. The standard explanation has been that repetition strengthens a memory trace or association. About the time that I entered graduate school, this hypothesis was under attack by proponents of all-or-none learning. In Bower's one-element model, for example, repetition simply provides multiple opportunities for a transition to take place, from an unlearned state to a learned state (Bower, 1961). In spite of the one-element model's successes, a strict two-state learning mechanism appears to be ruled out by effects of "overlearning" on retrieval latency and on the rate of forgetting. In Bower's multicomponent model, each repetition was assumed to lay down a separate memory trace (Bower, 1967). Although this multiple-trace assumption played only a minor role in the multicomponent model's predictions, it was central to a later model of recency discrimination (Flexser & Bower, 1974). In their network model of classification learning, by contrast, Gluck and Bower (1988) adopted a pure strength account of repetition's effects. So Bower's models have invoked at least three different mechanisms to explain the effects of repetition.

Shortly after I received my PhD, it occurred to me that evidence on repetition's effects might be obtained by showing experimental subjects a list that includes repetitions, and then having them respond to individual test items with judgments of presentation frequency (JOF). If repetition strengthens memory, strength approaches an asymptote, and subjects base JOF on memory strength, then JOF should increase with frequency only up to a point, and remain relatively constant thereafter. Neither my initial experiments (Hintzman, 1969) nor any others that I have seen since suggest that JOF approaches an asymptote. It just keeps going up with repetition.

To explain this outcome, I adopted a multiple-trace view of the effects of repetition. In support of the multiple-trace hypothesis, Rick Block and I showed that subjects could judge two different serial positions of a repeated word with some degree of independence, and that subjects could remember two different frequencies for a word as it appeared in two separate lists (Hintzman & Block, 1971). This led me to wonder how far the multiple-trace view could be pushed. Could a single memory store that lays down multiple traces and accounts for JOF also explain how abstract concepts are acquired through repetition? An affirmative answer might help the field avoid the proliferation of purported memory "systems" serving different functions—in this case, one system supporting episodic memories and another supporting generic or abstract memories. As a minimalist, in-principle demonstration that this could be done using a single memory store, I developed the Minerva 2 model (Hintzman, 1986, 1988).

Minerva 2 is based on a few simple assumptions. As in Bower's (1967) multi-component model, each item or event is represented as a vector of features, and the similarity of two events is reflected by the degree of overlap in their features. When an event occurs its vector is simply copied into memory, with some probability of encoding failure applied to each feature. A repetition of an item is treated exactly as the item's first presentation was, thus—as in Flexser and Bower (1974)—the traces of repetitions are separate and independent. Minerva 2 differs from Bower's models, however, in the way retrieval works. When a test vector is presented, it simultaneously contacts and activates all traces in the memory store. The degree of activation of an individual trace is a positively accelerated function of the trace's match to the test vector, so overall activation in the memory store is dominated by good matches. Performance on the episodic memory tasks of recognition memory and JOF are assumed to be based on the summed activation of all traces in the memory store in response to the test vector, a kind of familiarity measure called *echo intensity* (Hintzman, 1988). This property helps explain effects of similarity and repetition on recognition memory, and also the failure of JOF to asymptote with repetition.

Cued recall in Minerva 2 is based on a retrieved-feature vector called the *echo content*, which is also based on the summed activation of traces (Hintzman, 1986). Each of a trace's features contributes to the echo content in proportion to that trace's level of activation. If there are several traces strongly activated by the test vector, the echo content will tend to include the features that these traces have in common, and their individuating features will tend to cancel out. In principle, such a process might explain how a test word such as dog could retrieve the essence of what dogs are like from a store of individual traces, each conjoining the label dog with features of an individual animal. In principle also, such a system could retrieve different nuances, different levels of abstraction, or entirely different meanings of a word by addressing different subsets of stored contextual features. Simulations with Minerva 2 illustrated how this sort of abstraction might work in principle; however the model was not used to simulate the learning of such real-world concepts.

My efforts to test Minerva 2 experimentally have not been concerned with abstract concepts, but with the episodic-memory tasks of recognition memory and

JOF. Several different models have been proposed for the recognition task; but in the case of JOF, Minerva 2 has had essentially no competition. For this reason, I have not tried to compare Minerva 2's predictions with those of other models. Instead, I have tried to identify predictions that derive from core assumptions of the model, but that seem contrary to my subjective expectations. I describe a recent example, which derives from the central role the model assigns to echo intensity in both recognition and JOF.

There are three basic factors that affect the intensity of the echo in Minerva 2: the degree to which the traces in memory match the retrieval cue; the strength or completeness of each matching trace; and the number of matching traces. Echo intensity, in turn, is the sole determinant of recognition memory and also of JOF. As is routine in recognition memory models, recognition confidence ratings are assumed to be generated in relation to criterion settings distributed along the echo intensity (familiarity) scale. JOFs are assumed to be generated in the same way as confidence ratings, except that the criterion settings are different. So in Minerva 2, recognition confidence ratings and JOF are essentially two versions of the same task.

This set of assumptions achieves considerable parsimony, but it leads to the counterintuitive prediction that people should not be able to remember what combination of the three factors just mentioned produced a given echo intensity. According to the model, two manipulations that affect echo intensity should have proportionally the same effects on recognition confidence and JOF. Although Minerva 2 is a multiple-trace model, it produces a cumulative strengthlike output; and as was noted by Anderson and Bower (1972), strength is "ahistorical." Taking the inside perspective, this seems unlikely to be right. People understand the difference between a repeated event and an event with a long duration. How could people understand the difference if, as the model implies, they cannot remember the difference?

To test this counterintuitive implication of Minerva 2, I conducted an experiment that orthogonally varied the number of stimulus presentations and their durations, and tested subjects with either a recognition confidence rating task or a numerical JOF task (Hintzman, 2004). In agreement with intuition, JOF was more sensitive to repetition and less sensitive to exposure duration than recognition confidence was. But why? To try to answer this question, I plotted ROC curves for the two tasks. The curves for recognition confidence offered no surprises, but the curves for JOF appeared bizarre. To get slightly technical, I was especially puzzled by the slopes of the normalized ROCs. The slopes for recognition were around 0.70, which is typical for that task, but those for JOF were 1.0 or greater. The highest slope (around 1.5) was for items that had been seen just once in the study list.

Taking the usual reverse-engineering approach based on signal-detection theory, I tried to invent a set of underlying distributions that would produce such results, and assumptions that would explain the properties of those distributions.

Nothing made sense. Finally I abandoned this effort and switched to an inside perspective. I asked: What must a subject know in order to produce data like these, and how could the subject know it? This perspective made it clear that my subjects were particularly sensitive to a difference between items that had been repeated in the study list, versus items that had not been repeated (see Hintzman, 2004). It was clear also that such differentiating information could not be encoded until the item's second occurrence. I inferred that this encoded information must have been a *reminding*—that is, the awareness that the item was being repeated.

Years ago, my students and I had employed this idea to explain why, after seeing a list of words, subjects could judge the spacings between repetitions of a word or the spacings between associatively related words, but were unable to judge the spacings between words that were unrelated (Hintzman, Summers, & Block, 1975). The new idea that emerged was that the concept of reminding could be used to explain JOF. Suppose that what you encode in memory on a study trial is whatever you are consciously aware of on that trial, and that when the item is presented again later, it reminds you of your previous state of awareness. This, in its essence, is the concept of *recollection*. Although recollection was reported by early introspectionists (e.g., Strong & Strong, 1916), it was ignored for several decades. Only fairly recently has recollection reappeared in the recognition memory literature.

If you apply the concept of recollection repeatedly across multiple presentations of an item, you end up with a representation of the number of times the item occurred in the list, which I call *recursive reminding* (Hintzman, 2004). To put this in subjective terms, you can be reminded that you were reminded of being reminded ... and so on. According to the recursive reminding hypothesis, subjects in a JOF experiment intuitively know that the depth of recursion of this reminding record is diagnostic of the number of times the test item occurred in the list. JOF is hypothesized to be based primarily on this information.

So far recursive reminding is just a hypothesis, but as I discuss elsewhere, it appears to explain several findings from the JOF literature that are otherwise hard to understand (Hintzman, 2004). To give one of several examples, just as you would expect if reminding were an automatic process, experimental subjects accumulate information about frequency regardless of whether they are warned about the JOF task in advance (Flexser & Bower, 1975). A big project that remains is to integrate recursive reminding into a formal model of memory. I feel fairly confident that the hypothesis is on the right track, partly because I think I experience such remindings when I go through a list that includes repetitions. (Of course, my impressions could be influenced by knowledge of the hypothesis, so as always, objective evidence is needed.)

One implication of the recursive-reminding hypothesis is that memories of repeated and nonrepeated items differ in a qualitative way: A trace of a repeated item will include at least one reminding. This does not necessarily contradict either the strength hypothesis or the multiple-trace hypothesis, but it does imply an added layer of complexity. Contrary to virtually every memory theory, the hypothesis implies (and the data affirm) that the effects of repetition are qualitative, and not just quantitative.

Another implication of this perspective on repetition is that the psychology of memory might benefit from giving more attention to cognitive context and its role in recollection. Bower's (1972) description of the "internal monologue" may be a good place to start—although I doubt that the so-called monologue is strictly verbal, as the word suggests. Also, the standard theoretical division of the memory trace into features of the item and features of the context may be misleading. As the concept of recursive reminding illustrates, much cognitive context may be about the way particular items are embedded in the experimental context.

Finally, to return to the relation between the outside and the inside perspectives, the proliferation of cognitive models has brought to the forefront the question of how the models should be evaluated. Thought on this topic has been mostly concerned with the technical question of how models can be compared with each other in their ability to explain or fit data (e.g., Jacobs & Grainger, 1994; Pitt, Myung & Zhang, 2002). Without discounting the importance of such work, I suggest that it may be fruitful in some cases to supplement the model-comparison strategy with a strategy of pitting of a model—or even better, a set of models—against the researcher's first-person perspective. Core predictions of a model that seem to lack "psychological plausibility" are prime candidates for experimental test. In effect, one researcher can play the roles of both Hull and Tolman. If the model wins, confidence in the model increases. If the model loses, the field can narrow its theoretical search space to combinations of assumptions that avoid the failed predictions. One should not presume to know the answer in advance, as is shown by the examples I have cited in this chapter.

REFERENCES

Anderson, J. R., & Bower, G. H. (1972). Recognition and retrieval processes in free recall. *Psychological Review, 79,* 97–123.

Anderson, J. R., & Bower, G. H. (1973). *Human associative memory.* Washington, DC: Winston.

Black, J. B., Turner, T. J., & Bower, G. H. (1979). Point of view in narrative comprehension, memory, and production. *Journal of Verbal Learning & Verbal Behavior, 18,* 187–198.

Bloom, P. (2004). *Descartes' baby: How the science of child development explains what makes us human.* New York: Basic Books.

Bower, G. H. (1961). Application of a model to paired-associate learning, 26, 255–280.

Bower, G. H. (1967). A multicomponent theory of the memory trace. In K. W. Spence & J. T. Spence (Eds.), *The psychology of learning and motivation* (Vol. 1, pp. 229–325). New York: Academic Press.

Bower, G. H. (1970a). Imagery as a relational organizer in associative learning. *Journal of Verbal Learning and Verbal Behavior, 9,* 529–533.

Bower, G. H. (1970b). Organizational factors in memory. *Cognitive Psychology, 1*, 18–46.

Bower, G. H. (1972). Stimulus-sampling theory of encoding variability. In A. W. Melton & E. Martin (Eds.), *Coding processes in human memory* (pp. 85–123). Washington, DC: Winston.

Bower, G. H., & Bolton, L. (1969). Why are rhymes easy to learn? *Journal of Experimental Psychology, 82*, 453–461.

Bower, G. H., & Clark, M. (1969). Narrative stories as mediators for serial learning. *Psychonomic Science, 14*, 181–182.

Bower, G. H., Clark, M., Lesgold, A., & Winzenz, D. (1969). Hierarchical retrieval schemes of recall of categorized word lists. *Journal of Verbal Learning & Verbal Behavior, 8*, 323–343.

Bower, G. H., & Hilgard, E. R. (1981). *Theories of learning* (5 ed.). Englewood Cliffs, NJ: Prentice-Hall.

Bower, G. H., & Theios, J. (1964). A learning model for discrete performance levels. In R. C. Atkinson (Ed.), *Studies in mathematical psychology* (pp. 367–373). Stanford, CA: Stanford University Press.

Ericsson, K. A., & Crutcher, R. J. (1991). Introspection and verbal reports on cognitive processes—two approaches to the study of thinking: A response to Howe. *New Ideas in Psychology, 9*, 57–71.

Estes, W. K. (1955). Statistical theory of spontaneous recovery and regression. *Psychological Review, 62*, 145–154.

Feigenbaum, E. A. (1963). The simulation of verbal learning behavior. In E. A. Feigenbaum & J. Feldman (Eds.), *Computers and thought* (pp. 297–309). New York: McGraw-Hill.

Flexser, A. J., & Bower, G. H. (1974). How frequency affects recency judgments: A model for recency discrimination. *Journal of Experimental Psychology, 103*, 706–716.

Flexser, A. J., & Bower, G. H. (1975). Further evidence regarding instructional effects on frequency judgments. *Bulletin of the Psychonomic Society, 6*, 321–324.

Gilligan, S. G., & Bower, G. H. (1983). Reminding and mood-congruent memory. *Bulletin of the Psychonomic Society, 21*, 431–434.

Gillund, G., & Shiffrin, R. M. (1984). A retrieval model for both recognition and recall. *Psychological Review, 91*, 1–67.

Glanzer, M., & Adams, J. K. (1990). The mirror effect in recognition memory: Data and theory. *Journal of Experimental Psychology: Learning, Memory, and Cognition, 16*, 5–16.

Glenberg, A. M. (2001). What language needs from memory (and vice versa). In H. L. I. Roediger, J. S. Nairne, I. Neath, & A. M. Surprenant (Eds.), *The nature of remembering.* (pp. 351–368). Washington, DC: American Psychological Association.

Gluck, M. A., & Bower, G. H. (1988). Evaluating an adaptive network model of human learning. *Journal of Memory and Language, 27*, 166–195.

Hawkins, J. (2004). *On intelligence.* New York: Holt.

Hintzman, D. L. (1968). Explorations with a discrimination net model for paired-associate learning. *Journal of Mathematical Psychology, 5*, 123–162.

Hintzman, D. L. (1969). Apparent frequency as a function of frequency and the spacing of repetitions. *Journal of Experimental Psychology, 80*, 139–145.

Hintzman, D. L. (1986). "Schema abstraction" in a multiple-trace memory model. *Psychological Review, 93*, 411–428.

Hintzman, D. L. (1988). Judgments of frequency and recognition memory in a multiple-trace memory model. *Psychological Review, 95*, 528–551.

Hintzman, D. L. (1991). Why are formal models useful in psychology? In W. E. Hockley & S. Lewandowsky (Eds.), *Relating theory and data: Essays on human memory in honor of Bennet B. Murdock* (pp. 39–56). Hillsdale, NJ: Lawrence Erlbaum Associates.

Hintzman, D. L. (2003). Robert Hooke's model of memory. *Psychonomic Bulletin & Review, 10,* 1–14.

Hintzman, D. L. (2004). Judgment of frequency vs. recognition confidence: Repetition and recursive reminding. *Memory & Cognition, 32,* 336–350.

Hintzman, D. L., & Block, R. A. (1971). Repetition and memory: Evidence for a multiple-trace hypothesis. *Journal of Experimental Psychology, 88,* 297–306.

Hintzman, D. L., Summers, J. J., & Block, R. A. (1975). Spacing judgments as an index of study-phase retrieval. *Journal of Experimental Psychology: Human Learning and Memory, 1,* 31–40.

Jacobs, A. M., & Grainger, J. (1994). Models of visual word recognition—sampling the state of the art. *Journal of Experimental Psychology: Human Perception and Performance, 20,* 1311–1334.

Katona, G. (1940). *Organizing and memorizing.* New York: Columbia University Press.

Köhler, W. (1925). *The mentality of apes* (E. Winter, Trans.). New York: Harcourt, Brace & World.

Lachman, R., Lachman, J. L., & Butterfield, E. C. (1979). *Cognitive psychology and information processing: An introduction.* Hillsdale, NJ.: Lawrence Erlbaum Associates.

Levine, J. (1983). Materialism and qualia: The explanatory gap. *Pacific Philosophical Quarterly, 64,* 354–361.

Malle, B. F., & Hodges., S. D. (2005). *Other minds: How humans bridge the divide between self and others.* New York: Guilford.

Murdock, B. B., Jr. (1982). A theory for the storage and retrieval of item and associative information. *Psychological Review, 89,* 609–626.

Murray, D. J. (1995). *Gestalt psychology and the cognitive revolution.* Hemel Hempstead, England: Harvester Wheatsheaf.

Nisbett, R. E., & Wilson, T. D. (1977). Telling more than we can know: Verbal reports on mental processes. *Psychological Review, 84,* 231–259.

Owens, J., Bower, G. H., & Black, J. B. (1979). The "soap opera" effect in story recall. *Memory & Cognition, 7,* 185–191.

Pitt, M. A., Myung, I. J., & Zhang, S. (2002). Toward a method of selecting among computational models of cognition. *Psychological Review, 109,* 427–491.

Rescorla, R. A., & Wagner, A. R. (1972). A theory of Pavlovian conditioning: Variations in the effeciveness of reinforcement and non-reinforcement. In B. A. H. & W. F. Prokasy (Eds.), *Classical conditioning: II. Current research and theory* (pp. 64–99). New York: Appleton–Century–Crofts.

Rinck, M., Hähnel, A., Bower, G. H., & Glowalla, U. (1997). The metrics of spatial situation models. *Journal of Experimental Psychology: Learning, Memory, and Cognition, 23,* 622–637.

Ross, B. H., & Bower, G. H. (1981). Comparison of models of associative recall. *Memory & Cognition, 9,* 1–16.

Strong, M. H., & Strong, E. K. J. (1916). The nature of recognition memory and of the localization of recognitions. *American Journal of Psychology, 27,* 341–362.

Tolman, E. C. (1938). The determiners of behavior at a choice point. *Psychological Review, 45,* 1–41.

Trabasso, T., & Bower, G. H. (1968). *Attention in Learning.* New York: Wiley.

Winzenz, D., & Bower, G. H. (1970). Subject-imposed coding and memory for digit series. *Journal of Experimental Psychology, 83,* 52–56.

CHAPTER 3

On the Law of Primacy

Endel Tulving

There exists a highly familiar phenomenon in learning and memory: first encounters with new situations, people, events, objects, and facts have greater impact on subsequent thought and behavior than later encounters of similar kinds. These "primacy effects" are well known from everyday life: the first day of school, the first romantic kiss, the graduation day, the first scientific paper accepted for publication, and many other "firsts" of the same kind are remembered vividly, and sometimes for the rest of one's life.

Primacy effects have been intensely studied under the controlled conditions in the laboratory where they are ubiquitous. They are found in many kinds of memory tasks and situations as diverse as impression formation (Asch, 1946), absolute judgments (Bower, 1971), social judgments (Nisbett & Ross, 1980), updating of beliefs (Hogarth & Einhorn, 1992), abductive reasoning (Wang, Johnson, & Zhang, 2006), and "cognitive access" to unknown, abstract individuals mentioned in laboratory-made sentences (Gernsbacher & Hargreaves, 1988). Primacy effects are found in rats (Kesner, Measom, Forsman, & Holbrook, 1984), pigeons (Wright, Santiago, Sands, Kendrick, & Cook, 1985), and nonhuman primates (Castro & Larsen, 1992), as well as in various subgroups of humans, including amnesiacs (Baddeley & Warrington, 1970), people with frontal-lobe damage (Eslinger & Grattan, 1994), and people under the influence of alcohol (B. M. Jones, 1973).

Primacy represents such a pervasive, regular phenomenon in learned behavior that there ought to be a law of it. At an earlier age in the science of psychology there was, indeed, a law of primacy, along with many other laws. Over time, however, the popularity of psychological laws has waned to the extent that today few practitioners think of the law of primacy even when they are explicitly asked about laws (Teigen, 2002). These days psychologists in various subdisciplines are generating all sorts of phenomena, effects, functions, and principles, but few if any laws. Laws are a vanishing species, and it is a pity. It is true that psychology deals with a subject matter that is exceedingly complex and in which phenomena of interest are almost invariably determined by multiple variables and their interactions, a state of affairs that discourages laws. But surely underneath all the complexity there must be some regularity. It is just a matter of finding them and then taking them seriously. Some psychological laws are accepted even today (Teigen, 2002), and there must be others.

Here I propose that primacy is one such law. It can be thought of as a resurrected version of earlier laws of primacy, although it goes beyond the earlier ones in that it can be derived from a more general law, the law of camatotic encoding, explained later. The thesis of this chapter is that camatosis, as discussed in the latter half of this chapter, can account for the primacy effect in memory as well as a host of other interference-based and novelty-related behavioral phenomena.

This chapter consists of eight sections plus a summary. The sections are labeled law of primacy, serial position curves, events 1 and 2, hypothesis of camatosis, novelty, repetition suppression, and law of camatotic encoding.

THE LAW OF PRIMACY

Scientific laws, like most other things in life, come in different sizes, shapes, and styles. A basic distinction has to do with the generality of the law. Laws, by definition, are supposed to be "general," but generality, like most other concepts, is flexible. Newton's well-known laws of mechanics are very general, and in some sense can be thought of as universal. The economists' equally well-known "law of supply and demand" does not hold in the whole universe at all times but only right now in some parts of our world. And Herrnstein's well-known "matching law," which specifies the relation between rather specific variables in rather specific laboratory-based learning situations, is nevertheless general within the specified limits.

The law of primacy I would like to propose here is this:

Of two sequential events the second one tends to be retained less well.

The law is assumed to have some generality. It is meant to apply to all situations in which *perceived events* occur in succession and entail consequences for subsequent behavior that we classify as learning or remembering. This generality holds within the limited domain of behavior, broadly defined, of living creatures that are capable of perceiving events in their (external or internal) environment. Another limitation of this law is that it is assumed to be true only for long-term retention.

Note that this law describes a scenario containing only two events rather than a whole series of events. We return to this matter later in the chapter. Note also that this law does not define primacy directly but indirectly, in terms of the inferior retention of the later event rather than the superior retention of the earlier event. The reason for this wording becomes clear as we proceed. Some other obvious questions, concerns, and other forms of puzzlement and incredulity engendered from what I have written thus far are also dealt with presently.

SERIAL POSITION EFFECTS

Primacy effects have usually been observed and studied in situations in which there are also recency effects—higher recall of more recent than less recent events. Such situations involve list-learning and list-recall experiments that yield typical, U-shaped serial position curves (or bow-shaped when plotting "errors") that show graded performance or error scores over the first few and last few positions in the list (e.g., Murdock, 1962). The close proximity of the two empirical phenomena in the observing scientist's mind, plus the fact that both are defined in terms of temporal variables, have led many theorists to seek an explanation not of primacy and recency as two different phenomena, but rather an explanation of the overall phenomenon of "serial position effects."

Primacy and recency components of serial position curves in standard memory experiments have been shown to be differentially affected by certain independent variables (Baddeley & Warrington, 1970; Glanzer, 1972; B. M. Jones, 1973; Shallice, 1979). This fact justifies the theoretical treatment of primacy, separate from that of recency. However, recency as an empirical fact—the fact that under certain conditions recent events are better recalled than less recent ones—does become highly relevant to the assessment of the validity, or plausibility, of the law of primacy. As an astute reviewer of the first version of the chapter put it—"There is no generality to primacy; I remember my last night's dinner very much better than any dinner last week" (my paraphrase of his words).

The issue of the relation between primacy and recency is complex because, in terms of behavioral observations, it depends on a large number of variables and their interaction. A glimpse of the complexity is provided by the results of a series of clever experiments by Wright and his associates (1985). These investigators tested pigeons, monkeys, and human beings on a yes–no recognition task. On a given trial, the subject would see four visual patterns that they had never seen before, presented one at a time. The presentation series was followed by a single probe pattern that either matched ("old") or did not match ("new") one of the four presented patterns. The stimuli were colored "travel pictures" for the two non-verbal species and colored kaleidoscopic images for the humans. This latter feature was adopted to eliminate verbal mediation and to force the humans to rely on pure perceptual memory as did the pigeons and monkeys. The nonhuman animals were provided instructions as to the rules of the game through extensive practice that preceded the experiment proper whereas the humans were instructed verbally.

The critical independent variable manipulated in the Wright et al. (1985) studies was the length of the retention interval: the duration of the time between the presentation of the last item in the inspection (study) series and the test probe. This interval ranged from 0 to 10 seconds for pigeons, 0 to 30 seconds for monkeys, and 0 to 100 seconds for humans. Extensive data, systematically covering the intermediate stages of all these intervals, were collected.

The results, graphically summarized in Figure 3-1, were striking, remarkably consistent, and highly informative. (More complete data are reported in Wright et al., 1985.) They can be summarized by saying that all three species exhibited a "pure recency" effect when tested immediately after the presentation of the

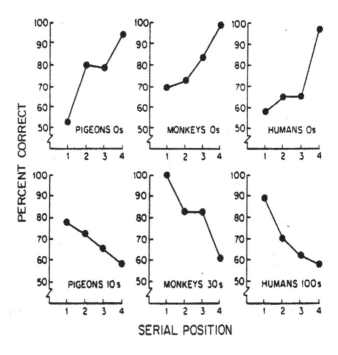

Figure 3–1.   Percentage of correct recognition (50 is chance) shown as a function of the serial presentation position of complex visual stimuli in pigeons, monkeys, and human beings as reported by Wright et al. (1985). Immediate tests (no retention interval, upper bank) yielded pure recency effects whereas delayed tests (longer retention intervals, lower bank) yielded pure primacy effects in all three species.

to-be-recognized visual patterns, that all three exhibited "pure primacy" effects when tested after a longer retention interval (the length of the interval varying with the species), and that all three species exhibited both primacy and recency with intermediate retention intervals (these latter data are not shown in Fig. 3-1).

Data rather reminiscent of those of Wright and colleagues (1985), but based on auditorily presented verbal paired associates, have been reported by Madigan, McCabe, and Itatani (1972): Immediate recall shows the primacy effect overshadowed by the recency factors, whereas delayed recall shows a pure primacy effect throughout the eight-pair list.

The Wright et al. (1985) findings provide at least four lessons relevant to the story told here.

First, the fact that clear primacy effects occur in birds and nonhuman primates is at variance with one of the most venerable and most popular explanations of primacy, namely that primacy results from rehearsal of the material. The rehearsal hypothesis can be saved only if one is willing to assume that pigeons and monkeys, and even humans, are capable of "rehearsing" complex colored patches of light.

Second, varying the length of the retention interval, while holding constant all other variables, produces either primacy, recency, or both. This general fact is not unknown (Neath & Crowder, 1990), but it is worth emphasizing in the present context.

Third, whatever processes determine recognition performance as measured immediately after the presentation of the four-item inspection series can completely overpower or overshadow the processes that subserve the primacy effect. Whatever these processes are, and however the overshadowing works—and a number of possibilities, as always, suggest themselves—the important lesson is to observe and measure primacy, one has to keep it out of the reach of recency. The situation is analogous, say, to the measurement of the power of the Earth to attract a paper clip: One should not do so when a magnet is near the clip. The law of primacy is limited to "long-term" retention to stay clear of the strong powers of the determinants of recency.

Fourth, the Wright et al. (1985) data are incompatible with the idea that primacy is a phenomenon of episodic memory (T. Jones & Roediger, 1995), unless one is willing to agree that pigeons possess episodic memory. This fact is worth noting, although its more detailed pursuit does not fit into the present chapter.

EVENTS 1 AND 2

The proposed law of primacy deals with two sequentially occurring events. This is the simplest situation in which primacy can be observed. Thus, one event occurs, then another, and the learner witnesses them. Call them Event 1 and Event 2. Some time after witnessing Event 2, the learner's knowledge of the fact of the occurrence of the two events is measured. Frequently the measurement takes the form of free recall, although other measures of retention such as cued recall, recognition, "remembering," "knowing," and judged confidence (Lockhart, 2000) may also be used. In what follows, I use the generic term recall as a placeholder for all measures. Higher recall of Event 1 than Event 2 is referred to as "primacy effect," or simply "primacy."

In the scenario as described, there can of course be many reasons why Event 1 is more memorable than Event 2, reasons orthogonal to the temporal relations of the two events. Many "material variables" that affect recall have been identified in memory research. If higher recall of Event 1 were attributable to such a material variable, it would be of little interest, and it should not be called primacy. Or, it could be that Event 1 might "catch" more attention than Event 2 because of its distinctive position at the beginning of some sequence. Or, Event 1 might receive more rehearsal, because the learner has greater opportunities to do so, with appropriate consequences for retention. Now, although there is no doubt that special attention and rehearsal can produce primacy effects, the Wright et al. (1985) data mentioned earlier in the chapter prove that rehearsal is not necessary for such effects. In cases where primacy appears as a result of such special processing, I would suggest that what looks like primacy is a mere side effect of more fundamental processes and therefore theoretically uninteresting.

Here I am concerned with "true" primacy, primacy that occurs solely in virtue of Event 1 preceding Event 2 in time, and nothing else. Keeping firmly in mind the standard *ceteris paribus* clause—that always, automatically, applies to any scientific laws—may help minimize misunderstanding in this respect.

The proposed law tolerates many variations of the basic scheme. The nature of the events does not matter, the length of the temporal intervals involved does not matter, cognitive environments in which Events 1 and 2 occur are not supposed to matter. The law says nothing about what qualifies as an event. In practice, an event can be defined in many ways. The presentation of a word in a word list could be an event; the first three adjectives in a description of a person could be one event, and the next three, as in classic experiments of Asch (1946), another; one whole to-be-learned list could be an event. Indeed, the first half of one's life could be one event and the second half another, although for practical reasons the memorability of these two "successive events" cannot always be compared. In principle, however, as far as the law of primacy is concerned, "anything goes." As long as Events 1 and 2 are objectively identifiable and their retention measurable—and the *ceteris paribus* clause satisfied—the law of primacy is expected to hold.

The first and second items in experimental lists conform to the paradigm of two successive events, and in that sense the explanation of primacy that we are seeking would have to apply to them, too. But the beginning of a typical list represents only a special instance of a more general case; it is simple to create primacy effects in the middle of a list, and it is this more general case that is the object of interest in the present story. And it better be, too, because there are no experimenter-made "lists" in real life, yet real life is replete with primacy effects, and we want to understand those as much as their laboratory analogues.

ACCOUNTS OF PRIMACY

Memory theorists have proposed explanations for findings that have been interpreted as primacy effects. These explanations have targeted the higher recall of earlier events rather than the lower recall of later ones, as I am doing here. That is, rather than targeting the impoverished recall of the later events, the perspective taken by the "camatosis hypothesis" I describe in the next section, explanations for primacy have focused on the superiority of recall for the earlier events. The most common and popular explanation of this sort is one that invokes the concept of "rehearsal." It comes in different varieties, but the basic idea is that the learner rehearses (thinks about, reviews in her mind) earlier list items while studying later ones. This kind of extra "practice" spent on the early items makes for stronger "memory traces" that translate into higher recall.

The rehearsal idea is one that is easy to think of because it is obviously true—surely extra practice spent on or extra thought paid to a to-be-remembered item helps its subsequent recall. The idea has been around from the 19th century (Madigan & O'Hara, 1992) and its popularity has continued unabated to this day. It has been bolstered by experiments in which the extent of item-by-item rehearsal is observed and has been seen to be correlated with recall (Rundus, 1971).

Problematic aspects of the rehearsal theory of primacy have also been registered from time to time, long before Wright and his colleagues reported their findings. In his classic book, *The Psychology of Human Learning* (1942), McGeoch writes that the suggestion is "frequently made that the rapid rate of learning at the initial position or positions may be a function of rehearsal" (p. 107). However, after considering the available evidence, especially the fact that the primacy effect occurs under conditions where materials are presented at rapid rates (thereby making rehearsal impossible), he gives the theory short shrift.

Similar doubts about the validity of the rehearsal theory of primacy continue to be expressed in our day and age (Sikstrom, 2006). However, in the absence of a better explanation, the intuitive appeal of the rehearsal theory of primacy has remained high.

An alternative approach to explaining primacy is based on the idea that items at the beginning and the end of a given list are more discriminable, or more distinctive, than those that come in the middle. As such, items that come earlier in a given list receive more "attention," making them more memorable (Johnson, 1991; McGeoch, 1942; Murdock, 1960; Ribback & Underwood, 1950). This type of explanation takes care of the situations in which primacy occurs in the absence of rehearsal. Like the rehearsal theory it, too, makes intuitively good sense: surely an item that receives extra attention, together with attendant extra "processing," has a memorial advantage over other items.

The discriminability theory also has the additional virtue of parsimony: it also explains the recency effect (Murdock, 1960).The discriminability idea has fared better than the rehearsal idea in the theoretical sweepstakes, although it too has some problems (Hunt, 2006). Apart from anything else, it is at odds with data from experiments where there are only two to-be-remembered events, which, according to the discriminability theory, occupy equally distinctive positions. These data show primacy: the first event is remembered better than the second. Moreover, there is nothing much that the experimenter or subject can do to change the inferiority of recall for the second event (Peterson & Peterson, 1962).

Because neither the rehearsal or discriminability ideas, the two main types of explanations for the primacy effect, are free from problems, more sober sugges- tions have been made to the effect that primacy is a result of multiple causes that include rehearsal and discriminability. In Anderson's ACT–R model, "The ten- dency for the earlier items to receive greater rehearsal is one factor that is pro- ducing the primacy effect. The other factor is the lower positional confusions among items at the beginning of the list" (Anderson, Bothell, Lebiere, & Matessa, 1998, p. 357). In Baddeley's view, the primacy effect "may reflect a number of variables, but in particular the tendency to give more attention and possibly more rehearsal to the initial item" (Baddeley, 2000, p. 79).

Most traditional explanations of primacy do not explain primacy as much as they explain primacy away. After they are finished there is no real phenomenon left to explain. Primacy is an "artifact," a product of more basic processes.

I believe that primacy is primary: it reflects a basic property of the brain. It can and does occur in situations where rehearsal, attention, and all variables other than the temporal relation between Events 1 and 2 are held constant. We consid- er this basic property next.

HYPOTHESIS OF CAMATOSIS

When a person witnesses an event, whether a miniature event (such as seeing a word on a display device in the laboratory setting) or a more complex one (like being involved in an automobile accident), information about many aspects of the event is encoded in long-term memory. This encoded or stored information (the memory trace or engram) is one of the critical determinants of what, and how well, the person remembers the event some time later.

Now, let us make a few rather reasonable assumptions. One, that the encoding process is subserved by the activity of (widely distributed, highly complex) cere- bral ensembles of neuronal networks. Two, that the isomorphic relation between the witnessed and "cognitively processed" event, on the one hand, and the corre- sponding widely distributed yet highly specific neural activity, on the other hand, applies to every single feature of the event. Three, as a result of its activity, a net- work becomes "fatigued," as do many other biological mechanisms and systems as a result of their operations.

Given these assumptions, the components of the network underlying the pro- cessing of Event 1 in our two-event scenario can also become fatigued. If now

Event 2 comes along whose processing for long-term retention requires the same components as Event 1, and if these components are in the refractory state engendered by the "fatigue," the encoding of Event 2 suffers, and so does the subsequent retention.

The kind of neuronal "fatigue" I am talking about here has been dubbed camatosis. The term is derived from kamatos, a word in classical Greek that can be translated into English as "tiredness" or "weariness".[1]

Camatosis is defined as a *"hypothetical (neurochemical?) process that causes specific activity-dependent reduction in the efficacy of a neuronal network."* One can assume that camatosis affects many different kinds of neural networks. For the sake of simplicity, in what follows in this chapter, however, whenever I use the term I mean camatosis of those networks that subserve *encoding of online information for long-term storage*. The concept of camatosis was initially introduced to account for the Von Restorff–type distinctiveness effects (Tulving & Rosenbaum, 2006). Its definition there was somewhat different from the one proffered here, but the general idea about it, and about its role in "causing" what appears as superior retention of certain items from within a collection, is very much the same.

Thus, according to the *camatosis hypothesis* proffered here, (true) primacy reflects the lowered memorability of Event 2 because of the "fatigue" of the neuronal networks underlying the processing of Event 1.

The camatotic effects of the processing of Event 1 on the processing of Event 2 depend on a number of variables, most of which remain to be identified in future research. A major determinant is the totality of similarity between Events 1 and 2. Such totality includes the context in which the events occur. Another major determinant is the length of the interval between the two events. Because "fatigue" in biological systems usually dissipates with inactivity (rest), it makes sense to assume that camatotic effects diminish over time. Camatosis is transitory. The rate of dissipation of the camatotic fatigue presumably depends on a number of variables, and it need not always be complete.

An explanation of primacy that is in some ways rather similar to the one that leans on the concept of camatosis has been proposed in a recent paper by Sikström (2006). Sikström, too, believes that the proper place to look for causes of apparent superiority of recall of certain kinds of events—those that are distinctive, or isolated, or those that appear at the beginning or end of a series—is the brain and its activity, rather than the deployment of attention and other cognitive capacities of the rememberer. Sikström's account is much more sophisticated and elaborate than the simple one I describe here. It is also more comprehensive. Among other things he proposes an objective, quantitative index of

---

[1]I am grateful to Professor Jaan Puhvel of UCLA for creating the term camatosis for the purpose of labeling the process described in this chapter.

primacy that is useful for comparing the magnitude of primacy in different situations, thereby helping adjudicate disputes having to do with issues such as whether or not some experimental treatment reduced or even eliminated primacy.

Here I proffer the camatosis hypothesis as an explanation of primacy in memory; however, the potential domain of application of this hypothesis is presumably larger, perhaps much larger, thereby crossing over the boundary of primacy. This is so, because all cognitively apprehended events, without a single exception, are always processed in the temporal context of other events that have preceded them. In the next section, I briefly consider one obvious target of the camatosis hypothesis—novelty.

NOVELTY AND RELATED PHENOMENA

The concept of camatosis—a hypothetical "fatigue" process that reduces the efficacy of specific task-relevant neuronal circuits—or something like it, may help us to understand numerous memory phenomena. These are phenomena that are covered by the umbrella term of "associative interference," phenomena explained by concepts such as unlearning, response competition, negative transfer, build-up of proactive inhibition, list-length effects in learning, ineffectiveness of massed repetition, cue overload, fan effect, and the like.

The concept of camatosis extends the concept of interference into the neural realm. It explains why one item, or one collection of items, or the carrying out of one task, interferes with another. We can assume that camatosis is the "cause," or one of the "causes," of behavioral and cognitive interference. Camatotic interference effects are more readily discerned in learning (at encoding) than in forgetting (at retrieval), but they are, presumably, always present whenever events occur and are cognitively "processed." This happens in the laboratory as well as outside it, on a minuscule as well as a broad scale. In my bolder moments, I can imagine that the impaired remembering of life's events by healthy older people may reflect camatosis of the neural networks subserving encoding of autobiographical happenings chronically built up over a lifetime. So might the impaired ability of the older folks to learn and remember new names—"name-encoding circuits are overloaded," as we might say.

Camatosis seems to be particularly relevant to the understanding of "novelty effects" in memory, the finding that novel events are remembered better than familiar ones (Kormi-Nouri, Nilsson, & Ohta, 2005.). Novelty is a concept that can assume many forms and that can be defined in a variety of ways, and camatosis need not apply to all of them. But it might apply to some.

Novelty in cognitive memory experiments is usually specified in terms of the appearance of a given item in the experimental situation. An item that appears for the very first time is novel whereas subsequent appearances are less so; they are said to be (more) "familiar."

Like primacy, novelty is a concept that can be defined only relationally. Primacy refers to higher recall of an earlier, relative to a later, event. Novelty refers to higher recall of a new, relative to an old, event. In relation to an imaginary baseline (the "default state" of the brain/mind; Raichle et al., 2001), primacy and novelty can come about because of the enhanced recall of the first or new event, the lowered recall of the subsequent or old event, or both.

In an earlier paper (Tulving & Kroll, 1995), it was suggested that "familiar items are less well recognized than novel items because the novelty-assessment system screens out familiar items from further processing for subsequent recognition at an early stage of encoding" (p. 389). This screening was assumed to involve the comparison of the incoming information with information already in the long-term memory store. Further processing (for encoding) was assumed to depend on the outcome of this global comparison.

This idea may have had some merit at the time, but it now appears less attractive. The postulated global comparison mechanism, although a popular idea that has found wide application in the cognitive literature (Farrell & Lewandowsky, 2002; Metcalfe, 1993), just sounds too cumbersome a neural mechanism. Comparison and screening may still occur, but a simpler way to produce data that look like better recognition of novel rather than familiar items would be not to encode the familiar information at all, or to encode it less efficaciously. This is where camatosis becomes relevant. For the brain, it is not a question of whether or not to encode some incoming information. The question is whether there are resources available to do so. If, and only, the resources are available, encoding occurs, always.

Thus, the concept of camatosis provides a solution to the problem of determining the novelty of incoming information, and it does so without postulating any global, systemwide comparison.

REPETITION SUPPRESSION AND CAMATOSIS

The thesis of this chapter is that camatosis explains primacy effect in memory, along with a host of other interference-based and novelty-related behavioral phenomena. In this last section of the chapter, I briefly summarize some of the available evidence for a neural process, or set of processes, that produce camatotic effects.

The evidence comes from situations in which a stimulus is presented to an experimental subject (Event 1) and then presented again (Event 2), or comparable situations in which Event 2 is similar to Event 1. Brain activity for the repeated event is compared with the brain activity observed for the original presentation. It is measured in a variety of ways—single-cell recording in experimental animals (Miller, Li, & Desimone, 1991), intracranial event-related potentials from depth electrodes in patients (Grunwald, Lehnertz, Heinze,

Helmstaedter, & Elger, 1998), scalp recording of electrical (Henson, Rylands, Ross, Vuillemier, & Rogg, 2004) and magnetic (Duzel et al., 2005) signals, as well as functional neuroimaging (positron emission tomography [PET] and functional magnetic resonance imaging [fMRI]) in human beings.A common observation in these situations is that the activity associated with the repeated stimulus (Event 2) is lower relative to that of Event 1. That is, primacy is commonly observed at the neural level.

Different names have been given to this kind of a finding by different investigators: "adaptive filtering" (Desimone, 1992), "adaptive mnemonic filtering" (Miller, Li, & Desimone, 1993), "stimulus specific adaptation" (Ringo, 1996), "repetition suppression" (Desimone, 1996), "decremental responses" (Brown & Xiang, 1998), "habituation" (Sohal & Hasselmo, 2000), "repetition priming" or "neural priming" (Wagner, Koutstaal, Maril, Schacter, & Buckner, 2000) or even just "priming," (Buckner & Koutstaal, 1998), "cortical activity reduction" (Dobbins, Schnyder, Verfaellie, & Schacter, 2004), plus, probably, a few others. In the remainder of this chapter, I follow others and use "repetition suppression," adopted from Desimone (1996), as a single, umbrella term for all forms of experimental observations where neural activity for the repeated stimulus is reduced in relation to that of the first (novel) stimulus.

The highlights of a rapidly growing literature on repetition suppression have recently been lucidly summarized by Grill-Spector, Henson, and Martin (2006). These writers propose several potential neural mechanisms underlying repetition suppression: firing-rate adaptation (reduced excitability of neurons), synaptic depression (reduction in presynaptic neurotransmitter release), long-term depression, and long-term potentiation. They also describe three models of repetition suppression—fatigue model, sharpening model, and facilitation model—that make different assumptions regarding the source or locus of reduced neuronal efficacy. In the present context, the interesting feature of these models of repetition suppression is that every single one of them would be equally appropriate as a summary description of camatosis.

Repetition suppression nicely parallels primacy and novelty effects: neural activity is reduced for the "repeated" stimulus in relation to the original stimulus, as does observed retention of Event 2 in relation to Event 1. But such an encouraging parallel is not sufficient to firmly associate neural repetition suppression to behaviorally observed primacy and novelty effects. A more direct link between the brain and the mind would be highly desirable, especially as there are popular theories that hold that repetition suppression expresses itself behaviorally in the phenomenon of priming, experience-based *enhanced* identification of the repeated stimulus (Schacter & Buckner, 1998; Wiggs & Martin, 1998). Although the priming story is not entirely clear (Habib, 2001; Henson & Rugg, 2003), it needs to be kept in mind as we explore the implications of the reduced memorability of repeated items.

A closer link between repetition suppression and reduced memorability of Event 2 in relation to Event 1 is provided by an ingenious experiment reported by Brenda Kirchhoff and her colleagues (Kirchoff, Wagner, Maril, & Stern, 2000). Using functional imaging, they demonstrated the existence of a number of cerebral regions in which novelty detection was found to be tied to effective encoding of to-be-remembered items (words and pictures).

Kirchhoff and her colleagues accomplished this feat by combining two powerful methods for studying the brain activity correlated with cognitive tasks. One of the methods (event-related fMRI) makes it possible to track neural activity, as reflected in changes in blood oxygenation, that accompanies the perceptual-cognitive processing of "single" events, such as the presentation of a word or a picture for study (encoding), and thereby provides the "neural signature" of the event (Buckner et al., 1996). The same kind of item-by-item analysis had been available earlier in electrophysiological recordings of event-related potentials, a method with high temporal, but not sufficiently fine spatial, resolution. The other method is dubbed "subsequent memory paradigm" (Paller & Wagner, 2002). It consists of the back-sorting of the "neuronal signatures" of single events recorded at one point in time, such as encoding, into different categories, depending on what happens at a later time, such as subsequent recognition or failure of recognition of the encoded item.

The procedure used by Kirchhoff and her colleagues essentially isolated two sets of brain regions of interest: first, "novelty regions" in which encoding activity (expressed in the BOLD signal) was reduced by virtue of an earlier appearance of, and camatosis engendered by, the same item; second, "encoding regions," in which the level of activity at encoding "predicted" subsequent recognizability of the item—"remembered" items versus "forgotten" items. These "encoding regions" were identified while novelty was held constant. The critical finding, supportive of the camatosis hypothesis, was the finding of considerable overlap between the novelty regions and encoding regions. The authors summarized the finding by saying that "the present results provide the first evidence that the same ventrolateral prefrontal and temporal regions that are sensitive to novelty also predict subsequent explicit memory, supporting the hypothesis that these regions contribute to encoding" (Kirchhoff et al., 2000, p. 6179).

Kirchhoff et al. (2000) focused on a restricted set of cerebral regions, prefrontal and temporal cortex, because they had been marked as "interesting" by the results of earlier encoding and novelty-related fMRI studies. Their full data set, however, reveals a number of additional novelty-encoding regions in other parts of the brain. (Note: I am grateful to Brenda Kirchhoff for making the complete data available for inspection and analysis.) Perhaps even more interesting, and important, is the fact that *none* of the "familiarity regions," regions in which repeated items showed greater activity than novel items, coincided with regions in which the encoding activity was higher for "remembered" than for "forgotten" item.

If one believes, as I do, that primacy and novelty reflect the same kind of selectively reduced camatosis-dependent encoding processes, then Kirchhoff's data on novelty encoding are also relevant to primacy. More direct applications of Kirchhoff's procedure, to the first few items in a to-be-remembered list, are awaiting experimenters. One relevant study has already been recently reported (Sommer, Rose, & Buchel, 2006; see also Strange, Otten, Josephs, Rugg, & Dolan, 2002).

CAMATOTIC LAW OF ENCODING

We are now in a position to contemplate the possibility of complementing the descriptive law of primacy with a higher level law that would explain primacy. The idea is that primacy, as manifested in many situations involving learning and memory, comes about because of a basic property of the brain labeled camatosis, a hypothetical neural process that causes specific activity-dependent fatigue-like reduction in the efficacy of the neural networks subserving perception and thought. Physiological research under the umbrella term of repetition suppression encourages me to believe that camatosis may be more than just an idea. At the least, it is not difficult to see how the patterns woven by psychological experiments on phenomena of learning and memory, such as distinctiveness, primacy, and novelty, fit comfortably into the patterns produced by recordings and images yielded by objectively measured activity of the brain.

It is against the backdrop of this kind of a reasonably coherent picture of the brain/mind that I would like to propose another broad generalization, or a law:

Of two events, the one whose encoding is more severely affected by camatosis is less likely to be retained.

We can of think of this as the *camatotic law of encoding*. A little thought reveals that it subsumes the descriptive law of primacy as presented earlier, and that it also explains some data that may seem to be at variance with the descriptive law. Further thought reveals that the camatotic law of encoding hides, within itself, a host of issues and questions that may be worth pursuing and that may not be pursued in the absence of the ideas contained in the law. If for no other reason, then, at least for this, the ideas I have presented here—which I know some of my best friends think are not that different from happenings on Alice's journey into the Wonderland—may turn out to have some merit.

ACKNOWLEDGMENTS

My research is supported by an endowment in support of cognitive neuroscience by Anne and Max Tanenbaum. I am grateful to Alice Kim for editorial assistance.

REFERENCES

Anderson, J. R., Bothell, D., Lebiere, C., & Matessa, M. (1998). An integrated theory of list memory. *Journal of Memory and Language, 38,* 341–380.

Asch, S. E. (1946). Forming impressions of personality. *Journal of Abnormal and Social Psychology, 41,* 258–290.

Baddeley, A. D. (2000). Short-term and working memory. In E. Tulving & F. I. M. Craik (Eds.), *The Oxford Handbook of Memory* (pp. 77–92). New York: Oxford University Press.

Baddeley, A. D., & Warrington, E. K. (1970). Amnesia and the distinction between long- and short-term memory. *Journal of Verbal Learning and Verbal Behavior, 9,* 176–189.

Bower, G. H. (1971). In M. H. Appley (Ed.), *Adaptation-level theory* (pp. 175–201). New York: Academic Press.

Bower, G. H., Thompson-Schill, S., & Tulving, E. (1994). On reducing retroactive interference: An interference analysis. *Journal of Experimental Psychology: Learning, Memory, and Cognition, 20,* 51–66.

Brown, M. W., & Xiang, J. Z. (1998). Recognition memory: Neuronal substrates of the judgment of prior occurrence. *Progress in Neurobiology, 55,* 184–189,

Buckner, R. L. Bandettini, P. A., O'Craven, K. M., Savoy, R. L., Petersen, S. E., Raichle, M. E., & Rosen, B. R. (1996). Detection of cortical activation during averaged single trials of a cognitive task using functional magnetic-resonance-imaging. *Proceedings of the National Academy of Sciences, 93,* 14878–14883.

Buckner, R. L. & Koutstaal, W. (1998). Functional neuroimaging studies of encoding, priming, and explicit memory retrieval. *Proceedings of the National Academy of Sciences, 95,* 891–898.

Castro, C. A., & Larsen, T. (1992). Primacy and recency effects in nonhuman primates. *Journal of Experimental Psychology: Animal Behavior Processes, 18,* 335–340.

Desimone, R. (1992). The physiology of memory: Recordings of things past. *Science, 258,* 245–246.

Desimone, R. (1996). Neural mechanisms for visual memory and their role in attention. *Proceedings of the National Academy of Sciences, 93,* 13494–13499.

Dobbins, I. G., Schnyer, D. M., Verfaellie, M., & Schacter, D. L. (2004). Cortical activity reductions during repetition priming can result from rapid response learning. *Nature, 428,* 316–319.

Düzel, E., Richardson-Klavehn, A., Neufang, M., Schott, B.J., Scholz, M., & Heinze, H. J. (2005). Early, partly anticipatory, neural oscillations during identification set the stage for priming. *Neuroimage, 25,* 690–700.

Eslinger, P. J., & Grattan, L. M. (1994). Altered serial position learning after frontal lobe lesion. *Neuropsychologia, 32,* 729–239.

Farrell, S., & Lewandowsky, S. (2002). An endogenous distributed model of ordering in serial recall. *Psychonomic Science & Review, 9,* 59–79.

Gernsbacher, M. A., & Hargreaves, D. J. (1988). Accessing sentence participants: The advantage of first mention. *Journal of Memory and Language, 27,* 699–717.

Glanzer, M. (1972). Storage mechanisms in recall. In G. H. Bower & J. T. Spence (Eds.), *The psychology of learning and motivation* (Vol. 5, pp. 129–193). New York: Academic Press.

Grill-Spector, K., Henson, R., & Martin, A. (2006). Repetition and the brain: Neural models of stimulus-specific effects. *Trends in Cognitive Sciences, 10,* 14–23.

Grunwald, T., Lehnertz, K., Heinze, H. J., Helmstaedter, C, & Elger, C. E. (1998). Verbal novelty detection with the human hippocampus proper. *Proceedings of the National Academy of Sciences, 95,* 3193–3197.

Habib, R. (2001). On the relation between conceptual priming, neural priming, and novelty assessment. *Scandinavian Journal of Psychology, 42,* 187–195.

Henson, R. N. A. (2003). Neuroimaging studies of priming. *Progress in Neurobiology, 70,* 53–81.

Henson, R. N. A., & Rugg, M. D. (2003). Neural response suppression, haemodynamic repetition effects, and behavioural priming. *Neuropsychologia, 41*(3), 263–270.

Henson, R. N. A., Rylands, A., Ross, E., Vuillemier, P., & Rugg, M. D. (2004). The effect of repetition lag on electrophysiological and haemodynamic correlates of visual object priming. *Neuroimage, 21,* 1674, 1689.

Henson, R. N. A., Shallice, T., Gorno-Tempini, M. L., & Dolan, R. J. (2002). Face repetition effects in implicit and explicit memory tests as measured by FMRI. *Cerebral Cortex, 12,* 178–186.

Hogarth, R. M., & Einhorn, H. J. (1992). Order effects in belief updating: The belief-adjustment model. *Cognitive Psychology, 24,* 1–55.

Hunt, R.R. (2006). The concept of distinctiveness in memory research. In R. R. Hunt & J. B. Worthen (Eds.), *Distinctiveness and memory* (pp. 3–25). New York: Oxford University Press.

Johnson G. J. (1991). A distinctiveness model of serial learning. *Psychological Review, 98,* 204–217.

Jones, B. M. (1973). Memory impairment on the ascending and descending limbs of the blood alcohol curve. *Journal of Abnormal Psychology, 82,* 24–42.

Jones, T., & Roediger, H. L., III. (1995). The experiential basis of serial position effects. *European Journal of Cognitive Psychology, 7,* 65–80.

Kesner, R. P., Measom, M. O., Forsman, S. L., & Holbrook, T. H. (1984). Serial-position curves in rats: Order memory for episodic spatial events. *Animal Learning and Behavior, 12,* 378–382.

Kirchhoff, B. A., Wagner, A. D., Maril, A., & Stern, C. E. (2000). Prefrontal-temporal circuitry for episodic encoding and subsequent memory. *Journal of Neuroscience, 20,* 6173–6180.

Kormi-Nouri, R., Nilsson, L. G., & Ohta, N. (2005). The novelty effect: Support for the novelty-encoding hypothesis. *Scandinavian Journal of Psychology, 46,* 133–143.

Lockhart, R. S. (2000). Methods in memory research. In E. Tulving & F. I. M. Craik (Eds.), *The Oxford handbook of memory* (pp. 45–57). New York: Oxford University Press.

Madigan, S.A. (1969). Intraserial repetition and coding processes in free recall. *Journal of Verbal Learning and Verbal Behavior, 8,* 828–835.

Madigan, S. A., McCabe, L., & Itatani, S. (1972). Immediate and delayed recall of words and pictures. *Canadian Journal of Psychology, 26,* 407–414.

Madigan, S., & O'Hara, R. (1992). Short-term memory at the turn of the century: Mary Whiton Calkins's memory research. *American Psychologist, 47,* 170–174.

Martin, S. J., & Morris, R. G. M. (2002). New life in an old idea: The synaptic plasticity and memory hypothesis revisited. *Hippocampus, 12,* 609–636.

McGeoch, J. A. (1942). *The psychology of human learning.* New York: Longmans Green.

Metcalfe, J. (1993). Novelty monitoring, metacognition, and control in a composite holographic associative recall model—implications for Korsakoff amnesia. *Psychological Review, 100,* 3–22.

Miller, E. K., & Desimone, R. (1994). Parallel neuronal mechanisms for short-term memory. *Science, 263,* 520–522.

Miller, E. K., Li, L., & Desimone, R. (1991). A neural mechanism for working and recognition memory in inferior temporal cortex. *Science, 254,* 1377–1379.

Miller, E. K., Li, L., & Desimone, R. (1993). Activity of neurons in anterior inferior temporal cortex during a short-term memory task. *Journal of Neuroscience, 13,* 1460–1478

Murdock, B. B. (1960). The distinctiveness of stimuli. *Psychological Review, 67,* 16–31.

Murdock, B. B., Jr. (1962). The serial position effect in free recall. *Journal of Experimental Psychology, 62,* 482–488.

Neath, I., & Crowder, R. G. (1990). Schedules of presentation and temporal distinctiveness in human memory. *Journal of Experimental Psychology: Learning, Memory, and Cognition, 16,* 316–327.

Nisbett, R. E., & Ross, L. (1980). *Human inference: Strategies and shortcomings of social judgment.* Englewood Cliffs, NJ: Prentice-Hall.

Paller, K. A., & Wagner, A. D. (2002). Observing the transformation of experience into memory. *Trends in Cognitive Sciences, 6,* 93–102.

Peterson, L. R., & Peterson, M. J. (1962). Minimal paired-associate learning. *Journal of Experimental Psychology, 63,* 521–527.

Raichle, M. E., MacLeod, A. M., Snyder, A. Z., Powers, W. J., Gusnard, D. A., & Shulman, G. L. (2001). A default mode of brain function. *Proceedings of the National Academy of Sciences, 98,* 676–682.

Ribback, A., & Underwood, B. J. (1950). An empirical explanation of the skewness of the serial position curve. *Journal of Experimental Psychology, 40,* 329–335

Ringo, J. L. (1996). Stimulus specific adaptation in inferior temporal and medial temporal cortex of the monkey. *Behavioural Brain Research, 76,* 191–197

Rundus, D. (1971). Analysis of rehearsal processes in free recall. *Journal of Experimental Psychology, 89,* 63–77.

Schacter, D. L., & Buckner, R. L. (1998). Priming and the brain. *Neuron, 20,* 185–195.

Shallice, T. (1979). Neuropsychological research and the fractionation of memory systems. In Nilsson, L.-G. (Ed.), *Perspectives in memory research* (pp. 193–218). Hillsdale, NJ: Lawrence Erlbaum Associates.

Sikström, S. (2006). The isolation, primacy, and recency effects predicted by an adaptive LTD/LTP threshold in postsynaptic cells. *Cognitive Science, 30,* 243–275.

Sohal, V. S., & Hasselmo, M. E. (2000). A model for experience-dependent changes in the responses of inferotemporal neurons. *Network, 11,* 169–190.

Sommer, T., Rose, M., & Büchel, C. (2006). Dissociable parietal systems for primacy and subsequent memory effects. *Neurobiology of Learning and Memory, 85,* 243–251.

Strange, B. A., Otten, L. J., Josephs, O., Rugg, M. D., & Dolan, R. J. (2002). Dissociable human perirhinal, hippocampal, and parahippocampal roles during verbal encoding. *Journal of Neuroscience, 22,* 523–528.

Teigen, K. H. (2002). One hundred years of laws in psychology. *American Journal of Psychology, 115,* 103–118.

Tulving, E., & Kroll, N. (1995). Novelty assessment in the brain and long-term memory encoding. *Psychonomic Bulletin & Review, 2,* 387–390.

Tulving, E., & Rosenbaum, R. S. (2006). What do explanations of the distinctiveness effect need to explain? In R. R. Hunt & J. B. Worthen (Eds.), *Distinctiveness and memory* (pp. 407–423). New York: Oxford University Press.

Underwood, B. J. (1970). A breakdown of total-time law in free-recall learning. *Journal of Verbal Learning and Verbal Behavior, 9,* 573–580.

Wagner, A. D., Koutstaal, W., Maril, A., Schacter, D. L., & Buckner, R. L. (2000). Task-specific repetition priming in left inferior prefrontal cortex. *Cerebral Cortex, 10,* 1176–1184.

Wang, H., Johnson, T. R., & Zhang, J. (2006). The order effect in human abductive reasoning; an empirical and computational study. *Journal of Experimental & Theoretical Artificial Intelligence, 18,* 215–247.

Wiggs., C. L., & Martin, A. (1998). Properties and mechanisms of perceptual priming. *Current Opinion in Neurobiology, 8,* 227–233.

Wright, A. A., Santiago, H. C., Sands, S. F., Kendrick, D. F., & Cook, R. G. (1985). Memory processing of serial lists by pigeons, monkeys, and people. *Science, 229,* 287–289.

4

Gordon and Me

Elizabeth F. Loftus
University of California–Irvine

A particularly terrifying life experience for many Stanford graduate students was the first time that you had to present your research findings at the Friday Seminar. It was my 1st year of graduate school, and I would be discussing my research project on computer-assisted instructed conducted under the supervision of my then-adviser Dick Atkinson. For much of the academic year, I'd watched "Dr. Bower" tear into my poor predecessors, and didn't have the confidence that I'd be able to withstand his aggressive questions. But I did quite well. In fact, my answers to Gordon's questions were downright excellent! I confessed, some 30 years later, how this was so. It turns out that Dick Atkinson was sitting next to me, whispering the answers to Gordon's questions in my ear. So Cyrano de Atkinson skated by the 1st year. That was the 1966–1967 academic year. How odd today to think of this, but Gordon-The-Terrible was only 7 years post-PhD.

Seven years post-PhD, and already Gordon had published extensively, including his chapter in the first volume of the prestigious Psychology of Learning and Motivation on a multicomponent theory of memory traces (Bower, 1967) and his revision of Jack Hilgard's Theories of Learning text (Hilgard & Bower, 1966)—required reading at the time. These publications encompassed Gordon's key interests in animal learning and in mathematical modeling. I, meanwhile, was struggling to finish my master's thesis on computer-assisted instruction, which was ultimately published a year later (Fishman, Keller, & Atkinson, 1968). No one that I know of was ever required to read that paper.

I was not Gordon's actual student at Stanford, and we never actually worked together. His time was taken by many other fortunate students, and mine was being spent primarily on computer-assisted instruction projects with Atkinson, and also Pat Suppes, who would become my PhD supervisor. But over the next several decades, Gordon would come to play an important role in my life, making appearances at unexpected times and places, at bad times and good ones. His role grew so large that when I'm now asked who was particularly important in my own career development, I invariably mention Gordon. This chapter provides a welcome opportunity to memorialize some of the appearances Gordon made, and some of the times I got to step on Bower Road (as he called it in his Memory Memoir, presented at the 2003 meeting of the Psychonomic Society, Bower, 2003).

LIFE AFTER STANFORD

After finishing graduate school, I moved to New York City, to begin teaching at the New School for Social Research, where the students were quite heterogeneous. I taught cognitive psychology. To my horror, one of the poorer students took a paper that he had submitted as a required class assignment, and, when the class was over, submitted it to the *Journal of Experimental Psychology* where it was promptly rejected by the then-editor David Grant from Wisconsin.

The student then sent the paper to Gordon, whose work he had learned about in my class, along with this note:

Nov. 12, 1972

Dear Dr. Bower:

The paper I am submitting to you was done in a seminar with Dr. E. Loftus. It would be greatly appreciated by the authors if you could look over the paper and make some brief comments. We would like to try and publish it, if this is possible. Dr. Loftus didn't really understand the paper, so I thought that I should send it to you for any comments that you wish to make in any form.

Very truly yours

(name omitted)

Gordon returned the letter with a handwritten note at the bottom—that perfect handwriting that Gordon has. He sent a copy to me:

"Dear (student):

I haven't the time nor energy to try to understand your paper. I agree with Dr. Loftus that it is very poorly written, and a sampling of its contents suggest to me that you probably mis-state or have misunderstood certain positions. I'm sorry, but I am terribly busy and must strictly curtail all nonessential work.

Gordon Bower

I've saved that letter all these years. ... God knows why. It still seems funny. I would learn much later that faculty sometimes get all kinds of requests like this one. Lately, scores of students from far away universities request via e-mail that I send them references for their papers, or sit for an interview, or design their class projects for them. One line from Gordon's reply comes in handy, and I should have begun using it earlier when these requests began mounting: "I'm sorry but I am terribly busy and must strictly curtail all nonessential work."

In those first few years post graduate school, I spent most of my time studying semantic memory, and then turned my attention to eyewitness testimony. I was eager to take up scientific issues that would have some obvious practical applications, and for a psychologist interested in memory, the study of witness memory seemed like a perfect application. I began showing subjects films of simulated accidents and crimes, and studying their memory for the details of those events.

Many cognitive psychologists at the time were studying memory for words, or pictures, or other simple stimuli. I was showing subjects films of complex events, and studying their memory for the details of those events. With various collaborators, we showed that you could change the memory for details of events rather easily. We made people believe they had seen yield signs rather than stop signs, curly hair rather than straight hair, all with simple postevent suggestions (e.g., Loftus, 1975; Loftus, Miller, & Burns, 1978).

I published my first book on eyewitness testimony in 1979 (Loftus, 1979). Considerable space was devoted to one of Gordon's studies (Bower & Karlin, 1974), one that was lesser known than many of his famous publications, but was one of my favorites. Although the paper described three experiments, was published in a prestigious basic research journal, and was meant to contribute to the then-popular depth of processing literature, I saw important practical implications. Imagine eyewitnesses to a robbery who might be engaging in a variety of activities—trying to figure out how to escape the dangerous situation, trying to remember the robber's face to help the police capture him, thinking about family members who would grieve if the event ended badly. Gordon's study allowed me to demonstrate that the activity that the witness engaged in at the time of the event might affect how well details were remembered. In that research, Gordon presented pictures of human faces while they performed one of several tasks. Some judged the sex of the face, a fairly superficial judgment. Others judged the likableness or honesty of the face, thought to be a deeper judgment. Later, when subjects had to identify the faces, subjects were better if they had earlier judged the faces for likableness or honest. The practical implications of these findings were apparent to the authors even then: "If you want to remember a person's face, try to make a number of difficult personal judgments about his face when you are first meeting him" (pp. 756–757).

Gordon's research on depth of processing and face memory represented an instance of his larger research interest in memory organization and mnemonics. His contributions showing how learning materials could be converted into visual images or other representations that enhance later memory were exciting to him at the time, and great lecture material grist for a gal like me who was always looking for applications of memory science to include in classroom and public lectures.

THE MEMORY WARS

By the 1990s, Gordon was getting particularly interested in emotion and cognition (Bower, 1992; Forgas, Bower, & Moylan, 1990), and I would turn my attention to a new problem that erupted in society. Thousands of people, mostly women, were "discovering" recent memories, mostly of sexual abuse, that had allegedly been repressed in the unconscious until certain psychotherapeutic procedures bought the memories into conscious awareness. Grown-up adults were now suing their parents, their other relatives, their former neighbors, or anyone, whom they claimed had abused them decades earlier. Some accused were criminally prosecuted, and more than a few innocent people went to jail (Loftus, 1993). Gordon took a stab at the concept of "repression" (Bower, 1990), discussing his perspective on it as an experimental psychologist. He talked about repression in the context of "motivated forgetting," accepting that motivated failures to remember can and do occur during initial learning, during storage, or during retrieval. He appreciated that a patient's claim of remembering long-repressed memories has a key problem, namely the difficulty of determining the accuracy of the "memory." I liked best his conclusion that "reliable evidence for unconscious repression, which is automatic with principal parts of it occurring outside awareness, is extremely meager, and its few apparent demonstrations are subject to alternative interpretations" (p. 223).

But the topic of repression would never take over Gordon's life the way it did mine. I scoured the literature looking for any evidence that one could repress a decade of cruel brutalization, be completely unaware that it had happened, and reliably recover it. To say that the evidence was "extremely meager" would be generous.

How, then, could someone "remember" in such detail, if the events never happened? I plunged into a new line of research designed to deliberately plant wholly false memories as a way of studying how this might happen. With collaborators, we developed a variety of paradigms for showing how suggestive interventions could lead to false childhood memories. Several of these are summarized in an article I wrote for Scientific American (Loftus, 1997), including the "lost-in-the-mall" study in which we seduced about 25% of adults into believing that, as children, they had been lost for an extended time, frightened, crying, and ultimately rescued by an elderly person and reunited with their families. Later, we showed that people could be led to believe that they had experienced implausible events as children, such as witnessing demonic possession (Mazzoni, Loftus, & Kirsch, 2001). We've even gotten people to remember impossible events, such as socializing with Bugs Bunny at a Disney Resort, an impossibility because Bugs is a Warner Bros. character and wouldn't be found at Disney (Braun, Ellis, & Loftus, 2002). We would ultimately call these "rich false memories" (Loftus & Bernstein, 2005). By this, we mean the subjective feeling that one is experiencing a genuine recollection, replete with sensory details, and even expressed with confidence and emotion, even though the event never happened. We had gone a long way from turning stop signs into yield signs.

Sometimes I would testify in court cases where a defendant had been accused of unspeakable crimes for which there was no other evidence but for the claim of repressed memory. It did not endear me to the repressed-memory patients or the therapists who helped them lift the veil of "repression" and become aware of their alleged victimization. People wrote to my university complaining about my behavior. People sent angry e-mails to my departmental colleagues. People tried to get professional organizations to rescind their invitations to have me speak. At some universities, armed guards were provided to accompany me during invited speeches after the universities received calls threatening harm if the talks were not canceled. People filed ethical complaints. In early 1996, I resigned from the American Psychological Association (APA) to devote my attentions to a society that I felt valued science more highly and consistently—the American Psychological Society. Shortly after my resignation, rumors circulated that I had left APA because of ethical complaints that had been filed by two repressed-memory patients. Nothing could be further from the truth, and yet I worried about the rumors and what havoc they might wreak. Gordon appeared on the scene with a comforting e-mail, particularly in its last line:

From: Gordon Bower

Sent: Monday, April 29, 1996 4:48 AM

To: Elizabeth Loftus

Subject: Replying to your Note of Monday 4/29

What to do about the "unethical behavior" complaints against you to the APA? Lobby APA so they don't get involved retroactively, since you're no longer a member. I'll try to do what I can to get APA to keep out of it. It's a sad commentary on the situation. I gather the clients and/or their attorneys claim that you misrepresented the facts of their cases in your later public (published) descriptions of them, albeit using veiled and anonymous references to their identities. Although I and your friends have faith in you and will all give you the benefit of the doubt, the probity of their claim, of course, requires a close reading of trial transcripts (which none of us have) alongside what you wrote.

The Psych Today editorial (?) is a point in your favor. But there's really not much you can do against a subrosa smear campaign except to keep defending your reputation, which among cognitive psychologists is still sterling and unsullied. The idea that someone would try to sue the Southeastern Psychological Association to keep you off the program strikes me as extremely bizarre. It can't succeed. I'm really sorry all this is happening to you; it seems the result of your sticking your head up above the crowd of cowering cowards.

Best wishes,

Gordon

It would not be the last e-mail that Gordon would send me when times got bad. Several years later, trouble brewed again. In the late 1990s, I read an article by a psychiatrist named David Corwin and his fellow therapist about a woman named Jane Doe. People were citing this case as proof that memories can be repressed and then reliably recovered. The psychiatrist's article described how Jane Doe's mother had sexually abused her in 1984, and then 11 years later, after Jane failed to remember the sexual abuse, she suddenly remembered. Captured on videotape, what could be better "proof." Using public records and other materials, the psychologist and lawyer Mel Guyer and I found evidence that cast doubt on whether the abuse had even happened. Jane Doe complained to my former university about an invasion of her privacy, and with 15 minutes' notice, the university seized my files on the case and denied me the right to talk about it or publish anything we had discovered. I was in hot water again. And Gordon was back with a comforting e-mail that came out of the blue, but with impeccable timing:

Date: Wed, 20 Sep 2000 12:31:53–0700

From: Gordon Bower <gordon@psych.Stanford.EDU>

To: Elizabeth F. Loftus <eloftus@u.washington.edu>

Subject: Your home page

Beth:

I just looked up your Web page and read the Psych Today story about you. It was truly wonderful and beautiful, and showed all of us the caring side of your hard-nosed intellectual persona. I am proud to know you and count you among my friends...and Sharon is just as strong in her love for you as I am.

I am glad for what you are.

Gordon

It was a bleak time. I felt betrayed by the university that I had so loyally served. But I was determined to leave my job if they tried to prevent me from publishing the Jane Doe exposé. Ten months after Gordon sent the "I am glad for what you are" e-mail, my university exonerated me. Guyer and I immediately published our work in the Skeptical Inquirer (Loftus & Guyer, 2002a, 2002b). Still bitter about the lack of real apology from the University of Washington, I accepted a dream offer from the University of California–Irvine—a Distinguished Professorship, a lab built to my specifications, with research funds to keep me going for the next half decade. I would learn that Gordon was one of the scientists who provided a letter of recommendation on my behalf. As if that wasn't enough, again he e-mailed his friendship directly:

Date: Fri, 28 Jun 2002 15:17:10–0700

From: Gordon Bower <gordon@psych.stanford.edu>

To: Elizabeth Loftus <eloftus@u.washington.edu>

Subject: Way to go, Girl!

Well, well, moving to Irvine—these are indeed scary and exciting times for you. Like being born again, getting wrenched out of your settled complacency, your smoothed accommodations to small details of living, getting a new gulp of fresh air in the brain, having to prove yourself all over again (not that there's any doubt about your ability to do so). Yes, I admire you for taking the leap, grabbing for new experiences, new colleagues, new challenges. You may even find new collaborators, new avenues of research you never knew existed, a new life.

Don't burn your Washington friendship-bridges behind you; but you might tell the Dean (or IRB Chair) who shat upon you to kiss your toukis.

Gordon

LIFE AT UNIVERSITY OF CALIFORNIA–IRVINE

Gordon was right on. At UC–Irvine I did find new experiences, new colleagues, new challenges. I continued my work on memory distortion (Loftus, 2003, 2005), but also found a new angle. With collaborators, I developed some new paradigms for examining the consequences of having a false memory. In one series of studies, we induced participants to believe that when they were children they got sick eating hard-boiled eggs (or, for other participants, that they got sick eating dill pickles). We accomplished this mental feat by gathering data from the participants and plying them with false feedback. We told them that a sophisticated computer program had analyzed their data and determined that they had had one of these "sick" experiences as a child. We found that those given the "dill pickle" feedback became more confident that they had had the experience as a child and those given the "hard-boiled egg" feedback became more confident of that experience. A significant minority of participants told us they actually had a memory or a belief that these had really happened to them.

But would the false belief lead to subsequent behavior change? Would they, for example, avoid these foods when given the opportunity to eat them? To find out, we gave participants a "Party Behavior" questionnaire. They imagined themselves at a large barbeque and had to indicate which foods they would like to eat. Those who were seduced by the dill-pickle feedback reported being less likely to want to eat pickles, whereas those who fell for the egg feedback reported being less likely to want to eat eggs (Bernstein, Laney, Morris, & Loftus, 2005b).

In a subsequent study, we showed that we could get similar results with a fattening food, namely strawberry ice cream (Bernstein, Laney, Morris, & Loftus, 2005a). People could be led to belief that they had gotten sick as children eating strawberry ice cream, and later they expressed less interest in eating the tasty dessert. Time magazine reported on the work, under the headline "The Mental Diet." In December 2005, the New York Times Magazine published a list of 78 of the "most noteworthy ideas" of 2005. One item that made the list was "The False Memory Diet," based on our research. The research was also featured in the January 2006 issue of *Discover* magazine. It was No. 48 on *Discover* magazine's 100 top science stories of 2005. So, much to my delight, the "new avenues of research" that Gordon forecast in his loving e-mail, had come through in less than 3 years.

THE ORGANIZATION PEOPLE

Gordon's prolific scientific career has flourished even though he's taken the time to tend to many other matters, including the professional organizations to which he belongs. I got to travel down this part of Bower Road (Bower, 2003) on several extended occasions. We both served as president of the American Psychological Society in its formative years. We were adjacent presidents of the Western Psychological Association (WPA) in the mid-2000s (a second term for both of us, because we had previously served in the 1980s).

During a recent WPA meeting, I was strolling through the book exhibits with Gordon, checking out the vast collection of new books. On Gordon's mind was the next year's program, and he was deeply interested in making the program as appealing as possible, but cognizant of WPA's limited funds to bring in speakers. His solution: He stopped at various booths to see if he could entice the publishers into flying one of their authors to the next WPA meeting to give an invited talk. Most of the recipients of his idea seemed to like it, and Gordon was on his way toward ensuring a successful meeting filled with more speakers than we could possibly afford. Some people talk of random acts of kindness; in Gordon, I see innumerable nonrandom acts of caring.

Gordon's Festschrift was held in May 2005 at Stanford, and I was honored to be invited to speak at the gala affair. It gave me a chance to show some of these valued communications that I had saved over all these years. I ended my talk with an e-mail that that spoke back to Gordon to convey, albeit briefly, what he has meant to me.

Date: Sat, 14 May 2005 11:31:53–0700

From: Elizabeth F. Loftus <eloftus@uci.edu>

To: Gordon Bower <gordon@psych.Stanford.EDU>

Subject: The Bowerfest

Gordon:

I can't believe I've known you for 38 years. In all that time, while being one of the world's leading experimental psychologists, you've been THE professor who is far more than a student could possibly hope for. In courses back then, and in exchanges since, you've taught me many of the skills of surviving in an academic world. But even more your support and mentorship in the worst of times, and in the best of times, is something I will always cherish.

I am glad for what you are.

Beth

REFERENCES

Bernstein, D. M., Laney, C., Morris, E. K., & Loftus, E..F. (2005a). False beliefs about fattening foods can have healthy consequences. *Proceedings of the National Academy of Sciences, 102,* 13724–13731.

Bernstein, D. M., Laney, C., Morris, E. K., & Loftus, E. F. (2005b). False memories about food can lead to food avoidance. *Social Cognition, 23,* 10–33.

Bower, G. H. (1967). A multicomponent theory of the memory trace. In K. W. Spence & J. T. Spence (Eds.), *The psychology of learning and motivation* (Vol. 1, pp. 229–325). New York: Academic Press.

Bower, G. H. (1990). Awareness, the unconscious, and repression: An experimental psychologist's perspective. In J. A. Singer (Ed.), *Repression and dissociation: Implications for personality theory, psychopathology, and health* (pp. 209–231). Chicago: University of Chicago Press.

Bower, G. H. (1992). How might emotions affect learning? In S-A. Christianson, *The handbook of emotion and memory: Research and theory* (pp. 3–31). Hillsdale, NJ: Lawrence Erlbaum Associates.

Bower, G. H. (2003, November). Memories of my memory research. Paper presented at the Psychonomic Society annual meeting, Vancouver, BC, Canada.

Bower, G. H., & Karlin, M. (1974). Depth of processing pictures of faces and recognition memory. *Journal of Experimental Psychology, 103,* 751–757.

Braun, K. A., Ellis, R., & Loftus, E. F. (2002). Make my memory: How advertising can change our memories of the past. *Psychology and Marketing, 19,* 1–23.

Fishman, E. F. (Loftus), Keller, L., & Atkinson, R. C. (1968). Massed vs. distributed practice in computerized spelling drills. *Journal of Educational Psychology, 59,* 290–296

Forgas, J. P., Bower, G. H., & Moylan, S. J. (1990). Praise or blame? Affective influences on attributions for achievement. *Journal of Personality and Social Psychology, 59,* 809–819.

Hilgard, E., & Bower, G. H. (1966). Theories of learning (3rd ed.). New York: Appleton–Century–Crofts.

Loftus, E. F. (1975). Leading questions and the eyewitness report. *Cognitive Psychology, 7,* 560–572.

Loftus, E. F. (1979). Eyewitness testmony. Cambridge, MA: Harvard University Press.

Loftus, E. F. (1993). The reality of repressed memories. *American Psychologist, 48,* 518–537.

Loftus, E. F. (1997). Creating false memories. *Scientific American, 277* (3), 70–75.

Loftus, E. F. (2003). Make-believe memories. *American Psychologist, 58,* 864–873.

Loftus, E. F. (2005). A 30-year investigation of the malleability of memory. *Learning and Memory, 12,* 361–366.

Loftus, E. F., & Bernstein, D. M. (2005). Rich false memories: The royal road to success. In A. F. Healy (Ed.), *Experimental cognitive psychology and its applications* (pp. 101–113). Washington, DC: American Psychological Association Press.

Loftus, E. F., & Guyer, M. (2002a). Who abused Jane Doe?: The hazards of the single case history (Part I). *Skeptical Inquirer, 26*(3), 24–32.

Loftus, E. F., & Guyer, M. J. (2002b). Who abused Jane Doe? (Part II). *Skeptical Inquirer, 26*(4), 37–40, 44.

Loftus, E. F., Miller, D. G., & Burns, H. J. (1978). Semantic integration of verbal information into a visual memory. *Journal of Experimental Psychology: Human Learning and Memory, 4,* 19–31.

Mazzoni, G. A. L., Loftus, E. F., & Kirsch, I. (2001) Changing beliefs about implausible autobiographical events. *Journal of Experimental Psychology: Applied, 7*(1), 51–59.

Towards Valued
Human Expertise

Alan Lesgold
University of Pittsburgh

In his valedictory invited address to the Psychonomic Society, Gordon Bower said, *"Read the experimental literature broadly, listen to your colleagues in other areas of psychology and appreciate their research, avoid specializing and getting stuck in one topic too soon, and expect to change research interests every 5 to 10 years."* I've tried to follow his advice. This has led me to do work in memory, reading, professional expertise, applications of artificial intelligence to training, assessment, and teacher preparation. In each area, I've benefited greatly from the mentoring that Gordon provided. He continually modeled the level of focus and discipline needed to do good research. He also passed on a spirit of adventure, as captured in a remark he made at a Western Psychological Association meeting over 35 years ago: *"Research assistants arise! You have nothing but your S–R bonds to lose."*

For many folks, the rise of the cognitive psychology era meant abandonment of all that we had learned before in experimental psychology. Another lesson from Gordon was that this was very wasteful. The real lesson is both to be adventurous and to retain in one's scientific ontology those parts of past thinking that still make sense. For Gordon, the joint anchors of emotion and association have both been important aspects of that foundation. I think we will find in the future that work in such novel areas as neuroeconomics will be most productive if it is similarly anchored.

Before turning to my own work, I would like to acknowledge one further contribution, from both Gordon and Sharon Bower. Both impressed upon me, through example and through coaching, the importance of scientific communication. We serve no one by just having brilliant ideas; science advances only when new ideas are communicated clearly as part of a longer community conversation. I owe much of whatever career successes I have enjoyed to Gordon's continual example of clear communication and to his and Sharon's coaching efforts.

Having had the good fortune of Gordon's shaping of my early career and of then joining a very tolerant university, I have been able to change my area of work several times. Throughout my career, though, I've been concerned with complex competence and how it is acquired. I have looked at several areas of competence, including reading, radiological diagnosis, teaching, and repairing failures of complex equipment. I have done this work in the context of a center dedicated to the improvement of learning and schooling. So, even though I was over in a corner looking mostly at adult competence, I continually was reminded both of everything I learned from Gordon and of the problems of American schools. Moreover, having always had a computational dark side, I keep being reminded that computers do many things that used to be the height of achievement for many well-employed humans. In this chapter, I would like to reflect on the roles computational machines are taking over and the human capabilities that will continue to be valued in the maturing information age. I suggest that future work on learning should focus on these capabilities. In the sections that follow, I first describe three basic capabilities that largely will remain the province of valued humans in the information age. I then consider how these capabilities might be acquired and why the approach I describe works. The chapter concludes with a brief discussion of the assessment of these valued human capabilities.

WHAT'S LEFT FOR HUMANS?

There is a striking parallel between the analytic skills of instructional developers and the skills of task analysts who work to develop expert systems and other intelligent systems. Both focus largely on identifying rules and associations that, if learned, can support intelligent activity. Though others (e.g., Fitts & Posner, 1967; Rasmussen, 1986) also have contributed to our understanding of the levels of knowledge and the learning mechanisms that support those levels, Gordon and his student John Anderson (Anderson & Bower, 1973) certainly have been central in helping us learn how to decompose complex capabilities into aggregations of rules and associations. Indeed, the analytic tools that have evolved from their analyses of cognitive competence have been much of the basis for the development of intelligent systems that can substitute for human capability in many situations.

Two basic analytic approaches have been especially important. First, there is the identification of IF–THEN rules that, when learned, allow an automated stream of reasoning toward decisions and actions. Today, rule-based systems help to identify the beginnings of epidemics (natural or human-made). They assure that patients in hospitals do not receive combinations of drugs that could be damaging. They decide who can get a mortgage and at what rate, and they do much of our income tax computation and reporting for us. When extended by feature-based recognition systems that are themselves partly informed by the analytic techniques developed for educators, these rule-based machines can be built to do virtually any routine cognitive work.

If the same analytic schemes used to shape human instruction also are used to design machines to replace humans, perhaps there is something we need to worry about. Could it be that almost all of schooling is aimed at levels of performance that machines can readily achieve? I personally believe this to be happening, and in some cases, the evidence is compelling. Much of elementary school mathematics can be done with a calculator costing less than we hope our children will earn in 1 hour as adults. Much of high school mathematics can be done by specialized calculators or consumer software that costs significantly less than we hope our children will earn in a day. The standards used by states to satisfy the No Child Left Behind Act tend to fall in between these two levels. Perhaps we are preparing our children only to be as valuable as the machine one could buy with half a day's pay. This could be a problem.

So, what is it that will remain a valued human capability in the information age? There may be a number of capabilities, but I focus on three: dealing with novel situations, learning new routines quickly, and mediating between one worldview or body of systematic knowledge and another. We can build machines to deal with any routine that we can teach explicitly. But, in our fast-moving world, we keep seeing situations arise that cannot be predicted well enough to be able to design effective rule systems to deal with them. Thus, humans will be valued if they can deal with novel and emergent situations. Also, as the artifacts and roles in our world change, there is a lot of work that is human work only temporarily. If routine work is required for very long, it will become the province of machines, but newly required work will be available to humans for a number of years until automated systems are developed. Finally, there are also uniquely human roles that involve reconciling the thinking of one system or organization or person with that of another.

The human roles discussed in this chapter bear considerable relationship to those discussed by Levy and Murnane (2005). They focus on our inability to represent emergent domains explicitly as quickly as they become economically important and the related inability to write rule systems to capture the expertise of some domains. I suspect that they are, with their two categories of human roles, describing roughly the same space I describe with my three.

To summarize, I suggest that in the future valued human work will be of three forms. First, there will be jobs that involve dealing with emergent and novel problems. Second, a substantial job niche will consist of new jobs requiring new learning that will persist for some number of years before being replaced by machines. Finally, there will be jobs involving mediation between two knowledge systems having different ontologies. Thus, I suggest, our children will need to become quick problem solvers, efficient learners, and skilled bridgers of content domains. Next, I consider each of these briefly, in turn.

DEALING WITH NOVEL SITUATIONS

Computers allow us to deal with ever larger systems and ever greater complexity. Moreover, our modern world is really a large community of systems, interacting in manners both predicted and not predicted. There are parallels to human systems. When writing about human interactions, Tolstoy[1] wrote: "Happy families are all alike; every unhappy family is unhappy in its own way." Basically, the various constraints of environment limit the number of ways a family can work out well. On the other hand, families are such complex systems that the number of ways they can fail is far too numerous to list. So also for systems of productive enterprise.

In our work teaching people how to diagnose and repair complex machines, colleagues and I had to cope with the same basic problem (Gott & Lesgold, 2000; Lesgold & Nahemow, 2001). One cannot list all the ways that an ion beam implant machine (used to "write" circuits onto computer chips) can fail, and thus one cannot write a complete repair manual.[2] Nor can we develop a set of rules complete enough to do all the diagnosis of such failures. Yet, people can become expert in such work, and we have learned a bit about how to train them.

The problem is not specific to repairing machines, by any means. The various mental health professions face similar difficulties. When a person is depressed, for example, this could be for any of a number of reasons. There might be an imbalance of neural transmitter substances. Or, a difficult work environment, a difficult home environment, or a recent mental or physical trauma may be the cause. There are other possibilities as well. One can develop protocols that can be learned and that often will lead to a solution to a given patient's depression problem. However, these protocols are far from universally successful and also can

---

[1]Tolstoy wrote *Anna Karenina,* from which I quote the first sentence, between 1875 and 1877.

[2]I note in passing that this problem also is arising in the auto repair world. Basically, the repairs that are charged a flat rate often are made by replacing more than is necessary, whereas those charged at an hourly rate require unpredictable diagnosis that goes far beyond the content of shop manuals.

lead to temporary states of affairs more painful than the initial symptoms (e.g., as different drug regimens are tried out). A few trained experts can figure out what is needed in a specific case without trying an excessive number of expensive alternative treatments. These experts are in short supply. Moreover, their decisions are hard enough to validate that health systems generally settle for more automated and less successful protocols. But, the best depression experts do quite well for themselves and are valued highly.

It is difficult to capture such expertise fully. Although the ACT formulations (Anderson & Bower, 1973; Anderson & Lebiere, 1998; Anderson et al., 2004) have made considerable progress in clarifying how the mind/brain does complex thinking, perhaps the least fully examined kinds of cognitive performances are the ones just described. Successfully solving a really difficult emergent problem tends to involve rather arbitrary combinations of production-based reasoning, associative remindings, inference from active memories, and metaphorical use of recollections of prior cases.

What must be learned, in fact, is not the specific set of cognitive rules to address a specific problem. Rather, one needs a set of metacognitive rules for experimentally trying various combinations of recognition, forward reasoning, and metaphorical reasoning combined with the efficient execution of appropriate subprocesses that can be highly trained in advance. These must work in tandem with a range of recognition capabilities acquired through extensive case experiences. From a more historical perspective, even though we know that "formal discipline" cannot be trained directly (Thorndike & Woodworth, 1901), managing the problem-solving processes that are partly empirical and that involve learning while acting is one of the most important cognitive functions left to humans.

LEARNING NEW ROUTINES
(BOTH "HOW TO" AND "WHY") QUICKLY

One might argue that if such complex activity is all that is left as a human province, then most humans are doomed to a life of lesser social significance. In fact, there are two other ways in which humans trump machines. One of these is the ability to learn quickly to do newly required tasks. These tasks may be routine enough to be done by expert systems. However, humans often do work that machines could do, simply because it is not yet "good business" to automate that work.

For example, one could, in principle, develop automated ticket takers for movie theaters, just as they already exist for subway and surface train systems. However, the surface area of a subway station is huge, making it sensible to automate ticket taking and still have security personnel and information/cashier staff. On the other hand, the average movie theater has a much smaller surface area. The ticket taker can double as most or all of the security staff and also can answer any customer questions. So, it is likely that humans will keep collecting tickets unless a change in the nature of movie theaters makes it worth investing in an automated ticket-taking apparatus.

Presumably, that will happen some day. Indeed, for the group of our fellow humans who take such jobs as movie ticket taking, an important survival skill is the ability to quickly learn new routines. Whenever the ticket taker job disappears, it is likely that other jobs available to people who have been ticket takers will be extremely different and require learning very different routines.

Even high-end jobs now have characteristics that make being a quick study an important survival skill. For example, suppose that one is an expert in Mandarin and gets work as an interpreter. The domains in which interpretation skills will be demanded will change over time, and the best interpreters will learn quickly what is needed for new assignments, whether it is specialized vocabulary or understanding of different work domains. Thus, one special and valued kind of complex, nonroutine performance is learning new routines.

MEDIATING BETWEEN WORLDVIEWS

Pushing this social skill-oriented view of new human competences one step further, there is one more capability that seems valued for humans in the information age, the ability to translate between two different communal views of a process. Much of value in products and services today comes from the ability to make a product useful to an individual person or organization. For example, where software companies once made their money primarily from selling a software package, today much of the yield is from consulting—helping a customer figure out how to use the software to advantage in his or her specific enterprise. This is fundamentally an act of translating or coordinating between the different ontologies and goal structures of different systems.

Sometimes this can be relatively simple and not involve much coordination— *I've got a hammer; let me help you find all your nails that can be pounded in.* Other times this can be very complex. For example, when a consultant helps a smaller company learn to use enterprise resource planning (ERP) software, much of the activity that is valued is efficient coordination of thinking between the ERP world and the company's traditional view of its core activities and business processes. In the consumer markets, the coordination that is valued often falls into the category of customer service, which essentially is mediating between the customer's world and the company's. Much of the increased value of many goods arises from the customer service provided with them.

Consider a simple case. A person gets a medical bill in the mail and believes that it should have been paid by his insurance company. He calls the customer service number of that insurance company to discuss his concern. The person he talks to can do several different things. One model often observed is the black box approach: *I checked, and your policy doesn't cover this.* Another approach is the customer advocate approach: I'll put it through again and change a few things; maybe it will go through this time. A third approach is the coordination approach: *Let me understand how you view this problem, after which I'll explain how the company views it, and maybe we can at least figure out how you can do better on getting future bills covered.* I suspect that the third approach is the most profitable, because it involves finding a win-win solution.

Which of these approaches do we prepare people for while they are in school? The first approach is the "mind your own business" model. Your job is to do what I teach you and nothing else. We certainly see some of schooling rehearsing this approach. But, a company that takes this approach can compete only on price, which means that the job of customer service will be under great pressure—customers do not value it highly, and if it is put offshore or simply not provided, the price can get lower.

The second approach, which often amounts to solving the customer's problem by gaming the system, might produce more happy customers willing to pay more for a product, but it fundamentally amounts to discounting (you didn't buy insurance that covers this case, but I'll pay off anyway to keep you as a customer) and may not be sustainable. Even it relies on a level of problem solving that we often don't teach well in school, and the problem solving does not sufficiently coordinate customer and company goals structures. The real value comes from solving a goal coordination problem that bridges between customer goals and company goals.

Goal bridging is a subset of a wider range of human activities that involve coordinating different knowledge structures and finding problem solutions that make sense within each of those disparate structures. Notice that writing rules to do this is inherently harder than writing rules to solve problems within a domain that has a unified knowledge structure. The problem, actually, is not so much the rules as the meanings associated with the symbols in those rules. In terms of both extension and intension, the same term may have different meaning in the two domains. For example, when a customer calls up an insurance company, the term insurance policy may not mean the same thing to the customer as to the company, especially in its intensions, that is, the associations that connect it to other concepts or experiences.

In the collaboration situations just discussed, there is already an implicit assumption of some need to establish shared meaning, to develop a common ground between people with different knowledge that can be the basis of joint activity. Indeed, part of effective collaborating is knowing what meaning is shared and what meaning is personal. With goal bridging, the successful goal bridger has at least part of both systems of thinking internalized. So, for example, the successful customer service representative at an insurance company has both a model of how customers often think (or several, if there are different groups of customers with different representations) as well as a model of what constitutes success for the insurance company and, to some extent, how the insurance company operates. Somehow, one of those models must be projected into the space of the other in order to find a win-win solution to a problem.

There certainly are simple bridging situations one could practice, even some that are simple in representation yet complex in solution, such as solving a Sudoku puzzle. However, these puzzle situations tend to involve the same basic kind of representation for each part of the puzzle. In contrast, human win-win solution seeking often involves the reconciliation of very different systems with very different representations. At the everyday end, there are situations such as the insurance example. At the more exotic end can be found evidence-based medical decisions that involve drugs that have a positive effect on one body system with possible negative effects on another (a simple example is a nonsteroid anti-inflammatory drug that may reduce fever and simultaneously stress the kidneys if taken in sufficient quantity).

As in the world of simple rule-based decision making, some goal bridging is amenable to machine solution, including some drug interaction problems. Where humans have sole dominion is when one or both systems to be reconciled are poorly understood or governed by conflicting principles. One example might be automobile design, which involves reconciling a constantly changing set of potentially inconsistent desires and beliefs on the part of customers with physical and business constraints on how a car can be configured.

Although this domain of goal bridging seems on the surface to be quite different from being a quick study or being able to deal with emergent problems, it may not be that different. At the very least, it is worth considering what kinds of experience in goal bridging would lead to the development of sufficiently powerful weak-method skills that would constitute competence in goal bridging. My colleagues and I came close to dealing in this realm in some of our technical-training work that used the coached-apprenticeship model described later. Specifically (Lesgold & Nahemow, 2001), we trained workers to deal with problems that might depend for solution on a mixture of tidbits of physical chemistry, silicon chemistry, quantum mechanics, optics, magnetics, and a few other science domains. What we found was that we could train workers to constrain the problem domain sufficiently that they only needed to consider a small number of relationships governed by these differing scientific theories. That is, the same basic approach of coached apprenticeship followed by reflection on problem solutions was quite salutary in developing problem-solving skills for dealing with complex, multifaceted systems that could transfer to very different kinds of problems.

COACHED APPRENTICESHIP

In our efforts to train people to cope with complex tasks for which effective routines cannot be learned explicitly, we have found that certain approaches work extremely well (see Gott & Lesgold, 2000, and Lesgold & Nahemow, 2001, for data). First, there are structuring routines that can help people learn to manage the complexity of these difficult work situations. Symptoms can be mapped onto possible causes, and these then become salient drivers of extended cognitive work. Computer tools make it easy to clearly record task steps taken so far and to review this record as needed. Knowledge of causal relationships can be the basis for some hypothesis testing and other inference. Previously experienced cases can be appealed to.

We have found that people best learn to deal with emergent and incompletely predictable problem situations by actually dealing with some. If coaching is available to provide help on demand, then even very difficult problems can and should be part of training. Moreover, a particularly effective way to practice solving extremely difficult problems is to cycle through the stages of planning, acting, and reflecting.[3] In such arrangements, coached practice in solving diagnostic problems is extremely productive. Furthermore, having learned (Katz, O'Donnell, & Kay, 2000) that trainees are especially able to learn from "why" information after solving a problem but want mostly "how" information while in the midst of problem solving, we have a pretty good sense of how to structure practice and the coaching of practice in solving very difficult problems in incompletely understood domains.

The scheme that seems to be extremely successful (Gott & Lesgold, 2000; Lesgold & Nahemow, 2001) involves giving trainees extremely difficult tasks, the hardest in the domain being trained. Ordinarily, this is not feasible, because the trainee will inevitably be discouraged or even repeatedly take nonproductive paths and hence learn to do poorly. However, we have been able, in simulated problem environments, to provide effective intelligent computer-based assistance, so that every problem is solvable, at least if the available help is consulted. After each problem is solved, we have found it productive to provide some form of postproblem reflection opportunity, such as an opportunity to compare one's own performance to that of an expert and even the opportunity to access more "why" information to explain the "how" assistance that might have been provided while trying to solve the problem.

There are several things to note about this approach. First, it is similar to the approaches that have evolved in some areas of high performance. Several years ago, when touring the facilities just built for the university football team, I was intrigued by how close the intelligent coached-apprenticeship approach that I was taking in the joint work with Intel (Lesgold & Nahemow, 2001) was to high-end football coaching. Football coaches give only terse, but often sufficient, advice during a football game. However, afterward, there often is a very structured film

---

[3]Donald Schön (1987) observed that the best professionals not only know what to do in a wide range of situations but also reflect regularly on their recent experiences and adapt in response to aspects of their work where they sense the opportunity for improvement.

review. Indeed, commercial software from firms like XOS and Avid is routinely used to produce comparative sequences of game plays and other objects to support reflection on the practice of football.

A second parallel is to hospital rounds. In teaching hospitals, senior attending physicians, fellows, other house staff, medical clerks, and often nursing staff gather to discuss cases. One format is the daily case conference, in which all the participants on a service gather to plan care for each patient on the service. Another format is grand rounds, where particularly interesting or difficult cases are presented, discussed, and diagnosed. Both formats provide the same sort of cycling of planning, action, and reflection that Schön (1987) described and that has been shown to be productive of learning in our own work (Lesgold & Nahemow, 2001).

Conceivably, the plan-act-reflect cycle is a good way to learn how to learn as well. After all, encountering a new learning need is similar to encountering a new problem. There are, however, some critical differences. First, the coached-apprenticeship scheme, at least in the forms colleagues and I have developed, assumes considerable declarative domain knowledge to have been acquired earlier. Second, we assume prior acquisition of considerable routine procedural knowledge as well. We have focused on taking people who can do routine jobs in a domain and preparing them to handle the nonroutine. Our schemes can be developed and fielded efficiently largely because we do not have to teach basic terms or concepts. Although the "why" part of our systems does indeed include a lot of underlying conceptual information, much has to be learned by the trainee before our systems will be usable. For example, in the case of our tutors for repair of ion deposition devices used at Intel, we assumed that the trainees knew every component of the devices. We also assumed they could carry out any part replacement or other basic process (such as establishing a clean environment inside the sealed chambers of the device) before beginning use of the training system. What we were teaching was how to decide efficiently (the cost of delay was roughly $150/minute) what was wrong and which part to replace.

One could, of course, argue that the job of making people quick studies for any given domain is the job of the trainer rather than that of the trainee. That is, one could conclude that the work of worker retraining requires doing the kinds of detailed task analyses and instructional design that have occupied a goodly part of our field for more than half a century. Of course, once we have the task analyses, we also have the basis for machine replacement of the human worker. Moreover, experience has shown that many potential workers should not be selected for training because they are not likely to progress through the training quickly enough. What more can we do for those people?

A generation ago, we would have concluded that they simply lacked the needed aptitude or that they were inadequately schooled. Today, this seems too much a blaming of the victims of changes in the nature of work. Still, we must consider what data was available to support earlier aptitude views. Essentially, the criterion variable for validity of tests like the SAT was grades in freshman courses. To the extent that grades in high school are given in a standard manner, they do about as good a job of predicting freshman college grades as the SAT. Not surprisingly, doing well in school predicts doing well in school. But, school is a rather artificial place, and doing well in being schooled may not be the only way to be ready for doing well in continual retraining as a worker. Indeed, doing well on the SAT does not, by itself, show clear readiness to learn certain subjects, like advanced mathematics or natural sciences. Many students come to the university with high test scores and do well, but often they succeed by shifting what they choose to study.

Another predictor of college success, perhaps the only one that adds significant prediction power beyond the SAT or high school grades, is persistence or follow-through in just about any extended activity that requires gaining expertise (Willingham, 1985), such as playing a musical instrument, being an athlete, or being on a debate team. So, we might hypothesize that if someone has become good at learning and also has learned to persist long enough in an activity to master it, then they will have the now-especially-adaptive ability to be a quick study and be readily retrainable as job requirements change in our information economy.

But, this still leaves us the question of how to help people become quick studies. There are, of course, a large number of books, including many written by learning psychologists, on this topic. Most, however, focus on the learning of school content, which is generally relatively unmotivated by obvious connections to real-world work needs. One possibility to consider that might be more effective in producing the ability to learn expeditiously might be to combine the best techniques proven for school learning with the basic approach of the coached-apprenticeship scheme. This idea has, of course, been put forward before (e.g., Collins, Brown, & Newman, 1989; Lave & Wenger, 1990), though for a slightly different purpose.

Coached apprenticeship is different from traditional apprenticeships that involve starting with the simplest tasks and building a progressively more expert set of routines. In coached apprenticeship, one works primarily with the very hardest tasks, relying on scaffolding and coaching by a human or an intelligent machine that provides enough assistance so that the task becomes manageable. In the kind of reformed schooling I have in mind, part of the purpose of schooling would be to stretch bodies of newly acquired knowledge and put that knowledge to use in realistic situations that challenge humans and go beyond the capabilities of machines. That is, schooling would be redesigned. Though part of it might still be practice, and even drill on procedural components, another part would be going beyond what is predictable, readily doable, or even fair to test. This would involve giving students very difficult tasks that, with great effort, can be addressed with existing knowledge plus some scaffolding. The idea is that the hidden curriculum of schooling might become that of learning to confront new learning demands, developing a plan for learning, applying techniques learned for finding new patterns in bodies of information, and developing plans for attacking emergent problems using both past knowledge and afforded scaffolding.[4]

Gardenförs (2004) has argued that a unique human ability is planning for future needs. Just as dealing with emergent needs is a special province for humans, perhaps another is the rapid development of plans for the unfolding of enterprises. Although this area has not been explored to my knowledge as an instructional issue, we can perhaps reach a few tentative hypotheses about what might be taught to our children to better prepare them to engage in this uniquely human enterprise of planning, especially group planning.

An individual person can have a mental model of an enterprise, and that model can include support for envisioning how the enterprise might unfold and even the multiple paths the unfolding might take. The representation might be symbolic, so that planning might involve letting a set of cognitive rules execute as the mental model is mentally "run." For bodies of experience not yet the object of symbolic representation, some amount of envisioning can occur through simple associations, of course, and also on representations best seen as spatial, such as prototypes and typical instances. Regardless of how one becomes able to envision the unfolding of a process or situation or enterprise, real human enterprises require coordination of such envisionments across multiple actors. Indeed, this is how symbolic representations tend to arise—naming is required in order for communication to occur, and communication is required in order for shared envisionments to occur, and shared envisioning is required in order for planned enterprises to occur (Gardenförs, 2004).

I suggest that part of preparation for active participation in new enterprises is coached opportunities to practice the language-driven coordinations required for such enterprises to take shape. It seems appropriate that part of the hidden curriculum of schooling include this kind of coached apprenticeship. In traditional schooling, this partly happens, but in very limited ways. For example, students in difficult courses often form study groups. Part of the task for such groups is to discover how to think about new bodies of knowledge and how to use that knowledge to solve problems or perform other school tasks. As students in such groups develop intuitions related to their learning goals, they learn partly by having to give linguistic voice to their intuitions so they can both share and confirm them.

Where we fail, in addition to not assuring that all students get regular practice in effective study groups, is in not going further to give group assignments specifically designed to allow students to practice developing shared knowledge and to help them learn to engage in this cooperative knowledge development and knowledge-sharing activity. One purpose of this brief sketch, then, is to prompt some discussion in the education world of what a school might be like if one of its goals was to help students develop the ability to collaborate in sense making, enterprise designing, and explicit planning for the future of enterprises. Perhaps this is

---

[4]See the reference to the unpublished paper of Peter Gardenförs in Levy and Murnane (2005).

simply a different cut on what a school that develops quick learners might be like, a cut that sees quick learning as a group enterprise rather than an individual one.

WHY MIGHT COACHED APPRENTICESHIP WORK?

This chapter puts forward two basic hypotheses. First, I argue that there are new capabilities that should be formed as part of schooling and that this formation should be a primary goal of education if our children are to fare well in the global information society. Second, I suggest, based on past work on coached apprenticeship, that this instructional method might be adaptable to produce an approach to schooling that is especially helpful in forming the needed capabilities. This leads to a suggestion for future research, which is to better understand, both theoretically and experimentally, how coached apprenticeship works.

My own thinking on this is that coached apprenticeship can be understood within the context of the Anderson et al. (2004) view of learning and thinking. Specifically, I think that coached apprenticeship depends first on a strong level of recognition knowledge and basic associative representations for a domain. On top of this basic knowledge, an apprentice must form a set of general rules that permit adding new knowledge quickly, solving novel problems, and building mappings from one ontological base to another.

The key to putting some flesh on this rather meager skeleton is to clarify, within the Anderson et al. (2004) formulation, what it might mean to have several different underlying ontological bases for knowledge. At the lowest level, I suspect that an ontological base might be thought of as a collection of associations that is relatively closed, that is, with lots of interconnecting associations and few associations extending outside of the collection. At a second level, one might imagine a set of symbols or nouns that have intensions into such a collection and that are referenced in a set of rules that are themselves relatively closed. The skill of bridging, then, would consist of a set of rules that can bind to nouns in two different collections and thus connect one to the other. If we add to the Anderson formulation some of the ideas of Forbus and Gentner (cf. Forbus, 2001), we have a strong start toward a theoretical basis for coached apprenticeship.

I suggest that research elaborating this basis is an important goal for instructional science, one with major social implications.

ASSESSMENT

For each of the three areas of valued competence that will remain within the human sphere, we also will need to develop adequate assessment schemes, if we are to make progress in transforming schooling to focus on them. Here, we run into some difficulties. All three areas include an important component of novelty. It is not merely knowing something in particular that we want for our children but rather the ability to learn new things quickly, the ability to master the hard parts of a job after quickly learning the routine parts, and the ability to connect any two different bodies of knowledge. This will require some changes in how we measure competence.

First, we will need to change our concepts of fairness. As I suggested some time ago (Lesgold, 1996), much of what is important to demonstrate in modern life would be considered unfair on a test, because the student is not fully prepared for the content ahead of time. We will need to develop a style of learning and of regular in-school testing that makes dealing with the novel a valued capability that society believes can be learned with effort, rather than an aptitude that not all children are expected to have. The comparison to football coaching might be exploited here as well. We have widely shared belief that the job of coaching a football team is to prepare them to play against other teams that may come up with new plays and other surprises. We need to convince the broader public— citizens, parents, teachers, school leaders, students—that the jobs of teaching and learning also mean getting ready for the unexpected. And, of course, we need to find ways to assure that the range of unexpected situations used in testing does not favor one or another experiential background.

This means that we will need to find ways to accumulate over time the results of large numbers of experiences dealing with the novel, so that everyone occasionally lucks out with a test that matches past experience but no one is especially favored or penalized overall. Such an approach may be incompatible with the current emphasis on cheap, relatively short tests that are given once a year. Dealing with the novel takes more time, which means that successful assessment strategies may need to summarize over a large number of novel learning situations a student experiences over a longer period of time, perhaps a quarter of a year or even a whole year (see Lesgold, in press, for further development of this idea).

The collaborative aspect of learning and performance will also require a change in the basics of testing. Currently, we test each person alone. If much of modern work involves working with teams and knowing how to develop shared understanding even when each team member has special and unique expertise, then testing situations will need to involve teamwork of one kind or another. One possibility is to have intelligent agents that represent the other team members, so that each student works alone in a communications environment that includes intelligent machines filling other roles. If this is possible, it could be the cleanest way to proceed, but the core argument made earlier about the special province of humans suggests that it is not entirely possible. The alternative is to learn how to estimate the contributions of a particular individual from a number of performances that involve working with different people on different occasions.

In addition to simply averaging performance over a number of different team situations, a new assessment approach might involve assessment rubrics specific to the particular expertise each person brings to a testing situation. In such a scheme, Person A might previously be taught one body of knowledge whereas

Person B is taught another. Rubrics might be developed to assess their joint performance in terms of adequate exploitation of the Person-A knowledge versus the Person-B knowledge.

A possible metaphor is the critic's review of a concert. Although the performance depends upon many players, it is still possible for the critic to comment both on individual contributions and on the overall effect. Again, if we can find ways to record data from standardized collaborative tasks that students complete in teams over the course of a year, we may be able to summarize each individual student's experience through a combination of rubric components for individual contributions summarized over the course of a year and an average of performance of the various groupings of which that student was part. This would be like saying of a violinist, for example, that she is known for her virtuoso handling of difficult passages but that many of the concerts in which she played showed a certain raggedness and lack of ensemble.

SUMMARY

To summarize, much of the psychology of learning has focused on the kinds of learning historically valued in schools, and much of the science of psychological measurement has focused on performances for which a test taker could prepare and then carry out on his or her own. Today, though, the roles we can expect to be valued for humans in the future involve quick learning, confronting the novel and emergent, and interconnecting domains of knowledge that lack common ontology. Developing a strong science of instruction for these newly critical human skills along with the ability to measure their acquisition will require substantial new work.

It's a good thing that Gordon Bower trained us all so well; we have plenty left to do!

REFERENCES

Anderson, J. R., Bothell, D., Byrne, M. D., Douglass, S., Lebiere, C., & Qin, Y. (2004). An integrated theory of the mind. *Psychological Review, 111*(4), 1036–1060.

Anderson, J. R., & Bower, G. H. (1973). *Human associative memory.* New York: Halstead.

Anderson, J. R., & Lebiere, C. (1998). *The atomic components of thought.* Mahwah, NJ: Lawrence Erlbaum Associates.

Collins, A., Brown, J. S., & Newman, S. E. (1989). Cognitive apprenticeship: Teaching the crafts of reading, writing, and mathematics. In L. B. Resnick (Ed.), *Knowing, learning, and instruction: Essays in honor of Robert Glaser* (pp. 453–494). Hillsdale, NJ: Lawrence Erlbaum Associates.

Fitts, P. M., & Posner, M .I. (1967). *Human performance.* Belmont, CA: Brooks Cole.

Forbus, K. (2001). Exploring analogy in the large. In D. Gentner, K. Holyoak, & B. Kokinov (Eds.), *The analogical mind: Perspectives from cognitive science* (pp. 23–58). Cambridge, MA: MIT Press.

Gardenförs, P. (2004). Cooperation and the evolution of symbolic communication. In K. Oller & U. Griebel (Eds.), *Evolution of communication systems: A comparative approach* (pp. 237–256). Cambridge, MA: MIT Press.

Gott, S. P., & Lesgold, A. M. (2000). Competence in the workplace: How cognitive performance models and situated instruction can accelerate skill acquisition. In R. Glaser (Ed.), *Advances in instructional psychology* (pp. 239–327). Mahwah, NJ: Lawrence Erlbaum Associates.

Katz, S., O'Donnell, G., & Kay, H. (2000). An approach to analyzing the role and structure of reflective dialogue. *International Journal of Artificial Intelligence in Education, 11(3),* 320–343.

Lave, J., & Wenger, E. (1990). *Situated learning: Legitimate peripheral participation.* Cambridge, England: Cambridge University Press.

Lesgold, A. (in press). Assessment to steer the course of learning: Dither in testing. In E. L. Baker, J. Dickieson, W. Wulfeck, & H. O'Neil (Eds.), *Assessment of problem solving using simulations.* Mahwah, NJ: Lawrence Erlbaum Associates.

Lesgold, A. (1996). Quality control for educating a smart work force. In L. B. Resnick, & J. Wirt, (Eds.), *Linking school and work: Roles for standards and assessment* (pp. 147–191). San Francisco: Jossey-Bass.

Lesgold, A., & Nahemow, M. (2001). Tools to assist learning by doing: Achieving and assessing efficient technology for learning. In D. Klahr & S. Carver (Eds.), Cognition and instruction: Twenty-five years of progress (pp. 3070–346). Mahwah, NJ: Lawrence Erlbaum Associates.

Levy, F., & Murnane, R. J. (2005). *The new division of labor: How computers are creating the next job market.* Princeton, NJ: Princeton University Press.

Rasmussen, J. (1986). *Information processing and human–machine interaction: An approach to cognitive engineering.* New York: North-Holland.

Schön, D. (1987). Educating the reflective practitioner. San Francisco: Jossey-Bass.

Thorndike, E. L., & Woodworth, R. S. (1901). The influence of improvement in one mental function upon the efficiency of other functions (I). *Psychological Review, 8,* 247–261.

Willingham, W. W. (1985). *Success in college: The role of personal qualities and academic ability.* New York: College Entrance Examination Board.

The Algebraic Brain

John R. Anderson
Carnegie Mellon University

My enduring intellectual interests were all formed in the 4 years of graduate education with Gordon Bower. I basically imprinted on the things he was interested in during the period 1968 to 1972. This included an interest in mathematical psychology, artificial intelligence, learning and memory, and applications of psychology to improving classroom performance. Whereas Gordon's interests have ranged far and wide over the decades, I have remained stuck on these topics. This chapter describes current work in my laboratory bringing these various threads together. I am going to describe a formal information-processing model of how children learn to solve linear equations and test predictions of this model for activation patterns in five brain regions.

THE EXPERIMENT AND THE ACT–R MODEL

In the experiment modeled in detail (Qin, Anderson, Silk, Stenger, & Carter, 2004), 10 students aged 11 to 14 spent 6 days practicing solving simple linear equations. The first day (Day 0) they were given private tutoring on how to solve a restricted set of equations and practiced paper-and-pencil solutions of such problems with a private human tutor. On the remaining 5 days, they practiced on a computer the solution of three classes of equations:

0-step: e.g., $1x + 0 = 4$

1-step: e.g., $3x + 0 = 12, 1x + 8 = 12$

2-step: e.g., $7x + 1 = 29$

Each day they went through 10 computer-administered blocks of such equations. Each block consisted of 16 trials with four instances of the four possible types of equations (there are two subtypes for the one-step equations). Figure 6–1 presents their latency and the predictions of a model implemented in the ACT–R architecture (Anderson et al., 2004).

The ACT–R Architecture

According to the ACT–R theory, cognition emerges through the interaction of a number of independent modules. Figure 6–2 illustrates the modules relevant to algebra equation solving:

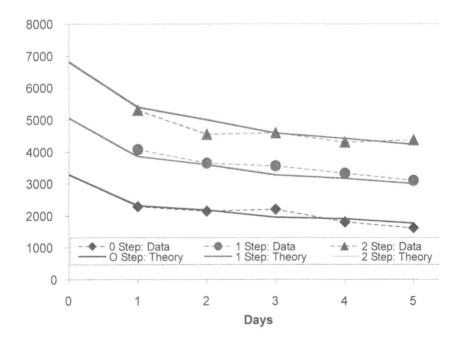

Figure 6–1.   Mean solution times (and predictions of the ACT–R model) for the three types of equations as a function of delay. Although the data were not collected, the predicted times are presented for the practice session of the experiment (Day 0).

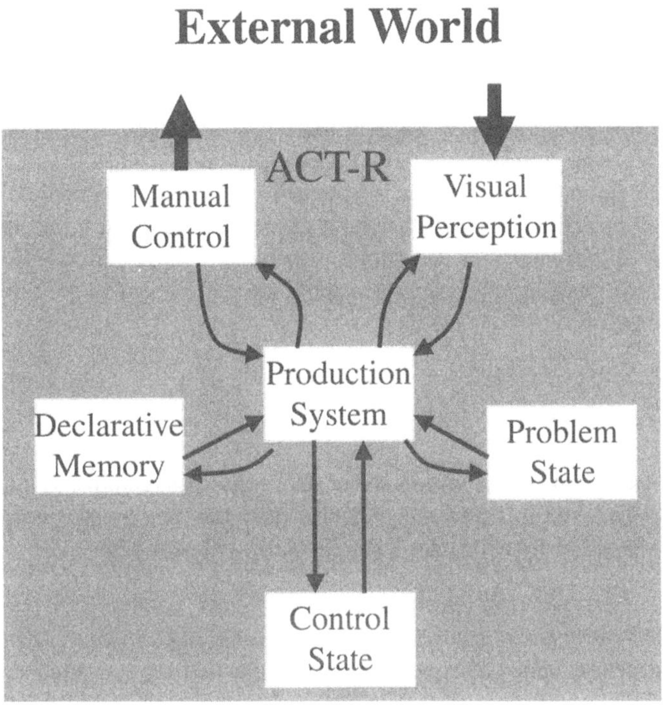

External World

Figure 6–2. The interconnections among modules in ACT–R 5.0.

1. A visual module that might hold the representation of an equation such as "$3x - 5 = 7$."
2. A problem state module (sometimes called an imaginal module) that holds a current mental representation of the problem. For instance, the student might have converted the original equation into "$3x = 12$."
3. A control module (sometimes called a goal module) that keeps track of one's current intentions in solving the problem—for instance, one might be trying to apply the unwind strategy described later.
4. A declarative module that retrieves critical information from declarative memory such as that $7 + 5 = 12$.
5. A manual module that programs the output such as "$x = 4$."

Each of these modules is capable of massively parallel computation to achieve its objectives. For instance, the visual module is processing the entire visual field and the declarative module searches through large databases. However, each of these modules suffers a serial bottleneck such that only a little information can be put into a buffer associated with the module—a single object is perceived, a single problem state represented, a single control state maintained, a single fact retrieved, or a single program for hand movement executed. Formally, each buffer can only hold what is called a "chunk" in ACT–R, which is structured unit bundling a small amount of information. ACT–R does not have a formal concept of a working memory, but the current state of the buffers constitutes an effective working memory. Indeed, there is considerable similarity between these buffers and Baddeley's (1986) working memory "slave" systems. Communication among these modules is achieved via a procedural module (production system in Fig. 6–2). The procedural module can respond to information in the buffers of other modules and put information into these buffers. The response tendencies of the central procedural module are represented in ACT–R by production rules.

The ACT–R Model

The ACT–R model begins with a set of declarative instructions, given in Table 6–1, that encode the unwind strategy. To illustrate how these instructions apply to example equations, first consider a simple 0-step equation like:

$$1 * x + 0 = 2.$$

These instructions imply a sequence of operations that can be summarized:

Instruction 1a: Create image " = 2."

Instruction 2b: Unwind-right "1 * x + 0."

Instruction 3a: Focus on "1 * x" and unwind it.

Instruction 2c: Unwind-left "1 * x."

Instruction 4a: Focus on "x" and unwind it.

Instruction 2a: The answer is 2.

Whereas for a two-step equation like

$$7 * x + 3 = 38$$

they imply a sequence of operations that can be summarized:

Instruction 1a: Create image " = 38."

Instruction 2b: Unwind-right "7 * x + 3."

Table 6–1

**English Rendition of Instructions Given to
ACT-R Model for Equation Solving**

1) To solve an equation, encode it and

   a). If the right side is a number then imagine that number as the result and focus on the left side and unwind it.

   b). If the left side is a number then imagine that number as the result and focus on the right side and unwind it.

2) To unwind an expression

   a). If the expression is the variable then the result is the answer.

   b). If a number is on the right unwind-right

   c). If a number is on the left unwind-left

3) To unwind-right, encode the expression (of the form "subexpression operator number") and

   a). If the operator is + or − and the number is 0 then focus on the subexpression and unwind it.

   b). Otherwise invert the operator, imagine it as the operator in the result, imagine the number of the expression as the second argument in the result, evaluate the result, and then focus on the subexpression and unwind it.

4) To unwind-left encode the expression (of the form "number operator subexpression") and

   a). If the operator is * and number 1 then focus on the subexpression and unwind it.

   b). Otherwise check that the operator is symmetric, invert the operator, imagine it as the operator in the result, imagine the number as the second argument in the result, evaluate the result, and then focus on the subexpression and unwind it.

Instruction 3b: Change image to " $= 38 - 3$ "; this to " $= 35$ "; and focus on "$7 * x$" and unwind it.

Instruction 2c: Unwind-left "$7 * x$."

Instruction 4b: Change image to " $= 35/7$ "; this to " $= 5$ "; and focus on x and unwind it.

Instruction 2a: The answer is 5.

Figure 6–1 shows that ACT–R is able to reproduce the speed-up seen in the participants. The key to understanding this speed-up in the ACT–R model is to understand how the preceding instructions were interpreted. These instructions are encoded as declarative structures and ACT–R has general interpretative productions for converting these instructions to behavior. For instance, there is a production rule that retrieves the next step of an instruction:

> IF one has retrieved an instruction for achieving a goal
> THEN retrieve the first step of that instruction.

There are also productions for retrieving particular arithmetic facts such as

> IF one is evaluating the expression "a operator b"
> THEN try to retrieve a fact of the form "a operator b = ?"

Using such general instruction-following productions is laborious and accounts for the slow initial performance of the task.

Though multiple types of learning are occurring in this experiment, it is mainly production compilation that is accounting for the speed-up (see Taatgen, 2005; Taatgen & Anderson, 2002). This is a process by which new production rules are learned that collapse what was originally done by multiple production rules. In this situation, the initial instruction-following productions are compiled over time to produce productions to embody procedures that efficiently solve equations. For instance, the following production rule is acquired:

> IF the goal is to unwind an expression
> and the expression is of the form "subexpression = 0"
> THEN focus on the subexpression.

Figure 6–3a illustrates a typical trial at the beginning of the Day 1 and Figure 6–3b illustrates a typical trial at the end of the Day 5. In both cases, the model is solving the two-step equation $7 * x + 3 = 38$. The figure illustrates when the various modules were active during the solution of the equation and what they were doing. The Day 1 trial (Fig. 6–3a) takes 6.1 seconds and the Day 5 trial (Fig. 6–3b) takes 4.1 seconds. However, these do not reflect the extremes of the learning curve according to ACT–R. The very first trial on Day 0 takes 8.4 seconds in the model. With an infinite amount of practice, the model would take 1.7 seconds during which it would only read the equation and type the answer, having compiled the answer into production rules for that problem. Still, the contrast between parts a and b of Figure 6–3 gives a sense for what is happening over the course of learning. It is worth emphasizing a number of general features of the activity in the figure before discussing the detail of what is happening in individual buffers:

1. Multiple modules can be active simultaneously. For instance, early on in the figure there is a point where the goal module is noting that it is implementing

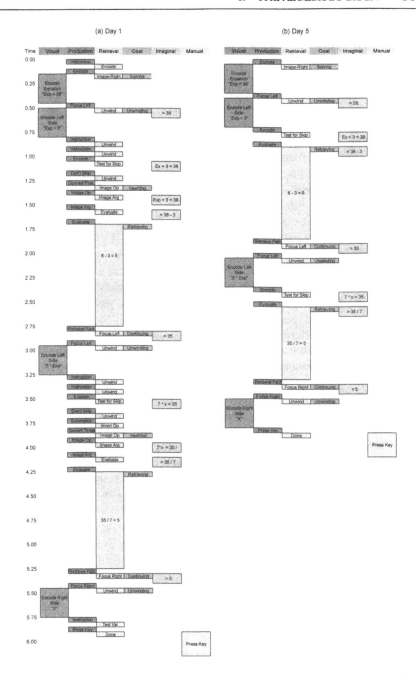

Figure 6–3.   Comparison of the module activity in ACT–R during the solution of a two-step equation on Day 1 (part a) with a two-step equation on Day 5 (part b). In both cases the equation being solved is $7 * x + 3 = 38$.

the unwind strategy, while an image of the right-hand side of the equation (" = 38") is being encoded in the imaginal buffer, while the next step in the unwind strategy is being retrieved, and while the visual system is encoding the left-hand side of the equation. Certain of these activities tend to be on the critical path because they are taking longer than the other processes and further processing has to wait for them to complete. In these cases, the times of the other operations have no effect on total time. For instance, often the visual encoding of the equation is holding up other operations and the durations of these other operations do not matter.

2. Much of the speed-up in processing is driven by collapsing multiple steps into single steps. A particularly dramatic instance of this is noted in Figure 6–3 where five production firings, five retrievals, two control settings of the goal, and two imaginal transformations are compressed into one production, one retrieval, one control setting, and one imaginal transformation.[1] Production compilation can compress these internal operations without limit. What it cannot collapse are the external operations such as visual encodings or manual operations. These external operations define the bounds of the compilation. Whereas the example in Figure 6–3 shows multiple productions being collapsed, the actual learning proceeds slowly in ACT–R and takes all 5 days to achieve the transformation in Figure 6–3. Given enough practice, ACT–R would collapse all equation solving simply into a series of visual encodings and manual operations and there would be no effect of equation complexity (nor any real thought occurring). However, to do so ACT–R would have to essentially build into production rules the capacity to recognize each possible equation and produce its solution. The combinatorics of this are so overwhelming (so many different possible equations) that it would never happen in the normal course of learning to solve equations.

3. A second, lesser source of speed-up is the reduction of retrieval times. This reflects an increase in the base-level activation of the facts used in this experiment and as such it is an example of subsymbolic activation learning. This subsymbolic learning is a relatively minor contributor to the learning in Figure 6–1 for two reasons. First, the basic instructions get used over and over again and are already strongly encoded during Day 0 and there is not that much room for further speed-up. Second, the arithmetic facts do not repeat very often over the course of the experiment and are getting little practice over their baseline. In other situations, subsymbolic activation processes can have a major effect on performance. However, over the period of time studied

---

[1]Although this is a particularly dramatic example of production compilation, there are many other instances in Figure 6–3 that I have not noted to avoid overly cluttering the figure.

in this experiment, the major learning is happening at the symbolic level in terms of creating new production rules.

Comments on the Model

The model has some considerable virtues. It actually interacts with the same software as the participants and so really does the task—there are no vague, unspecified bridging assumptions in its predictions. The model is not handcrafted to do the task but learns from instruction. Moreover, it is has the same model of instruction following that has been used in a number of other efforts in our lab (Anderson et al., 2004, Anderson, Taatgen, & Byrne, 2005). Only two parameters were estimated to fit the data. One was a scale factor that determines the length of the retrieval episodes and the other was the time for encoding a fragment of an equation from the screen (300 ms.). Although the fit to Figure 6–1 is pretty good, the reader might well harbor some doubt about whether this really justifies all the detail in the model in Figure 6–3. There are many unseen steps of processing. We have been engaged in a program of brain imaging to try to bring some converging data to bear on these assumptions.

USING fMRI TO TEST ACT–R MODELS

We have now completed a large number of functional magnetic resonance imaging (fMRI) studies of many aspects of higher level cognition (Anderson, Qin, Sohn, Stenger, & Carter, 2003; Anderson, Qin, Stenger, & Carter, 2004; Qin et al., 2003; Sohn, Goode, Stenger, Carter, & Anderson, 2003; Sohn, Goode, Stenger, Jung, Carter, & Anderson, 2005) and based on the patterns over these experiments we have made the following associations between a number of brain regions and modules in ACT–R. In this chapter, we are concerned with five brain regions and their ACT–R associations:

1. **Caudate (Procedural):** Centered at Talairach coordinates $x = -5$, $y = 9$, $z = 2$. This is part of a set of subcorticial structures called the basal ganglia that we associate with the procedural system.
2. **Prefrontal (Retrieval):** Centered at $x = -40$, $y = 21$, $z = 21$. This includes parts of Brodmann Areas 45 and 46 around the inferior frontal sulcus.
3. **Anterior Cingulate (Goal):** Centered at $x = -5$, $y = 10$, $z = 38$. This includes parts of Brodmann Areas 24 and 32.
4. **Parietal (Problem State or Imaginal):** Centered at $x = -23$, $y = -64$, $z = 34$. This includes parts of Brodmann Areas 39 and 40 at the border of the intraparietal sulcus.

5. **Motor (Manual):** Centered at $x = -37$, $y = -25$, $z = 47$. This includes parts of Brodmann Areas 3 and 4 at the central sulcus.

Predicting the BOLD Response

We have developed a methodology for relating the profile of activity in modules like those in Figure 6–3 to Blood Oxygen Level Dependent (BOLD) responses from the brain regions that correspond to these modules. Figure 6–4 illustrates the proportion of time that a particular module was active at various points during a

(a)

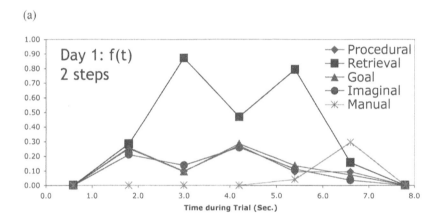

b)

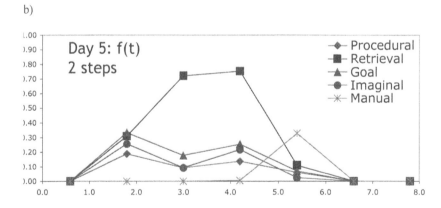

Figure 6–4.   The degree of engagement of the various modules during a trial on Day 1 (part a) and Day 5 (part b).

trial on Day 1 (Part a) and Day 5 (Part b) for the two-step equations. These numbers would be directly obtainable from Figure 6–3, except that Figure 6–4 reflects the average engagement over the whole day not just at the beginning of Day 1 (Fig. 6–3a) and the end of Day 5 (Fig. 6–3b). The basic model we have developed of the BOLD response claims that the while a module is engaged it is producing a hemodynamic response in the corresponding region. We have adopted the standard gamma function that other researchers (e.g., Boyton, Engle, Glover, & Heeger, 1996; Cohen, 1997; Dale & Buckner, 1997; Glover, 1999) have used for the BOLD response. If the module is engaged it will produce a BOLD response t time units later according to the function:

$$B(t) = m \left(\frac{t}{s}\right)^a e^{-(t/s)}$$

where m governs the magnitude, s scales the time, and the exponent a determines the shape of the BOLD response such that with larger a the function rises and falls more steeply. The time to peak for the BOLD response is $a * s$ and the magnitude area under the curve is $m * s * \Gamma(a)$ where Γ is the gamma function ($\Gamma(a) = (a - 1)!$) The BOLD response accumulates whenever the region is engaged. Thus, if $f(t)$ is an engagement function giving the probability that the region is engaged at time t, then the cumulative BOLD response can be obtained by convolving the two functions together:

$$CB(t) = \int_0^t f(x) B(t - x) dx$$

This is the observed BOLD response. Its area is proportional to the total time that the region is engaged. Thus, if a module is active for T seconds, then the area under the BOLD response is $T*m*s*\Gamma(a)$.

In summary, a model for the time course (Fig. 6–3) of this task yields engagement functions $f(t)$ like those in Figure 6–4. By convolving the engagement functions with the BOLD function, one can obtain predictions for the BOLD response in the regions associated with the modules. Most of the parameters of this model are set according to prior values established for ACT–R, but fitting the latency in Figure 6–1 did require estimating parameters for the time to encode the equation and the duration of the retrievals. Having now committed to the time course of each module, predictions immediately follow for the time course of the BOLD response. The exact height and shape of the BOLD response depends on the magnitude (m), the scale (s), and the exponent (a) for the region that corresponds to that module. However, the strong parameter-free prediction is that the relative areas under the BOLD responses in two conditions for a region will reflect the relative amounts of time this region is engaged in these two conditions. Thus, the BOLD response provides a direct check on assumptions about the amount of time various modules are engaged in doing a task.

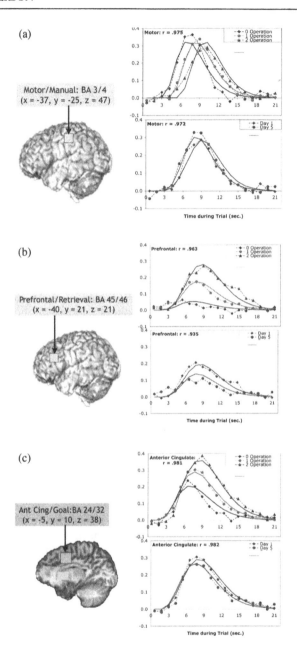

Figure 6–5.   Use of module behavior to predict BOLD response in various regions: (a) Manual module predicts motor region; (b) Retrieval Module predicts prefrontal region; (c) Control/Goal module predicts anterior cingulate region

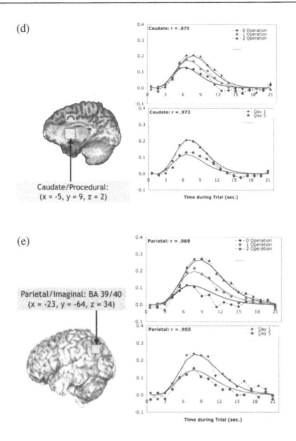

Figure 6–5. *(continued)* (d) Imaginal/Problem State module predicts parietal region; (e) Procedural module predicts caudate region.

Table 6–2 gives the estimated parameters for the BOLD response and Figure 6–5 shows how well this model predicts the BOLD responses in the six conditions achieved by crossing day and number of steps of transformation for each of the five associated regions. To simplify matters and to make the functions more comparable, the exponent of the BOLD response was set to 3 for all regions. To keep the data presentation readable and get better estimates, Figure 6–5 averages either over days or over conditions.[2]

---

[2]In fact, none of the regions showed a significant interaction between practice and number of steps or between practice, number of steps, and scan.

Table 6-2

Parameters Estimated and Fits to the Bold Response

	Motor/ Manual	Prefrontal/ Retrieval	Parietal/ Imaginal	Cingulate/ Goal	Caudate/ Procedural
Magn(m)	0.531	0.073	0.231	0.258	0.207
Exponent(a)	3	3	3	3	3
Scale(s)	1.241	1.545	1.645	1.590	1.230
Correlation	0.975	0.963	0.969	0.981	0.975
Chi-square (105 *df*)	88.93	82.60	95.21	123.27	81.03

Characterizing the Differences Among the Brain Regions

The first impression one probably gets from Figure 6–5 is that the BOLD responses for the five regions look a lot alike. All show a characteristic hemodynamic response that goes up and comes down with the trial structure. Furthermore, most regions show a stronger response for more transformations and a stronger response on Day 1. This is quite characteristic of imaging results where disparate regions of the brain give quite similar responses to the material. Without a strong theory to guide one's expectations, one is in danger of missing the differences and concluding that the whole brain (or at least those regions that respond—not all regions in the brain respond to the task structure in this experiment) is reflecting a global response to the task. However, if one knows where to look, there are characteristic differences. Although this one experiment does not reveal all the differences in the behavior of all five regions, it does reflect many of the important differences that we have identified over our experiments. These are enumerated next.

First, and most apparent, in Figure 6–5a the motor region is giving basically the same hemodynamic response in all conditions. The effect of the slower conditions is to delay when that hemodynamic response occurs. This is what would be expected given a relatively strong understanding of what regions of the brain control the hand. Although the motor region is transparently giving a different response than the other regions (on both theoretical and observational grounds), its correlation with the BOLD responses in other regions averages .66. Thus even it might be confused with the other regions unless one had a theory to tell one where to look to find the relevant differences.

Two of the other regions have distinct signatures. The prefrontal region (Fig. 6–5b) is distinguished by the very weak response it generates in the case of

0 steps. According to the model, this case involves some brief retrievals of instructions but no retrieval of number facts. We have often modeled this condition by assuming no retrieval and predicted a flat function but a slight rise can be discerned. The striking feature of the anterior cingulate (Fig. 6–5c) is that there is almost no effect of learning whereas there is a robust effect of number of steps on magnitude of the response. The goal component in ACT–R is engaged in maintaining state at points where the system is engaged in a retrieval of an arithmetic fact (this is because the retrieval buffer cannot be used to hold the next step of instruction). Every time it engages in retrieval of an arithmetic task it must note this so that it will wait for the fact before going on. Once the fact is retrieved it must reset the state so that it can proceed with solving the equation. Thus, the number of retrieval operations is one factor influencing the number of state-setting operations in the goal buffer. The number of arithmetic retrievals changes in this experiment with the number of steps in solving the equation since each step requires retrieval of a fact. However, there is little reduction in these retrievals with practice. In principle, with enough practice they would eventually drop out but there are so many individual facts that they just do not repeat enough in equation solving.

The other two regions (the parietal in Fig. 6–5d and the caudate in Fig. 6–5e) can be distinguished from the other three regions because they lack the features that identify the other three. However, there is little difference in the response that we see in these two regions. They approximately reflect the average response of all the areas, showing substantial effects of both number of steps of transformations and days of practice. The caudate is fit according to the number of rules that fire, which naturally increases with steps and decreases with days. The parietal is fit according to number of mental re-representations of the equation, which also increases with steps and decreases with days. There is a subtle difference between the two with the caudate showing a relatively larger effect of days and the parietal showing a relatively larger effect of steps. We find differences between these two regions in experiments that vary modality of presentation from visual to aural with the parietal responding less to auditory presentation than visual and the caudate responding more (Sohn et al., 2005). Note that in the comparisons of Figures 6–5d and 6–5e, the caudate gives a relatively weak response and has a poorer signal-to-noise ratio. This is unfortunate because according to the theory it should be the one region that is involved in all cognitive tasks, reflecting number of production rules fired.

Assessing Goodness of Fit

The figures contain measures of correlations between the predictions and observed behavior. These are averaged over either days or operations but Table 6–2 gives correlations among all 108 points for each region. Although this is a conventional measure of quality of fit, it has a number of problems. For instance, correlation is only sensitive to whether the shapes match up and not to whether the actual predicted numbers match up.

The quantitative correspondence can be assessed by the chi-square statistics in the table, which measure the degree of mismatch against the noise in the data. They are calculated as

$$\chi^2 = \frac{\sum_i (\hat{X}_i - \overline{X}_i)^2}{S_{\overline{X}}^2}$$

where the denominator is estimated from the interaction between conditions and participants. This has 105 degrees of freedom, calculated as 108 minus the 3 parameters estimated for the BOLD function. By this measure, all of the areas are being modeled as well as can be expected because they all yield nonsignificant chi-squares (it would have to be 130 or greater to be significant at the .05 level).

Table 6–3 reports the outcome of trying to fit each module to each region's activation profile and calculating a chi-square measure of misfit. With 105 degrees of freedom, the 5-percentile tails for the chi-square distribution are at 82 and 130. As we noted with respect to Table 6–2, all the modules give acceptable fits (less than 130) to their ascribed regions. A few other modules give acceptable fits to other regions although not as good. In particular, the modules other than the manual module all give approximately equal fits to the parietal and caudate regions. As noted, these regions approximately show the average response of all the regions.

Table 6–3
Chi-Square Measure of Fits between Regions and Modules

	Motor	Prefrontal	Cingulate	Parietal	Caudate
Manual	88.93	452.05	724.66	426.40	333.89
Retrieval	493.22	82.60	350.32	101.88	133.13
Goal	255.91	194.94	123.27	171.74	111.01
Imaginal	384.66	125.66	210.47	95.21	101.82
Procedural	347.05	163.76	286.28	114.93	81.03

CONCLUSIONS

We should note that there is no reason why such data and methodology should be limited to testing the ACT–R theory. Many other information-processing theories could be tested. The basic idea is that the BOLD response reflects the duration for which various cognitive modules are active. The typical additive-factors information-processing methodology has studied how manipulations of various cognitive components affect a single aggregate behavioral measure like total time. If we can assign these different components to different brain regions, we have essentially a separate dependent measure to track each component. Therefore, this methodology promises to offer strong guidance in the development of any information-processing theory.

ACKNOWLEDGMENTS

This research was supported by the NSF Grant ROLE: REC—0087396 and ONR Grant N00014–96–1–0491.

REFERENCES

Anderson, J. R. (in press). Using brain imaging to guide the development of a cognitive architecture. In W. E. Gray (Ed.), *Integrated models of cognitive systems.* New York: Oxford University Press.

Anderson, J. R., Bothell, D., Byrne, M.D., Douglass, S., Lebiere, C., & Qin, Y. (2004) An integrated theory of mind. *Psychological Review, 111,* 1036–1060.

Anderson, J. R., Qin, Y., Sohn, M-H., Stenger, V. A., & Carter, C. S. (2003) An information-processing model of the BOLD response in symbol manipulation tasks. *Psychonomic Bulletin & Review, 10,* 241–261.

Anderson, J. R., Qin, Y., Stenger, V. A., & Carter, C. S. (2004). The relationship of three cortical regions to an information-processing model. *Cognitive Neuroscience, 16,* 637–653.

Anderson, J. R., Taatgen, N. A., & Byrne, M. D. (2005). Learning to achieve perfect time sharing: Architectural implications of Hazeltine, Teague, & Ivry. *Journal of Experimental Psychology: Human Perception and Performance, 31,* 749–761.

Baddeley, A. D. (1986). *Working memory.* Oxford, England: Oxford University Press.

Boyton, G. M., Engel, S. A., Glover, G. H., & Heeger, D. J. (1996). Linear systems analysis of functional magnetic resonance imaging in human V1. *Journal of Neuroscience, 16,* 4207–4221.

Dale, A. M., & Buckner, R. L. (1997) Selective averaging of rapidly presented individual trials using fMRI. *Human Brain Mapping, 5,* 329–340.

Glover, G. H. (1999). Deconvolution of impulse response in event-related BOLD fMRI. *NeuroImage, 9,* 416–429.

Qin, Y., Anderson, J. R., Silk, E., Stenger, V. A., & Carter, C. S. (2004). The change of the brain activation patterns along with the children's practice in algebra equation solving. *Proceedings of National Academy of Sciences, 101,* 5686–5691.

Qin, Y., Sohn, M.-H., Anderson, J. R., Stenger, V. A., Fissell, K., Goode, A., & Carter, C. S. (2003). Predicting the practice effects on the blood oxygenation level-dependent (BOLD) function of fMRI in a symbolic manipulation task. *Proceedings of the National Academy of Sciences of the United States of America, 100*(8), 4951–4956.

Sohn, M.-H., Goode, A., Stenger, V. A, Carter, C. S., & Anderson, J. R. (2003). Competition and representation during memory retrieval: Roles of the prefrontal cortex and the posterior parietal cortex, *Proceedings of National Academy of Sciences, 100,* 7412–7417.

Sohn, M.-H., Goode, A., Stenger, V. A, Jung, K.-J., Carter, C. S., & Anderson, J. R. (2005). An information-processing model of three cortical regions: Evidence in episodic memory retrieval. *NeuroImage, 25,* 21–33.

Taatgen, N. A. (2005) Modeling parallelization and speed improvement in the skill acquisition: from dual tasks to complex dynamic skills. *Cognitive Science, 29,* 421–456.

Taatgen, N. A., & Anderson, J. R. (2002). Why do children learn to say "Broke"? A model of learning the past tense without feedback. *Cognition, 86,* 123–155.

Remembering Images

Stephen M. Kosslyn
Harvard University

Gordon H. Bower had a profound influence on my eventual academic fate, well before I actually met him. When I arrived at Stanford in 1970, Gordon was on sabbatical (teaching in Austria, as I recall). One of the other faculty members gave me a preprint of an article he wrote, "Mental Imagery and Associative Learning," later to appear in the volume edited by Gregg (1972). In that paper, a single line struck me right between the eyes (I vividly remember reading it, late at night in the original Stanford coffee house). He said something to the effect that "If images are like pictures, and can be scanned and otherwise inspected ... ." This throwaway thought from Gordon (which he valued so little that he deleted it from the final version) instantly led me to have two ideas. First, I realized that— exactly analogous to the now-famous "mental rotation" experiments of Lynn Cooper, Jackie Metzler, and Roger Shepard (see Shepard & Cooper, 1982)—I could measure how much time people required to respond when they had to scan different distances across a drawing they were visualizing. If Gordon were correct, more time should be required to scan greater distances across an imaged object. Second, I also realized that I could use such response times more generally, as a kind of "mental tape measure," to assess structural properties of the underlying representation. The thought was that if image representations (the short-term memory representations, which somehow give rise to the experience of "seeing with the mind's eye") were in some sense pictorial, then space in the representation should embody actual space. If so, I conjectured, then the time to scan from one point to another on the image should directly reflect the distance between the points on the corresponding object.

I did in fact carry out the experiment I conceived that night, as my 1st-year project, and it was eventually published in 1973. Little did I realize, but a single fragment of a line from one of Gordon's papers essentially determined the next 35 years of my research life. When Gordon returned from his sabbatical, it wasn't long before we were talking and he was having a personal impact on my research. Gordon's incisive, sometimes very critical (but always constructive) feedback whipped me into intellectual shape. In those days, there was nothing like being the object of Gordon's full attention; he listened very carefully, and followed the implications of ideas to their logical conclusions. If you wanted to avoid embarrassment, you tried to do the same thing—before the conversation!

In this short chapter, I wish to outline where I've ended up in the line of research that Gordon inspired. Although much of my recent research has focused on the neural bases of imagery (for review, see Kosslyn, Thompson, & Ganis, 2006), I've also continued to develop theories and studies of the role of imagery in information processing.

THE REALITY SIMULATION PRINCIPLE

For the past 35 years, I've often begun presentations by asking the audience a simple question: What shape are a German shepherd dog's ears? I'm not really interested in the answer, but rather in what seems to go on when people try to answer. Namely, they often report that they visualize the dog's ears, and "see" their shape in the mental image. By "mental image" I mean a short-term memory representation that depicts information; in a depiction, each part of the representation corresponds to part of the represented object such that the distances among the parts of the representation preserve the corresponding distances among the parts of the object itself (see Kosslyn et al., 2006). A "mental" image is an image that arises from stored information, not directly from sense organs (which produce perceptual, not mental, images).

If the common introspection about the dog's ears can be taken at face value, performing this task is perhaps the simplest example of what I've come to call the reality simulation principle (RSP) at work. The RSP states that mental imagery mimics the corresponding events in the world. As such, imagery can be used to simulate the consequences of performing an action or observing an action. The virtue of such mental simulations is that they make accessible and explicit information that may be inaccessible and implicit in long-term memory (such as, for most of us, the shape of an animal's ears). However, I must note from the outset that these mental simulations are only as good as the underlying knowledge or beliefs that guide them; images are not like objects, which are rigid and must obey the laws of physics. Rather, one of the strengths of mental images is that we can alter them at will, and image transformations are guided by information stored or computed—and the more complex and unfamiliar the type of situation, the more likely it is that our mental simulations will fail to operate appropriately (e.g., Caramazza, McCloskey, & Green, 1981). Fortunately for the use of imagery in recalling information, one need only simulate the act of looking at an object or event, which does not draw on complex physical principles and hence is less likely to fall prey to mistaken beliefs or misguided theories.

Perhaps the earliest documented example of the RSP at work traces back to the fifth-century BCE bard Simonides of Ceos, who described the use of mental imagery in remembering (see Yates, 1966). The story goes that Simonides was entertaining at a banquet when he was summoned to go outside to receive a message. At just that moment, the ceiling collapsed, killing all the diners and mangling them beyond recognition. Relatives, friends, and (presumably) tax collectors anxiously awaited news of the identities of the victims. When asked about the guest list, Simonides found that he could recall perfectly who was at the feast simply by visualizing the banquet table and imagining that he was shifting his mental gaze from person to person, recognizing each in turn.

When you use imagery to remember the shape of an animal's ears or people who were sitting around a table, the RSP is at work. You run a mental simulation of what you would see if you were actually seeing the dog or people, and voila! You remember information even if you didn't know you knew it. Simply by perceiving an object or event, you typically will automatically store information about it, but not necessarily in a form that is explicit or accessible. Images, unlike words and descriptions, are rich in incidental detail, capable of being mined in ways not considered when they were originally stored. To discover the role that imagery plays in remembering, let's take a closer look at what goes on the first time someone considers the shape of that canine's ears.

MENTAL IMAGE REPRESENTATIONS

When I first asked my favorite question, about the dog's ears, if you were like most people you used imagery to answer. How do we produce mental images when we need them? A Buddhist monk I know told me that after training, mental images "spring to mind like a fish leaping out of water." I love this simile, which not only summarizes the idea succinctly and elegantly, but is so poetic. However, that said, although the fish may seem to be formed all at once, it is possible that it is built up a bit at a time—a fin here, gills there, and so on—but so quickly that even a well-trained monk would not notice the piecemeal construction process. Moreover, the simile doesn't explain what's different about air and water, what's different before and after the image was brought to mind. In order to understand how mental images are created, we first need to consider what's happening behind the scenes in the brain, which ultimately produces our mental images.

Surface Versus Deep Representations

Let's start with a simple and uncontroversial observation: You don't have any particular mental image all the time. Until I ask you to tell me in which hand the
Statue of Liberty holds the torch or to recall the color of the inside of a lime, you
don't have an image of the monument or the fruit. Where did the image come
from? Clearly, the image isn't coming from something in front of you at the time
(if it did, we would be discussing perception, not imagery), and thus the image
must arise from information stored in memory. In my 1974 PhD dissertation, I
adapted some then-current ideas from linguistics to mental imagery, and distinguished between a *surface representation,* which is an image that you experience
as if you were perceiving, and a *deep representation,* which is the unconscious
information stored in memory that allows you to create the surface representation.

The distinction between a surface representation and a deep representation is
exactly parallel to the difference between a picture on a computer screen (surface representation) and the information on a DVD disk (deep representation),
or between a song played from a speaker (surface representation) and the information on a CD or in an MP3 file (deep representation). In fact, I initially used
a very similar metaphor when I first began to study imagery (in 1970, before
PCs, DVDs, or CDs existed). In my metaphor, I identified surface representations with displays on a cathode-ray tube (a computer's screen), and deep representations with files that a computer program uses to create such displays (see
Kosslyn, 1975).

However, this metaphor may convey two misleading ideas. First, it seems to
suggest that surface representations are created simply by playing back stored
information. This notion would fit the leaping fish metaphor. However, there is an
enormous amount of data indicating that images are *constructed* on the basis of
deep representations (e.g., see Kosslyn, 1980, 1994). Forming an image isn't really
like playing a DVD. It's more like assembling pieces of a puzzle, a part at a time.
Thus, images built up over time, and there's ample opportunity for slippage—but
also ample opportunity for novel twists and creative turns. Second, the metaphor
would seem to play into the hands of Zenon Pylyshyn's (1973) original critique
of imagery, which was titled "What the Mind's Eye Tells the Mind's Brain." Who
(or what) would look at the screen? Unlike when we play a DVD or CD, there's
no person waiting to see the picture or hear the sound. There's no "little man" in
the head, munching popcorn as he watches mental images scroll by on a mental
TV screen. Instead, the image representation is processed so that signals are sent
to other parts of the brain, and these signals are interpreted.

In the following sections, I want to provide an overview of the picture I see
emerging from the last 35 years of research on the nature of mental imagery. In
so doing, I map the metaphors into the brain, thereby removing the whiff of
untestable mentalism that so bothered the behaviorists.

Four Key Facts About the Visual Brain

Instead of using the neural mechanisms of perception for that one purpose alone, this machinery has been pressed into doing double-duty—serving in both perception and mental imagery. In fact, we have found that the vast majority of brain areas activated during visual perception are also activated during visual mental imagery (Ganis et al., 2003; Kosslyn, Thompson, & Alpert, 1997). Researchers have gained considerable leverage in understanding imagery by considering the neural mechanisms that give rise to it.

Let's start by focusing on four important facts about the visual system as it operates during perception. Following this, I suggest how these facts bear on imagery.

Fact 1: *The brain has many areas that depict shapes.* In vision, light striking the retina causes impulses to be sent to the *primary visual cortex,* at the back of the brain (e.g., Heegar et al., 1999; Sereno et al., 1995; Tootell et al., 1984). A striking feature of this brain area is that the pattern of light that strikes the retinas produces a corresponding pattern of activation on the surface of the brain itself; the shape of the stimulus is physically laid out on the surface of the brain. Such brain areas are said to be *retinotopically organized.* The neurons are arranged so that their physical organization corresponds to the locations of the points on the retina that stimulates them. In other words, the physical structure of cortex mirrors (to some degree of accuracy) the physical structure at the back of the eye. And because an image is projected onto the retina, the pattern on cortex is also an image. The patterns of activation in retinotopically organized brain areas literally depict shapes.

The monkey brain has some 15 such areas; we don't yet know how many the human brain has, but we know for sure it has several (e.g., Sereno et al., 1995; Slotnick & Yantis, 2003). I refer to the ensemble of retinotopically organized visual areas in the occipital lobe as the *visual buffer.* (I use the term buffer because it is a repository of information that is stored only briefly, and that information can be operated on in various ways.) In a very concrete sense, we have "pictures in the head."

But it's one thing for researchers, as outside observers, to see an image on the surface of the brain, and quite another for that image to be used by the brain itself. By analogy, if a TV camera weren't hooked up to something else, the images it captured would be irrelevant. Perhaps what we see on the brain is the equivalent of the image in the disconnected camera. Perhaps the image in the brain is just a byproduct of processes that create languagelike representations of objects and events (as many computer vision programs are designed to do); in this case, the image would be like the lights that flashed on the outsides of the earliest computers, which took no part in the computational process itself.

Before being convinced that activity in a particular brain area plays a role in a particular type of processing, we need two kinds of evidence: First, the area must become activated during the appropriate sort of processing; and second, if the area is damaged, the relevant sorts of processing should be disrupted. Both conditions are met for inferring that retinotopically organized brain areas depict shapes in the human brain:

1. When people view objects, these areas are activated—and the precise pattern of activation depends on the shape of the object. For example, using functional magnetic resonance imaging (fMRI), researchers observed a precise circular pattern activated in primary visual cortex when participants viewed a circle (Heegar et al., 1999).
2. In addition, brain damage reveals that these areas depict shape. For example, retinotopically organized brain areas sometimes were damaged in wars of bygone eras, when bullets were sufficiently slow that a soldier could sustain a head wound and live to be seen by a neurologist. If the bullet punched a hole in one of the retinotopically organized areas, it produced a blind spot (i.e., a *scotoma*). In fact, two nearby holes in a retinotopically organized brain area will produce two nearby blind spots, whereas two relatively distant holes in the brain area will produce two relatively distant blind spots. As you would expect, given these findings, when neural activity in these brain areas is temporarily dampened down (by administering brief pulses of strong magnetic stimulation), perception is impaired (e.g., see Kosslyn et al., 1999).

Fact 2: *The visual areas are organized into separate major systems.* The visual buffer merely organizes input, and represents it as a depiction; the visual buffer does not recognize the depicted objects or specify relative locations among them. Patterns of activation in this structure, like electrical patterns produced in a TV camera, must be further processed in order for us to recognize the shape of a dog's ears or know where they are located relative to the head. The situation is like that old conundrum, "If a tree falls in the forest but there's no one there to hear it, is there a sound?" From the perspective of a psychologist, the answer is clear: No. "Sound" is more than compressed waves, propagating through the air or some other medium. To have a sound, a brain must register the waves. Similarly, if patterns of neural activation in retinotopically organized areas had no effects at all on any other parts of the brain, then they may as well not exist.

The brain areas that implement the visual buffer are in the occipital lobe, at the back of the brain. When the visual buffer is active, it is not like a tree falling in the wilderness. It is "heard" by other systems, which are implemented in two major neural pathways. The *ventral system,* which relies on the temporal lobes (so named because they are located under the temples), processes information about what an image is. In contrast, the *dorsal system,* which relies on portions of the parietal lobes (so named because they are under the os parietale bone, located at the top rear of the head), processes information about where an object is (and spatial properties more generally, such as size; see Haxby et al., 1991; Ungerleider & Mishkin, 1982). The dorsal system plays a special role in guiding actions (Milner & Goodale, 1996).

To get a sense of the role of the ventral ("what") system in perception, it is illuminating to observe the problems that patients experience when this brain area is damaged. I vividly recall one patient who had brain damage that effectively disconnected the input from the occipital lobes to the temporal lobes. This particular patient was being examined for a class I was teaching, to allow the students to see how brain damage can affect mental processes and behavior. This patient, let's call him J.M., had suffered a stroke, which often is caused by a blood clot that cuts off the supply of blood (and its life-giving oxygen and nutrients) to specific parts of the brain—causing those brain cells to die. J.M.'s stroke profoundly affected his visual abilities, but only in selective ways. The fact that J.M. was not completely blind was evident the instant that he was wheeled into the room. As soon as J.M. saw the mass of 40 or so students, intently watching his every move, he twisted around and looked back the way he came. He was clearly well-oriented in space. J.M. began to complain, fluently and very coherently, wondering what was going on. He evidently had no problem expressing himself in words. The neurologist who was going to examine him reminded him that these students were considering becoming physicians, and that J.M. had agreed to be examined in front of them, and then asked if that was still OK. Hearing this, the patient relaxed and averred that he remembered and was still willing to participate.

And so the examination began. After showing that J.M. had knowledge of common facts that he had learned prior to his injury (the capitols of major states and relatively recent current events), the neurologist held up a comb and asked him what it was. J.M. said, "I have no idea." "Guess," said the neurologist. "I have no idea," J.M. repeated. "Please take a guess." "OK ... a shoe?" At this point, the neurologist asked him to reach out and touch it. J.M. reached unerringly, and immediately upon touching it he said, "Oh, it's a comb." This same pattern—failure to recognize when looking, precise reaching followed by quick and confident recognition when touching—was repeated with several other objects. The class was transfixed. The point was not lost on them: J.M. was utterly at sea when he had to name objects by sight, but as competent as anyone in the room at reaching and at identifying objects by touch.

What was going on here? J.M's stroke had destroyed critical connections between the retinotopically organized areas in the occipital lobes (which organize the input into figure vs. ground, as well as extract color and various other properties of shapes) and the brain areas in the ventral system—which is the seat of visual memories. In order to recognize something, we need to access memory: When we recognize an apple, we have matched what we perceive to a representation stored in memory; there's nothing inherent in that shape that makes it meaningful—it's only our past experiences with others of its kind that lends meaning to the current shape we see. Because the sensory input in J.M.'s brain was not able to access his visual memories, he could not recognize objects he saw (see Farah, 1990). But the connections from the parts of his brain that process tactile input were intact, and thus he had no problem using that route to access stored memories.

We can also learn a lot by observing the effects of damage to the brain areas that compose the dorsal system. Some patients with damage in the dorsal system have exactly the opposite problem as J.M.; they can easily identify objects, but cannot locate them in space. These patients typically have trouble when they must use vision to guide reaching (De Renzi, 1982). Moreover, they cannot direct their gaze toward named objects, cannot navigate effectively through a room, and cannot estimate how far away objects are from them.

As the effects of brain damage so dramatically illustrate, the brain contains numerous different systems involved in memory. Sticking with the ventral system, we can distinguish between two sorts of memory representations. On the one hand, modality-specific memories allow us to *recognize* objects by sight. After first encountering an object, we typically store a visual representation of its shape. Later, when we see objects, the input is compared to shapes stored in memory. If a match is obtained, we recognize the object. In this use of the term recognition, all we know after recognition is that the object is familiar—it matches a stored shape, and hence we are assured that we have seen it before.

On the other hand, we also can *identify* objects. After we have identified an object, we know various facts about it that we've previously learned, such as categories it belongs to, common contexts in which it occurs, and all manner of other associated facts. The memories that we use to identify an object are not modality specific, and are not stored in either the ventral or dorsal systems. Instead, such memories are stored in a long-term associative memory that retains abstract representations, and can be accessed following recognition in any modality. For example, you can recognize a cat by the way it looks, by hearing its meow, or by feeling it rub against your shins. But once you recognize it, you can then identify it—and have access to the same set of associated information (such as the facts that it is a mammal and likes to drink milk), regardless of how it was recognized (see Kosslyn, 1994). Patient J.M. could not recognize visual input, but could recognize tactile input—and once recognized, could then identify the object (which is required in order to retrieve its name). Long-term associative memory relies on cortex in various places in the brain, including Area 19 (which includes what classically was called "association cortex") and parts of the anterior temporal lobes.

In short, the visual buffer sends input to two separate systems, the ventral system (which processes and stores visual memories of shapes and shape-related properties, such as color) and the dorsal system (which processes and stores spatial properties). Moreover, information from these two streams converges to access a long-term associative memory, which is crucial for identifying the input.

Fact 3: *Visual memories are not stored as images.* At least in the monkey brain (about which we know much more than we do about the human brain), the areas of the ventral system that actually store modality-specific visual memories do not depict information. Instead, such memories are stored in a kind of "compressed code" (as are images stored in a computer or on a DVD, perhaps for similar reasons—but the brain's compression system looks very different from that used in computer graphics; see Fujita, Tanaka, Ito, & Cheng, 1992; Tanaka, 1996). This code leaves implicit many of the precise aspects of an object's shape. We can recognize objects because the same compression process is used every time we see an object, and thus what is stored in memory will match what is it produced when we see the object again. By analogy, if you had two pictures on two different DVDs, you could compare the patterns of 0's and 1's on the disks to determine whether they were the same.

Fact 4: *Virtually all of visual areas are reciprocally connected.* Virtually every visual brain area that projects fibers to another area also receives fibers from that area. In fact, the feedback connections are about the same size as those that feed forward—an enormous amount of information flows backward in the visual system! Specifically, brain areas in both the ventral system and the dorsal system have massive connections going backward, to the areas that implement the visual buffer (see Felleman & Van Essen, 1991; Suzuki, Saleem, & Tanaka, 2000). And it is this backward-flowing information that allows us to create visual mental images.

IMAGERY AND TOP-DOWN PERCEPTION

And now for my hat trick—these four facts about perception are the key to understanding how our brains can use deep representations to create surface images. The essential idea is that imagery arises directly out of perception—in fact, the two activities meld into one another. Specifically, during perception, the reverse connections between brain areas allow stored information to supplement what you see, filling in missing information. Consider the act of seeing a dog behind a picket fence. What we actually see of the dog is a set of vertical patches of different extents, colors, and textures—and we not only succeed in organize them, but we also recognize the organized shape. In order to accomplish this truly amazing feat, we use a mixture of bottom-up (driven by the sensory input) and top-down (driven by stored knowledge, goals, or beliefs) processing.

Specifically, during perception we do not simply wait, seeing what our eyes happen upon; we are not like some kind of cognitive sponge, waiting passively for what floats by us. Rather, we are active viewers, and as soon as an object begins to look like an animal, we search for animal parts. When we find enough information to implicate a particular object, we not only recognize it but actively begin to fill in what we don't actually see. When we finally see a dog behind the fence, our brains will supply edges that aren't actually there. Our imagery is playing a role in perception itself. The shape we perceive is an amalgam of information coming from the eyes and information coming from memory.

Although using mental imagery to classify a German shepherd dog's ears from memory may seem very different from the act of recognizing a partially obscured dog, I claim that many common processes are involved in accomplishing the two tasks. Here's the central idea: During perception, information flows downstream in cascade—earlier processes send partial results to subsequent processes; the earlier systems do not "wait to finish" before sending output, the way a subroutine in a computer program would do. And as soon as the subsequent areas receive input, they reflexively project information backward, using top-down processing to assist the earlier areas. (In terms of neural net models, a feedback loop supplements the input, resulting in "vector completion.") Such feedback may always occur as a kind of verification step; if you've in fact recognized an object correctly, then feedback from the ventral system should correspond to the pattern in the visual buffer. We don't usually notice such feedback processes because we have in fact successfully recognized the object, and thus the information projected backward does in fact correspond to the representation in the visual buffer.

From this perspective, visual mental imagery would rely on such backward projections. In fact, when we compared brain activation when people saw degraded pictures (and hence presumably needed to complete them) to an imagery task (where their eyes were closed), approximately 92% of the same voxels were activated in the two conditions (Ganis et al., 2003). But more than that, virtually all of the same voxels were activated in the frontal lobes; the difference between the two conditions was primarily in the occipital lobes, which were activated more strongly in perception. Top-down filling-in is not as strong as bottom-up perception, nor should it be: We do not want to hallucinate, seeing objects or characteristics that we expect to see but that are not in fact present.

In short, I argue that the top-down processes that fill in missing portions of representations during perception also underlie *image generation*—the act of creating a surface representation on the basis of information stored in a deep representation, which is what you probably did when first thinking about the German shepherd's ears. I argue that we cannot directly reinterpret stored deep representations any more than we can gaze at the silvery surface of a DVD and know what pictures and sounds it stores. Rather, to derive novel information from deep representations we first must use them to produce surface representations, and then reinspect these surface representations. Visual memories—deep representations—are stored in the ventral system, and massive connections run backward, from these areas in the temporal lobes to those that compose the visual buffer in the occipital lobes (Rockland & Drash, 1996). The connections allow a deep representation to be used to create a surface representation in the visual buffer. This general idea is not new; in fact, William James (1890) discussed something very much like this notion in his *Principles of Psychology.*

To consider the relationship between top-down processing during perception and image generation, consider the following anecdote: I was helping a friend search for a black purse in her apartment, and went into her bedroom. I recall triumphantly announcing "Victory!" and then sheepishly realizing my error: What I took to be a purse sitting in a corner was in fact her black cat, curled up asleep. I was unconsciously expecting to see a purse so strongly that I actually imposed my image onto the cat, seeing him as a purse. This incident illustrates the intimate relationship between *anticipating* seeing something and generating a mental image. When unconscious processes lead us to anticipate seeing something, parts of the frontal lobes trigger representations in the ventral system, getting us ready to see the object. This preparatory activity is a form of *priming:* We are unconsciously warming up the system, just beginning to engage it so that it can be more easily recruited when the time comes. I want to argue that such priming can be so strong that the feedback connections fill in a pattern of activity in the retinotopically organized areas of the visual buffer. Such *hyperpriming,* as I call it, underlies image generation: This pattern of activity created in the visual buffer is the surface representation, the image itself (see Kosslyn, 1994; McDermott & Roediger, 1994).

These notions lead us to expect the frontal lobes to be used when we see degraded pictures but know what they might depict, and when we form visual mental images; in fact (as noted earlier), virtually identical activation is observed in the two cases. Moreover, and more controversial, we also expect the retinotopically organized areas that implement the visual buffer to be used in imagery, and indeed they are. Going back to the two criteria I noted earlier: First, when people form visual mental images of objects and "look" for details, retinotopically organized brain areas are activated in humans (Kosslyn & Thompson, 2003). Moreover, the precise pattern of activation during imagery, as during perception, depends on the size and shape of the imaged object (Klein et al., 2004; Slotnick, Thompson, & Kosslyn, 2005). In fact, the activation of primary visual cortex during imagery can be remarkably similar to what is found when the participants are actually looking at the stimuli, not visualizing them (Klein et al., 2004). Second, researchers have found that when the occipital lobe in one hemisphere is removed, the horizontal extent of imaged objects is reduced by half (Farah, Soso, & Dashief, 1992). The occipital lobes contain retinotopically organized areas, but each lobe contains areas that depict the opposite side of space. Thus, removing a lobe should reduce the extent of space in which an image can occur, if images do indeed rely on this cortex. And this is just what has been found. Moreover, when neural activity in primary visual cortex is temporarily dampened down (by administering brief pulses of strong magnetic stimulation), imagery is impaired—just as is found in perception. In fact, such magnetic pulses disrupt imagery and perception to equal extents, as we would expect if these brain areas are used in both activities (Kosslyn et al., 1999).

The possibility of generating a surface representation on the basis of stored deep representations is crucial for memory because retinotopically organized areas make the shape of an object explicit and accessible for further processing; once you've visualized an object, you can "look again," and notice aspects of the object's appearance that were only implicit in the deep representation. Signals from the visual buffer go to the ventral and dorsal systems, just as in perception, which allows new characteristics of objects to be recognized or spatial relations to be detected. Moreover, representations in retinotopically organized areas truly depict information: They support actual images, not descriptions. The fact that such areas support mental image representations is inconsistent with propositional theories, which claim that all representations in the brain are like those that underlie language (e.g., Pylyshyn, 1973).

However, I now must add a wrinkle to the story: The occipital lobe is not always used in imagery. This conclusion is implied by results from neuroimaging studies (e.g., for review, see Kosslyn & Thompson, 2003) and studies of the effects of brain damage. In fact, some patients with damage to the occipital lobe can perform imagery tasks (e.g., Behrmann, Winocur, & Moscovitch, 1992; Chatterjee & Southwood, 1995; Jankowiak, Kinsbourne, Shalev, & Bachman, 1992). We can explain such results by appeal to a feature of the ventral system. The lowest level retinotopically organized areas include neurons that have very small receptive fields (i.e., the part of space in which a stimulus will trigger the neuron). In other words, they register variations in space with high resolution. In contrast, retinotopically organized areas later in the processing stream include neurons with larger receptive fields, and presumably they register variations in space with lower resolution. It is possible that imagery tasks that do not require high resolution can be performed on the basis of these later areas. If so, then damage to the earlier areas would not affect performance of such tasks.

SHAPE VERSUS SPATIAL IMAGERY

We've been focusing on mental images of shape, but activating stored spatial information can generate an image of where things are in space (right now, think of what is behind you). In fact, brain-damaged patients have been described who have trouble visualizing shapes, but do not have trouble visualizing relative locations. And other patients have been described who have the reverse problems (Levine, Warach, & Farah, 1985). When the ventral system is damaged, patients cannot tell you about characteristics of objects that require imagery (such as the shape of animals' ears; Farah, 1995). When the dorsal system is damaged, patients cannot judge relative locations (e.g., as required to decide whether Utah is west of Nevada), they get lost, and they cannot sketch a map or give directions to someone else. Moreover, neuroimaging studies have shown that the dorsal system can support spatial images (Thompson & Kosslyn, 2000). Clearly, the ventral and dorsal systems are used not only in perception, but also in imagery.

The idea that we can have mental images of spatial relations leads to a second way to explain why some patients with damage to the occipital lobes can nevertheless perform imagery tasks. It is possible that many imagery tasks can be performed on the basis of the spatial relations among parts of an object. For instance, consider a patient I once tested, who had occipital damage. I asked her to perform a simple imagery task, deciding from memory whether the uppercase version of letters, printed in a standard font, has only straight lines (e.g., *A, E*) or contains any curved lines (e.g., *B, C*). She performed this task by using her right-hand index finger to "draw the letters in the air." Presumably, spatial information alone could guide such movements, and once they were produced she could note whether a curved movement had occurred. This process was very slow, however, compared to normal. To my knowledge, response times were not collected in any of the studies in which brain-damaged patients were shown to be able to perform imagery tasks.

Moreover, Kozhevnikov, Hegarty, and Mayer (2002; see also Kozhevnikov, Kosslyn, & Shephard, 2005) found that some perfectly normal people, with intact brains, are especially good at *object imagery*—constructing vivid and detailed images of the shapes and surface characteristics of objects—whereas others are good at *spatial imagery*—representing spatial relationships between objects and imagining spatial transformations (such as imagining rotating an object). They also found that the two types of imagery ability rarely go together. In fact, people who are good at one type tend to be relatively poor at the other.

Just as there are many specialized systems and subsystems that underlie perception, I expect researchers to discover many specialized systems and subsystems in imagery. Cognitive neuroscience has dramatically shown that faculties (such as memory, perception, and imagery) that may at first glance seem to be unitary and undifferentiated are in fact complex systems with rich underlying structure. Imagery is not "one thing," and part of the challenge for future research will be to understand how the various types and aspects of imagery work together when one performs a specific type of task.

CONCLUDING REFLECTIONS

The discoveries about how mental images arise in the brain allow us to put to rest—finally!—a nagging concern about imagery. I noted before that the DVD analogy was flawed because it seemed to suggest that there's a little man "watching" our mental images. For centuries, the very idea of mental images was a bit dodgy because such images seemed to require such a little man (formally known as a *homunculus*) to look at them—and then there would need to be another "little man" in that little man's head, and so on and so on. But where's the little man in what we've just discussed? Nowhere. We don't need to posit one in imagery any more than we need to posit one in perception. No matter how hard you look, you won't find a little man (even a very very tiny little man) sitting in the brain looking at pictures in the visual buffer. If we don't need a little man in perception proper, we don't need one in imagery. In both imagery and perception, patterns of neural activity underlie internal representations, and activation patterns allow information regarding such representations to be propagated through the system (cf. Barsalou, 1999; Chapter 14, this volume); moreover, other areas can act to alter the activity the underlies representations, thereby transforming the representation in specific ways. The basic idea is simple and straightforward; there's nothing mystical or inherently unscientific in the very idea of mental imagery.

Gordon Bower's interest in imagery was focused on memory, and I've focused here on the use of imagery to retrieve stored information. Let me illustrate a final point about the role of imagery in memory with one last anecdote. Some years ago I had the great honor of discussing scientific research on mental imagery with His Holiness the Dalai Lama. By now you won't be surprised to learn that I began by trying to give him a sense of the phenomena, and asked him to recall the shape of an animal's ears. I replaced my German shepherd with a cat (which I was told were common in Tibet). When I first posed this question, his response was to ask what kind of cat I had in mind. A "house cat" I replied. (Although the Dalai Lama understands and speaks English well, he relied on his translator once I started asking bizarre questions.) His Holiness said he really didn't know about the shape of its ears, but he could visualize a furry head, which made him feel "peaceful." A few minutes later, I asked whether he minded my asking a somewhat personal question, and he consented. So I asked how many windows were in his bedroom. His eyes moved as if he were scanning an image, but he again said he really didn't know. I was astonished. I've asked this question to literally hundreds of people, and never received that response. But since then I've learned that the Dalai Lama simply doesn't care about such things. He was happy to indulge my interests in cats' ears and windows, but his focus is elsewhere. I also discovered that His Holiness can form extremely vivid, highly detailed images of more than 700 Buddhist deities. These images are remarkably complex; for example, one is a person with three heads (each of which symbolizes a different quality) and six arms, with each holding a different object (such as a sword with a red tip). But the details of cats and bedrooms? Of no interest.

This encounter underscores the fact that we will be able to form a mental image only of what we have paid attention to and stored in as a deep representation. For most of us, living the relatively unstructured lives of the West, it makes good sense to graze widely and store incidental details that may be of no interest at the time. Just as a cow can chew its cud, we can recall this information later if we need it. But describing every little detail would be extraordinarily time consuming, both at the time the information is stored and later, if inferences need to be drawn on the basis of what has been stored. Storing deep representations requires little effort, and allows us later to reconstruct a vast array of information, ranging from the trivial (such as the shapes of animal's ears) to the profound (such as the images that garnish Proust's writing).

In short, what we register and store about the world constrains both our memories and what we can think about. The RSP plays a role in memory, but it is probably even more important in problem solving and creative thought. In fact, many aspects of memory meld into problem solving; for instance, retracing your steps from memory is solving a kind of problem. My hope is that the insights we have gained into the basic mechanisms of imagery will in turn help us to understand not only its roles in cognition, but the nature of cognition itself.

ACKNOWLEDGMENTS

Preparation of this chapter was supported by the following grants: National Space Biomedical Research Institute NCC 9–58–193; National Science Foundation REC–0411725; National Institute of Health 2 R01 MH060734–05A1; Defense Advanced Research Projects Agency FA8750–05–2–0270. I thank Larry Barsalou and Berhe Mehreteaband for helpful comments.

REFERENCES

Barsalou, L. W. (1999). Perceptual symbol systems. *Behavioral and Brain Sciences, 22*, 577–602.

Behrmann, M., Winocur, G., & Moscovitch, M. (1992). Dissociation between mental imagery and object recognition in a brain-damaged patient. *Nature, 359*, 636–637.

Bower, G. H. (1972). Mental imagery and associative learning. In L. Gregg (Ed.), *Cognition in learning and memory* (pp. 51–88). New York: Wiley.

Caramazza, A., McCloskey, M., & Green, B. (1981). Naive beliefs in "sophisticated" subjects: Misconceptions about trajectories of objects. *Cognition, 9*, 117–123

Chatterjee, A., & Southwood, M. H. (1995). Cortical blindness and visual imagery. *Neurology, 45*, 2189–2195.

De Renzi, E. (1982). *Disorders of space exploration and cognition.* New York: Wiley.

Farah, M. J. (1990). *Visual agnosia: Disorders of object recognition and what they tell us about normal vision.* Cambridge, MA: MIT Press.

Farah, M. J. (1995). Current issues in the neuropsychology of image generation. *Neuropsychologia, 23*, 1455–1472.

Farah, M. J., Soso, M. J., & Dasheiff, R. M. (1992). Visual angle of the mind's eye before and after unilateral occipital lobectomy. *Journal of Experimental Psychology: Human Perception and Performance, 18*, 241–246.

Felleman, D. J., & Van Essen, D. C. (1991). Distributed hierarchical processing in primate cerebral cortex. *Cerebral Cortex, 1,* 1–47.

Fujita, I., Tanaka, K., Ito, M., & Cheng, K. (1992). Columns for visual features of objects in monkey inferotemporal cortex. *Nature, 360,* 343–346.

Ganis, G., Thompson, W. L., & Kosslyn, S. M. (2004). Brain areas underlying visual mental imagery and visual perception: An fMRI study. *Cognitive Brain Research, 20,* 226–241.

Haxby, J. V., Grady, C. L., Horwitz, B., Ungerleider, L. G., Mishkin, M., Carson, R. E., Herscovitch, P., Schapiro, M. B., & Rappaport, S. I. (1991). Dissociation of object and spatial visual processing pathways in human extrastriate cortex. *Proceedings of the National Academy of Sciences, USA, 88,* 1621–1625.

Heeger, D. J. (1999). Linking visual perception with human brain activity. *Current Opinion in Neurobiology, 9,* 474–479.

James, W. (1890). *The principles of psychology* (Vol. 2). New York: Dover.

Jankowiak, J., Kinsbourne, M., Shalev, R. S., & Bachman, D. L. (1992). Preserved visual imagery and categorization in a case of associative visual agnosia. *Journal of Cognitive Neuroscience, 4,* 119–131.

Klein, I., Dubois, J., Mangin, J. M., Kherif, F., Flandin, G., Poline, J. B., Denis, M., Kosslyn, S. M., & Le Bihan, D. (2004). Retinotopic organization of visual mental images as revealed by functional magnetic resonance imaging. *Brain Research Reviews, 22,* 26–31.

Kosslyn, S. M. (1973). Scanning visual images: Some structural implications. *Perception and Psychophysics, 14,* 90–94.

Kosslyn, S. M. (1975). Information representation in visual images. *Cognitive Psychology, 7,* 341–370.

Kosslyn, S. M. (1980). *Image and mind.* Cambridge, MA: Harvard University Press.

Kosslyn, S. M. (1994). *Image and brain: The resolution of the imagery debate.* Cambridge, MA: MIT Press.

Kosslyn, S. M., & Thompson, W. L. (2003). When is early visual cortex activated during visual mental imagery? *Psychological Bulletin, 129,* 723–746.

Kosslyn, S. M., Pascual-Leone, A., Felician, O., Camposano, S., Keenan, J. P., Thompson, W. L., Ganis, G., Sukel, K. E., & Alpert, N. M. (1999). The role of area 17 in visual imagery: Convergent evidence from PET and rTMS. *Science, 284,* 167–170.

Kosslyn, S. M., Thompson, W. L., & Alpert, N. M. (1997). Neural systems shared by visual imagery and visual perception: A positron emission tomography study. *NeuroImage, 6,* 320–334.

Kosslyn, S. M., Thompson, W. L., & Ganis, G. (2006). *The case for mental imagery.* New York: Oxford University Press.

Kozhevnikov, M., Kosslyn, S. M., & Shephard, J. M. (2005). Spatial versus object visualizers: A new characterization of visual cognitive style. *Memory and Cognition, 33,* 710–726.

Kozhevnikov, M., Hegarty, M., & Mayer, R. E. (2002). Revisiting the visualizer-verbalizer dimension: Evidence for two types of visualizers. *Cognition & Instruction, 20,* 47–78.

Levine, D. N., Warach, J., & Farah, M. J. (1985). Two visual systems in mental imagery: Dissociation of "what" and "where" in imagery disorders due to bilateral posterior cerebral lesions. *Neurology, 35,* 1010–1018.

McDermott, K. B., & Roediger, H. L. (1994). Effects of imagery on perceptual implicit memory tests. *Journal of Experimental Psychology: Learning, Memory and Cognition, 20,* 1379–1390.

Milner, A. D., & Goodale, M. A. (1996). *The visual brain in action.* Oxford, England: Oxford University Press.

Pylyshyn, Z. W. (1973). What the mind's eye tells the mind's brain: A critique of mental imagery. *Psychological Bulletin, 80,* 1–24.

Rockland, K. S., & Drash, G. W. (1996). Collateralized divergent feedback connections that target multiple cortical areas. *Journal of Comparative Neurology, 373,* 529–548.

Sereno, M. I., Dale, A. M., Reppas, J. B., Kwong, K. K., Belliveau, J. W., Brady, T. J., Rosen, B. R., & Tootell, R. B. (1995). Borders of multiple visual areas in humans revealed by functional magnetic resonance imaging. *Science, 268,* 889–893.

Shepard, R. N., & Cooper, L. A. (1982). *Mental images and their transformations.* Cambridge, MA: MIT Press.

Slotnick, S. D., Thompson, W. L., & Kosslyn, S. M. (2005). Visual mental imagery induces retinotopically organized activation of early visual areas. *Cerebral Cortex, 15,* 1570–1583.

Slotnick, S. D., & Yantis, S. (2003). Efficient acquisition of human retinotopic maps. *Human Brain Mapping, 18,* 22–29.

Suzuki W., Saleem K. S., & Tanaka, K. (2000). Divergent backward projections from the anterior part of the inferotemporal cortex (area TE) in the macaque. *Journal of Comparative Neurology, 422,* 206–228.

Tanaka, K. (1996). Inferotemporal cortex and object vision. *Annual Review of Neuroscience, 19,* 109–139.

Thompson, W. L., & Kosslyn, S. M. (2000). Neural systems activated during visual mental imagery: A review and meta-analyses. In A. W. Toga & J. C. Mazziotta (Eds.), *Brain mapping: The systems* (pp. 535–560). San Diego, CA: Academic Press.

Tootell, R. B. H., Silverman, M. S., Switkes, E., & De Valois, R. L. (1982). Deoxyglucose analysis of retinotopic organization in primate striate cortex. *Science, 218,* 902–904.

Ungerleider, L. G., & Mishkin, M. (1982). Two cortical visual systems. In D. J. Ingle, M. A. Goodale, & R. J. W. Mansfield (Eds.), *Analysis of visual behavior* (pp. 549–586). Cambridge, MA: MIT Press.

Yates, F. A. (1966). *The art of memory.* London: Routledge & Kegan Paul.

8

Sharing Landmarks and Paths

Barbara Tversky
Stanford University

We all know that life is a journey, rolling our eyes when we hear it yet another time. I apologize. Journeys are made of paths and landmarks, and journeys can intersect. Remembered journeys are inevitably nostalgic. Here, I reminisce over the landmarks, the intersections of Gordon's journeys and mine, both geographic and intellectual. The geographic landmark is, of course, Stanford. Within Stanford, more landmarks. Jordan Hall, where the yoyo some giddy graduate students hung from the statue (of Jordan?) outside the third floor is long gone. Room 100, the now-gone home of the venerable Friday Seminar, the site of so many brilliant talks by poised graduate students whose testimonies of fear and dread belied their performances. Room 358, the site of numerous brown bags and dissertation orals, with ideas vying for the floor with humor. Gordon's office, at the opposite end of the corridor from mine, so that his deliberate footfalls announced his approach, never without a purpose. The intellectual landmarks are the stops that follow.

The intellectual journeys began first, a rising young professor at Stanford and a graduate student at the University of Michigan. It is not surprising that the graduate student was acquainted with Gordon's research. More surprising is that Gordon was acquainted with my meager output. As a contrary graduate student skeptical of the claims of her elders, my dissertation challenged the idea that memory for the visuospatial world had to be transformed to a linguistic code to achieve permanence (Tversky, 1969). I like to say that Gordon discovered me, though not at the proverbial Hollywood coffee shop but through a mailing list. The Human Performance Center, where I was a student, sent copies of dissertations to a wide group that included Gordon Bower, and he read them! I was soon astonished to see that work described in a seminal chapter he wrote on imaginal representations and mnemonic devices (Bower, 1972).

Gordon's physical presence, almost the scale of his intellectual presence, was to enter my life soon after. He sponsored me as a postdoc at Stanford in 1970–1971. No sooner did I arrive than he left on sabbatical. Because my Michigan adviser had been off-campus most of the time I was in his lab, because I had been off-campus most of my last 2 years in graduate school, and because I still had that contrariness, I expected to work alone. Even in his physical absence, Gordon's intellectual presence was palpable: the issues that attracted him—memory and mental representations, the clear-headed analyses, the rapid-fire generation of experiments, the encyclopedic knowledge; the incisive critical mind, turned as readily to his own work as to that of others. Stanford was an especially exciting destination at that time. Other cognitive faculty included Roger Shepard, Herb Clark, Dick Atkinson, and Ed Smith, and among the graduate students were Steve Kosslyn, John Anderson, Keith Holyoak, Beth Loftus, Geoff Loftus, Bobbie Klatzky, Lynn Cooper, and Arnie Glass.

Years later, I returned to Stanford; this time on sabbatical from the Hebrew University of Jerusalem. In one of those unanticipated turns life journeys can take, I stayed at Stanford more than 25 years, becoming first a colleague of Gordon's and then a friend. I am fortunate, grateful, and enriched for the roles Gordon has played in my life.

Although we never collaborated, the influences had only a short distance to travel, and travel they did, in both directions. But when they arrived, they were transformed.

Imaginal Representations.   It is hard to imagine now how biased cognition and memory were against anything but words. My own work was a reaction to this. It showed that not only could people retain visual codes of visual stimuli, in this case, schematic faces, but also that people could generate visual codes from linguistic stimuli, in this case, the names of the faces, and retain the visual codes instead of the verbal codes, when it was advantageous to performance to use a visual. At about the same time, Allan Paivio was showing that pictures of things yielded better recall than their names, and that the more vivid and imaginable the names, the better the recall (1971, 1986). Gordon characteristically picked up findings that opened new ways of thinking and advanced them. He extended Paivio's methods, and expanded them to an analysis of the effectiveness of mnemonic devices in a paper that has become a classic (1970). I suspect that this was the beginning of his continuous interest in the establishment and nature of mental representations and how they serve memory. After that came his work with John Anderson, a propositional account of memory and mental representations (Anderson & Bower, 1973), followed by work with John Black and others on scripts (Bower, Black, & Turner, 1979), and then work with Dan Morrow and Mike Rinck on what we called spatial mental models (e.g., Morrow, Bower, & Greenspan, 1979; Rinck, Hahnal, Bower, & Glowalla, 1997). It was here that our work again intersected. But first some background.

Mental Representations of the Visuospatial World.   I had always believed that the propositional analyses of mental representations that derived from thinking about the structure of language were not appropriate for analyzing mental representations of the visuospatial world. The visuospatial world has its own structure, different from the structure of language. What's more, knowledge of the visuospatial world preceded language evolutionarily. It seemed more likely that whatever mental structures developed to behave in the visuospatial world would serve as a basis for the structure of language and even thought, rather than the opposite. The dissertation study had juxtaposed verbal and visual similarity to show that both verbal and visual mental representations existed and could be translated one to the other. Studies done during my postdoctoral year at Stanford showed that the encoding strategies effective for remembering words—finding meaningful relations among them—were not the same as those that facilitated remembering pictures—finding distinctive features (Tversky, 1973). The same studies showed that rather than being on a continuum, recognition and recall were qualitatively different, in part a deflected echo of Gordon's ongoing project on recognition and recall memory with John Anderson.

Categories and Parts.   On my return to Stanford as a colleague of Gordon's, it seemed that nearly everyone at Stanford in the 1970s and early 1980s was studying categorization. Much of the impetus came from across the Bay, from Rosch's path-breaking work (e.g., Rosch, 1978). Gordon's lab, too, was working on categorization, including Larry Barsalou, Mark Gluck, and John Clapper. Naturally, we began with the visuospatial aspects of categories. Hemenway and I were intrigued by the special status of basic-level categories. What was it that privileged the level of *table* and *dog*? Hemenway and I found that what characterized the basic level was the salience knowledge of parts, the legs and top of a table, the legs, head, and body of a dog (Tversky, 2004; Tversky & Hemenway, 1984). We observed that parts were at once features of perception and of function, and proposed that they formed a bridge between perception and function, allowing inferences from observable perceptual features to not always observable functional ones. This analysis, though developed for object categories, could be extended to more abstract categories like organizations, which also have parts.

Cognitive Maps.   Always on the alert for research showing special characteristics of representations of the visuospatial world, I was struck by Stevens and Coupe's (1979) finding that students in San Diego thought that Reno is east of San Diego when in fact it is west of San Diego. Stevens and Coupe's explanation is compelling: that instead of remembering all the spatial relations among all pairs of cities, people remember the spatial relations among states, and use those to infer the spatial relations of the cities contained by the states. Because Nevada is east of California, people infer that all the cities in Nevada are east of all the cities in California. Stevens and Coupe argued that spatial memory, like verbal memory, can be regarded as a hierarchically organized network.

The contrarian in me saw another explanation, (for this example, though not for others presented by Stevens and Coupe), derived from thinking about how the mind organizes the visuospatial world, distinguishing figures from grounds, locating them relative to reference frames and other figures, approximating and categorizing their shapes and the spatial relations among them. The coast of California, for one, runs west as it runs north, though people think of it as running primarily north; this, and a presumption that the east and west borders of California are roughly parallel, would yield Stevens and Coupe's error, of thinking that San Diego is west of Reno. Studies tapping geographical knowledge, old and new, and selecting between correct and distorted maps and blobs showed systematic errors in memory attributable to perceptual organizing principles, to the ways visuospatial information is encoded, organized, and represented (Tversky, 1981, 199, 200, 2005a, 2005b, 2005d). One basic finding was that geographic entities, whether land masses like the Bay Area or streets, were remembered as more aligned with their reference frames than they actually are. The geographic entities induce their own axes, and the mind organizes those axes with respect to the axes of the reference frame. This phenomenon, termed *rotation,* accounts for the tendency of people to "upright" South America and to report that Berkeley is east of Stanford, when it is actually west. Another basic finding was that two grouped geographic entities are remembered as more grouped, a phenomenon termed *alignment.* Alignment led a majority of participants to select an incorrect map of the Americas as the true map, a map in which South America was moved westward to be more directly south of North America than it actually is. Indeed, Gordon and Ian Moar, a postdoc of his, replicated some of these findings (Moar & Bower, 1983). Because the various errors cannot be reconciled in a Euclidean representation, we observed that cognitive maps are essentially impossible figures. Because spatial knowledge consists of bits and pieces, such as memory for maps, memory for routes traveled, memory for routes explained, and more, a better metaphor for geographic memory than cognitive map is *cognitive collage* (Tversky, 1993).

Systematic Distortions in Memory.   Although this work firmly established that the processes and representations underlying memory of the visuospatial world are distinctly different from those for memory of the linguistic world, they also showed that mental representations of the visuospatial world systematically distorted metric relations of the actual world. These distortions were a consequence of the way disparate memories were integrated to provide a judgment of direction or distance or size (see Tversky, 2003, 2005c, for an analysis of why mental representations may be distorted but behavior quite accurate). These conclusions were resisted indeed, often ignored, by researchers of mental imagery. Many working on mental imagery were also keen to show that mental images differ from linguistic or propositional representations, but they did this by showing that qualities of mental images are like qualities of pictures and transforming mental images is like perceiving visual transformations in the world (e.g., Kosslyn, 1980, 1994; Shepard, 1975; Shepard & Podgorny, 1978). That enterprise emphasized the richness and veracity of mental images. Of course those enterprises were directed at accounting for different phenomena, such as the construction and use of images in information retrieval or judgment, and they elegantly accounted for them. Nonetheless, research showing that visuospatial representations were systematically distorted did not fit the conception of imagery as internalized perception and suggested other processes at work.

Spatial Mental Models.   From the small-scale visuospatial domain of faces and objects and the large-scale visuospatial domain of the geographic world, we next turned to the human scales of the world around the body, and then the body. Each of these spaces has a different basis in perception and in action, with consequent differences in mental representations (see Tversky, 2005a, 2005d). The research had dual aims: to investigate the nature of mental representations of that space, and to do so using narratives and no special instructions. Much of the classical (Shepard/Kosslyn) work on imagery had relied either on visual stimuli or on instructions to image and practicing imaging. We wanted to study the movie that spontaneously runs through the mind while reading evocative prose. Gordon's influences are evident; not only had he and his students been studying narrative comprehension, but they had shown costs in reading time when spatial point of view was changed (Black, Turner, & Bower, 1979).

Stanford blessed me not only with wonderful colleagues like Gordon but also gifted students, beginning with Kathy Hemenway. Some of those students found their ways to both Gordon and me, among them, Nancy Franklin, David Bryant, Scott Mainwaring, Ellen Levy, Jessica Lang, Elizabeth Marsh, and Lera Boroditsky. This two-way path between Gordon's office and mine, from one end of the hallway to the other, was unique even at Stanford, where multiple collaborations are fostered.

Nancy Franklin, Holly Taylor, and I began studying spatial mental models induced by narratives. Holly and I varied the spatial perspective of the narratives, either embedded in the scene, describing landmarks with respect to the left and right of a traveler moving through the environment (route), or over the scene, describing landmarks with respect to each other in terms of the cardinal directions (survey) (Taylor & Tversky, 1992b). What was significant was that after several readings of a narrative from one of the perspectives, participants were as fast and accurate to verify inference statements from either perspective, indicating that they had formed perspective-free mental representations. The analogy that seems apt is to an architect's three-dimensional (3-D) model of a building, a physical representation that allows many different perspectives on it. Later, Lee and I investigated online formation of mental models from descriptions. We found perspective-bound mental representations initially. However, after a few test questions even from the same perspective, the representations appeared to be perspective-free in that questions from either perspective were answered with the same speed and accuracy (Lee & Tversky, 2005).

Nancy and I, and later, David Bryant, explored the mental representations of the space immediately around the body, the space in reach of eye or hand (e. g., Franklin and Tversky, 1990). Participants read narratives that placed them in a 3-D world, with objects located to their front, back, head, feet, left, and right. After they had learned the environments, participants were told they turned to face another object, and were then probed for the objects currently located to all sides of their bodies. Accuracy was nearly perfect; it was the pattern of reaction times that concerned us. Again, the pattern did *not* conform to what a classical imagery account would predict, that participants would mentally scan the environments, so that objects requiring less rotation of the body to locate would be faster than those requiring more rotation of the body. Instead, the reaction times conformed to what we called the *spatial framework* account. According to this account, participants associate the objects to a mental framework composed of extensions of the three body axes, head/feet, front/back, and left/right. Accessibility of objects is determined by the salience of the body axes and their correspondence to the salient axes of the world. In both cases, asymmetry increases salience, so that for the upright observer of the scene, head/feet would be most salient and accessible because it is an asymmetric axis of the body and correlated with the only asymmetric axis of the world, that of gravity. The patterns of retrieval times corresponded to that predicted by the spatial framework model in more than a dozen studies, many of which examined variations of the standard situation (e.g., Bryant & Tversky, 1999; Bryant, Tversky, & Franklin, 1992; Franklin, Tversky, & Coon, 1992). In one, participants were told that they were in a special room built by NASA. On some trials, they were told that they moved to face a new object but on other trials, they were told that the room rotated so that now they were facing a new object. They pressed a button when they were reoriented. Although the two situations are formally identical, participants took twice as long to readjust when told the room moved than when told they moved.

These findings are counter to a propositional account as well, because according to a propositional account, it should make no difference whether the room moves or the observer moves.

Down the hall, Gordon, along with Dan Morrow and later Mike Rinck, was investigating spatial mental models using a priming paradigm (Morrow, Bower, & Greenspan, 1989; Rinck, Bower, & Wolf, 2002; Rinck et al., 1997). Participants first memorized a spatial layout. Then they read narratives describing an actor navigating the environment. They were probed about the locations of objects at various points in the narrative. The closer the actor was to the probed object, the faster the response time. Early on, the correlation between priming and distance appeared to be Euclidean, which seemed improbable to me given that the systematic errors we had studied showed that people's knowledge of space was not strictly Euclidean. Later, however, the group indeed demonstrated that spatial priming they had found was not only not strictly Euclidean, but had temporal influences as well (Rinck et al., 2002).

Event Perception and Cognition. From space to time, from objects to events. Jeff Zacks led me on this part of the journey (Zacks & Tversky, 2001; Zacks, Tversky, & Iyer, 2001), but of course Gordon had been there first. He and his collaborators had set the stage for this enterprise with their work on scripts showing that people have readily available hierarchical knowledge of common events, such as going to a restaurant or the doctor (Bower, Black, & Turner, 1978). The hierarchy underlying scripts or event knowledge is one of parts, a partonomy, in contrast to the taxonomic hierarchy underlying categorical knowledge. We turned to study bottom-up perception of events, borrowing a technique of Newtson (1973). Participants watched films of events rated as familiar (e.g., making a bed) and unfamiliar (e.g., assembling a saxophone) twice. On one viewing, they segmented the events into the largest units that made sense to them; on another viewing (order counterbalanced), they segmented into the smallest units that made sense to them. Half the participants gave a play-by-play description of the event segments as they segmented. Not only were the small and large units organized hierarchically, but also the degree of hierarchical organization increased when participants described the actions as they watched, suggesting the interplay of bottom-up perceptual and top-down conceptual factors in event perception and understanding.

A later graduate student, Bridgette Martin Hard, pursued these findings, showing that participants organized even abstract events—movements of geometric figures—hierarchically, and that bottom-up information, namely, degree of change of movement of the figures, determined segmentation (Hard, Tversky, & Lang, in press). Sandra Lozano then arrived at Stanford, and joined the effort. Together, they have shown that degree of hierarchical organization predicts action learning (Hard, Lozano, & Tversky, in press; Lozano, Hard, & Tversky, in press-a).

Their work has united space and time, demonstrating the influence of spatial perspective taking; taking the actor's perspective, by either description or imitation, rather than one's own perspective, augments action learning (Lozano, Martin, & Tversky, 2005).

Rest Stop.   Neither journey is over, but we have reached the here and now. From space and the objects in it to time and the events in it. And this description has been schematic, highlighting common landmarks and paths, but by no means all of them. Our journeys began separately, but it was my good fortune to join Gordon's.

ACKNOWLEDGMENTS

Preparation of this chapter and/or some of the research reported were supported by the following grants: NSF Grant BNS 8002012; Air Force Office of Scientific Research Grant AFOSR 89–0076; the Edinburgh–Stanford Link through the Center for the Study of Language and Information at Stanford University, Office of Naval Research, Grants NOOO14-PP–1-O649, N000140110717, and N000140210534; and NSF Division of Research, Evaluation, and Communication Grant REC–0440103 to Stanford University.

REFERENCES

Anderson, J., & Bower, G. H. (1973). *Human associative memory.* Washington, DC: Winston.

Black, J., Turner, T., & Bower, G. H. (1979). Point of view in narrative comprehension, memory and production. *Journal of Verbal Learning and Verbal Behavior, 18,* 187–199.

Bower, G. H. (1972). Mental imagery and associative learning. In L. Gregg (Ed.), *Cognition in learning and memory* (pp. 51–88). New York: Wiley.

Bower, G. H. (1970). Analysis of a mnemonic device. *American Scientist, 58,* 496–519.

Bower, G. H., Black, J. B., & Turner, T. J. (1979). Scripts in memory for text. *Cognitive Psychology, 11,* 179–220.

Bryant, D. J., & Tversky, B. (1999). Mental representations of spatial relations from diagrams and models. *Journal of Experimental Psychology: Learning, Memory and Cognition, 25,* 137–156.

Bryant, D. J., Tversky, B., & Franklin, N. (1992). Internal and external spatial frameworks for representing described scenes. *Journal of Memory and Language, 31,* 74–98.

Byrant, D. J., Tversky, B., & Lanca, M. (2001). Retrieving spatial relations from observation and memory. In E. van der Zee & U. Nikanne (Eds.), *Conceptual structure and its interfaces with other modules of representation* (pp. 116–139). Oxford, England: Oxford University Press.

Franklin, N., & Tversky, B. (1990). Searching imagined environments. *Journal of Experimental Psychology: General, 119,* 63–76.

Franklin, N., Tversky, B., & Coon, V. (1992). Switching points of view in spatial mental models acquired from text. *Memory and Cognition, 20,* 507–518.

Hard, B. M., Lozano, S. C., I Tversky, B. (in press). Hierarchical encoding: Translating perception into action. *Journal of Experimental Psychology: General.*

Hard, B. M., Tversky, B., & Lang, D. (in press). Making sense of abstract events: Building event schemas. *Memory and Cognition.*

Kosslyn, S. M. (1980). *Image and mind.* Cambridge, MA: Harvard University Press.

Kosslyn, S. M. (1994). *Image and brain: The resolution of the imagery debate.* Cambridge, MA: MIT Press.

Lee, P. U., & Tversky, B. (2005). Interplay between visual and spatial: The effects of landmark descriptions on comprehension of route/survey descriptions. *Spatial Cognition and Computation, 5(2 &3),* 163–185.

Lozano, S. C., Hard, B. M., & Tversky, B. (in press-a). Perspective-taking promotes action understanding and learning. *Journal of Experimental Psychology: Human Perception and Performance.*

Lozano, S. C., Hard, B. M., & Tversky, B. (in press-b). Putting action in perspective. *Cognition.*

Lozano, S. C., Martin, B. A., & Tversky, B. (2005). Perspective taking: A helpful hand in action understanding and learning. In *Proceedings of the Cognitive Science Society* (p. 2517). Mahwah, NJ: Lawrence Erlbaum Associates.

Lozano, S. C., & Tversky, B. (2005). People's gestures change how and what they learn. In *Proceedings of the Cognitive Science Society* (p. 1337). Mahwah, NJ: Lawrence Erlbaum Associates.

Lozano, S. C., & Tversky, B. (in press). The cognitive function of communicative gestures. *Journal of Memory and Language.*

Moar, I., & Bower, G. H. (1983). Inconsistency in spatial knowledge. *Memory & Cognition, 11,* 107–113.

Morrison, J. B., & Tversky, B. (2005). Bodies and their parts. *Memory & Cognition, 33,* 696–709.

Morrow, D. G., Bower, G. H., & Greenspan, S. L. (1989). Updating situation models during narrative comprehension. *Journal of Memory and Language, 28,* 292–312.

Newtson, D. (1973). Attribution and the unit of perception of ongoing behavior. *Journal of Personality & Social Psychology, 28,* 28–38.

Pylyshyn, Z. W. (1981). The imagery debate: Analogue media versus tacit knowledge. *Psychological Review, 88,* 16–45.

Rinck, M., Bower, G. H., & Wolf, K. (2002). Temporal and spatial distance in situation models. *Memory & Cognition, 28(8),* 1310–1320.

Rinck, M., Hahnal, A., Bower, G. H., & Glowalla, M. (1997). The metrics of spatial situation models. *Journal of Experimental Pschology: Learning, Memory, and Cognition, 23,* 622–637.

Rosch, E. (1978). Principles of categorization. In E. Rosch & B. B. Lloyd (Eds.), *Cognition and categorization* (pp. 27–48). Hillsdale, NJ: Lawrence Erlbaum Associates.

Schiano, D., & Tversky, B. (1992). Structure and strategy in viewing simple graphs. *Memory & Cognition, 20,* 12–20.

Shepard, R. N. (1975). Form, formation, and transformation of internal representations. In R. Solso (Ed.), *Information processing and cognition: The Loyola symposium* (pp. 87–122). Hillsdale, NJ: Lawrence Erlbaum Associates.

Shepard, R. N., & Podgorny, P. (1978). Cognitive processes that resemble perceptual processes. In W. K. Estes (Ed.), *Handbook of learning and cognitive processes* (Vol. 5. pp. 189–237). Hillsdale, NJ: Lawrence Erlbaum Associates.

Taylor, H. A., & Tversky, B. (1992a). Descriptions and depictions of environments. *Memory & Cognition, 20,* 483–496.

Taylor, H. A., & Tversky, B. (1992b). Spatial mental models derived from survey and route descriptions. *Journal of Memory and Language, 31,* 261–282.

Tversky, B. (1981). Distortions in memory for maps. *Cognitive Psychology, 13,* 407–433.

Tversky, B. (1989). Parts, partonomies, and taxonomies. *Developmental Psychology, 25,* 983–995.

Tversky, B. (2000). Remembering space. In E. Tulving & F. I. M. Craik (Eds.), *Handbook of memory* (pp. 363–378). New York: Oxford University Press.

Tversky, B. (2001). Spatial schemas in depictions. In M. Gattis (Ed.), *Spatial schemas and abstract thought* (pp. 79–111). Cambridge, MA: MIT Press.

Tversky, B. (2003). Navigating by mind and by body. In C. Freksa, W. Brauer, C. Habel, & K. F. Wender (Eds.), *Spatial cognition III: Routes and navigation, human memory and learning, spatial representation and spatial reasoning* (pp. 1–10). Berlin: Springer Verlag.

Tversky, B. (2004). Form and function. In L. A. Carlson & E. van der Zee (Eds.), *Functional features in language and space: Insights from perception, categorization and development* (pp. 331–347). Oxford, England: Oxford University Press.

Tversky, B. (2005a). Functional significance of visuospatial representations. In P. Shah & A. Miyake (Eds.), *Handbook of higher-level visuospatial thinking.* Cambridge, England: Cambridge University Press.

Tversky, B. (2005b). How to get around by mind and body: Spatial thought, spatial action. In A. Zilhao (Ed.), *Cognition, evolution, and rationality: A cognitive science for the XXIst century.* London: Routledge.

Tversky, B. (2005c). La cognition spatiale: Incarnee et desincarnee [Spatial cognition: embodied and disembodied]. In A. Berthoz & R. Recht, *Les Espaces de l'homme* (pp. 161–184). Paris: Odile Jacob.

Tversky, B. (2005d). Visualspatial reasoning. In K. Holyoak & R. Morrison, (Editors). *Handbook of reasoniong* (pp. 209–249). Cambridge, England: Cambridge University Press.

Tversky, B., & Hemenway, K. (1983). Categories of scenes. *Cognitive Psychology, 15,* 121–149.

Tversky, B., & Hemenway, K. (1984). Objects, parts, and categories. *Journal of Experimental Psychology: General, 113,* 169–193.

Tversky, B., Kim, J., & Cohen, A. (1999). Mental models of spatial relations and transformations from language. In C. Habel & G. Rickheit (Eds.), *Mental models in discourse processing and reasoning* (pp. 239–258). Amsterdam: North-Holland

Tversky, B., Kugelmass, S., & Winter, A. (1991).Cross-cultural and developmental trends in graphic productions. *Cognitive Psychology, 23,* 515–557.

Tversky, B., & Lee, P. U. (1998). How space structures language. In C. Freksa, C. Habel, & K. F. Wender (Eds.), *Spatial cognition: An interdisciplinary approach to representation and processing of spatial knowledge* (pp. 157–175). Berlin: Springer-Verlag.

Tversky, B., & Lee, P. U. (1999). Pictorial and verbal tools for conveying routes. In C. Freksa & D. M. Mark (Eds.), *Spatial information theory: Cognitive and computational foundations of geographic information science* (pp. 51–64). Berlin: Springer.

Tversky, B., Morrison, J. B., & Zacks, J. (2002). On bodies and events. In A. Meltzoff & W. Prinz (Eds.), *The imitative mind: Development, evolution and brain bases* (pp. 221–232). Cambridge, England: Cambridge University Press.

Tversky, B., & Schiano, D. (1989). Perceptual and conceptual factors in distortions in memory for maps and graphs. *Journal of Experimental Psychology: General, 118,* 387–398.

Tversky, B, Zacks, J., Lee, P. U., & Heiser, J. (2000). Lines, blobs, crosses, and arrows: Diagrammatic communication with schematic figures. In M. Anderson, P. Cheng, & V. Haarslev (Eds.), *Theory and application of diagrams* (pp. 221–230). Berlin: Springer.

Tversky, B., Zacks, J. M., Morrison, J. B., Martin, B. A., & Lozano, S. C. (in press). Talking about events. In E. Pederson, J. Bohnemeyer, & R. Tomlin (Eds.), *Event representation.* Cambridge, England: Cambridge University Press.

Zacks, J., & Tversky, B. (1999). Bars and lines: A study of graphic communication. *Memory & Cognition, 27,* 1073–1079.

Zacks, J. M., & Tversky, B. (2001). Event structure in perception and conception. *Psychological Bulletin, 127,* 3–21.

Zacks, J., Tversky, B., & Iyer, G. (2001). Perceiving, remembering, and communicating structure in events. *Journal of Experimental Psychology: General, 130,* 29–58.

9

Evidence of All-or-None Learning from a Repetition Detection Task

Arnold L. Glass
Rutgers University

Arild Lian
Bredtvet Resource Center, Oslo

The all-or-none theory of learning is unparalleled in its simplicity elegance, and in the preciseness and accuracy of its predictions for tasks measuring the basic elements of learning. Forty years after being abandoned it is again being investigated empirically. Recent evidence of all-or-none learning comes from trigram detection in a continuous recognition task. Subjects were told to respond with a button press every time a repeated trigram was seen. If a subject responded to a repeated trigram, it was not repeated again. However, if a subject did not respond to a repeated trigram, then it was repeated again at the same interval for up to three repetitions. The probability of noticing a repeated trigram did not increase with the number of repetitions. The results demonstrate that a repeated input does not leave a permanent trace in memory that increments in strength until the trigram is recognized.

It is not sufficient for a scientific theory to be true in order for it to be accepted as true. There must be some way to test the theory and by confirming its predictions demonstrate that it is true. Sometimes a theory may be premature because it is first proposed at a time when there is inadequate methodology to determine its validity. Consider the case of all-or-none learning theory. Forty years ago it appeared to promise a firm foundation for a comprehensive quantitative description of learning. Yet it was proposed and abandoned within a single decade. Recently, it has been reintroduced in the context of a new experimental paradigm. This review considers its history and its current prospects. We begin with the classic literature on all-or-none paired-associate learning. Next, recent research on all-or-none recognition of visual patterns is described. Then new research on all-or-none recognition of consonant trigrams across the lifespan is presented. Finally, future directions for all-or-none learning research are suggested.

ALL-OR-NONE PAIRED-ASSOCIATE LEARNING

Traditionally, learning has been regarded as a process of gradual improvement (Kintsch, 1977, p. 69). However, between 1957 and 1962, four separate reports (Bower, 1961, 1962; Estes, 1960; Rock 1957) raised the possibility that learning actually occurs in discrete all-or-none increments. That is, on a single-study trial, an input either leaves a trace in memory or it does not. All four reports discussed all-or-none learning within the context of the paired-associate learning task, which was then the dominant method for studying learning and memory.

Consider a paired-associate learning task of alternating study and test trials. On a study trial, Rock (1957) presented 12 A-B study pairs and on a test trial the 12 A terms were presented. The study–test sequence was repeated until all 12 B response terms were correctly reported. Rock tested the all-or-none learning hypothesis by modifying this (control) procedure. In the replacement condition, if the B response was not given on the test trial then the A-B study pair was repeated with an all-new C-D study pair on the next presentation of the study list. The results were that the mean number of trials required to achieve the criterion of all 12 responses correctly reported did not differ between the control and replacement procedures. Rock argued, therefore, that the subjects must not have developed any associative strength between the stimulus and response terms for the items missed. Had such associative strength developed, the elimination of the missed pairs should have retarded overall learning because for the new pairs the associative strength would have to be built up from "scratch." The fact that the insertion of new items did not slow down learning was taken to mean that no strength was built up for the missed pairs and consequently the association must be an all-or-none affair.

Estes (1960) responded to Rock's (1957) finding by considering the results of a variety of experimental learning paradigms: paired-associate learning, classical conditioning, and free recall. These paradigms had always produced incremental improvements in performance over study trials as predicted by an incremental theory of learning. However, Estes examined the results of selected experiments in more detail than previously with particular attention to response contingencies for successive trials. For example, suppose that on a given test trial 50% of the subjects generated a particular correct response. The interpretation within the framework of incremental learning theory is that all the subjects had a 50% probability of generating that response. So if exactly the same item were tested again, half of the subjects who produced the correct response should again produce it, and half of the subjects who had not produced the correct response should produce it for the first time. In contrast, the interpretation within the framework of all-or-none learning theory is that the subjects who had produced the response had learned it and those who had not produced the response had not learned it. So if exactly the same item were tested again, most of those subjects who previously produced the response should do so again (except for loss through forgetting) and none of the subjects who had previously failed to produce the response should now be able to do so without another study trial. Estes found results much closer to the prediction of the all–none than the incremental hypothesis. He called for a further investigation into the matter.

Estes' call was answered by Bower (1961, 1962) in two seminal papers. Bower used a simple Markov model to predict the precise distribution of errors in several paired-associate learning tasks. A Markov model is simply a model that consists of discrete states such that each state determines its possible set of successor states. By assigning probabilities to state transitions, Bower was able to make and verify extremely detailed and precise predictions about when and where errors would occur during paired-associate learning. These predictions were completely inconsistent with the predictions of an incremental theory. Bower's model and methods were widely adopted and over the next few years it became clear that the results of simple paired-associate learning tasks were predicted in detail by Bower's model. Discontinuities in response times (Millward, 1964) and the galvanic skin response to study items appeared to mark the boundary between the unlearned and learned states (Kintsch, 1965). Finally, the incremental learning of more complicated study items than simple paired associates could be described as the all-or-none learning of their components (Bower, 1967). Kintsch (1970) concluded a sympathetic review of the all-or-none literature with, "This approach offers considerable promise, especially when the stages or subprocesses can be given a psychological interpretation" (p. 85). However, by the time the review appeared, Bower's Markov models were no longer widely applied and all-or-none learning was no longer under active consideration as a psychological theory. Kintsch (1977, p. 85) concluded a revised review of the all-or-none literature by calling the question of whether learning is discrete or incremental a "dead issue."

There had been an immediate, large-scale, empirical effort in response to Rock's (1957) report in addition to the theoretical response of Estes (1960) and

Bower (1961). As a result of this effort, three flaws in his design had been discovered. The first flaw was an item-selection effect uncovered by Underwood, Rehula, and Keppel (1962) and Postman (1962). In a learning task involving a set of items, it is usually the case that some items are easier to learn than others and it is the easier items that are learned first. When Rock replaced unlearned items with new ones, he replaced more difficult items with items that were on average potentially a little easier to learn. The second flaw was an unequal-practice effect, uncovered by Underwood et al. and Postman. The novel items in the replacement condition appeared to receive more rehearsals than the old unlearned items in the control condition and rehearsal is the engine of learning. So new items in the replacement condition both were potentially easier and received more rehearsals, allowing subjects to learn the list with replacement items as fast as the control list. When subjects were prevented from rehearsing some items more than others by a distracter task, the subjects seeing the new items appeared to learn slightly slower. So Rock's studies do not provide evidence of all-or-none learning.

The third flaw was that the paired-associate learning task used by Rock (1957), the other tasks reviewed by Estes (1960), and the paired-associate tasks used by Bower (1960, 1961) tended not to elicit the kinds of partially correct responses that would be evidence of incremental learning. These tasks were all deliberately designed to be simple in order to study basic processes of learning. Hence, on any given trial, a subject almost always either produced the correct response or no response at all. Generally, when a learning task was designed so that a subject almost always produced one of two responses, one that was correct and one that was not correct, all-or-none learning theory provided an excellent fit to the data. However, it is possible to design a task in which more than two responses are probable, for example, a task where a subject selects the correct response from a set of three or more alternatives. Dinnerstein and Egeth (1962) pointed out that if the all-or-none hypothesis is correct, then a subject who makes an incorrect response is guessing. Consider all the subjects who select the incorrect response from among three alternatives. If these subjects are given a second chance at selecting the correct response, they should select it half the time from the remaining two alternatives. However, when Dinnerstein and Egeth gave subjects a second chance, the correct response was selected above chance. This result is inconsistent with all-or-none learning and consistent with incremental learning. Binford and Gettys (1965) replicated this finding.

In fact, the criticisms of Underwood et al. (1962) and Postman (1962) were not empirical refutations of all-or-none learning theory. They merely demonstrated a particular experimental test of the theory that appeared to support it was flawed. Three subsequent studies of all-or-none learning that controlled both rehearsal and item learnability found all-or-none free recall of words (Murdock & Babick, 1961), consonant trigrams (Nelson & Batchelder, 1969), and digit sequences (Nelson, 1971). Though Dinnerstein and Egeth's (1962) result does undermine a very simple application of the all-or-none learning hypothesis to the experimental task, it can easily be accommodated by an elaboration of the hypothesis. Essentially, instead of assuming that a subject is learning a single element or association, it is assumed that a subject is learning two things, each in an all-or-none manner. This makes it possible to describe states in which only parts of a study item is learned. Furthermore, except for very simple study items, it seems quite reasonable to assume that in fact such partial learning often occurs. Why then did interest in all-or-none learning theory decline so fast?

Part of the appeal of the Markov model instantiation of all-or-none learning theory was that an extremely simple model could accurately predict data both precisely and in detail. To the extent that the model became more complicated it became less appealing. The developers of the all-or-none learning models were good enough mathematicians to know that if they allowed themselves to assume a sufficient number of learning elements, two, three, four, whatever was necessary, they could precisely fit any set of experimental data. They were good enough psychologists to know that every elaboration of the model, from one to two to three elements, and so forth, implied another processing stage that required independent experimental verification. The instrumentation necessary to provide this verification was beyond the technology of the time. So instead, the all-or-none versus incremental alternatives were reinterpreted within an instrumental framework. According to the instrumental view of science, models are useful generalizations about data rather than mirrors of reality. According to this view, because within one set of experimental conditions an all-or-none model gave better predictions, it should be used there. Because within another set of experimental conditions an incremental model gave better predictions, it should be used there. However, neither model could claim to be a psychological theory of learning.

In retrospect, it can be seen that the decision in the 1960s to abandon an all-or-none model as a psychological learning principle was entirely correct. At the time, the appealing simple model was used to explain data from what was believed to be an equivalently simple task: paired-associate learning. We now know that the apparent simplicity of the task is deceptive because the underlying learning and retrieval processes are complex. Today there is considerable data that two distinct systems are involved in the encoding and retrieval of words and word pairs. One system increments the perceived familiarity of the item and the other associates it with its learning context (Yonelinas, 2002). Obviously, more than two states are required to describe two distinct learning and retrieval systems. So as a general explanation of learning, Bower's (1961, 1962) model was doomed from the start.

It is easy to understand why the instrumental view dominated at the time. There was then no obvious way to distinguish between the alternative models. However, the instrumental view has sometimes led to the illicit conclusion that, because any all-or-none model can be mimicked by an incremental model, there is no way to chose between them. Quite the opposite conclusion is the case.

According to the all-or-none hypothesis, either a trace is in memory or it is not. If it is in memory, then every time the same test cue is presented, the same response will be made. In contrast, according to the incremental hypothesis, the retrieval of a trace in memory is a stochastic process modulated by a characteristic of the trace called its strength. The greater the strength of the trace, the more likely it is to be retrieved. The more often a trace is retrieved, the greater is its strength. It should be clear from this example that the all-or-none hypothesis is the limiting case of the incremental hypothesis in which the strength of a trace must be either zero or one. So it must be the case that the predictions of any all-or-none model can be mimicked by a more complicated incremental model. However, it must be the case that for every true scientific theory there are an indefinitely large number of alternative more complicated theories that can exactly mimic its predictions. In this situation, science always selects the simplest explanation. So if an all-or-none learning model can be shown to be completely adequate, an insistence on a more complicated incremental alternative is outside the realm of science.

Hence, the reality of all-or-none learning remains an empirical question. In retrospect, the theoretical structure introduced by Bower (1961, 1962) was sound but premature. Though the tasks he applied it to were simple, the underlying processing used by subjects to perform the tasks was not simple. Furthermore, the complexity of the underlying processes was not appreciated at the time. Recall, including cued recall, requires a three-part encoding and a three-part retrieval process. Suppose that a cue-target study pair is presented and then at test the cue is presented and the correct response is the target. At study, a participant must encode the cue, encode the target, and encode an association between the cue and the target that makes it possible to generate the target. At test, when the cue is presented the subject must be able to recognize it and then use the association to generate the target (or the cue must somehow automatically activate the association and then the target). Hence, recall will fail if the cue, or the target, or the association between them was not encoded. Within the context of Bower's (1961) paradigm, it was simply assumed that the cue and the target were always encoded and the probability of recall directly measured the probability of encoding the association between them. For the simple task that Bower used, even if the target and cue are not always completely encoded, the effect on the results should be small. However, the results consistent with all-or-none learning should not generalize to more complicated tasks involving multiple responses, which is in fact what happened. Second, besides the association between the cue and target encoding during the study trial, there may already exist or be encoded associations between the cue and other nontarget representations in memory. These additional associations may influence the retrieval of the target when the cue is presented at test, so a pure measure of the probability of encoding the association is not obtained. Third, the probability of encoding an association between a cue and target is dependent on the number and distribution of rehearsals given them as a unit. If different study items are given different numbers of rehearsals and the number of rehearsals for each item is not known, then the effect of a single rehearsal, hence whether it is all-or-none or incremental, cannot be determined.

The task with which to study processes of learning so basic that their discrete all-or-none nature can be divined is not recall, but a continuous recognition task. In this task, a sequence of study items are presented in rapid succession and an observer must respond immediately when ever an item is presented that was shown before. Each item has an equal chance of being repeated, so that there is no advantage to rehearsing any one item more than any other. Furthermore, if a rapid rate of presentation is used, an observer will only have an opportunity to attend to the current item and no other. Finally, a correct response, that is, a hit, presumably occurs when a study item matches a representation in memory. Whenever the study items are all novel, it is extremely unlikely that a false match will occur to another representation in memory for an unrepeated study item. So if in fact the study items are encoded in an all-or-none manner, the task should be sensitive enough to produce a response for an encoded item and not produce a response for an unencoded item.

Forty years after Bower's (1961) seminal paper the question of all-or-none learning has been reopened. This time a continuous recognition test has been used to determine whether learning is all or none. Item learnability was controlled in two ways. First, the task required only limited and equal rehearsal of all study items. Second, all the study items were equally novel.

ALL-OR-NONE RECOGNITION OF
NOVEL VISUAL PATTERNS

If an event is repeated within the experience of an individual, that individual comes to recognize the event as a repetition. For example, if a person sees a sequence of trigrams and a particular trigram is repeated, then after a certain number of repetitions the person comes to notice that the trigram has been seen before. This simple account leaves many questions unanswered about the shape of the learning curve and the factors that influence it. For example, consider a trigram that has been repeated several times at a constant interval of m trials. First, consider the probability that it is recognized as a repetition the first time it is repeated. Let us call this probability p_1. Similarly, call p_2 the probability that it is recognized as a repetition the second time that it is repeated given that it is not recognized as a repetition the first time it is repeated. Finally, call p_3 the probability that it is recognized as a repetition the third time that it is repeated given that it is not recognized as a repetition the first two times it is repeated. The question this experiment addresses is whether $p_1 = p_2 = p_3$ or $p_1 < p_2 < p_3$.

Pretheoretically, either result is possible. It could be the case that a trace of the trigram is encoded into a short-term memory and decays after a certain number of seconds if it is not refreshed by either an external re-presentation or internal rehearsal, either one of which might count as a repetition. Furthermore, each repetition may transfer the trigram to long-term memory with some probability. According to this view, if a repetition of a trigram went unnoticed, this would indicate that it was absent from short-term memory and had not been matched in long-term memory. Hence, the effect of the presentation would be the effect for a "new" item uncontaminated by any previous memory trace. So it would be the case that $p_1 = p_2 = p_3$.

Alternatively, it could be the case that each repetition of the trigram is matched to its trace in long-term memory and a match between a memory trace and an input causes the activation level of the memory trace to increase. So each repetition strengthens the trace such that the next time the consonant trigram is presented its activation is higher. When the activation produced by the match of an input with its memory trace exceeds some criterion, the input is recognized as a repetition. According to this view, every repetition increases the baseline activation level of its memory trace whether or not the trigram is recognized. So it would be the case that $p_1 < p_2 < p_3$.

The two hypotheses described previously may be characterized as all-or-none versus incremental learning. Glass, Lian, and Lau (2004) performed an experiment to determine the effect of unnoticed repetitions on the probability of detecting a target and the interaction of this variable with the interval between repetitions of the target. Presumably, target detection would be a negative function of repetition interval because the greater the number of intervening distracters, the greater the interference with the target's representation. Within the framework of the incremental hypothesis, hit rate should be positively correlated with the number of target repetitions (and negatively correlated with repetition interval if forgetting occurs between target repetitions). In contrast, the all-or-none hypothesis predicts a slope of zero at all repetition intervals.

The items composing the trigrams were 20 novel patterns designed to have the same number of line segments as letters but to be entirely novel. Notice that the patterns are of equal complexity. Initially a circle, diamond, or square was selected for generating the shape. Then one side was deleted from the figure. Then a vertical or horizontal line was added from the center to a side for the square and diamond shapes. For the circle shape, two lines were added from the center to the sides. This was because when the shapes were pretested, circles with only a single center line were found to be slightly more memorable than the squares and diamonds, but circles with the second line were not.

The trigrams were presented visually, one at a time. Subjects were told to respond with a button press every time a repeated trigram was seen. If a subject responded to a repeated trigram, it was not repeated again. However, if a subject did not respond to a trigram, then it was repeated again. Finally, trigrams were repeated at intervals of 0, 1, or 2 items. If a trigram was not detected, it was repeated at the same interval. For example, if a target trigram was presented and then after an interval of two distracters it was repeated but not detected, it was repeated again after another two distracters, until it was detected. A 2,800-ms study interval was used so that there would be no question that the subject had sufficient time to encode the study item. Pattern trigrams rather than words were used so that there would not be an effect of prior familiarity with the study item. Because the patterns were of equal complexity, they should have been equally learnable. The results are shown in Figure 9–1. As can be seen from the figure, the probability of detecting a target did not increase as a function of the number of undetected repetitions. Learning was apparently all-or-none, not incremental. A false-alarm rate of .15 did vary across conditions. So a figure for d' would be indistinguishable from Figure 9–1, which shows hits.

Notice from Figure 9–1 that probability of a repetition detection was less when two distracters intervened between target repetitions than when only one distracter intervened between target repetitions. Presumably this is because some forgetting is occurring over the interval. The short retention interval raises the question of whether short-term or long-term retention is being measured. This question was addressed by Glass et al. (2004) in another experiment in which the test items were consonant trigrams and retention intervals of up to 16 items were used. The results are shown in Figure 9–2, and as can be seen from the figure,

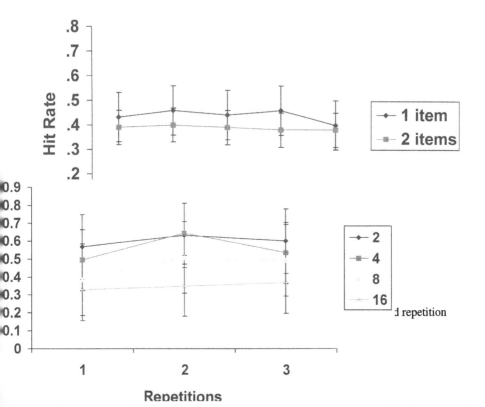

there was no effect of repetition regardless of the number of intervening items. A false-alarm rate of .13 did not vary across conditions. So a figure for d' would be indistinguishable from Figure 9–2, which shows hits.

Notice the regularities in Figure 9–2. The probability of indicating that a consonant trigram is a repetition is a function of both the number of repetitions and the interval between the trigrams. First, notice that the probability of a hit declines as a function of retention interval, but at no interval does the probability of a hit increase monotonically as a function of the number of unnoticed repetitions. Even at an interval of 16 intervening trigrams the probability of detecting a repetition is over twice the false-alarm rate and is constant across number of repetitions. Hence long-term retention is being measured. Let us consider how Bower's (1961) Markov model accounts for these results when applied at the consonant level. The model has four assumptions:

1. When a trigram, t_i, is presented, none, one, two, or all three of its consonants are encoded in a single trigram representation.
2. On a subsequent trial, $k > i$, if a trigram, t_k, is encoded, it may cause some or all of the consonants in the representation of trigram t_i to become unencoded, that is, forgotten.
3. When a trigram, t_i, is represented, it is compared with representations of all previously presented trigrams, which each may consist of up to three consonants. If the two trigram representations have the same consonant in the same position, then a consonant match is made with a probability of 1.0. If the two

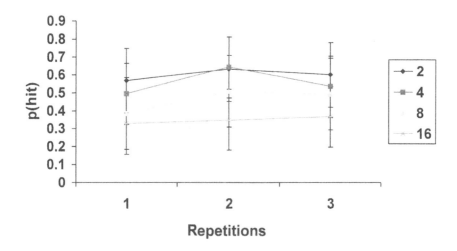

Figure 9–2.   Probability of a hit as function of number of repetitions and repetition interval for consonant trigrams. Bars show 95% confidence intervals (Glass et al., 2004).

trigram representations have different consonants in the same position, then a consonant match is made with a probability of 0. If a consonant in t_i is compared with an empty position in the other trigram representation, then a consonant match is made with a probability of C.

4. If three consonant matches are made between two trigrams then a trigram match is made and the trigram is perceived as repeated.

We derive a predictive equation for the model as follows:

1. According to the classic all-or-none Markov model, a consonant must be in either of two states: learned or unlearned. Every time a consonant trigram is presented, each consonant that it contains changes from the unlearned to the learned state with a probability of E. This means that it is available for comparison with consonants in the same position of subsequent trigrams. Otherwise, if the consonant remains unlearned, then it is not available for comparison with subsequent trigrams and that position of the trigram representation remains empty.

2. Classic all-or-none learning theory did not include a forgetting parameter. However, the data in Figure 9–2 clearly requires one. Hence, suppose that a consonant, $c_{p,i}$ in position p of the trigram presented on trial i is in the encoded state. On a subsequent trial k, $i < k \leq i + j$ if a different consonant, $c_{p,k}$, of a subsequent trigram is encoded in the same position then it returns $c_{p,i}$ to its unlearned state with probability M. Hence, the probability of a representation of a consonant encoded on trial i being available for comparison on trial $i + j + 1$ is $E * [(1 - E * M)]^j$.

3. Suppose that on trial $i + j + 1$ the same consonant is presented in the same position as on trial i. If the representation of the consonant presented on trial i is available for comparison on trial $i + j + 1$, then the probability of a match being found is assumed to be 1.0. Otherwise, the probability of a match being found is assumed to be C. Hence, if the same consonant appears in the position of a consonant trigram on trial i and on trial $i + j + 1$, the probability of a match being found is $P_j = E * [(1 - E * M)]^j + [1 - [E * [(1 - E * M)]^j]] * C$.

4. A trigram is recognized only when all three of its consonants are found to match consonants presented in the same positions of a previous trigram. Hence, if the same trigram is re-presented after an interval of j intervening trigrams, its probability of recognition is P_j^3. The probabilities of (incorrectly) recognizing trigrams with only two, one, or no consonants in the same position are $P_j^2 * C$, $P_j * C^2$, and C^3, respectively.

Using this model, we can set the values of parameters E, M, and C and then predict the results shown in Figure 9–2. When $E = 0.75$, $M = .04$, and $C = 0.45$, the correlation between the predicted and observed values is $r = 0.993$, hence $r^2 = 0.986$.

ALL-OR-NONE RECOGNITION OF CONSONANT
TRIGRAMS ACROSS THE LIFE SPAN

If repetition detection is all-or-none, then it is potentially useful as a diagnostic research tool for decomposing more complex learning tasks and as a diagnostic clinical tool for measuring an individual's ability to encode information. To address both issues, the repetition detection of consonant trigrams was replicated with an age-stratified sample.

We wanted to see whether performance on a learning task that did not involve either rehearsal or recall would nevertheless decline with age. Cross-sectional studies find a decline in learning ability with age (Zelinski, Gilewski, & Schaie, 1993). For example, Raanaas, Nordby, and Magnussen (2002) tested students and faculty in the 20 to 29, 40 to 49, and 60 to 69 age groups on immediate ordered recall of visual and auditory digit strings. They found that the two younger groups performed better than the oldest group for eight-digit strings. In particular, Shimamura, Berry, Mangels, Rusting, and Jurica (1995) performed an innovative cross-sectional study of only highly educated, healthy individuals: 72 professors from the University of California at Berkeley who ranged in age from 30 to 71. Performance declined with age for paired-associate learning; however, there was not a decline with age for prose recall. As mentioned earlier, paired-associate learning reflects both complex learning and retrieval processes so that an explanation of the age decrement as a result of a decrement in retrieval processes cannot be ruled out. This is also the case for ordered recall. Because the repetition detection task puts minimal demands on retrieval, it was an open question whether performance would decline with age.

To this end, we examined the performance of highly educated individuals in the second, fourth, and sixth decades of their lives on the consonant-trigram repetition detection task. Furthermore, to assess whether a decrement in performance could be attributed to a decrement in attention, they also performed the Paced Auditory Serial Addition Task (PASAT), to assess attention. In the PASAT (Diehr, Heaton, Miller, & Grant, 1998), an individual hears a sequence of numbers and must continuously respond by reporting the sum of the two most recently heard numbers. The decline of performance on this task with age is well-established (Diehr et al., 1998).

Method

Subjects.   Eighteen subjects, nine females and nine males between the ages of 21 and 65, participated in the experiment. Six subjects were between the ages of 20 and 29, six were between the ages of 40 and 49, and six were between the ages of 60 and 69. Eleven were native speakers of Norwegian, five were native speakers of English, and one was a native speaker of Czech who was also fluent in English. All subjects were either studying for advanced degrees or on the faculty at the University of Oslo except for one subject who was a senior administrator at the university. All of the subjects were healthy and had not used alcohol or drugs or suffered from migraine in the previous 48 hours. Two additional subjects who performed the task were excluded from the analysis. One reported a history of depression and one reported an occurrence of a headache within the previous 24 hours. An additional subject withdrew from the experiment in the middle of the task.

Design.   Each subject was tested during a single session. During the session, consonant trigrams were presented one at a time at a stimulus onset asynchrony (SOA) of 1,300 ms on the monitor of a personal computer. The subject was instructed to press a key whenever a trigram that had been shown earlier was repeated. A session contained 20 block sequences, separated by pauses of at least 30 seconds. During a pause, the monitor screen remained blank until the subject continued the task by pressing a key. Each block sequence contained four blocks, and each contained a single repeated target trigram. Hence, over the course of the entire session, repetitions of 80 different target trigrams were presented.

From the perspective of the subject, each block sequence was a continuous performance task during which trigrams were randomly repeated. However, in fact, the block sequence consisted of four blocks of trials. During each block of trials, a single target trigram was repeated after every m intervening distracter trigrams until it was detected. In each of the four blocks, $m = 0, 2, 4,$ or 8. The order of the four blocks within the block sequence was randomly generated.

Each block consisted of a study sequence followed by one or more test sequences. At the beginning of the study sequence, a number from 1 to 10 was randomly selected and that number of randomly generated consonant trigrams was presented. Then the target trigram was randomly generated and presented. The presentation of the target trigram concluded the study sequence. Next, for an interval of m, m randomly generated consonant trigrams were presented, and then the target trigram was re-presented. For example, if $m = 2$, then two randomly generated consonant trigrams were presented before the target trigram was repeated a first time. If the subject responded with a button press indicating that the target trigram was a repetition, this ended the block. Otherwise, if the subject did not respond, another m randomly generated consonant trigrams followed, and the target trigram was again presented. Additional test sequences were generated in this way until the target trigram was detected.

Trigrams were generated without replacement. That is, except for target repetitions, each trigram appeared no more than once during a session. In generating a trigram, the consonants were selected without replacement so that a trigram always consisted of three different consonants. Also, the completed trigram was compared with a list of familiar consonant trigrams, for example, BMW, and if it was on list, then the trigram was not presented and another trigram was presented instead.

Procedure.   Each subject filled out a brief health questionnaire. Subjects were asked to report the overall quality of their health: excellent, good, fair, or poor; any current or recent health problems; the amount and date of the most recent consumption of alcohol; and the type and date of most recent medication. Each subject was first given a Snellen eye chart test at a distance roughly equivalent to their distance from the computer screen. All subjects had 20–20 vision on the test. Also, all subjects were questioned about their health and habits.

Then a subject sat before the computer and self-initiated the repetition detection task. First, the instructions appeared and then when any key was pressed the task began. A consonant trigram appeared for 200 ms, followed by three underline symbols in the same location for 1,100 ms to bring the total SOA to 1,300 ms. Because the size of each study sequence and the order of the intervals was randomly selected, a subject could not predict when a target repetition would occur. Also, because the size of each study sequence could be between 1 and 10 trigrams and each test sequence could occur one or more times, the total number of trigrams presented during a session varied.

After the repetition detection task, each subject performed the PASAT. In this task, the subject heard a continuous sequence of digits at an interval of one digit every second and had to respond with the sum of the last two numbers heard. Hence, each digit was used to compute two sums before it was discarded. The native Norwegian speakers heard the test in Norwegian and the native English speakers and Czech speaker heard the test in English.

Results

All subjects reported good or excellent health. No subjects reported health problems within the previous year, nor alcohol consumption or medication within the previous 72 hours. An analysis of variance (ANOVA) was performed in which the factors were repetition interval and age and the dependent measure was hit rate. An alpha level of .05 was adopted for this and all subsequent analyses. Hit rate declined significantly as repetition interval increased, $F(3, 66) = 57.5$. Furthermore, the hit rate for the zero-item interval was significantly greater than for the other intervals when tested by orthogonal contrasts, $F(1, 66) = 419$. Also, hit rate declined with age, $F(2, 66) = 5.7$. The false-alarm rate was .18 for the youngest group, .17 for the middle group, and .21 for the oldest group, which was not a significant difference, $F(2, 15) = .974, p = .41$.

An ANOVA was performed in which the factors were repetition interval, age, and whether the response was a hit or false alarm and the dependent measure was reaction time (RT). There was a significant interaction between interval and whether the response was a hit or false alarm, $F(3, 132) = 24.9$. Hits were only faster than false alarms at the zero-item interval. Together, the much higher hit rates and faster responses for the zero-item interval condition demonstrate that this was not a memory task but a perceptual task. So subsequent analyses of the relationship between hit rate and number of repetitions excluded the zero-item interval.

Figure 9–3 shows hit rate as a function of number of repetitions for intervals with two, four, and eight intervening items. A false-alarm rate of .19 did not vary across conditions. So a figure for d' would be indistinguishable from Figure 9–3.

An ANOVA was performed on the slopes in which age group and repetition interval were the factors. The effect of repetition interval was not significant, $F(1, 15) = 1.57$, $p = .280$; however the effect of age group was significant $F(2, 15) = 5.29$, $p = .018$. However, as can be seen from Figure 9–4, hit rate was actually higher for the oldest age group than for the middle age group and the middle and oldest age groups did not differ significantly from each other. Furthermore, the false-alarm rates were .18, .17, and .21 for the youngest, middle, and oldest age groups, respectively. When d' was computed, again the youngest group differed from the two other age groups, which did not differ from each other. The mean slopes and 95% confidence intervals (CI) for each group were .093 (CI = .041, .145) for 20- to 29-year-olds, −.018 (CI = −.070, .033) for 40- to 49-year-olds, and .030 (CI = −.021, .082) for 60- to 69-year-olds.

Finally, correlations were computed for PASAT, several measures of performance on the repetition detection task, and the age of the subject. Specifically, the variables were hit rate for the zero-item interval (HR-zero), hit-rate for intervals with intervening items (HR-nonzero), hit RT for the zero-item interval, RT for hits and false alarms for all intervals (All RT), and the age of the subject. The PASAT was significantly correlated with age, HR-zero, and Hit RT.

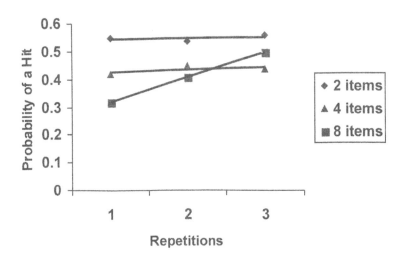

Figure 9–3.   The probability of a hit as a function of number of repetitions for two, four, and eight intervening items.

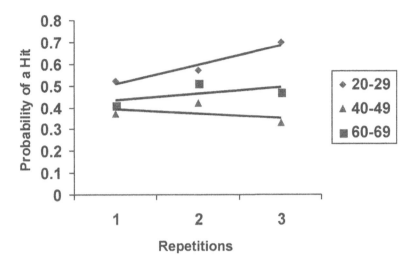

Figure 9–4.   The probability of a hit as a function of number of repetitions for each age group.

DISCUSSION

Though repetition did not have a significant effect on target detection, there was a slight nonsignificant increase for two of the three groups, which is consistent with encoding at the level of the consonant rather than at the level of the trigram. Although there was an effect of age on repetition, detection was higher for the oldest than for the middle-aged subjects. Perhaps this is a result of the lack of power due to the small number of subjects. However, it deserves further investigation. For now the question of the extent to which age-related task decrements that are attributed to encoding failure are actually the result of retrieval failure remains open. Finally, performance on repetition detection was not correlated with performance on the PASAT. Notice that the independence between these tasks cannot be attributed to lack of power, ceiling, or floor effects. Though the PASAT was not correlated with repetition detection for nonzero intervals, it was correlated with repetition detection for the zero interval as well as the hit RT for the zero interval. Hence PASAT performance was correlated with precisely those portions of the repetition detection task that were assumed to require visual attention but not learning and memory. This result suggests that individual differences in performance on the repetition detection task were not the result of differences in attention.

FUTURE DIRECTIONS FOR RESEARCH INTO ALL-OR-NONE LEARNING

Forty years ago the attempt to decompose learning into the all-or-none components failed not because of any specific empirical disconfirmation but because models of the necessary complexity to describe the data appeared to be ad hoc. They appeared to be ad hoc because ideas about representation and retrieval were underdeveloped and because there was not an independent measure of encoding beyond the behavioral data. Today, there are detailed hypotheses about representation and retrieval of both novel items and familiar items such as words and faces. We can ask whether the natural parts and features of these items are learned in an all-or-none or incremental manner. Because the parts and features of the items are specified by the theory of representation, the predictions of the learning model, regardless of number of parts, are a priori rather than ad hoc.

Finally, event-related potentials and the imaging of brain processes provide a new source of converging evidence for encoding. The rediscovery of all-or-none learning will be complete when the neural activity associated with the subset of study trials shown to be learning events is also shown to be all-or-none.

REFERENCES

Binford, J. R., & Gettys, C. (1965). Non-stationarity in paired-associate learning as indicated by a second-guess procedure. *Journal of Mathematical Psychology, 2,* 190–195.

Bower, G. H. (1961). Applications of a model to paired-associate learning. *Psychometrika, 26,* 255–280.

Bower, G. H. (1962). A model of response and training variables in paired-associate learning. *Psychological Review, 69,* 34–53.

Bower, G. H. (1967). A multicomponent theory of the memory trace. In K.W. Spence & J. T. Spence (Eds.), *The psychology of learning and motivation: Advances in research and theory* (Vol. 1, pp. 299–325). New York: Academic Press.

Diehr, M. C., Heaton, R. K., Miller, W., & Grant, I. (1998). The Paced Auditory Serial Addition Task (PASAT): Norms for age, education, and ethnicity. *Assessment, 5,* 375–387.

Dinnerstein, D., & Egeth, H. (1962). On the development of associations. *Psychologische Beitrage, 6,* 544–552.

Estes, W. K. (1960). Learning theory and the new "mental chemistry." *Psychological Review, 67,* 207–223.

Glass, A. L., Lian, A., & Lau, J. (2004). Detection of repeated trigrams: Evidence for all-or-none learning. *American Journal of Psychology, 117,* 497–515.

Kintsch, W. (1965). Habituation of the GSR component of the orienting reflex during paired-associate learning before and after learning has taken place. *Journal of Mathematical Psychology, 2,* 330–331.

Kintsch, W. (1970). *Learning memory and conceptual processes.* New York: Wiley.

Kintsch, W. (1977). *Memory and cognition.* New York: Wiley.

Millward, R. (1964). Latency in a modified paired-associate learning experiment. *Journal of Verbal Learning and Verbal Behavior, 3,* 309–316.

Murdock, B. B., & Babick, A. J. (1961). The effect of repetition on the retention of individual words. *American Journal of Psychology, 74,* 596–601.

Nelson, T. O. (1971). Transfer of serial information from short-term to long-term memory: Toward the locus of the repetition effect. *Psychonomic Society, 25,* 344–345.

Nelson, T. O., & Batchelder, W. H. (1969). Forgetting in short-term recall: All-or-none or decremental? *Journal of Experimental Psychology, 82,* 96–106.

Postman, L. (1962). Repetition and paired-associate learning. *American Journal of Psychology, 75,* 372–389.

Raanaas, R. K., Nordby K., & Magnussen S. (2002). The expanding telephone number—Part 2: Age variations in immediate memory for multiple-digit numbers. *Behavior & Information Technology, 21,* 39–45.

Rock, I. (1957). The role of repetition in associative learning. *American Journal of Psychology, 70,* 186–193.

Shimamura, A. P., Berry, J. M., Mangels, J. A., Rusting, C. L., & Jurica, P. J. (1995). Memory and cognitive abilities in university professors: Evidence for successful aging. *Psychological Science, 6,* 271–277.

Underwoood, B. J., Rehula, R., & Kepel, G. (1962). Item-selection in paired-associate learning. *American Journal of Psychology, 75,* 353–371.

Yonelinas, A. P. (2002). The nature of recollection and familiarity: A review of 30 years of research. *Journal of Memory and Language, 46,* 441–517.

Zelinski, E. M., Gilewski, M. J., & Schaie, K. W. (1993). Individual differences in cross-sectional and 3-year longitudinal memory across the adult life span. *Psychology and Aging, 8,* 176–186.

CHAPTER 10

Relations in Semantic Memory: Still Puzzling After All These Years

Keith J. Holyoak
University of California, Los Angeles

Gordon Bower's article in the first issue of the new journal *Cognitive Psychology* began, "A modest revolution is afoot today within the field of human learning, and the rebels are marching under the banner of 'cognitive organization'" (1970, p. 18). Bower's organizational manifesto signaled a sea change in memory research, moving beyond a narrow focus on undifferentiated associations between elements to a concern with the structural organization of material. The bases for organization included what he termed "relational rules" that constrained the range of potential responses to a stimulus, and hierarchical systems of categories that could be used to impose a preexisting organization on newly presented material.

The new concern with conceptual hierarchies and relations as tools for encoding new episodes dovetailed nicely with the emerging field of *semantic memory*, which was explicitly concerned with the organization of the vast store of concepts and relations that constitute a human being's knowledge of the world (Tulving, 1972). When I began graduate school at Stanford in 1972, semantic memory had already emerged as one of the hottest topics in the young field of cognitive psychology. Two major competing theoretical accounts of how categorical relations are stored and evaluated in semantic memory had been proposed: search in a hierarchical network (Collins & Quillian, 1969) versus computation from elemental features (Schaeffer & Wallace, 1970). I soon teamed up with my fellow graduate student Arnold Glass and began a program of research testing an augmented network model (Glass & Holyoak, 1974, 1975; Glass, Holyoak, & O'Dell, 1974; Holyoak & Glass, 1975; for francophones, our work was summarized in Holyoak, Glass, & Bower, 1976). At the opposite end of the third floor of Jordan Hall, Ed Smith and his graduate students, Lance Rips and Ed Shoben, were hard at work developing more sophisticated feature-comparison models (Rips, Shoben, & Smith, 1973; E. E. Smith, Shoben, & Rips, 1974). For young researchers working in a new field, in the first flush of intellectual excitement, it was easy to imagine that a clear understanding of how semantic relations are coded in human memory was within our reach, if not our grasp.

But by the time I left Stanford with my PhD in 1976, the field of semantic memory as we had known it was dead. Most research fields go out with a whimper rather than a bang, and indeed the lingering death rattles of semantic memory continued to appear in the journals for a few more years. But this was a case where the death knell sounded with the kind of clarity that establishes flashbulb memories. For those of us in the field back then, the end came when we opened the final issue of Psychological Review for 1975, and perused a new model of semantic verification offered by Collins and Loftus. Their "spreading-activation theory of semantic processing" incorporated a long list of assumptions (ominously, 13 in total) that in essence captured the union of all previous models of semantic verification. All-embracingly catholic, the resulting proposal comprehensively explained previous empirical findings, and appeared irrefutable by any imaginable future data. As Kintsch (1980) rather archly observed, this was "the semantic memory model to end all models" (p. 602). In the aftermath, confronted by an impressive yet apparently untestable model, an active research field effectively closed down. To this day, although semantic memory remains a standard topic in cognitive textbooks, those of us who worked in the field decades past find it hard to shake a sense of failure. Medin and Rips (2005), for example, bemoan the setbacks that "left semantic memory theory in the unenviable position of being unable to explain either semantics or memory" (p. 44).

In the remainder of this essay, I look back at the field of semantic memory from the perspective gained by letting three decades slip by. My review is selective and a bit idiosyncratic. In particular, I focus on issues related to the representation and processing of conceptual *relations*—knowledge of how one type of entity enters into systematic roles with respect to other entities. Conceptual relations are exemplified by the types of categorical statements that were used in "classic" speeded semantic-verification paradigms: "A robin is a bird," "All flowers are roses," "Some trees are people." My aim is to give a sense not only of what went wrong with the early field of semantic memory, but also what was learned in the process, and how some of the core issues might be reframed in light of current conceptions of relational knowledge representation. For what in the late 1970s seemed like the end was in fact the beginning of new directions of inquiry that have shed new light on semantic memory. Indeed, more recent work raises the possibility that the ideas culminating in the Collins and Loftus (1975) model still deserve serious consideration. My retrospective has been guided by three excellent review articles, each roughly covering one of the intervening decades: Chang (1986) represents the 1980s, Kounios (1996) the 1990s, and Thompson-Schill (2003) the early years of the new millennium.

SEMANTIC VERIFICATION:
EARLY MODELS AND PHENOMENA

In the Beginning

People have a vast amount of conceptual knowledge available in memory. An important subset of this knowledge concerns relationships between concepts within a hierarchy of categories. We know that a robin is a bird, an animal, and a living thing; when asked to evaluate the truth of such categorical statements, people make decisions quickly and accurately, yet with systematic differences in verification times. For cases such as the "bird" hierarchy, when the subject concept is held constant, reaction time (RT) increases as the predicate category becomes more abstract (i.e., "A robin is a bird" is verified most quickly, "A robin is a living thing" most slowly). Similarly, people tend to verify properties more quickly if they would be plausibly stored at lower levels of the hierarchy. For example, "A robin has wings" would be verified relatively quickly, as "has wings" is a property specifically of birds, whereas "A robin has skin" would take longer, as "has skin" is plausibly a property of the more abstract category of animal. Such differences in verification times figured prominently in many of the earliest studies (Collins & Quillian, 1969, 1970; Landauer & Freedman, 1968; Meyer, 1970), and led to the proposal that semantic memory was organized in accord with a principle of "cognitive economy"—a property is normally stored with the most abstract category for which it holds, then inferred as needed when queried at a more specific level (Collins & Quillian, 1969).

In hindsight, both the initial seductiveness of research on semantic verification, and the roots of the disillusionment to which it eventually led, are evident in these earliest studies. The seductiveness stemmed from the hope that reliable RT differences (varying in magnitude from tens to hundreds of milliseconds) obtained with syntactically simple sentence frames could reveal the structure of human categories and their organization within long-term memory. Key semantic relations, such as "is a," would do double duty as the basis for conceptual organization and as pathways for memory retrieval. By understanding how simple generic truths are stored and accessed, cognitive psychology could provide a unified framework for understanding memory, inference, and language.

It was a pipe dream. The class of semantic relations being explored was, in retrospect, remarkably narrow—instance–category relations such as "A robin is a bird," sometimes enlivened by varied quantifiers ("Some birds are robins" indeed, but "All birds are robins" claims too much), with a few property statements thrown in for good measure ("Robins have wings," and "can fly"). Left in the background, almost totally ignored, were causal relations ("A spark can cause a fire"), the multiple kinds of semantic entailments ("Fred killed Bill" entails "Bill is dead"; "Betty sold her car to Susan" entails "Susan, not Betty, now owns the car"), and the vast, nebulous realm of inductive inference (discovering that "Mary is over 40 years old" increases confidence that "Mary is, or has been, married"). Early on there was some hope that semantic memory research could usefully focus on the "mental dictionary" of knowledge comprising word meanings, for the time being setting aside the open-ended "mental encyclopedia." But in practice that boundary proved too amorphous ("Robins are living things" vs. "Robins breathe oxygen," perhaps?), and indeed cogent linguistic arguments cast doubt on the possibility of an autonomous theory of semantics (Bolinger, 1965). Thus even if a compelling model of the verification of categorical statements had been established, it would have provided at most a beachhead on an unexplored continent.

But the situation was much worse. Beneath their apparent simplicity, categorical statements conceal an ominous methodological pitfall: All verification data concerning such sentences is inherently correlational. So, "A robin is a bird" is verified more quickly than "A robin is a living thing"—what does that mean? The category "living thing," being more abstract than "bird," is logically defined by fewer features (easier to compare?), but includes more instances (harder to search among?). "Robin," a nice typical bird, is presumably more typical of, more related to, more similar to "bird" than "living thing." If asked, "What is a robin?" people will generate "bird" sooner and more frequently than "living thing." The latter category is also a bit less familiar overall, and less rich in perceptual information. In sum, we can readily discern a small host of stimulus variables, all naturally confounded to some degree, any or all of which might plausibly impact verification times for categorical statements.

Searching Networks, Comparing Features

Still, the initial hope was that careful experimentation could sort it all out. Stimulus variables were correlated, but not perfectly; some variables could be held constant, others varied with some degree of independence. And theories could be made, and these would guide the experiments.

From the beginning, two rival metaphors drove two guiding theoretical frameworks. The first metaphor was search in a conceptual network; the second was comparison of sets of conceptual features. Most cognitive textbooks continue to reprint a famous hierarchical diagram from Collins and Quillian (1969) showing a fragment of knowledge about birds and fish. It was a localist semantic network, with nodes representing concepts at various levels of abstraction, properties attached to nodes, and "is a" links interconnecting the nodes. Similar networks provided the basis for broader models of memory for propositions developed in the early 1970s, notably Anderson and Bower (1973) and Rumelhart, Lindsay, and Norman (1973) (both of which, I recall, were covered in a class I took during my first quarter at Stanford). Knowledge retrieval was based on search through the network. For example, to verify "A robin is an animal," search would start from the given concepts, robin and animal, and continue until an intersection is discovered, after which the resulting path would be evaluated to decide whether the stated categorical relation holds.

The second metaphor was based on the intuition that categorical relations can be computed from elemental features of concepts. Rather than prestoring "is a" links from robin to bird, and bird to animal, a person might compute the robin–animal relation by comparing the features of each concept. In general, the features of more abstract categories will form a subset of the features of more specific concepts. For example, animals have skin, and move around; robins have all the "core" features of animal; so a robin must be an animal. Early feature-comparison models (Schaeffer & Wallace, 1970) quickly were augmented by the hypothesis that category instances vary in their "typicality" with respect to categories (Rips et al., 1973; Rosch, 1973), and that concepts included features characteristic of typical instances in addition to more strictly "defining" features. Verification times would therefore depend on the similarity of the concepts being compared, as measured by feature overlap.

E. E. Smith et al. (1974) proposed a two-stage feature-comparison model, which remains the high-water mark of theoretical development based on that metaphor. In the first stage of the model, all features (both characteristic and more strictly defining) of the subject and predicate concepts are used to assess overall similarity of the two concepts. If the similarity value exceeds an upper decision threshold, a quick "true" judgment is made; if the value is below a lower threshold, a quick "false" judgment is made. If the similarity value falls in the intermediate range, a second stage is invoked, in which defining features of the predicate are isolated and matched to the features of the subject, thereby computing the logical relationship between the two concepts. Although the model made claims about factors that should affect second-stage processing time, in practice its empirical successes simply required that intermediate similarity should lead to longer RTs—that is, Stage 1 responses are fast, whereas Stage 2 responses take extra time.

Empirical Phenomena, Theoretical Challenges

As Chang (1986) observed, the network-search and feature-comparison models were remarkably complementary in their empirical strengths and weaknesses. Even though no unified model gave a coherent account of the entire set of phenomena discovered in empirical studies of semantic verification, each guiding metaphor was relatively "comfortable" with just those findings that seemed awkward for the other.

Table 10–1 provides a list of major phenomena involving verification and falsification of categorical relations. To begin with, each metaphor was associated

Table 10–1
Reaction Time to Verify or Falsify Semantic Relations:

Verification

V1) High frequency of generation (production frequency) and/or high relatedness ratings (typicality) leads to fast "true" decisions (e.g., Conrad, 1972; Freedman & Loftus, 1971; Glass et al., 1974; Rips et al., 1973; Rosch, 1973). E.g., "A robin is a bird" is verified more quickly than "A chicken is a bird."

V2) Asymmetries in generation frequency yield order effects in instance-category judgments (Loftus, 1973). E.g., butterfly-insect (high instance-to-category generation frequency) yields faster RT than insect-butterfly (lower category-to-instance frequency).

V3) Generation frequency and relatedness ratings yield moderate to high correlations; regression analysis found generation frequency to be the more effective predictor of RT (Smith et al., 1974, Expt. 1).

V4) "True" RTs are slower when "difficult" false sentences of the same syntactic type are included in the stimulus set (Glass & Holyoak, 1974; Rips, 1975; McCloskey & Gluckeberg, 1979; Lorch, 1981).

Falsification

F1) Anomalous sentences (e.g., "Canaries are cars") are rejected most quickly (Collins & Quillian, 1969; Glass et al., 1974; Holyoak & Glass, 1975; Rips et al., 1973; Wilkins, 1971).

F2) For "sensible" false sentences, RT decreases with increased generation frequency, or for close rather than far coordinates (Glass et al., 1974, 1979; Gruenenfelder, 1986; Holyoak & Glass, 1975; Lorch, 1978, 1981). E.g., "All girls are boys" is rejected more quickly than "All girls are brothers."

F3) For universally-quantified sentences, RT decreases with the availability of a counterexample, as measured by generation frequency (Holyoak & Glass, 1975). E.g., "All countries have presidents" (counterexample: England) is rejected more quickly than "All countries have ports" (counterexample: Switzerland).

with one of two major stimulus variables, which create a "natural confounding" with one another. Generation measures involve presenting a concept as a cue and asking respondents to generate concepts in some specified relationship to the cue; for example, given the category "bird" as a cue, generate instances of it. Generation frequency (also called "production frequency") predicted "true" RT (Phenomenon V1). For example, people proved faster to verify "A robin is a bird" (high generation frequency) than "A chicken is a bird" (lower generation frequency). Because generation tasks plausibly require directed search through semantic memory, it is relatively straightforward to interpret generation frequency as a measure of time to search through a network. Notably, generation frequency did not always neatly correspond to logical distance in a category hierarchy (e.g., people more frequently generate "animal" than "mammal" as a category of which "dog" is an instance; Conrad, 1972). Thus cognitive economy had to be interpreted as a default, rather than a strict requirement for memory storage (which to be fair, had been pointed out by Collins and Quillian, 1969, in their original statement of their network model). Moreover, generation frequency often varies among instances of a given category, as in the robin/chicken example. Thus network models had to include the assumption that links vary systematically in their strength (Collins & Loftus, 1975; Holyoak & Glass, 1975).

If generation measures led to some increase in the complexity of network models, they were more problematic for feature-comparison models. In particular, it was far from clear how a process of feature comparison could be adapted so that one concept could be used to generate another (because the "comparison" metaphor presupposes that there are two concepts already available to compare). However, setting aside the question of how people can perform structured generation at all, proponents of feature-comparison models observed that generation frequency is generally correlated with rating measures based on questions such as, "How typical is a robin/chicken as an instance of a bird?" Thus feature-comparison models could account for V1 by assuming that the observed RT differences are attributable to variations in typicality (which happens to be correlated with generation frequency).

Although V1 thus appeared to yield a rough "draw" between the two metaphors, V2 and V3 favored the network metaphor. Loftus (1973) identified asymmetries in RT to make instance-category judgments that were predictable from parallel asymmetries in generation frequency. For example, given the cue "butterfly," the category "insect" is commonly produced; but given the cue "insect," the instance "butterfly" is less commonly produced. As would therefore be expected (assuming search tends to proceed from subject to predicate), people verify a category relationship more quickly when the pair is ordered *butterfly-insect* rather than *insect-butterfly*. Although feature comparisons might be somehow asymmetrical, no compelling account of Phenomenon V2 was offered. In addition, E. E. Smith et al. (1974, p. 230) used regression analyses in an effort to tease apart the predictive power of generation frequency and typicality ratings; the frequency measure proved more potent (Phenomenon V3).

The final verification phenomenon in Table–1, V4, concerns context effects on decision time. The presence of "difficult" false sentences of a given syntactic type slows the verification of "true" sentences of that same type. For example, early work (Meyer, 1970) suggested that statements with the quantifier *some* are verified more quickly than statements with the quantifier *all* (e.g., "Some rubies are stones" vs. "All rubies are stones"). However, this apparent difference in "true" RTs was later shown to be due to Meyer's inclusion of highly plausible but false *all* statements (e.g., "All stones are rubies") in the absence of similarly demanding false *some* statements (Glass & Holyoak, 1974). When the difficulty of "false" sentences for each quantifier was controlled, the RT difference between "true" *all* and *some* statements was reversed. Such findings (see Chang, 1986, for a thorough review) indicate that any model of semantic verification will need to include a flexible decision process that adapts to the difficulty of discriminating "true" from "false" sentences.

The bottom half of Table 10–1 summarizes three phenomena related to the falsification of category statements. These phenomena support the prescient observation made by Collins and Quillian (1969) in their seminal paper: "The process by which a person decides that a statement is false does not seem to be very simple" (p. 246). Phenomenon F1 is a clear "win" for the feature-comparison metaphor: Anomalous sentences, in which the subject and predicate concepts have minimal feature overlap (e.g., "A truck is a flower") are rejected more quickly than any other type of "false" sentence. From the point of view of the E. E. Smith et al. (1974) two-stage model, V1 and F1 are the flip sides of the same coin: High relatedness yields fast "true" RT (V1), and low relatedness yields fast "false" RT (F1) because in both cases a decision can be made based on Stage 1 processing. In contrast, F1 is a blatant embarrassment to network models. When the two concepts are far apart in a conceptual network, it should take a long time to find their intersection; hence anomalous sentences should be slow to reject. Advantage, feature comparison.

But the picture is more complex: For "false" sentences, the overall relationship between relatedness and RT proved to be nonmonotonic. Arnold Glass and I, in a rather bizarre twist of the usual method of obtaining generation frequencies to predict "true" RTs, asked college students to generate completions that would make sentence frames *false*. It was far from obvious that we would obtain any systematic data; after all, almost any completion selected at random will make a false statement. For example, if given "Some girls are_____," suitable completions would include "trees," "cameras," "armadillos," and any of a host of similarly unrelated nouns. (Caveat: semantic-memory verification is to be performed with a straight face—metaphors are not welcome.) But in fact, the most common completion was "boys"—false to be sure, but clearly highly related. Lewis Carroll once remarked that the opposite of a cat is a dog; and indeed, our subjects completed "All cats are _____" with "dogs." Armed with such "false" generation measures, Glass and I compared falsification times for sentences that were "sensible," but varied in generation frequency of the predicate. Over several studies (Glass & Holyoak, 1975; Glass, Holyoak, & Kiger, 1979; Holyoak & Glass, 1975), we found that people rejected statements based on high-frequency completions (often direct antonyms) more quickly than those based on lower-frequency (but nonanomalous) completions (F2). Thus falsification time appears to be related to the availability of a contradiction between the subject and predicate concepts. Moreover, parallel differences were obtained with 6-year-old children using error rates as the dependent measure, indicating that young children's semantic judgments are also sensitive to the availability of contradictions (Glass, Holyoak, & Kossan, 1977).

In a similar vein, we used a generation measure to predict "false" RT to universally quantified statements, such as "All animals are birds," that would be true if the quantifier were *some*—that is, sentences that did not involve any kind of inherent contradiction between the two concepts. We found (Phenomenon F3) that falsification time decreased with the availability of *counterexamples,* as measured by the frequency with which relevant disconfirming instances were generated in norms collected for corresponding true *some* statements (Holyoak & Glass, 1975). Thus "All animals are birds" (counterexample: mammals) was rejected more quickly than "All animals are males" (counterexample: females). Both F2 and F3, which reveal dependencies between falsification times and structured semantic relationships among concepts, seemed more consistent with the network metaphor than with feature comparison. In any case, the apparent nonmonotonic relationship between relatedness and "false" RTs indicates that falsification depends on more than an assessment of the overall similarity of the two concepts.

AFTER THE FALL: WHAT HAVE WE LEARNED SINCE THE 1970S?

Although research using speeded sentence-verification paradigms waned as the 1970s came to a close, work on semantic memory has certainly continued up to the present day, using other paradigms. One early trend was that attention shifted from the verification of known semantic relations to the related topic of learning to classify novel instances of artificial concepts, defined by similarity of perceptual or verbal features. Many sophisticated models of classification were constructed, based on comparison to stored instances (Medin & Schaffer, 1978), Bayesian inference over feature distributions (Fried & Holyoak, 1984), connectionist learning rules (Gluck & Bower, 1988), and combinations of these approaches (Kruschke, 1992; Nosofsky & Palmeri, 1994). One of the most influential models was a simple application of parallel distributed processing to a toy categorization problem involving members of two hypothetical gangs, the "Sharks and Jets" (Rumelhart, McClelland, & Hinton, 1986), which was used to illustrate some of the attractive properties of connectionist learning and classification. In general terms, the models of artificial concept learning were consistent with the feature-comparison metaphor, indirectly lending credence to the feature-based approach to semantic verification. However, the artificial concept-learning paradigms seldom involved the acquisition of multileveled hierarchies, or any sort of structured relations between concepts; hence the ultimate relevance of this work to semantic verification is questionable.

Evidence From Speed–Accuracy Decomposition

Another trend (one that was most welcome) was to broaden the scope of dependent variables used to assess models of semantic judgments. In my view, the most important work on semantic memory in the last 30 years was done by John Kounios and his colleagues (Kounios, 1993; Kounios & Holcomb, 1992; Kounios, Osman & Meyer, 1987; see Kounios, 1996, for a review). Previous studies of sentence verification had been limited to a focus on mean RTs, and error rates. Building on the theoretical work of Meyer, Irwin, Osman, and Kounios (1988), this group of investigators exploited a new method of speed–accuracy decomposition (SAD). The basic idea is to collect RT data using a paradigm in which "regular" verification trials, on which subjects are instructed to respond quickly but accurately, are randomly interspersed with "response–signal" trials, on which the subject is required to immediately make a "best guess" under maximal speed stress. Using the resulting data from both types of trials, mathematical techniques developed by Meyer et al. can be used to derive a partial-information accumulation function, which describes the accumulation of partial information over the course of an average trial.

This method made it possible to test an apparent prediction of the network search metaphor. Kounios and colleagues reasoned that in a "pure" search model, based on localist nodes representing concepts, and with unitary "is a" links interconnecting them, the subject should not have any information about the truth of a semantic relation until the search of memory is complete. Such an all-or-none process would predict that no partial information, as measured by the SAD technique, will be accumulated prior to termination of search. In fact, however, Kounios et al. (1987) found clear evidence of partial information being accumulated for categorical statements such as "All dogs are animals," All animals are dogs," and "All dogs are clothes." Moreover, similar results were obtained for sentences based on "ownership" relations, such as "Many people own computers" (Kounios, Montgomery, & Smith, 1994). The latter finding contradicted the conjecture that complex relations such as "ownership" will be retrieved in an all-or-none fashion (Glass & Holyoak, 1975). Nor was it simply the case that all verification tasks would yield evidence of partial-information accumulation: R. W. Smith and Kounios (1996) found clear support for all-or-none processing in an anagram task.

The SAD paradigm yielded two additional important findings concerning semantic verification. First, information begins to accumulate at about the same point in time regardless of the type of sentence being verified, and grows at an approximately linear rate (in units of d'). In other words, variables such as generation frequency, typicality, and truth value apparently affect the asymptote of information accumulation, but not its initiation or rate of accrual (also see Lorch, 1982). Second, at least for some types of sentences, extrapolation of partial-information accumulation underpredicts the level of accuracy actually achieved on "regular" RT trials. Kounios (1993) obtained evidence suggesting that this underprediction may reflect the operation of two parallel verification mechanisms: a computational process based on feature-level processing, which yields partial-information accumulation but is slow to reach asymptote; and a discrete-search process, all-or-none in nature, whicih may return a decision before the computational process is completed. Thus the SAD paradigm provided tantalizing evidence that the kind of integrated model proposed by Collins and Loftus (1975), combining some sort of feature-comparison process with some sort of network search, may in fact be viable (and testable) after all.

Neural Substrate of Semantic-Memory Verification

Other sources of data on semantic-memory verification have emerged with the rise of cognitive neuroscience. Fischler and his colleagues (Fischler, Bloom, Childers, Roucos, & Perry, 1983; see Fischler & Raney, 1991, for a review) pioneered the use of event-related potentials (ERPs) to investigate verification of categorical statements. Their focus was on a component of the ERP waveform known as N400, a negative component peaking about 400 ms after the onset of a test stimulus. Kutas and Hillyard (1980; see Kutas & Federmeier, 2000, for a recent review) had found that a strong N400 was triggered by sentences made anomalous by their final word (e.g., "He spread the warm butter with socks"). Fischler et al. (1983) found that N400 to the predicate term in a sentence was especially large for anomalous sentences, such as "A canary is a rock," relative to sensible sentences such as "A canary is a bird." Importantly, the N400 was independent of the truth value of the statement, being strong not only after "A canary is a rock," but also after "A canary is not a rock." Similarly, Kounios and Holcomb (1992) found that predicate N400 is greatest when the two concepts are unrelated, and is independent of variations in quantifier that reverse truth value (e.g., "Some dogs are furniture" vs. "No dogs are furniture"). These ERP studies mesh well with the findings from the SAD paradigm, suggesting that semantic verification is based in part on a fast process of feature comparison. This process appears to be nonpropositional, in that concepts with minimal feature overlap trigger a large N400 regardless of logical quantifiers that ultimately determine the truth value of the presented statement. As Kounios (1996) argued, these findings suggest that propositions must be actively constructed on the basis of more primitive semantic information that initially is retrieved. (See Kounios, 2007, for a review of the use of ERP methods to identify and isolate transient functional modules for processing semantic information.)

Whereas ERP provides fine-grained temporal resolution but weak spatial resolution, the more recent methodology of functional imaging has the complementary strength and weakness. Thompson-Schill (2003) provides a recent review of neuroimaging studies of semantic memory, with the hopeful subtitle, "Inferring 'How' From 'Where'." But her review reveals that the "where" is rather indefinite—"The search for the neuroanatomical locus of semantic memory has simultaneously led us nowhere and everywhere" p. 288)—whereas the "how" remains as much a mystery as before the advent of functional magnetic resonance imaging. The major "region of interest" for semantic verification is the ventral temporal cortex, which appears to be organized by clusters of semantic features. In addition, prefrontal cortex (specifically, the left inferior frontal gyrus) appears to be involved in a general-purpose selection mechanism that often is useful for semantic judgments. Converging neuropsychological evidence has been found in a study of performance on simple verbal analogies, which must be solved using stored semantic relations (Morrison et al., 2004). Patients with either temporal- or frontal-lobe degeneration are impaired in solving verbal analogies, but in different ways: Temporal patients show general loss of the relevant semantic relations, whereas frontal patients are more selectively impaired when confronted by semantically related, but nonanalogical, foils.

More generally, Thompson-Schill (2003) concludes that semantic memory is based on a highly distributed network across many brain regions. Interestingly, various regions associated with quasi-perceptual semantic features (e.g., color, form) have been located somewhat anterior to their corresponding primary sensorimotor regions. This "anterior shift" may be related to a process of abstraction that generates semantic features on the basis of sensorimotor information. Thompson-Schill argues that the apparent coherence of semantic knowledge is in some sense a construction arising from complex neural interactions (cf. Kounios, 1996). Other evidence indicates that different types of semantic judgments (e.g., typicality vs. pleasantness) made about the same set of concepts can yield distinct patterns of neural activations (Grossman et al., 2006; cf. Saptute et al., 2005). Thus neuroimaging evidence provides (at best) extremely indirect clues to the localization of semantic knowledge and to the mechanisms that operate on it.

Neuropsychological studies, coupled with computational modeling of their findings, provide further support for a distributed representation of semantic knowledge. Patients with damage to anterior temporal cortex exhibit various symptoms of "semantic dementia," including loss of comprehension of concepts and categories, and associated difficulty in naming pictures of objects (Hodges, Graham, & Patterson, 1995). One of the most striking aspects of semantic dementia is its "concrete to abstract" pattern of progression. For example, the patient may lose the name "sheep," calling a picture of a sheep "dog" (a similar but more familiar concept) instead, or using the more abstract category name "animal." Rogers et al. (2004) provided a distributed connectionist model of semantic knowledge, which hypothesizes that neurons in anterior temporal cortex, functioning as "hidden units" in a parallel distributed processing model, constitute amodal semantic features that serve to integrate inputs from different sensory modalities. The pattern of semantic loss observed in cases of semantic dementia was simulated simply by removing increasing proportions of weights in the entire network. Interestingly, the concrete-to-abstract pattern of conceptual loss in semantic dementia runs opposite to the standard verification pattern observed in normals (i.e., faster verification of more specific than of more general categories; Collins & Quillian, 1969). It seems that in general, concrete concepts in normals have a richer semantic representation than do more abstract concepts, giving the former an advantage in speed of verification. However, the more diffuse representations associated with abstract concepts, by virtue of their interconnectivity with numerous specific concepts, are relatively robust as semantic weights deteriorate.

NOW WHAT? SEMANTIC RELATIONS IN A SYMBOLIC-CONNECTIONIST FRAMEWORK

If we survey the debates about network search versus feature comparison as metaphors for semantic verification, it is striking that the same key distinctions have figured prominently in broader discussions of symbolic representation. Roughly, network models have been associated with *localist* representations that encode *explicit* semantic relations, whereas feature-comparison models have been associated with *distributed* representations that represent relations only *implicitly* (e.g., Rogers et al., 2004). The long-standing notion that network and feature · models need to be integrated somehow (Collins & Loftus, 1975) therefore has a natural kinship with what has been termed *symbolic connectionism*—neural-networks models that integrate distributed representations of meaning with explicit representation of relations and the roles that comprise them (Holyoak, 1991; Hummel & Holyoak, 1997, 2003).

Explicit semantic relations, in which entities are bound to specific roles, are critical to seeing analogies between disparate situations (see Doumas & Hummel, 2005; Holyoak, 2005). In work more closely related to traditional semantic-memory paradigms, priming experiments have shown that structured relations of the sort used in semantic-verification studies play a role in activating concepts stored in semantic memory. Spellman, Holyoak, and Morrison (2001) found that pairs of words such as *bird-nest,* referring to entities bound to the respective roles of the "lives in" relation, could prime analogous pairs such as *bear-cave* in both naming and lexical decision tasks. "Intact" primes, such as the preceding example, were significantly more effective than "scrambled" primes such as *bird-desert* (formed by recombining the entities in *bird-nest* and *camel-desert*). Similar stimuli that revealed relational priming were formed using other relations, including "is part of," "works in," "is a," and "is opposite to." Spellman et al. found that relational priming was not fully automatic; rather, it was obtained only when participants were instructed to "note and use" the relations.

The fact that attention plays an important role in relational priming is consistent with the hypothesis that structured relations must be represented somehow not only in semantic (long-term) memory, but also in working memory. It follows that decision times for relation verification will depend on the degree of match between the roles of cues in working memory and their relational roles in semantic memory. Fenker, Waldmann, and Holyoak (2005) found evidence for such relational matching in a task requiring verification of causal relations using semantic knowledge. In a series of experiments, participants read pairs of words describing events that referred to either a cause (e.g., *spark*) or an effect (e.g., *fire*). When asked whether or not the two concepts had a causal relation to one another, participants responded more quickly when the first word referred to a cause and the second word to its effect (*spark-fire*) than vice versa (*fire-spark*). In contrast, no such asymmetry was observed when the question simply asked if the two concepts were "associated." In a related study using neuroimaging, decisions about whether two words were causally related activated additional neural regions (in particular, dorsolateral prefrontal cortex and precuneus) beyond those activated by decisions about whether the identical words were simply "associated" (Satpute et al., 2005). Importantly, the dorsolateral prefrontal cortex has been implicated in many other tasks, including high-level relational reasoning, that depend on working memory (see Waltz et al., 1999).

Theoretically, judging whether a structured relation, such as cause-effect or instance-category, holds between two concepts would be expected to require (a) forming a working-memory representation of the relational query, in which each concept is bound to a specific role in the relevant relation, and (b) matching this active representation against relational knowledge stored in semantic memory. The evidence for a feature-comparison process (fast rejection of anomalous false sentences, strong N400 for anomalous sentences independent of quantifier, independence of the onset of information accrual from type of sentence, concrete-to-abstract progression of semantic dementia) implicates a "fast and easy" mechanism for making decisions that do not require representing explicit relational roles in working memory. However, when an accurate decision necessitates evaluation of relational roles, a more demanding process dependent on working memory appears to be required (as evidenced by data on falsification of sensible "false" sentences, underprediction of "regular" verification accuracy by partial-information accumulation, relational priming, and neurobehavioral differences between judgments of causal vs. associative relations). Attention to explicit role bindings will typically be required in verification tasks when the truth values of statements vary with the logical quantifier, or with the specific relation linking concepts. Computational models in which role bindings are dynamically formed in working memory on the basis of neural synchrony (Hummel & Holyoak, 1997, 2003; Shastri & Ajjanagadde, 1993) may have the potential to integrate multiple processes for evaluating semantic relations.

So, where do we go from here? Three decades on, one might even argue that research on semantic verification in the 1970s was ahead of its time. The core issue—how structured relations are stored in memory and used to judge the truth of simple propositions—is still basic to understanding human thinking. The evidence at the time pointed toward an integrative, multiprocess account (Collins & Loftus, 1975). This track still seems like the right one; what was lacking back then were empirical methods more incisive than mean reaction time, and computational mechanisms more precise than diagrams showing nodes and arrows. After all these years, semantic memory is still worth puzzling over.

ACKNOWLEDGMENTS

Preparation of this chapter was supported by NIH Grant MH072613, NSF Grant SES–0350920, and Institute of Education Sciences Grant R305H030141. I thank John Hummel for many helpful discussions, and John Anderson, Arnold Glass, and John Kounios for comments on an earlier draft. Most of all, I thank Arnold Glass and Gordon Bower for making graduate school at Stanford back in the 1970s a whole lot of fun.

REFERENCES

Anderson, J. R., & Bower, G. H. (1973). *Human associative memory.* Washington, DC: Winston.

Bolinger, D. (1965). The atomization of meaning. *Language, 41,* 555–573.

Bower, G. H. (1970). Organizational factors in memory. *Cognitive Psychology, 1,* 18–46.

Chang, T. M. (1986). Semantic memory: Facts and models. *Psychological Bulletin, 99,* 199–220.

Collins, A. M., & Loftus, E. F. (1975). A spreading-activation theory of semantic processing. *Psychological Review, 82,* 407–428.

Collins, A. M., & Quillian, M. R. (1969). Retrieval time from semantic memory. *Journal of Verbal learning and Verbal Behavior, 8,* 240–248.

Collins, A. M., & Quillian, M. R. (1970). Does category size affect categorization time? *Journal of Verbal Learning and Verbal Behavior, 9,* 432–438.

Conrad, C. (1972). Cognitive economy in semantic memory. *Journal of Experimental Psychology, 92,* 149–154.

Doumas, L. A. A., & Hummel, J. E. (2005). Approaches to modeling human mental representations: What works, what doesn't, and why. In K. J. Holyoak & R. G. Morrison (Eds.), *The Cambridge handbook of thinking and reasoning* (pp. 73–91). Cambridge, England: Cambridge University Press.

Fenker, D. B., Waldmann, M. R., & Holyoak, K. J. (2005). Accessing causal relations in semantic memory. *Memory & Cognition, 33,* 1036–1046.

Fischler, I., Bloom, P. A., Childers, D. G., Roucos, S. E., & Perry, N. W. (1983). Brain potentials related to stages of sentence verification. *Psychophysiology, 20,* 400–409.

Fischler, I., & Raney, G. E. (1991). Language by eye: Behavioral, autonomic and cortical approaches to reading. In J. R. Jennings & M. G. H. Coles (Eds.), *Handbook of cognitive psychophysiology: Central and autonomic nervous system* (pp. 511–574). New York: Wiley.

Freedman, J. L., & Loftus, E. F. (1971). Retrieval of words from long-term memory. *Journal of Verbal learning and Verbal Behavior, 10*, 107–115.

Fried, L. S., & Holyoak, K. J. (1984). Induction of category distributions: A framework for classification learning. *Journal of Experimental Psychology: Learning, Memory and Cognition, 10*, 234–257.

Glass, A. L., & Holyoak, K. J. (1974). The effect of *some* and *all* on reaction time for semantic decisions. *Memory & Cognition, 2*, 436–440.

Glass, A. L., & Holyoak, K. J. (1975). Alternative conceptions of semantic memory. *Cognition, 3*, 313–339.

Glass, A. L., Holyoak, K. J., & Kiger, J. I. (1979). Role of antonymy relations in semantic judgments. *Journal of Experimental Psychology: Human, Learning and Memory, 5*, 598–606.

Glass, A. L., Holyoak, K. J., & Kossan, N. E. (1977). Children's ability to detect semantic contradictions. *Child Development, 48*, 279–283.

Glass, A. L., Holyoak, K. J., & O'Dell, C. (1974). Production frequency and the verification of quantified statements. *Journal of Verbal Learning and Verbal Behavior, 13*, 237–254.

Gluck, M. A., & Bower, G. H. (1988). Evaluating an adaptive network model of human learning. *Journal of Memory and Language, 27*, 166–195.

Grossman, M., Koenig, P., Kounios, J., McMillan, C., Work, M., & Moore, P. (2006). Category-specific effects in semantic memory: Category–task interactions suggested by fMRI. *Neuroimage, 30*, 1003–1009.

Gruenenfelder, T. M. (1986). Relational similarity and context effects in category verification. *Journal of Experimental Psychology: Learning, Memory, and Cognition, 12*, 587–599.

Hodges, J. R., Graham, N., & Patterson, K. (1995). Charting the progression in semantic dementia: Implications for the organization of semantic memory. *Memory, 3*, 463–495.

Holyoak, K. J. (1991). Symbolic connectionism: Toward third-generation theories of expertise. In A. Ericsson & J. Smith (Eds.), *Toward a general theory of expertise: Prospects and limits* (pp. 301–355). Cambridge, England: Cambridge University Press.

Holyoak, K. J. (2005). Analogy. In K. J. Holyoak & R. G. Morrison (Eds.), *The Cambridge handbook of thinking and reasoning* (pp. 117–142). Cambridge, England: Cambridge University Press.

Holyoak, K. J., & Glass, A. L. (1975). The role of contradictions and counterexamples in the rejection of false sentences. *Journal of Verbal Learning and Verbal Behavior, 4*, 215–239.

Holyoak, K. J., Glass, A. L., & Bower, G. B. (1976). Les processus de décision dans la mémoire sémantique. In S. Ehrlich & E. Tulving (Eds.), *La mémoire sémantique* (pp. 92–101). Paris: Bulletin de Psychologie.

Hummel, J. E., & Holyoak, K. J. (1997). Distributed representations of structure: A theory of analogical access and mapping. *Psychological Review, 104*, 427–466.

Hummel, J. E., & Holyoak, K. J. (2003). A symbolic-connectionist theory of relational inference and generalization. *Psychological Review, 110*, 220–264.

Kintsch, W. (1980). Semantic memory: A tutorial. In R. S. Nickerson (Ed.), *Attention and performance VIII* (pp. 595–620). Hillsdale, NJ: Lawrence Erlbaum Associates.

Kounios, J. (1993). Process complexity in semantic memory. *Journal of Experimental Psychology: Learning, Memory, and Cognition, 19*, 338–351.

Kounios, J. (1996). On the continuity of thought and the representation of knowledge: Electrophysiological and behavioral time-course measures reveal levels of structure in semantic memory. *Psychonomic Bulletin and Review, 3,* 265–286.

Kounios, J. (2007). Modularity of semantic memory revealed by event-related potentials. In J. Hart (Ed.), *Neural basis of semantic memory* (pp. 65–104). Cambridge, England: Cambridge University Press.

Kounios, J., & Holcomb, P. J. (1992). Structure and process in semantic memory: Evidence from event-related brain potentials and reaction times. *Journal of Experimental Psychology: General, 121,* 459–479.

Kounios, J., Montgomery, E. C., & Smith, R. W. (1994). Semantic memory and the granularity of semantic relations: Evidence from speed-accuracy decomposition. *Memory & Cognition, 22,* 729–741.

Kounios, J., Osman, A. M., & Meyer, D. E. (1987). Structure and process in semantic memory: New evidence based on speed-accuracy decomposition. *Journal of Experimental Psychology: General, 116,* 3–25.

Kutas, M., & Federmeier, K. D. (2000). Electrophysiology reveals semantic memory use in language comprehension. *Trends in Cognitive Sciences, 4,* 463–470.

Kutas, M., & Hillyard, S. A. (1980). Reading senseless sentences: Brain potentials refelect semantic incongruity. *Science, 207,* 203–205.

Kruschke, J. K. (1992). ALCOVE: An exemplar-based connectionist model of category learning. *Psychological Review, 99,* 22–44.

Landauer, T. K., & Freedman, J. L. (1968). Information retrieval from long-term memory: Category size and recognition time. *Journal of Verbal learning and Verbal Behavior, 7,* 291–295.

Loftus, E. F. (1973). Category dominance, instance dominance, and categorization time. *Journal of Experimental Psychology, 97,* 70–74.

Lorch, R. F., Jr. (1978). The role of two types of semantic information in the processing of false sentences. *Journal of Verbal learning and Verbal Behavior, 17,* 523–537.

Lorch, R. F., Jr. (1981). Effects of relation strength and semantic overlap on retrieval and comparison processes during sentence verification. *Journal of Verbal learning and Verbal Behavior, 20,* 593–610.

Lorch, R. F., Jr. (1982). Priming and search processes in semantic memory: A test of three models of semantic activation. *Journal of Verbal learning and Verbal Behavior, 21,* 468–492.

McClelland, J. L., Rumelhart, D. E., & Hinton, G. E. (1986). The appeal of parallel distributed processing. In D. E. Rumelhart, J. L. McClelland, & the PDP Research Group, *Parallel distributed processing: Explorations in the microstructure of cognition* (Vol. 1, pp. 3–44). Cambridge, MA: MIT Press.

McCloskey, M. E., & Glucksberg, S. (1979). Decision processes in verifying category membership statements: Implications for models of semantic memory. *Cognitive Psychology, 11,* 1–37.

Medin, D. L., & Rips, L. J. (2005). Concepts and categories: Memory, meaning, and metaphysics. In K. J. Holyoak & R. G. Morrison (Eds.), *The Cambridge handbook of thinking and reasoning* (pp. 37–72). Cambridge, England: Cambridge University Press.

Medin, D. L., & Schaffer, M. M. (1978). Context theory of classification learning. *Psychological Review, 85,* 207–238.

Meyer, D. E. (1970). On the representation and retrieval of stored semantic information. *Cognitive Psychology, 1,* 242–300.

Meyer, D. E., Irwin, D. E., Osman, A. M., & Kounios, J. (1988). The dynamics of cognition and action: Mental processes inferred from speed-accuracy decomposition. *Psychological Review, 95,* 183–237.

Morrison, R. G., Krawczyk, D. C., Holyoak, K. J., Hummel, J. E., Chow, T. W., Miller, B. L., & Knowlton, B. J. (2004). A neurocomputational model of analogical reasoning and its breakdown in frontotemporal lobar degeneration. *Journal of Cognitive Neuroscience, 16,* 260–271.

Nosofsky, R. M., & Palmeri, T. J. (1994). Rule-plus-exception model of classification learning. *Psychological Review, 101,* 53–79.

Rips, L. J. (1975). Quantification and semantic memory. *Cognitive Psychology, 7,* 307–340.

Rips, L. J., Shoben, E. J., & Smith, E. E. (1973). Semantic distance and the verification of semantic relations. *Journal of Verbal learning and Verbal Behavior, 12,* 1–20.

Rogers, T. T., Ralph, M. A. L., Garrard, P., Bozeat, S., McClelland, J. L., Hodges, J. R., & Patterson, K. (2004). Structure and deterioration of semantic memory: A neuropsychological and computational investigation. *Psychological Review, 111,* 205–235.

Rosch, E. (1973). On the internal structure of perceptual and semantic categories. In T. E. Moore (Ed.), *Cognitive development and acquisition of language* (pp. 111–144). New York: Academic Press.

Rumelhart, D. E., Lindsay, P. H., & Norman, D. A. (1972). A process model for long-term memory. In E. Tulving & W. Donaldson (Eds.), *Organization of memory* (pp. 197–246). New York: Academic Press.

Satpute, A. B., Fenker, D. B., Waldmann, M. R., Tabibnia, G., Holyoak, K. J., & Lieberman, M. D. (2005). An fMRI study of causal judgments. *European Journal of Neuroscience, 22,* 1233–1238.

Schaeffer, B., & Wallace, R. (1970). The comparison of word meanings. *Journal of Experimental Psychology, 86,* 144–152.

Shastri, L., & Ajjanagadde, V. (1993). From simple associations to systematic reasoning: A connectionist representation of rules, variables and dynamic bindings using temporal synchrony. *Behavioral and Brain Sciences, 16,* 417–494.

Smith, E. E., Shoben, E. J., & Rips, L. J. (1974). Comparison processes in semantic memory. *Psychological Review, 81,* 214–241.

Smith, R. W., & Kounios, J. (1996). Sudden insight: All-or-none processing revealed by speed–accuracy decomposition. *Journal of Experimental Psychology: Learning, Memory, and Cognition, 22,* 1443–1462.

Spellman, B. A., Holyoak, K. J., & Morrison, R. G. (2001). Analogical priming via semantic relations. *Memory & Cognition, 29,* 383–393.

Thompson-Schill, S. L. (2003). Neuroimaging studies of semantic memory: Inferring "how" from "where." *Neuropsychologia, 41,* 280–292.

Tulving, E. (1972). Episodic and semantic memory. In E. Tulving & W. Donaldson (Eds.), *Organization of memory* (pp. 381–403). New York: Academic Press.

Waltz, J. A., Knowlton, B. J., Holyoak, K. J., Boone, K. B., Mishkin, F. S., de Menezes Santos, M., Thomas, C. R., & Miller, B. L. (1999). A system for relational reasoning in human prefrontal cortex. *Psychological Science, 10,* 119–125.

Wilkins, E. J. (1971). Conjoint frequency, category size, and categorization time. *Journal of Verbal Learning and Verbal Behavior, 10,* 382–385.

CHAPTER 11

Using Cognitive Theory to Reconceptualize College Admissions Testing

Robert J. Sternberg
Tufts University

In my 1st-year project, done with Gordon Bower (Sternberg & Bower, 1974), I learned that negative transfer has deleterious effects on performance without one's even realizing it. In my work on intelligence, I have had many opportunities to observe such negative transfer at work.

The business of ability testing in the 20th century was largely atheoretical, as I learned in my dissertation, done under Bower (Sternberg, 1977). Unfortunately, this lack of theory in ability testing became a basis for negative transfer that spilled over into college admissions testing. University admissions testing in the 20th century was dominated by pragmatically derived tests. These tests, such as the SAT, ACT, GRE, and GMAT, measure cognitive and academic skills important for success in university settings. But the lack of a theoretical base has several disadvantages.

The first disadvantage is a disconnection between cognitive theory and the practice of psychology. To the extent one views practice as, ideally, emanating from and unified with theory, such a disconnection is less than ideal (Sternberg &

Grigorenko, 2000). The second is the possibility that the ceiling on validity coefficients that has been obtained (Sternberg, 1997) in such testing may derive, in part, from the absence of a universe of cognitive and academic skills that a psychological theory can specify. The third is that it is unclear how adequately to validate such tests in the absence of a theory. Construct validation is the simultaneous validation of a theory and a test, and in the absence of a theory, satisfactory construct validation is impossible. These tests have been used rather frequently in the United States as well as abroad as one basis for making high-stakes decisions about educational opportunities, placements, and diagnoses. To the extent that the tests cannot be adequately construct-validated, one must question whether they quite reach the ideal we would set for such tests.

In this chapter, I describe a relatively large-scale admissions-testing projects in which we at the Center for the Psychology of Abilities, Competencies, and Expertise (PACE Center) have been involved. The project is the Rainbow Project (Sternberg & The Rainbow Project Collaborators, 2005, 2006; Sternberg, The Rainbow Project Collaborators, & University of Michigan Business School Project Collaborators, 2004), which was designed to provide assessments to augment the SAT (an acronym that originally stood for Scholastic Aptitude Test but that now stands for nothing in particular). A related project, the University of Michigan Business School Project (Hedlund, Wilt, Nebel, Ashford, & Sternberg, 2006), which was designed to provide assessments to augment the GMAT (Graduate Management Admissions Test), is described elsewhere. The theoretical basis for both projects is the theory of successful intelligence.

THE THEORY OF SUCCESSFUL INTELLIGENCE

Here I briefly describe the theory of successful intelligence. More details regarding the theory of successful intelligence and its validation can be found in Sternberg (1985, 1997, 1999) and Sternberg, Lautrey, and Lubart (2003).

The Definition of Successful Intelligence

1. *Intelligence is defined in terms of the ability to achieve success in life in terms of one's personal standards, within one's sociocultural context.* The field of intelligence has at times tended to put "the cart before the horse," defining the construct conceptually on the basis of how it is operationalized rather than vice versa. This practice has resulted in tests that stress the academic aspect of intelligence, or intelligence relevant only to the classroom, which is not surprising given the origins of modern intelligence testing in the work of Binet and Simon (1905/1916) in designing an instrument that would distinguish children who would succeed from those who would fail in school. But the construct of intelligence needs to serve a broader purpose, accounting for the bases of success in all of one's life.

The use of societal criteria of success (e.g., school grades, personal income) can obscure the fact that these criteria often do not capture people's personal notions of success. Some people choose to concentrate on extracurricular activities such as athletics or music and pay less attention to grades in school; others may choose occupations that are personally meaningful to them but that never will yield the income they could gain doing work that is less personally meaningful. In the theory of successful intelligence, however, the conceptualization of intelligence is always within a sociocultural context. Although the processes of intelligence may be common across such contexts, what constitutes success is not. Being a successful member of the clergy of a particular religion may be highly rewarded in one society and viewed as a worthless pursuit in another culture.

2. *One's ability to achieve success depends on one's capitalizing on one's strengths and correcting or compensating for one's weaknesses.* Theories of intelligence typically specify some relatively fixed set of skills, whether one general factor and a number of specific factors (Spearman, 1904), seven multiple factors (Thurstone, 1938), eight multiple intelligences (Gardner, 1983, 1999), or 150 separate intellectual abilities (Guilford, 1982). Such a specification is useful in establishing a common set of skills to be tested. But people achieve success, even within a given occupation, in many different ways. For example, successful teachers and researchers achieve success through many different blendings of skills rather than through any single formula that works for all of them.

3. *Balancing of skills is achieved in order to adapt to, shape, and select environments.* Definitions of intelligence traditionally have emphasized the role of adaptation to the environment ("Intelligence and Its Measurement," 1921; Sternberg & Detterman, 1986). But intelligence involves not only modifying oneself to suit the environment (adaptation), but also modifying the environment to suit oneself (shaping), and sometimes, finding a new environment that is a better match to one's skills, values, or desires (selection).

   Not all people have equal opportunities to adapt to, shape, and select environments. In general, people of higher socioeconomic standing tend to have more opportunities and people of lower socioeconomic standing have fewer. The economy or political situation of the society also can be factors. Other variables that may affect such opportunities are education and especially literacy, political party, race, religion, and so forth. For example, someone with a college education typically has many more possible career options than does someone who has dropped out of high school in order to support a family. Thus, how well an individual adapts to, shapes, and selects environments must always be viewed in terms of the opportunities the individual has.

4. *Success is attained through a balance of three aspects of intelligence: analytical, practical, and creative skills.* Analytical skills are the skills primarily measured by traditional tests. But success in life requires one not only to analyze one's own ideas as well as the ideas of others, but also to generate ideas

and to persuade other people of their value. This necessity occurs in the world of work, as when a subordinate tries to convince a superior of the value of his or her plan; in the world of personal relationships, as when a child attempts to convince a parent to do what he or she wants or when a spouse tries to convince the other spouse to do things his or her preferred way; and in the world of the school, as when a student writes an essay arguing for a point of view.

Defining the Three Aspects of Successful Intelligence

According to the proposed theory of human intelligence and its development (Sternberg, 1980, 1984, 1985, 1990, 1997, 1999), a common set of processes underlies all aspects of intelligence. These processes are hypothesized to be universal. For example, although the solutions to problems that are considered intelligent in one culture may be different from the solutions considered to be intelligent in another culture, the need to define problems and translate strategies to solve these problems exists in any culture. However, although the same processes are used for all three aspects of intelligence universally, these processes are applied to different kinds of tasks and situations depending on whether a given problem requires analytical thinking, practical thinking, creative thinking, or a combination of these kinds of thinking.

Analytical Intelligence.   Analytic intelligence is involved when skills are used to analyze, evaluate, judge, or compare and contrast. It typically is involved when processing components are applied to relatively familiar kinds of problems where the judgments to be made are of a fairly abstract nature.

Creative Intelligence.   Creative intelligence is involved when skills are used to create, invent, discover, imagine, suppose, or hypothesize. Tests of creative intelligence go beyond tests of analytical intelligence in measuring performance on tasks that require individuals to deal with relatively novel situations. My colleagues and I have shown that when one enters the range of unconventionality of the conventional tests of intelligence, one starts to tap sources of individual differences measured little or not at all by the tests (e.g., Sternberg, 1985). Thus it is important to include problems that are relatively novel in nature. These problems can be either convergent or divergent in nature.

Practical Intelligence.   Practical intelligence is involved when skills are utilized, implemented, applied, or put into practice in real-world contexts. It involves individuals applying their abilities to the kinds of problems they confront in daily life, such as on the job or in the home. Practical intelligence involves applying the components of intelligence to experience so as to (a) adapt to, (b) shape, and (c) select environments. Adaptation is involved when one changes oneself to suit the environment. Shaping is involved when one changes the environment to suit oneself. And selection is involved when one decides to seek out another environment that is a better match to one's needs, abilities, and desires. People differ in their balance of adaptation, shaping, and selection, and in the competence with which they balance among these three possible courses of action.

Practical intelligence often has been equated with the notion of "common sense." It involves knowing how to navigate effectively through the problems of everyday life. Individuals who are successful at solving these everyday problems also are said to rely, to some extent, on their "intuition." In other words, they develop effective solutions to problems without necessarily being able to explain or justify their decisions. This "intuition" or "common sense" has been attributed in the practical intelligence literature to tacit knowledge (see Polanyi, 1976). The concept of tacit knowledge reflects the idea that much of the knowledge relevant to real-world performance is acquired through everyday experiences without conscious intent. Tacit knowledge guides action without being easily articulated.

We have defined this construct as the knowledge needed in order to work effectively in an environment that one is not explicitly taught and that often is not even verbalized (Sternberg et al., 2000; Sternberg & Hedlund, 2002; Sternberg & Wagner, 1993; Sternberg, Wagner, Williams, & Horvath, 1995; Wagner, 1987; Wagner & Sternberg, 1986). We (Sternberg & Horvath, 1999; Sternberg et al., 2000) have focused on tacit knowledge as a means of providing insight into practical intelligence. We have studied tacit knowledge in domains as diverse as bank management, sales, academic psychology, primary education, clerical work, and military leadership (Hedlund et al., 2003; Sternberg & Wagner, 1993; Sternberg et al., 1995; Wagner, 1987; Wagner & Sternberg, 1985; Wagner et al., 1999).

The measurement of tacit knowledge derives from an assessment of how individuals rate responses to practical problems. The format on tacit-knowledge (TK) tests is akin to that on situational-judgment tests. Individuals are presented with a brief problem description and are asked to evaluate the quality of potential solutions to the problem. For example, in a hypothetical situation presented to a business manager, a subordinate whom the manager does not know well has come to him for advice on how to succeed in business. The manager is asked to rate each of several responses (usually on a 1 = low to 9 = high scale) according to its importance for succeeding in the company. Examples of responses might include (a) setting priorities that reflect the importance of each task, (b) trying always to work on what you are in the mood to do, and (c) doing routine tasks early in the day to make sure you get them done. TK tests typically consist of several problem situations. Responses are scored by comparing an individual's ratings on all the alternatives to a standard based on expert or consensus judgment.

The score an individual receives on a TK test is viewed as an indicator of his or her practical ability. Previous research has examined the relationship of TK scores to domain-specific experience, general cognitive ability, and various indicators of performance. Generally, individuals with greater experience in a domain (e.g., business managers vs. business students) receive higher TK scores (Sternberg &

Wagner, 1993; Wagner, 1987). TK scores also correlate fairly consistently with performance across a variety of domains. Individuals with higher TK scores have been found to have higher salaries, better performance ratings, more productivity, and to work in more prestigious institutions (Hedlund et al., 2003; Sternberg & Wagner, 1993; Sternberg et al., 1995; Wagner, 1987; Wagner & Sternberg, 1985).

Finally, TK tests appear to tap abilities that are distinct from those measured by traditional intelligence or ability tests. The correlations between scores on TK tests and scores on traditional intelligence tests have ranged from negative to moderately positive (Sternberg et al., 2000, 2001; Sternberg & Wagner, 1993; Wagner & Sternberg, 1985). More important, TK scores have been found to explain performance above and beyond that accounted for by tests of general cognitive ability (Hedlund, et al., 2003; Wagner & Sternberg, 1990). Thus, TK tests offer a promising approach for assessing an individual's practical abilities.

THE RAINBOW PROJECT

The project described here applied the theory of successful intelligence in the creation of tests that capture analytic, practical, and creative skills. Our main goal in this project was to enhance college admissions testing using the theory of successful intelligence. In the project, a test battery was administered to over a thousand students at a variety of institutions across the country, and was used to predict success in school as measured by grade point average (GPA). The hypotheses were twofold: First, we expected that the battery of tests based on the theory of successful intelligence would predict a substantial proportion of variance in GPA above and beyond that captured by the SAT. Second, we expected that this battery of tests would reduce ethnic-group differences in scores that are typically found in current standardized college entrance exams such as the SAT.

We are not assuming that there are no inherent differences in scores among different ethnic groups. Rather, our past research suggests that there are differences, but that these differences are, at least in part, differences in score patterns. Different groups tend to do well on different kinds of assessments (Sternberg, 2004; Sternberg & Grigorenko, 2004). Many of these studies, however, were outside the United States. So we are particularly interested in finding out whether, in the United States as well as abroad, different groups show different average patterns of scores when diverse tests of cognitive abilities are deployed.

The Rainbow measures supplement the SAT-I. The SAT-I is a 3-hour examination measuring verbal comprehension and mathematical thinking skills, with a writing component added after this project was done. A wide variety of studies have shown the utility of the SAT as a predictor of college success, especially as measured by GPA (e.g., Bridgeman, McCamley-Jenkins, & Ervin, 2000).

Kobrin, Camara, and Milewski (2002) examined the validity of the SAT for college admissions decisions in California and elsewhere in the United States. They found that, in California, SAT-I and SAT-II both showed moderate correlations with family income (in the range of .25 to .55 for SAT-I). Correlations with parental education ranged from .28 to .58. These findings indicate that SAT scores tend to covary with social class. Predictive effectiveness of the SAT was similar for different ethnic groups; however, there were important mean differences for the different ethnic groups on the SAT (see also Bridgeman, Burton, & Cline, 2001). The group differences are reflected by the number of standard deviations away from the White students' mean each group scored. On average, African American students scored about one full standard deviation below the White students on both the verbal and mathematics tests. Latino students scored about three-fourths of a standard deviation lower than the White students, and Native Americans scored about one-half of a standard deviation lower than White students on the two tests. Asian students scored higher than White students by about a third of a standard deviation on the math test but about a third lower on the verbal test.

These data suggest reasonable predictive validity for the SAT in predicting college performance. Indeed, traditional intelligence or aptitude tests have been shown to predict performance across a wide variety of settings (Brody, 1997; Schmidt & Hunter, 1998). But as is always the case for a single test or type of test, there is room for improvement. The theory of successful intelligence (Sternberg, 1997, 1999) provides one basis for improving prediction and possibly for establishing greater equity. It suggests that broadening the range of skills tested to go beyond analytic skills, to include practical and creative skills as well, might significantly enhance the prediction of college performance beyond current levels. Thus, the theory does not suggest *replacing,* but rather, *augmenting* the SAT in the college admissions process. A collaborative team of investigators sought to study how successful such an augmentation could be.

We have had some past experience in such work. In one study (Sternberg, Grigorenko, Ferrari, & Clinkenbeard, 1999), we used the so-called Sternberg Triarchic Abilities Test (STAT; Sternberg, 1993) to investigate the internal validity of the theory. Three hundred twenty-six high school students, primarily from diverse parts of the United States, took the test, which comprised 12 subtests in all. There were four subtests each measuring analytical, creative, and practical abilities. For each type of ability, there were three multiple-choice tests and one essay test. The multiple-choice tests, in turn, involved, respectively, verbal, quantitative, and figural content:

1. Analytical-Verbal: Figuring out meanings of neologisms (artificial words) from natural contexts. Students see a novel word embedded in a paragraph, and have to infer its meaning from the context.
2. Analytical-Quantitative: Number series. Students have to say what number should come next in a series of numbers.
3. Analytical-Figural: Matrices. Students see a figural matrix with the lower right entry missing. They have to say which of the options fits into the missing space.
4. Practical-Verbal: Everyday reasoning. Students are presented with a set of everyday problems in the life of an adolescent and have to select the option that best solves each problem.

5. Practical-Quantitative: Everyday math. Students are presented with scenarios requiring the use of math in everyday life (e.g., buying tickets for a ballgame), and have to solve math problems based on the scenarios.
6. Practical-Figural: Route planning. Students are presented with a map of an area (e.g., an entertainment park) and have to answer questions about navigating effectively through the area depicted by the map.
7. Creative-Verbal: Novel analogies. Students are presented with verbal analogies preceded by counterfactual premises (e.g., money falls off trees). They have to solve the analogies as though the counterfactual premises were true.
8. Creative-Quantitative: Novel number operations. Students are presented with rules for novel number operations, for example, "flix," which involves numerical manipulations that differ as a function of whether the first of two operands is greater than, equal to, or less than the second. Participants have to use the novel number operations to solve presented math problems.
9. Creative-Figural: In each item, participants are first presented with a figural series that involves one or more transformations; they then have to apply the rule of the series to a new figure with a different appearance, and complete the new series.

We found that the data were supportive of the triarchic theory of human intelligence, yielding separate and uncorrelated analytical, creative, and practical factors. The lack of correlation was due to the inclusion of essay as well as multiple-choice subtests. Although multiple-choice tests tended to correlate substantially with multiple-choice tests, their correlations with essay tests were much weaker. We found the multiple-choice analytical subtest to be most highly related to the analytical factor, but the essay creative and performance subtests to be most highly related to their respective factors. Thus, measurement of creative and practical abilities probably ideally should be accomplished with other kinds of testing instruments that complement multiple-choice instruments.

In a second and separate study, conducted with 240 freshman-year high school students in the United States, Finland, and Spain, we used the multiple-choice section of that STAT to compare five alternative models of intelligence. A model featuring a general factor of intelligence fit the data relatively poorly. The triarchic model, allowing for intercorrelation among the analytic, creative, and practical factors, provided the best fit to the data (Sternberg, Castejón, Prieto, Hautamäki, & Grigorenko, 2001), although other related models fit the data nearly as well.

Methodological Considerations

Data were collected at 15 schools across the United States, including 8 four-year colleges, 5 community colleges, and 2 high schools (see Acknowledgments).

There were 1,013 students predominantly in their 1st year of college or their final year of high school. In this report, we discuss analyses only for college students because they were the only ones for whom we had available college performance. The final number of participants included in these analyses was 793.

Baseline measures of standardized test scores and high school GPA were collected to evaluate the predictive validity of current tools used for college admission criteria, and to provide a contrast for our current measures. Students' scores on standardized college entrance exams were obtained from the College Board.

Measuring Analytical Skills.   The measure of analytical skills was provided by the analytical items of the STAT (Sternberg, 1993) as described earlier.

Measuring Creative Skills.   Creative skills were measured by STAT multiple-choice items, as described previously, and by performance-based items. Creative skills also were measured using open-ended measures. One measure required writing two short stories with a selection from among unusual titles, such as "The Octopus's Sneakers," one required orally telling two stories based upon choices of picture collages, and the third required captioning cartoons from among various options. Open-ended performance-based answers were rated by trained raters for novelty, quality, and task appropriateness. Multiple judges were used for each task and satisfactory reliability was achieved.

Measuring Practical Skills.   Multiple-choice measures of practical skills were obtained from the STAT. Practical skills also were assessed using three situational-judgment inventories: the Everyday Situational Judgment Inventory (Movies), the Common Sense Questionnaire, and the College Life Questionnaire, each of which tap different types of tacit knowledge. The general format of tacit-knowledge inventories has been described in detail elsewhere (Sternberg et al., 2000), so only the content of the inventories used in this study is described here. The movies presented everyday situations that confront college students, such as asking for a letter of recommendation from a professor who shows, through nonverbal cues, that he does not recognize you very well. One then has to rate various options for how well they would work in response to each situation. The Common Sense Questionnaire provided everyday business problems, such as being assigned to work with a coworker whom one cannot stand, and the College Life Questionnaire provided everyday college situations for which a solution was required.

Unlike the creativity performance tasks, in the practical performance tasks the participants were not given a choice of situations to rate. For each task, participants were told that there was no "right" answer, and that the options described in each situation represented variations on how different people approach different situations.

All materials were administered either in paper-and-pencil format (for the college students, $N = 325$) or on the computer via the World Wide Web (for the college students, $N = 468$). Participants were either tested individually or in small groups. During the oral-stories section, participants who were tested in the group situation either wore headphones or were directed into a separate room to not disturb the other participants during the story dictation.There were two discrete sessions, conducted one directly after the other, for each participant. The first session included the informed-consent procedure, demographics information, the movies, the STAT batteries, and the cartoons, followed by a brief debriefing period. The second session included obtaining consent again, followed by the rest of the demographics and "additional measures" described earlier, the Common Sense or College Life Test (depending on the condition), the Written or Oral Stories (depending on the condition), and ending with the final debriefing. The order was the same for all participants. No strict time limits were set for completing the tests, although the instructors were given rough guidelines of about 70 minutes per session. The time taken to complete the battery of tests ranged from 2 to 4 hours.

As a result of the lengthy nature of the complete battery of assessments, participants were administered parts of the battery using an intentional incomplete overlapping design, as described in McArdle and Hamagami (1992; see also McArdle, 1994). The participants were randomly assigned to the test sections they were to complete. Details of the use of the procedure are in Sternberg and the Rainbow Collaborators (2003).

What We Found

Basic Statistics.   When examining college students alone, one can see that this sample also shows a slightly higher mean level of SAT than that found in colleges across the country. Our sample means on the SATs were, for 2-year college students, 490 verbal and 508 math, and for 4-year college students, 555 verbal and 575 math. These means, although slightly higher than typical, are within the range of average college students.

There is always a potential concern about restriction of range in scores using the SAT when considering students from a select sample of universities, especially when the means run a bit high. However, our sample was taken from a wide range in selectivity of institutions, from community colleges to highly select 4-year institutions. Additionally, the standard deviation of the SAT scores (for the college sample, $SD_{SAT\ Verbal} = 118.2$, and $SD_{SAT\ Math} = 117.5$) was comparable to the standard deviation of the SAT tests in the broader population. If anything, an analysis of variance test suggests that the variance for the sample for these items is statistically larger than for the typical population of SAT examinees. For these reasons, the concern of restriction of range of SAT scores across the whole sample is reduced.

Factor Structure of the Rainbow Measures.   An exploratory factor analysis was conducted to explore the factor structure underlying the Rainbow measures.

Three factors were extracted. One factor represented practical performance tests. A second, weaker factor represented the creative performance tests. A third factor represented the multiple-choice tests (including analytical, creative, and practical). Thus, method variance proved to be very important in this as in past studies (Sternberg et al., 1999). The results show the importance of measuring skills using multiple formats, precisely because method is so important in determining factorial structure.

Predicting College GPA.[1]   In order to test the incremental validity provided by Rainbow measures above and beyond the SAT in predicting GPA, a series of hierarchical regressions was conducted that included the items analyzed above in the analytical, creative, and practical assessments.

In one set of hierarchical regressions, the SAT-V, SAT-M, and High School GPA were included in the first step of the regression because these are the standard measures used today to predict college performance. Only High School GPA contributed uniquely to R^2. In Step 2 we added the analytic subtest of the STAT, because this test is closest conceptually to the SAT tests. The analytical subtest of the STAT slightly increased R^2, with a statistically significant beta-weight. In Step 3, the measures of practical ability were added, resulting in a small increase in R^2. Notably, the latent variable representing the common variance among the

---

[1]One problem when using College GPA from students across different colleges is that a high GPA from a less selective institution is equated to a high GPA from a highly selective institution. One could make the argument that the skills needed to achieve a high GPA at a selective college are greater than the skills needed to achieve a high GPA at a less selective college. There are a number of ways one could account for this problem of equated GPAs. For instance, one could assign a weight to GPA based on the selectivity of the students' institution, such that more selective institutions are given a weight that increases the GPA relative to less selective institutions. However, this procedure assumes that the variables used to predict GPA are measured independently of the weight, namely selectivity of the school. Because SAT is used to determine the selectivity of the school to which a student matriculates, and therefore results in a violation of independence of independent and dependent variables, we could not run this procedure because it would artificially inflate the relationship between SAT and weighted GPA. Adjusting for the SAT–Selectivity relationship by partialing out selectivity from the SAT would artificially deflate the relationship between SAT and weighted GPA. A second procedure would be to standardize all scores, including the dependent variable and all independent variables, within levels of selectivity of the institution, or even within each school, and then run these scores together in all analyses. This standardization procedure effectively equates students at highly selective institutions with students from less selective institutions, and produces results that would be essentially a rough summary of the analyses done within each level of selectivity or within each school. One problem with this procedure is that it loses the elegance of involving schools in a large range of selectivity (e.g., University of California–Santa Barbara vs. Mesa Community College), if all students become equated by standardization. Nevertheless, when this procedure is run, the pattern of results is essentially the same as an analysis that does not use a standardization adjustment to the data; in fact, the only substantive change is that, across the board, all coefficients become attenuated (including correlations, beta coefficients, R^2, etc.). Consequently, we have chosen to report the results based on scores that are unadjusted for institutional selectivity.

practical performance measures and High School GPA were the only variables to significantly account for variance in College GPA in Step 3. The inclusion of the creative measures in the final step of this regression indicates that, by supplementing the SAT and High School GPA with measures of analytical, practical, and creative abilities, a total of 22.4% of the variance in GPA can be accounted for. Inclusion of the Rainbow measures in Steps 2, 3, and 4 represents an increase of about 8.0% (from .164 to .244) in the variance accounted for over and above the typical predictors of College GPA. Including the Rainbow measures without High School GPA, using only SAT scores as a base, represents an increase in percentage variance accounted for of about 9.2% (from .096 to .188). Looked at in another way, this means that the Rainbow measures almost doubled prediction versus the SAT alone.

In another set of hierarchical regressions, SAT and High School GPA were entered in the last steps. These regressions showed that SAT did not add significant incremental validity above and beyond the Rainbow measures in the penultimate step, although High School GPA did in the final step. Approximately 20% of the variance in College GPA could be accounted for by using Rainbow measures alone. With the addition of High School GPA in the last step, at least one task from each of the Rainbow components also contributed to the incremental prediction of College GPA above and beyond High School GPA and the SAT.

These multiple regression analyses pose some concern because of the large number of measures used representing each of analytic, creative, and practical skills. This risks a great deal of construct overlap. To account for this problem, a final multiple regression analysis was conducted that included only High School GPA, SAT, and one measure from each of analytic, creative, and practical skills. For analytic skills, we used the only measure available from the new measures, the $STAT_{Analytical}$. For creative skills, we used the only statistically significant predictor, the oral-stories measure. For practical skills, we used the methodology that did not overlap with other methodologies in the study, namely the practical-performance measures as represented by the practical-performance latent variable. The results from this analysis support the claim that measuring analytic, creative, and practical skills using different methodologies can substantially improve on predicting College GPA beyond High School GPA and the SAT. All three representatives of the Rainbow measures and High School GPA maintained a statistically significant beta coefficient.

Group Differences.   With respect to group differences, there were two general findings. First, the Rainbow tests appear to reduce race and ethnicity differences relative to traditional assessments of abilities like the SAT. Second, the Latino students benefit the most from the reduction of group differences. The Black students, too, seem to show a reduction in difference from the White mean for most of the Rainbow tests, although a substantial difference appears to be maintained with the practical performance measures. Important reductions in differences can also be seen for the Native American students relative to White. Indeed, their median was higher for the creative tests. However, the very small sample size suggests that any conclusions about Native American performance should be made tentatively.

Although the group differences are not perfectly reduced, these findings suggest that measures can be designed that reduce ethnic and racial group differences on standardized tests, particularly for historically disadvantaged groups like Black and Latino students, at the same time that the tests *increase* prediction of college success. These findings have important implications for reducing adverse impact in college admissions.

Implications

The SAT is based on a conventional psychometric notion of cognitive skills. Using this notion, it has had substantial success in predicting college performance. But perhaps the time has come to move beyond conventional theories of cognitive skills. Based on multiple regression analyses, the Rainbow measures alone nearly double the predictive power of College GPA when compared to the SAT alone (comparing R^2 of .188 to .096, respectively). Additionally, the Rainbow measures predict an additional 8.0% of College GPA beyond the initial 16.4% contributed by the SAT and High School GPA. These findings, combined with encouraging results regarding the reduction of between-ethnicity differences, make a compelling case for furthering the study of the measurement of analytic, creative, and practical skills for predicting success in college.

One important goal for the current study, and future studies, is the creation of standardized test measures that reduce the different outcomes between different groups as much as possible to maintain test validity. Our measures suggest results toward this end. Although the group differences in the tests were not reduced to zero, the tests did substantially attenuate group differences relative to other measures such as the SAT. This finding could be an important step toward ultimately ensuring fair and equal treatment for members of diverse groups in the academic domain.

Although this first study presents a promising start for the investigation of an equitable yet powerful predictor of success in college, the study is not without its share of methodological problems. Better tests and scoring methods, larger samples, and more representative samples all are needed in future work. Future development of these tests will help sort out some of the problems borne out of the present findings.

In sum, the theory of successful intelligence appears to provide a strong theoretical basis for augmented assessment of the skills needed for college success. There is evidence to indicate that it has good incremental predictive power, and serves to increase equity. As teaching improves and college teachers emphasize more the creative and practical skills needed for success in school and life, the predictive power of the test may increase. Cosmetic changes in testing over the last century have made relatively little difference to the construct validity of assessment procedures. The theory of successful intelligence could provide a new opportunity to increase construct validity at the same time that it reduces differences in test performance between groups.

The most important lesson I learned from Gordon Bower is that what matters most is not whether you do research, or even how much research you do, but instead, the scientific and possibly even the societal impact that your research has. Whether the Rainbow Project will have such impact remains to be determined. What is clear, though, is that times have changed greatly since the early 1900s, but ability testing has not. It is time for cognitive theory, whether the theory of successful intelligence or some other theory, to have an impact on such testing.

ACKNOWLEDGMENTS

The research described here was a collaborative effort. Rainbow Project Collaborators included (in alphabetical order): Damian Birney, Brent Bridgeman, Anna Cianciolo, Wayne Camara, Michael Drebot, Sarah Duman, Richard Duran, Howard Everson, Ann Ewing, Edward Friedman, Elena L. Grigorenko, Diane Halpern, P. J. Henry, Charles Huffman, Linda Jarvin, Smaragda Kazi, Donna Macomber, Laura Maitland, Jack McArdle, Carol Rashotte, Jerry Rudmann, Amy Schmidt, Karen Schmidt, Brent Slife, Mary Spilis, Steven Stemler, Robert J. Sternberg, Carlos Torre, and Richard Wagner. University of Michigan Business School Collaborators (in order of authorship on the original report of the data): Jennifer Hedlund, Jeanne Wilt, Kristina Nebel, and Robert J. Sternberg. Other contributors to this project were Kevin Plamondon, Andrea Sacerdote Eric Goodrich, Weihua Niu, Melissa Droller, Evonne Plantinga, Mengdan Chu, Kathryn Rado, Julie Goodrich, Lisa Morgan, Donna Vann, and Robert Silaghi. Former Dean Joseph White and former Senior Associate Dean Susan Ashford of the University of Michigan Business School provided invaluable support and input on the project.

Participating institutions in the Rainbow Project included Brigham Young University; Florida State University; James Madison University; California State University–San Bernardino; University of California–Santa Barbara; Southern Connecticut State University; Stevens Institute of Technology; Yale University; Mesa Community College; Coastline Community College; Irvine Valley Community College; Orange Coast Community College; Saddleback Community College; Mepham High School; and Northview High School. Participating institution in the University of Michigan Business School Project was the University of Michigan.

REFERENCES

Binet, A., & Simon, T. (1916). *The development of intelligence in children.* Baltimore: Williams & Wilkins. (Original work published 1905)

Bridgeman, B., Burton, N., & Cline, F. (2001). *Substituting SAT II: Subject Tests for SAT I: Reasoning Test: Impact on admitted class composition and quality* (College Board Report No. 2001-3). New York: College Entrance Examination Board.

Bridgeman, B., McCamley-Jenkins, L., & Ervin, N. (2000). *Predictions of freshman grade-point average from the revised and recentered SAT I: Reasoning test* (College Board Report No. 2000-1). New York: College Entrance Examination Board.

Brody, N. (1997). Intelligence, schooling, and society. *American Psychologist, 52,* 1046–1050.

Gardner, H. (1983). *Frames of mind: The theory of multiple intelligences.* New York: Basic Books.

Gardner, H. (1999). *Intelligence reframed: Multiple intelligences for the 21st century.* New York: Basic Books.

Guilford, J. P. (1982). Cognitive psychology's ambiguities: Some suggested remedies. *Psychological Review, 89,* 48–59.

Hedlund, J., Forsythe, G. B., Horvath, J., Williams, W. M., Snook, S., & Sternberg, R. J. (2003). Identifying and assessing tacit knowledge: Understanding the practical intelligence of military leaders. *The Leadership Quarterly, 210,* 1–24.

Hedlund, J., Wilt, J. M., Nebel, K. R., Ashford, S. J., & Sternberg, R. J. (2006). Assessing practical intelligence in business school admissions: A supplement to the graduate management admissions test. *Learning and Individual Differences, 16,* 101–127.

Intelligence and its measurement: A symposium. (1921). Journal of Educational *Psychology, 12,* 123–147, 195–216, 271–275.

Kobrin, J. L., Camara, W. J., & Milewski, G. B. (2002). *The utility of the SAT I and SAT II for admissions decisions in California and the nation* (College Board Report No. 2002-6). New York: College Entrance Examination Board.

McArdle, J. J. (1994). Structural factor analysis experiments with incomplete data. *Multivariate Behavioral Research, 29*(4), 409–454.

McArdle, J. J., & Hamagami, F. (1992). Modeling incomplete longitudinal and cross-sectional data using latent growth structural models. *Experimental Aging Research, 18*(3), 145–166.

Polanyi, M. (1976). Tacit knowledge. In M. Marx & F. Goodson (Eds.), *Theories in contemporary psychology* (pp. 330–344). New York: Macmillan.

Schmidt, F. L., & Hunter, J. E. (1998). The validity and utility of selection methods in personnel psychology: Practical and theoretical implications of 85 years of research findings. *Psychological Bulletin, 124,* 262–274.

Spearman, C. (1904). "General intelligence," objectively determined and measured. *American Journal of Psychology, 15*(2), 201–293.

Sternberg, R. J. (1977). *Intelligence, information processing, and analogical reasoning: The componential analysis of human abilities.* Hillsdale, NJ: Lawrence Erlbaum Associates.

Sternberg, R. J. (1980). Sketch of a componential subtheory of human intelligence. *Behavioral and Brain Sciences, 3,* 573–584.

Sternberg, R. J. (1984). Toward a triarchic theory of human intelligence. *Behavioral and Brain Sciences, 7,* 269–287.

Sternberg, R. J. (1985). *Beyond IQ: A triarchic theory of human intelligence.* New York: Cambridge University Press.

Sternberg, R. J. (1993). *Sternberg Triarchic Abilities Test.* Unpublished test.

Sternberg, R. J. (1997). *Successful intelligence.* New York: Plume Books.

Sternberg, R. J. (1999). The theory of successful intelligence. *Review of General Psychology, 3,* 292–316.

Sternberg, R. J. (2004). Culture and intelligence. *American Psychologist, 59*(5), 325–338.

Sternberg, R. J., & Bower, G. H. (1974). Transfer in part–whole and whole–part free recall: A comparative evaluation of theories. *Journal of Verbal Learning and Verbal Behavior, 13,* 1–26.

Sternberg, R. J., Castejón, J. L., Prieto, M. D., Hautamäki, J., & Grigorenko, E. L. (2001). Confirmatory factor analysis of the Sternberg triarchic abilities test in three international samples: An empirical test of the triarchic theory of intelligence. *European Journal of Psychological Assessment, 17*(1) 1–16.

Sternberg, R. J., & Detterman, D. K. (Eds.). (1986). *What is intelligence?* Norwood, NJ: Ablex.

Sternberg, R. J., Forsythe, G. B., Hedlund, J., Horvath, J., Snook, S., Williams, W. M., Wagner, R. K., & Grigorenko, E. L. (2000). *Practical intelligence in everyday life.* New York: Cambridge University Press.

Sternberg, R. J., & Grigorenko, E. L. (2000). *Teaching for successful intelligence.* Arlington Heights, IL: Skylight Training and Publishing.

Sternberg, R. J., & Grigorenko, E. L. (2004). Intelligence and culture: how culture shapes what intelligence means, and the implications for a science of well-being. Philosophical Transaction: *Biological Sciences, 359*(1449), 1427–1434.

Sternberg, R. J., Grigorenko, E. L., Ferrari, M., & Clinkenbeard, P. (1999). A triarchic analysis of an aptitude-treatment interaction. *European Journal of Psychological Assessment, 15*(1), 1–11.

Sternberg, R. J., & Hedlund, J. (2002). Practical intelligence, g, and work psychology. *Human Performance 15*(1/2), 143–160.

Sternberg, R. J., & Horvath, J. A. (Eds.). (1999). *Tacit knowledge in professional practice.* Mahwah, NJ: Lawrence Erlbaum Associates.

Sternberg, R. J., Lautrey, J., & Lubart, T. I. (2003). Where are we in the field of intelligence, how did we get here, and where are we going? In R. J. Sternberg, J. Lautrey, & T. I. Lubart (Eds.), *Models of intelligence: International perspectives* (pp. 3–26). Washington, DC: American Psychological Association.

Sternberg, R. J., Nokes, K., Geissler, P. W., Prince R., Okatcha, F., Bundy, D. A., & Grigorenko, E. L. (2001). The relationship between academic and practical intelligence: A case study in Kenya. *Intelligence, 29,* 401–418.

Sternberg, R. J., & the Rainbow Project Collaborators (2005). Augmenting the SAT through assessments of analytical, practical, and creative skills. In W. Camara & E. Kimmel (Eds.). *Choosing students: Higher education admission tools for the 21st century* (pp. 159–176). Mahwah, NJ: Lawrence Erlbaum Associates.

Sternberg, R. J., & The Rainbow Project Collaborators (2006). The Rainbow Project: Enhancing the SAT through assessments of analytical, practical and creative skills. *Intelligence, 34*(4), 321–350.

Sternberg, R. J., The Rainbow Project Collaborators, & University of Michigan Business School Project Collaborators. (2004). Theory based university admissions testing for a new millennium. *Educational Psychologist, 39*(3), 185–198.

Sternberg, R. J., & Wagner, R. K. (1993). The geocentric view of intelligence and job performance is wrong. *Current Directions in Psychological Science, 2,* 1–5.

Sternberg, R. J., Wagner, R. K., Williams, W. M., & Horvath, J. A. (1995). Testing common sense. *American Psychologist, 32,* 912–927.

Thurstone, L. L. (1938). Primary mental abilities. Chicago: University of Chicago Press.

Wagner, R. K. (1987). Tacit knowledge in everyday intelligent behavior. *Journal of Personality and Social Psychology, 52,* 1236–1247.

Wagner, R. K., & Sternberg, R. J. (1985). Practical intelligence in real-world pursuits: The role of tacit knowledge. *Journal of Personality and Social Psychology, 49*, 436–458.

Wagner, R. K., & Sternberg, R. J. (1986). Tacit knowledge and intelligence in the everyday world. In R. J. Sternberg & R. K. Wagner (Eds.), *Practical intelligence: Nature and origins of competence in the everyday world* (pp. 51–83). New York: Cambridge University Press.

Wagner, R. K., & Sternberg, R. J. (1990). Street smarts. In K. E. Clark & M. B. Clark (Eds.), *Measures of leadership* (pp. 493–504). West Orange, NJ: Leadership Library of America.

Moving Cognition

David A. Rosenbaum
Pennsylvania State University

Shortly after I arrived at Stanford to begin my graduate work in experimental psychology, a just-published book was making the rounds of Jordan Hall. It was *Human Associative Memory,* by John Anderson and Gordon Bower (1973). John had recently received his PhD from Stanford, having completed his thesis under Gordon's direction. *Human Associative Memory* was based on John's doctoral dissertation.

I read the book not just to learn what John and Gordon had been thinking about, but also to see what was expected of a typical Gordon Bower graduate student—a comprehensive theory of an entire body of literature, replete with equations and beautiful diagrams showing theoretical structures and predicted as well as obtained data patterns for scores of well-crafted experiments. The book was about 525 pages long. Rumor had it that the volume was revolutionary. It occurred to me that if this was the sort of thing I was supposed to produce as a graduate student under Gordon, I was in deep trouble.

As I dug deeper into the book, focusing more on what it had to say than on the fears it aroused in me, I realized that for all its profundity, the theory was somewhat limited in scope. It focused on memory for sentences—an important topic to be sure, but obviously not the only thing human associative memory was about. In particular, it ignored what for me was an extremely important feature of memory—the capacity to learn and refine perceptual-motor skills. The reason this particular feature of memory was important to me was that I was then, and still am today, a serious amateur violinist. Since age 9, I have practiced the violin on a regular basis, played with orchestras and chamber groups, and even given some recitals (mostly to forgiving friends). Learning to play the violin, and seeking to learn to play particular pieces of increasing difficulty, has been a lifelong endeavor for me. The fact that some of the pieces I have tried to learn were only mastered (to the extent they were) late in life explains why I have earned my living as an experimental psychologist rather than as a concert musician.

The material in *Human Associative Memory* did have things to say about learning to play the violin because violin playing relies on human memory, and aspects of violin playing are associative. For example, the right hand is associated with bowing whereas the left hand is not. For the left hand, a given pitch is played on a given string at a particular point along the length of the string, although a given point along the length of a string need not be played with a particular finger. Playing a piece from memory entails recalling which fingers go down where on the four strings of the violin, not to mention the timing and dynamics of both the left and right hands.

As I considered the cognitive substrates of violin playing, letting my thinking wander from John and Gordon's book, I realized that what excited me most was not how any given piece of music is *recalled,* but how it is played for the first time, whether improvised or, more commonly, read from a score. In reading music, one rarely sees fingerings; that is, seldom does one see numbers above notes, indicating which finger should be pressed on which string. Instead, the player is on his or her own. He or she must not only determine which finger should be placed on which string for an individual note; he or she must look ahead and create a plan that takes into account the past and future demands of the piece to be played. For instance, if note n will be an octave above note $n-1$, it may be best to play note $n-1$ note with the index finger on one string so note n can be played with the little finger on the next higher string. Much of the skill of violin playing is reflected in the ability to plan effectively for entire sequences of notes.

The same sort of planning is called for in other musical domains. A familiar example is deciding which fingering to use while playing the piano. More broadly, the problem of motor planning arises in everyday activities. Deciding how to lift a glass, pick coffee beans, make a bed, dig a ditch, or clear dishes are all cognitively demanding planning tasks. That people who earn their livings performing these tasks are paid poorly does not diminish the computational challenges the tasks present. An indication of the computational difficulty of such tasks is that no modern robots can perform them under autonomous control in cluttered or unpredictable environments.

FEATURES AND EDITING

Appreciating that perceptual-motor performance relies on sophisticated cognitive capacities, I decided at the end of my first year of graduate school to devote my research to the planning and control of physical actions. Gordon was kind enough to sanction my foray into this topic though he was aware that very little had been done on it. He encouraged me to get in touch with others who had already recognized the potential value of a cognitive approach to motor planning and control. At the same time, he indicated that because this topic was so little studied, I would be forgiven for not ending my graduate days with a monograph on the scale of his and John's magnum opus (or a draft thereof).

As I began to study the literature on motor control and consulted with the few others who had delved into this topic—notably Steven Keele at the University of Oregon and Stuart Klapp at Cal State Hayward—I came to think that it would be useful to think of motor programming (the planning and preparation of movements) in terms of the specification of desired movement features.

Selective Adaptation

I pursued this idea in three ways. One was to adapt a method used by perceptionists for studying perceptual features. The method is called selective adaptation. A well-known example is related to the waterfall illusion. If one stares at a waterfall and then gazes at a stationary scene, that scene seems, paradoxically, to move upward. The illusion has been ascribed to mechanisms specialized for upward visual motion that "take over" for mechanisms specialized for downward visual motion after the latter mechanisms have become selectively adapted as a result of prolonged activation. Applying this procedure to movement, I found that a similar effect could be observed in the motor domain, at least using the rate at which one could perform a repetitive task as a proxy for an observer's phenomenal experience (Rosenbaum, 1977).

I asked Stanford undergraduates to turn a crank as quickly as possible for a brief period, either in the clockwise direction or in the counterclockwise direction and with either the left hand or right. I found that the participants could turn the crank more quickly if they had just turned it in the opposite direction (clockwise or counterclockwise) with the other hand than if they had just turned it in the same direction with the other hand. This outcome was consistent with the hypothesis that selective adaptation applies to movement as well as to the visual perception of movement. To the extent that selective adaptation could be ascribed to mechanisms associated with particular features of motor output, one could hypothesize that such mechanisms exist for clockwise versus counterclockwise movements of the arm.

Precuing

The selective adaptation procedure does not allow one to draw inferences about the time course of feature activation during movement programming. Such inferences are important if one wants to understand the translation of intentions into physical actions, which I did in this period, in the heyday of information-processing psychology.

The question I sought to answer was this: If one is going to move one's hand in some direction over some extent, when is it determined which hand should be used, which direction should be pursued, and which extent should be covered? The hypothesis I considered was that the three putative movement features of hand, direction, and extent are specified in an order that corresponds to the difficulty of correcting possible mistakes in their specification. For a task in which it is critical to move just one hand and not the other, it is impossible to correct a hand mistake once the switch for a wrong hand is opened. Thus, it is very important to get the hand choice correct. It is easier to correct a direction error than a hand error, and it is easier still to correct an extent error than a direction error (Megaw, 1972; Vince & Welford, 1967). If hand, direction, and extent are specified in an order that corresponds to their ease of error correction, one would p r edict these features to be specified in a fixed order: hand, then direction, and then extent.

I tested this prediction using a method I called the movement precuing technique (Rosenbaum, 1980, 1983). The method, as instantiated in the main experiment I performed, had subjects rest their left and right index fingers on two buttons, after which a stimulus was presented that signaled the subjects to reach one of eight targets distinguished by the hand to be used (left or right), the direction to be pursued (away from the torso or toward the torso), and the extent to be c overed (long or short). Subjects were told to minimize the time between the onset of the signal and placement of the appropriate finger (left or right index) on the designated target. Before the "go" stimulus was presented, a precue wa s given about some, none, or all of the features of the movement that would be called for. All possible combinations or zero, one, two, and three features were precued.

The experiment had three main outcomes. First, movement initiation times increased as fewer features were precued. Second, for a given number of precued features, movement initiation times were shortest when hand was precued and were longest when extent was precued. Third, times to specify the features that were not precued, as estimated by differences in choice reaction times, were additive.

I interpreted these outcomes as follows. The third outcome suggested that the features were specified serially, the second outcome suggested that it took more time to specify hand than direction and more time to specify direction than extent, and the first outcome argued against the fixed-order hypothesis: If the features had to be specified in a fixed order, subjects would have been equally slow to start whenever the first feature was omitted from the precue, regardless of whether the second or third feature was also precued. Likewise, if the features had to be specified in a fixed order, subjects would have been equally slow to start whenever the second feature was omitted from the precue regardless of whether the third feature was also precued.

If the features of the motor program were specified serially but not in a fixed order, they must have been specified one at a time and in a variable order. What might be the advantage of a variable order? I suggested that motor programming works by changing just those features that distinguish the motor act to be performed from the motor act that was just performed. This proposed method is computationally more efficient than generating the next needed motor program from scratch regardless of its relation to the movement that was just performed.

Parameter Remapping

If motor programming works by changing features that distinguish what needs to be done from what one has just been done, it should take less time to perform motor sequences that entail few feature changes than many. I had an experience playing the violin that confirmed this prediction.

At a rehearsal of a community orchestra, we violinists were supposed to play a passage of alternating bowstrokes over and over again very quickly with the following pattern: (a) long down; (b) short up, short up; (c) short down, short down; (d) long up; (e) short down, short down; (f) short up, short up. Playing the passage was very difficult. What made it so? The passage was not hard because we had to alternate up and down bow strokes. That is something even beginning players can do. What made it hard was that the associations between stroke directions and stroke durations kept changing. Changing stroke durations is not hard in and of itself, for when we played patterns fully defined by a long downstroke followed by two short upstrokes or vice versa, we could do so easily, presumably because the associations between bow directions and bow durations were fixed.

If changing associations between aspects of successive movements affects the speed with which those movements can be made, one should be able to obtain more than anecdotal evidence for the effect. Furthermore, one should be able to find evidence for the effect in domains other than community-orchestra violin playing.

My colleagues and I obtained such evidence in a series of experiments on rapid speech and button pushing (Rosenbaum, Weber, Hazelett, & Hindorff, 1986). The results of one of the rapid speech experiments is shown in Figure 12–1. Here, college students tried to repeat the first n letters of the alphabet over and over as quickly as possible under the stipulation that they always alternated between stressed and unstressed pronunciations. When n was even, the mappings between stress levels and letters remained the same in successive cycles (e.g.,

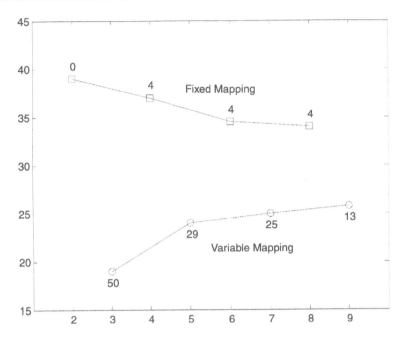

Figure 12–1.   Mean number of letters recited in 10 seconds of rapid speech when successive letters were stressed or unstressed. Number of errors are listed with each point. For even-length lists, the mapping of stress level to letters was fixed, but for odd-length lists, the mapping of stress level to letters was variable. From Rosenbaum et al. (1986). Adapted by permission.

AbCdAbCd …). However, when n was odd, the mappings between stress levels and letters changed in successive cycles (e.g., AbCaBbC …).

As shown in Figure 12–1, subjects performed most poorly when they had to say the first $n = 3$ letters of the alphabet over and over again in this alternating-stress task. By contrast, they performed the best when n equaled 2. In general, when n was odd, mean recitation rate increased with n. When n was even, mean recitation rate decreased with n.

It is easy to account for these results in terms conducive to the inspiration for the experiment. The more recently a letter was spoken, the greater the benefit of being able to say it with the same stress level as before, but the greater the cost of having to say it with a *different* stress level. Evidently, the need to change associations slows performance, regardless of whether the associations involve bow directions and bow durations, letters and stress levels, or, as shown in other experiments reported in our 1986 paper, buttons and number of button presses.

HIERARCHICAL CONTROL

If motor programming is achieved by changing features of successive movements, there must be a way of controlling those changes. Some plan must guide the changes. What are its properties?

A popular and, I think, useful hypothesis about plans for movement sequences is that they are hierarchical. There is an intuitive basis for this suggestion: One has an overarching objective, and for that overarching objective to be achieved, subordinate objectives must be achieved. The notion of hierarchy dates back at least to Bryan and Harter (1897) and finds support in errors made in speech (Garrett, 1975), typewriting (Cooper, 1983), and other action domains (Norman, 1981). In the case of speech, distinct levels of representation for language production have been inferred from semantic errors ("Professor, I really hated ... I mean I really liked your course"), syntactic errors ("I'm writing a mother to my letter"), morphological errors ("slicely thinned bread"), and phonological errors ("flow snurries"). These sorts of errors as well as other features of speech suggest that words are assembled out of their constituents during production. The fact that the errors appear to be of distinct types and that exchanges almost always involve the same types of constituents (Garrett, 1975) suggest that the assembly of words occurs at each of a number of levels. Similar findings apply to typewriting (Cooper, 1983) and other activities (Norman, 1981).

There is another source of support for hierarchical organization of movement-sequence plans—the times involved in generating the sequences. If one assumes that sequences of movements are governed hierarchically, times between movements should be longer at major chunk boundaries than at minor chunk boundaries. Analyses of times to generate sequences of movements from memory bear out this prediction. These analyses were inspired by studies of timing in more classical cognitive domains. When chess experts return chess pieces to a board after the pieces have been removed from a midgame configuration, the pieces are returned with short pauses within chunks and with long pauses between chunks (Simon, 1972). Similar results come from studies of verbal recall of semantically organized lists (Reitman & Rueter, 1980). The latter results indicate that hierarchical organization not only increases the likelihood that word lists will be recalled correctly (Bower, Clark, Lesgold, & Winzenz, 1969). It also influences the way the lists are "unpacked" in real time.

Rapid Finger Tapping

In 1983, I coauthored a paper (Rosenbaum, Kenny, & Derr, 1983) showing that the timing of rapid keyboard sequences also relies on hierarchical plans. Our subjects memorized simple finger-tapping sequences that they performed with their left and right index and middle fingers. One such sequence was *MmMmIiIi*, where *M* and *I* denote the right middle and index fingers, and *m* and *i* denote the left middle and index fingers. This sequence, like the others in the experiment, was repeated over and over as quickly as possible from memory. All the sequences alternated between the left and right hands and repeated the finger of a hand before the other finger of that same hand was used again.

It is natural to break *MmMmIiIi* into two groups of four responses each, and to break each of these four-response groups into 2 two-response groups. Participants in our study seemed to do this, for the times between their key presses depended on the putative change in levels associated with the transitions. Interresponse intervals (IRIs) were longest in going from the first half of the sequence to the second and in going from the last half of the sequence back to the first half. Similarly, the IRIs were shorter in going from the first quarter of the sequence to the second quarter and in going from the third quarter to the fourth. Finally, the IRIs were shortest for the remaining transitions. We modeled the IRIs in terms of a tree-traversal process, which is a systematic procedure for unpacking chunks into their constituents. The errors we recorded were consistent with this model.

The results of the study by Rosenbaum et al. (1983), along with other results published around the same time (Povel & Collard, 1982), indicated that hierarchical organization is not limited to verbal categories or to symbolic categories such as chess positions, but extends as well to rapid finger tapping. This outcome pointed to a cognitive basis for motor control (Rosenbaum, Carlson, & Gilmore, 2001). Furthermore, the fact that the IRIs in the study of Rosenbaum et al. (1983) were close to a tenth of a second indicates that the mental operations associated with access to hierarchical plans can be very rapid.

Hierarchical Editing

How are hierarchical plans formed? Later experiments, summarized in a volume edited by Gordon Bower (Rosenbaum, 1987), addressed this question. These experiments, like the ones by Rosenbaum et al. (1983) and Povel and Collard (1982), used rapid finger tapping. In contrast to the earlier studies, the later experiments did not have participants simply tap out sequences from memory. Instead, participants memorized two possible sequences and waited for a choice signal to indicate which sequence had to be performed in a given trial. The idea behind the procedure was that holding two possible sequences in mind and having to choose between them might yield patterns of choice reaction times that could shed light on the dynamics of motor planning.

Two findings were of special interest. One was that the time to make the first response of the chosen sequence increased as the two possible sequences got longer. Second, the time to make the first response of the chosen sequence was affected by the similarity of the two possible sequences. If the two possible sequences began the same way, the more initial responses they shared, the shorter was the choice time.

A model that could account for these findings was a slightly elaborated version of the tree-traversal model described above. According to the elaborated model, motor plans are represented hierarchically and are unpacked via tree-traversal. Furthermore, choosing between one sequence and another is achieved by descending the hierarchy as much as possible until a point of uncertainty is reached, whereupon the choice of how to proceed awaits identification of the choice signal. Once the choice is made, the chosen path is descended further, and all subsequent choice points are checked so any other initially uncertain choices are resolved. After this first edit pass through the hierarchy, control returns to the top of the tree and the plan is executed via traversal of the now pruned tree.

This *hierarchal editor* model, as I called it, accounted for the data from the sequence choice experiments my colleagues and I conducted. The first finding reviewed earlier, that choice RT increased as sequence length increased, was explained by the depth of the tree that had to be traversed during the edit pass. The second finding, that choice RT decreased as the serial position of the first uncertain receded from the starting position, was explained by the fact that a shorter edit pass was needed for sequence choices that had many shared initial responses than for sequence choices that had few shared initial responses.

KEYFRAMES

At least two unresolved questions remain from the preceding discussion. One is whether the hierarchical editor model generalizes to other sorts of movements. The other is whether the editing described in connection with the hierarchical editor model is the same as the editing described earlier in connection with precuing and the parameter remapping effect, where I used the term "editing" to refer to changing features of just-used plans to specify next-used plans.

The answer to both questions can be linked to a single concept: keyframes (see Figure 12–2). Keyframes are used in computer animation (Lasseter, 1987). They constitute critical images, between which intermediate images or "interframes" are inserted. Animation procedures that use keyframing rely on techniques for forming series of interframes. Computer programs for running keyframe-based animations (stored in .mpg format) use much less memory than programs that fully describe each frame (stored in .avi format).

Editing and Keyframing

Keyframing provides an answer to the question raised earlier about the nature of editing: There are two kinds of editing in keyframing and, one could say, in motor programming as well. One kind occurs at the level of keyframes. The other kind occurs at the level of interframes. Editing at the level of keyframes involves specifying subgoals between which movements are made. Editing at the level of

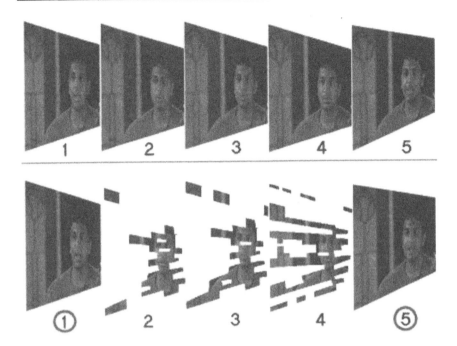

Figure 12–2. Two methods of computer animation. Top panel: Storing every frame completely. Bottom panel: Using keyframes along with interframes that only contain successive differences. From public-domain Web site http://nickyguides .digital-digest.com/keyframes.htm.

interframes defines the movements to be made. In terms of the tree-structure metaphor used previously, editing at the level of keyframes amounts to specifying the nodes of the tree. The information in these nodes either can specify the contents beneath them or they can specify how each node differs from the node before. The latter method is the one suggested by my work with parameter remapping and movement precuing.

The Generality of Keyframing

Can one validate the distinction between keyframes and interframes in the domain of motor control? My colleagues and I have approached this question while trying to address the other question raised earlier: Does hierarchical editing generalize to other sorts of movements? We have pursued these issues by studying reaching and grasping. Specifically, we have examined anticipatory effects in object manipulation, for reasons given later, and we have developed a computational model of reaching control that relies on the distinction between keyframes and interframes.

Anticipatory Effects in Reaching

If the keyframing perspective applies to motor control, future states of the body should be represented. In connection with reaching and grapsing, people should grasp objects differently depending on what they will do with the objects.

In agreement with this prediction, we have found that anticipatory effects are widespread in object manipulation. In one study (Rosenbaum et al., 1990), we asked college students to reach out for a rod lying flat on two small cradles. In one condition, the subjects were told before reaching the rod that they would place the *left* end of the rod onto a horizontal surface. In another condition, they were told before reaching the rod that they would place the *right* end of the rod onto a horizontal surface (see Fig. 12–3). We asked our participants to grasp the rod firmly with the right hand, and we found that all participants grasped the rod with an overhand grip when the right end of the rod was to be placed on the surface, and all participants grasped the rod with an underhand grip when the left end of the rod was to be placed on the surface. Whether the horizontal surface was on the left or right did not affect the probability of overhand or underhand grasps.

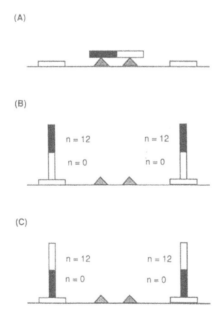

Figure 12–3.   Object manipulation tasks and results. (A) A rod lying on two cradles. (B) When the white end was brought down onto a surface on the left or right, all 12 subjects took hold of the rod with the right thumb pointing toward the black end of the rod (overhand grasp). (C) When the black end was brought down onto the left or right surface, all 12 subjects took hold of the rod with the right thumb pointing toward the white end of the rod (underhand grasp). From Rosenbaum et al. (1990). Copyright 1990 by Lawrence Erlbaum Associates.

The explanation we gave for subjects' grasp choices was that subjects tolerated initial discomfort for the sake of final comfort or control. Lifting the rod with a comfortable (overhand) grasp was consistent with final comfort or control when the *right* end of the rod was brought down to a target, but lifting the rod with an overhand grasp was inconsistent with final comfort or control if the left end of the rod was brought down onto a target. Participants' ratings of comfort confirmed that overhand grasps were more comfortable than underhand grasps and that thumb-up grasps were more comfortable than thumb-down grasps. Apparently, subjects tolerated initial discomfort for the sake of final comfort, consistent with the idea that keyframes were established for the task.

These findings were replicated and extended in other studies, both in our lab and elsewhere (see Rosenbaum, Cohen, Meulenbroek, & Vaughan, 2006, for a review). The anticipatory effects were not restricted to choices of overhand or underhand grasps. In another series of experiments (Cohen & Rosenbaum, 2004), we found that participants grasped a standing cylinder at different heights depending on the height to which they would next bring the cylinder (Fig. 12–4). Our interpretation of this result was that participants sought to avoid extreme joint angles at the ends of the object transport maneuvers, just as they sought to avoid uncomfortable postures at the ends of the rod placement maneuvers summarized in Figure 12–3.

A Computational Model of Reaching

If the distinction between keyframes and interframes is correct, it should be possible to show that the distinction provides a basis for an effective computational model of movement generation. My colleagues and I have developed such a model and have found that it does a reasonably good job of simulating observed movements (Jax, Rosenbaum, Vaughan, & Meulenbroek, 2003; Rosenbaum, Meulenbroek, Vaughan, & Jansen, 2001; Rosenbaum et al., 1995).

The core concept of the model is that movements provide bridges between goal positions. Said another way, the motor system specifies goal positions before specifying movements to those goal positions. Movements, in the model, are treated as interpolations or interframes between goal positions (cf. Bullock & Grossberg, 1988; Latash, 1993).

Our model has other components as well. One is that goal positions are not just defined in terms of spatial coordinates, but are also defined in terms of body coordinates. Goal positions defined in terms of spatial coordinates are places one wants to go. Goal positions defined in terms of body coordinates are postures one wants to assume. Goal postures are needed to define movements.

Another component of the model is its way of specifying goal postures and movements. These are not specified by optimization, as in other models of movement generation (Todorov, 2004), but by satisficing (i.e., finding adequate solutions; Simon, 1955). Our model relies on satisficing because optimization can be computationally taxing, at least given known methods of optimizing multiple

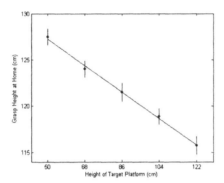

Figure 12–4. Grasping a cylinder (a bathroom plunger) at different heights depending on the height to which it will be brought. Top panel: The author testing a participant who has just taken hold of the cylinder at its constant home position before placing the cylinder on the top target platform (122 cm above the floor). The participant gave permission to be shown here. Bottom panel: Mean grasp heights (±1 SE) as a function of the height of the target platform. Bottom panel from Cohen and Rosenbaum (2004).

costs (cf. Dornay, Uno, Kawato, & Suzuki, 1996). In our model, satisficing is done with respect to prioritized constraints defining each task to be performed (Tversky, 1972).

The final component of the model mentioned here is the model's method for interpolating between goal postures. By default, we assume straight-line trajectories through joint space from starting postures to goal postures. The spacing of the points along the trajectory yields a bell-shaped speed profile (Hogan, 1984). However, if the forthcoming movement is predicted to result in an unwanted collision or to have an unwanted shape (e.g., a straight line when one wants to draw a curved line), the movement can be shaped accordingly (see Rosenbaum et al., 2001, for details).

A detailed review of the strengths and weaknesses of the model is impossible here, although it is important to note, in the spirit of full disclosure, that, for computational convenience only, the model has so far been restricted to kinematics (i.e., positions without regard to forces and torques). Forces and torques have yet to be incorporated but ultimately they must be.

Apart from the possibility that all the model's achievements must be taken with a grain of salt until forces and torques have been dealt with, the list of behaviors it can simulate and findings it can explain are encouraging. Here, I mention four such signs.

One is that the model can generate writing that looks the same no matter which effectors are used to produce it (Meulenbroek et al., 1996). This result constitutes a possible solution to a long-standing problem in motor control—the problem of *motor equivalence:* How does one manage to produce writing that maintains one's personal style even when different muscle groups are used to produce it (e.g., on a bank check or scrawled across a blackboard)? As far as I know, our model is the first and, so far, only model that can solve this problem.

Second, our model can generate realistic simulations of reach-and-grasp movements, including reaches around obstacles (Fig. 12–5). A detailed, quantitative

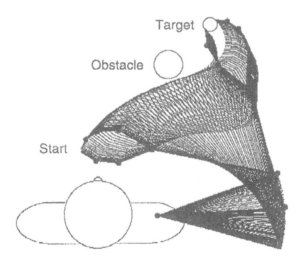

Figure 12–5. Simulated reach for an object after avoiding an obstacle. From Rosenbaum et al. (2001). Copyright 2001 by the American Psychological Association. Reprinted by permission. Third, the model provides a way of explaining how actors can compensate immediately for changes in the mobility of individual joints. Such compensation is easily achieved because the model relies on goal postures. If it becomes difficult to rotate a joint because of a sore tendon, say, a goal posture is selected that requires little rotation of that joint. This approach to compensation is simpler and more robust than other methods (cf. Mussa-Ivaldi, Morasso, & Zaccaria, 1988), an outcome that is attributable to the models' reliance on keyframing (i.e., specification of goal postures followed by specification of moves to those goal postures).

analysis of the similarities between modeled reach-and-grasp movements and actual reach-and-grasp movements showed that the model's reaches were very similar to those of human subjects (Rosenbaum et al., 2001).

Fourth and finally, our model provides an account of the finding that variability of hand positions increases as the hand leaves for a target and then decreases as the hand approaches the target. This nonmonotonic relation, which holds even when the movement is made without visual feedback (Darling & Cooke, 1987; Harris & Wolpert, 1998), is just what one would expect if there were a level of representation for terminal positions (keyframes) and a subordinate level for movements between those terminal positions (movements or interframes).

CONCLUSIONS

This chapter has reviewed some of the research by one of Gordon Bower's former students. A noteworthy feature of the research is that it is a bit removed from the work that Gordon has pursued himself. That Gordon countenanced my excursion into the field of motor control is a tribute to his open-mindedness and trust, both of which were important to me as I began the journey that has kept me, my colleagues, and my students (some of Gordon's academic "grandchildren") busy.

I would like to close this chapter with three final observations. One is that the problem that got me interested in motor control in the first place—understanding violin playing—has remained a goal of my scientific work. In this connection, it is gratifying that colleagues of mine in the Netherlands recently applied our model to the analysis of guitar fingering (Heijenk & Meulenbroek, 2002).

My second final observation pertains to the growing appreciation of motor imagery and internal simulation of action for understanding external events, including language (Barsalou, 1999; Glenberg & Kaschak, 2002; Zwaan & Taylor, 2006). It is heartening to me as a motor-control researcher that investigators concerned with higher level cognition see the relevance of movement to their concerns. On the other hand, it is important not to view movement generation, whether overt and covert, as a panacea. Generating the right movement is nontrivial, and it remains to be seen whether generating movement or the experiencing already generated movement promotes comprehension.

My final observation is triggered by the reference earlier to academic grandchildren. Gordon was the academic grandchild of John B. Watson, who was the most avid, or some might say most rabid, advocate of behaviorism. Watson and his disciples wanted rigor in behavioral science, a value Gordon and his students adopted, though in different form from Watson's. Surprisingly, Watson, or more specifically B. F. Skinner, was less interested in the detailed bodily expression of behavior than most people realize. Skinner, in particular, was avowedly uninterested in movement per se because all that he (or his theory) cared about were the instrumental outcomes of behavior. It was Gordon's adviser, Neil Miller, who became one of the most "body-centered" researchers in 20th century American psychology. Neil Miller's orientation, coupled with Gordon's own early career as an almost-big-league-baseball player, may have predisposed Gordon to include the psychological analysis of motor control in his portfolio of well-supervised research.

REFERENCES

Anderson, J. R., & Bower, G. H. (1973). *Human associative memory.* Washington, DC: Winston.

Barsalou, L. W. (1999). Perceptual symbol systems. *Behavioral and Brain Sciences, 22,* 577–660.

Bower, G. H., Clark, M., Lesgold, A., & Winzenz, D. (1969). Hierarchical retrieval schemes in recall of categorized word lists. *Journal of Verbal Learning and Verbal Behavior, 8,* 323–443.

Bryan, W. L., & Harter, N. (1897). Studies in the physiology and psychology of the telegraphic language. *Psychological Review, 4,* 27–53.

Bullock, D., & Grossberg, S. (1988). Neural dynamics of planned arm movements: Emergent invariants and speed–accuracy properties during trajectory formation. *Psychological Review, 95,* 49–90.

Cohen, R. G., & Rosenbaum, D. A. (2004). Where objects are grasped reveals how grasps are planned: Generation and recall of motor plans. *Experimental Brain Research, 157,* 486–495.

Cooper, W. E. (Ed.). (1983). *Cognitive aspects of skilled typewriting.* New York: Springer-Verlag.

Darling, W. G., & Cooke, J. D. (1987). Changes in the variability of movement trajectories with practice. *Journal of Motor Behavior, 19,* 291–309.

Dornay, M., Uno, Y., Kawato, M., & Suzuki, R. (1996). Minimum muscle-tension change trajectories predicted by using a 17-muscle model of the monkey's arm. *Journal of Motor Behavior, 2,* 83–100.

Garrett, M. F. (1975). The analysis of sentence production. In G. H. Bower (Ed.), *Psychology of learning and motivation* (Vol. 9, pp. 133–177). New York: Academic Press.

Glenberg, A. M., & Kaschak, M. P. (2002). Grounding language in action. *Psychonomic Bulletin & Review, 9,* 558–565.

Harris, C. M., & Wolpert, D. M. (1998). Signal-dependent noise determines motor planning. *Nature, 394,* 780–784.

Hogan, N. (1984). An organizing principle for a class of voluntary movements. The *Journal of Neuroscience, 4,* 2745–2754.

Jax, S. A., Rosenbaum, D. A., Vaughan, J., & Meulenbroek, R. G. J. (2003). Computational motor control and human factors: Modeling movements in real and possible environments. *Human Factors, 45,* 5–27.

Lasseter, J. (1987). Principles of traditional animation applied to 3D computer animation. *Computer Graphics, 21,* 35–44.

Latash, M. L. (1993). *Control of human movement.* Champaign, IL: Human Kinetics.

Megaw, E. D. (1972). Direction and extent uncertainty in step-input tracking. *Journal of Motor Behavior, 4,* 171–186.

Meulenbroek, R. G. J., Rosenbaum D. A., Thomassen, A. J. W. M., Loukopoulos, L. D., & Vaughan, J. (1996). Adaptation of a reaching model to handwriting: How different effectors can produce the same written output, and other results. *Psychological Research, 59,* 64–74.

Mussa-Ivaldi, F. A., Morasso, P., & Zaccaria, R. (1988). Kinematic networks: A distributed model for representing and regularizing motor redundancy. *Biological Cybernetics, 60,* 1–16.

Norman, D. A. (1981). Categorization of action slips. *Psychological Review, 88,* 1–15.

Povel, D.-J., & Collard, R. (1982). Structural factors in patterned finger tapping. Acta *Psychologica, 52,* 107–124.

Reitman, J. S., & Rueter, H. H. (1980). Organization revealed by recall orders and confirmed by pauses. *Cognitive Psychology, 12,* 554–581.

Rosenbaum, D. A. (1977). Selective adaptation of "command neurons" in the human motor system. *Neuropsychologia, 15,* 81–91.

Rosenbaum, D. A. (1980). Human movement initiation: Specification of arm, direction, and extent. *Journal of Experimental Psychology: General, 109,* 444–474.

Rosenbaum, D. A. (1983). The movement precuing technique: Assumptions, applications, and extensions. In R. A. Magill (Ed.), *Memory and control of action* (pp. 231–274). Amsterdam: North-Holland.

Rosenbaum, D. A. (1987). Successive approximations to a model of human motor programming. In G. H. Bower (Ed.), *Psychology of learning and motivation* (Vol. 21, pp. 153–182). Orlando, FL: Academic Press.

Rosenbaum, D. A., Carlson, R. A., & Gilmore, R. O. (2001) Acquisition of intellectual and perceptual-motor skills. *Annual Review of Psychology, 52,* 453–470.

Rosenbaum, D. A., Cohen, R. G., Meulenbroek, R. G., & Vaughan, J. (2006). Plans for grasping objects. In M. Latash & F. Lestienne (Ed.), *Motor control and learning over the lifespan* (pp. 9–25). New York: Springer.

Rosenbaum, D. A., Kenny, S., & Derr, M. A. (1983). Hierarchical control of rapid movement sequences. *Journal of Experimental Psychology: Human Perception and Performance, 9,* 86–102.

Rosenbaum, D. A., Loukopoulos, L. D., Meulenbroek, R. G. M., Vaughan, J., & Engelbrecht, S. E. (1995). Planning reaches by evaluating stored postures. *Psychological Review, 102,* 28–67.

Rosenbaum, D. A., Marchak, F., Barnes, H. J., Vaughan, J., Slotta, J., & Jorgensen, M. (1990). Constraints for action selection: Overhand versus underhand grips. In M. Jeannerod (Ed.), *Attention and performance XIII: Motor representation and control* (pp. 321–342). Hillsdale, NJ: Lawrence Erlbaum Associates.

Rosenbaum, D. A., Meulenbroek, R. G., Vaughan, J., & Jansen, C. (2001). Posture-based motion planning: Applications to grasping. *Psychological Review, 108,* 709–734.

Rosenbaum, D. A., Weber, R. J., Hazelett, W. M., & Hindorff, V. (1986). The parameter remapping effect in human performance: Evidence from tongue twisters and finger fumblers. *Journal of Memory and Language, 25,* 710–725.

Simon, H. (1955). A behavioral model of rational choice. *Quarterly Journal of Economics, 69,* 99–118.

Simon, H. A. (1972). Complexity and the representation of patterned sequences of symbols. *Psychological Review, 79,* 369–382.

Todorov, E. (2004). Optimality principles in sensorimotor control. *Nature Neuroscience, 7,* 907–915.

Tversky, A. (1972). Elimination by aspects: A theory of choice. *Psychological Review, 79,* 281–299.

Vince, M. A., & Welford, A. T. (1967). Time taken to change the speed of a response. *Nature, 213,* 532–533.

Zwaan, R. A., & Taylor, L. J. (2006). Seeing, acting, understanding: Motor resonance in language comprehension. *Journal of Experimental Psychology: General, 135,* 1–11.

13

Imaginary Worlds

John B. Black
Teachers College, Columbia University

Leaders today seem to be suffering from what might be called a failure of the imagination. We seem to be continually finding ourselves in situations where the leaders say something like "no one could have imagined that this would happen." For example: Who could imagined that Hurricane Katrina would breach the levies in New Orleans; who could have imagined that an insurgency would arise from the U.S. invasion of Iraq; who could have imagined that falling foam could critically damage a space shuttle; who could have imagined that people would crash airplanes into buildings; and so forth. Some time after such statements were made it has turned out that people did imagine such possibilities, so it was humanly possible, but the decision makers were committed to one way of thinking about these things and so did not imagine alternative ways that the world might turn out than what they expected. For several years I have been studying various aspects of imaginary worlds, when and how people construct and use them; but in looking back now I see that the seeds of this work were laid in the story understanding and memory research I did with Gordon Bower in the later 1970s.

Particularly striking in retrospect is a paragraph that appeared in a paper we published in the journal *Poetics* in 1980 (Black & Bower, 1980). The initial parts of this paper critiqued the extant story grammar theories of story understanding and memory, then proposed that the structure of stories could be characterized as one or more story characters acting on the world of the story trying to move the state of that world from the initial state to a goal state (i.e., problem solving in the Newell & Simon, 1972, sense) and that the critical path of state transitions (actions and events) that described the change that did occur would be the best remembered (and the further off that path the worse the memory). We presented a variety of data to support our approach, and it was our version of the basic proposal originally made by Schank (1975) that story memory is a causal and intentional network of actions, events, and states. I have done subsequent research that supports this basic idea (e.g., Black & Bern, 1981), but it has since been formalized and much more extensively researched by Trabasso, Graesser and their colleagues (see Goldman, Graesser, & Van den Broek, 1999).

However, the paragraph that struck me in a recent reading appeared near the end of the paper where, perhaps inspired by being in a journal called *Poetics*, we took poetic license (going beyond our existing formal research) and said the following in a section labeled "Storyworld" (pp. 247–248):

> Readers report that they construct visual images of the scenes being described in stories. They say they use the text to construct and enact a play in the theater of their mind's eye. Perhaps they even sit on top of the shoulders of the characters with whom they identify. We could dismiss such introspections as irrelevant epiphenomena if we could be sure that our theoretically reconstructed hierarchy of propositions and plans characterizing the subject's story knowledge were a complete rendering. However, it is likely that the subject's image of the storyworld has information implicit in it beyond that available in the propositional listing of the scene. The subject can up-date and "see" dynamic changes of characters, objects, and locations in his storyworld: he has available for inspection not only the starting and ending state of a character's motion but also intermediate points along the dynamic path. The reader can "see" that objects afford or suggest certain actions and prevent others. Furthermore, the reader's storyworld model allows him to experiment with hypothetical changes in his imagination. So he can imagine what would have happened had circumstances been different in the storyworld. Thus, readers can answer questions like, "How could this story have been different if Superman had been unable to fly?", or "If St. George hadn't had a lance, how might he have overpowered the dragon? Could he have pacified and domesticated it?". By such questions we can learn something about the reader's model of the story world and of the characters in it.

Thus, this paragraph proposes that there is a level of memory representation for a story (the Storyworld) that provides a referent world for the symbols and relations in the propositional content of the story text to refer to, and thus adds the referent aspect of meaning to the sense aspect of meaning provided by the causal network of propositions (Carnap, 1956). This same general idea was also proposed shortly thereafter by the mental-model proposals by Johnson-Laird (1983) and Gentner and Stevens (1983), and the situation model proposal by Van Dijk and Kintsch (1983). However, there is also more: Specifically, the Storyworld proposal involves visual and spatial imagery, which not all the other proposals did, and in addition the idea that the Storyworld provided an ability to imagine how things could have been different from the way the story played out. This perspective on story understanding thus seems to have the flexibility of a modern video game where the players make different choices and the game narrative then proceeds differently (Black, 2006).

FROM STORYWORLDS TO IMAGINARY WORLDS

Earlier, we had done a series of studies showing spatial-layout effects in comprehension and memory of simple compound sentences and sentence pairs using deictic terms for the spatial manipulation (Black, Turner, & Bower, 1979). For example, college undergraduates would take longer to read a shift in point of view (e.g., " John was working in the front yard, then he came inside"; the readers have to shift the perspective point from which they are viewing this scene), than a consistent point of view with only one word change ("John was working in the front yard then he went inside")—they also misremembered the point of view shift sentences as being consistent instead (i.e., misremembered "came" as "went"). Thus even in this minimal situation, these college undergraduates (skilled readers) would set up a sketchy spatial layout for a sketchy story. In later research, Bower and Morrow (1990) showed that if study participants memorized the floor plan of a building (including the relevant objects in the building), then they used imagery to track a narrative protagonist as they moved through this building in the narrative: that is, as they moved through the Storyworld.

IMAGINING THE WORLD OF A CATHEDRAL

Recent research I have done seems to indicate that there is more to these Storyworlds than just objects laid out in space (Van Esselstyn & Black, 2001). Also, it seems unlikely that humans would have evolved a cognitive mechanism only for stories, so at this point I want to shift the terminology to calling them Imaginary Worlds and extending their application to content beyond stories (as indeed the mental-model theories cited earlier did). In this research, we were interested in whether using new technology that allowed learners to take virtual tours of three-dimensional (3-D) virtual spaces would allow them to remember facts and spatial relations about those spaces better than presenting the same content in a purely textual form or in a text and pictures form. In technology terms, we were comparing learning from hypertext, hypermedia, and virtual reality. We thought that providing the 3-D virtual tours would help the learners to construct the Imaginary World that would then provide an effective way to organize the content for later memory retrieval because moving through the 3-D virtual worlds on the computer would correspond more exactly to moving through a 3-D mental world.

For content we used St. John's Cathedral, which is conveniently located adjacent to the Columbia University campus, but is rich in historical, architectural, and art history details (it is the largest gothic cathedral in the world, but still unfinished after more than 100 years). The basic design of the computer system we created is shown in Figure 13–1. There are three key areas of the screen: The rectangular area at the bottom of the screen presents the facts about the area of the cathedral that is shown in the picture and marked on the floor plan, the area on the right-hand side shows the floor plan of the cathedral with dots marking the key areas and where the learner is virtually located, and the picture is in the upper left-hand corner.

Across three experiments, we compared various combinations of this interface design to examine their effectiveness for helping learners remember the facts present in the text, the spatial location of a given item, and the spatial direction one would move to go from one item to another (spatial relations). We had a text-only condition, a text-plus-floor-plan condition, a text-plus-floor-plan-plus-static-picture condition, and a text plus floor plan plus a virtual tour picture condition. The virtual tour picture moved the learner through the cathedral as they moved the computer mouse. All the conditions, except the text only, could also move around the cathedral by pointing and clicking on one of the dots on the floor plan.

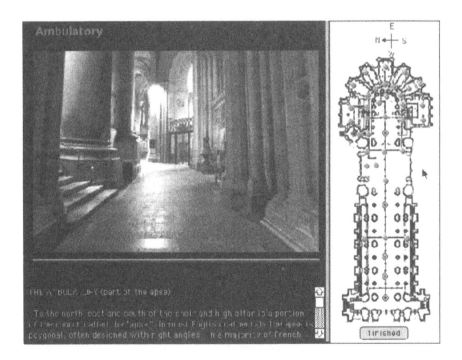

Figure 13–1.   Cathedral multimedia program.

In the first two experiments, the text-only condition did very poorly but to our surprise there wasn't much difference between the text, text-plus-picture, and text-plus-virtual-tour groups as long as the floor plan was there to provide a spatial context. There was a slight difference in favor of adding pictures but not much, and the virtual tour was no better than the static pictures. Thus, our learners (and they were Columbia U. students) were able to construct a spatial imaginary world with minimal input (text plus a floor plan). We didn't examine whether these results varied with visual and spatial abilities (e.g., were high–visual and spatial ability learners better able to use minimal input), but these differences were probably muted here because we were dealing with high-ability learners (however, see the Constructing Imaginary Worlds section later in this chapter).

In a third experiment, we added some text to all conditions explaining why the cathedral is laid out spatially the way it is—that is one reason we chose the cathedral content, because it has a strong spatial design rationale. The pattern of results was the same, except that now the virtual tour group did much better than the others. This suggests that the most effective imaginary worlds are the ones where the spatial layout has a meaning and is not just arbitrary.

IMAGINING MARS COLONIES

In 2000, we had an opportunity to see what kinds of imaginary worlds middle school students in New York City would construct. This opportunity was provided by the nationwide Mars Millennium Project being pushed by several government agencies including NASA and the Clinton White House. This project was supposed to use the landing of two space probes on Mars to motivate precollege students to learn more about Mars and science in general by designing Mars Colonies. Unfortunately, these probes did not have the intended motivational effects because they crashed rather than landing—but the kids still seemed somewhat interested in the topic. Fortunately for our purposes, NASA put a lot of information about Mars on their Web sites for the kids to access as part of this project. We used this material together with discussions to inform the students we were working with in a South Bronx middle school, and then had them create their designs for Mars Colonies using paper and pencil.

We then scored those designs for how many entities were there, how many relations were specified between these entities, and whether they described how the Mars Colony would work in terms of physical (e.g., how are we going to get power like electricity), biological (e.g., how are we going to get air and water), and social (e.g., how are the colonists going to make decisions) systems. Crucial for specifying these systems is describing the kinds of functional relations that describe how entities move through space and affect each other (Hachey, Tsuei, & Black, 2001). The Mars Colonies designed by the students were completely disconnected and disjointed: They had almost no relations of any kind (much less dynamic functional relations); they merely laid out a bunch of entities spatially (e.g., the apartment building goes here, the McDonald's restaurant goes here, etc.). Thus, these students needed help to learn how to design dynamic imaginary worlds that had not just a surface but also functional relations behind the scenes that allow them to function and allowed reasoning about how the functioning might differ in different circumstances (as described in the Storyworld quote earlier).

Fortunately, we got another shot at fostering middle school students' abilities to imagine Mars Colonies because NASA tried again in 2004 and managed to land two terrific and very motivating Mars Rovers that are still going today, long after their anticipated lifetimes are over. We went back to the same school (but different students), but now prepared them to think in terms of dynamic imaginary worlds by having them learn to diagram dynamic earth science phenomena (e.g., how volcanoes work) using system diagrams like the one shown in Figure 13–2.

More formal system diagramming (e.g., *Stella II*) has proven too difficult for precollege students, but this system, designed by Lisa Tsuei, worked well for these middle school students. This system-diagramming approach uses different

Figure 13–2.   System diagram with different kinds of functional links.

kind of arrows to represent different kinds of relations: The wavy arrows indicate the functional relation of moving entities (e.g., lava flow), whereas the dashed lines indicate the functional relations of changes in entity state (e.g., lava cools from liquid to solid), and the solid lines indicate propositional relations between entities (e.g., the mantle has magma). After experience with these system diagrams in an earth science unit, the students transferred these concepts when asked to design Mars Colonies later: Now their Mars Colony designs represented dynamic Imaginary Worlds and colonies that worked (Tsuei & Black, 2006).

IMAGINARY WORLDS IN SCIENTIFIC INQUIRY

Efforts to improve the scientific reasoning skills of middle school students, or even adults like community college students, can be frustrating because people are resistant to applying simple scientific-reasoning rules like variable isolation— the idea that to conclude that a factor is causally related to another factor one has to vary the independent factor, keeping others constant, while looking for corresponding changes in the target dependent factor. People have a tendency to want to change more than one factor at a time, probably in an attempt to get a bigger effect, but it makes causal inferences problematic.

For example, we used a computer simulation of flooding to examine middle school students investigating what causes flooding (Kuhn, Black, Kesselman, & Kaplan, 2000). The cover story of this simulation game was that the students were developers trying to figure out how high off the ground they needed to build cabins on sites around lakes in the mountains so that the cabins would not be flooded. Figure 13–3 shows the basic elements of the computer screen design (this system has several kinds of screens but this is the main design). The box in the upper left-hand corner lists the candidates for factors that may cause an increase in flooding (water pollution in the lake, lake water temperature, soil depth, soil type, and site elevation). The students specify the values of the factors for a given site and the flooding level they expect, then the system tells them the actual flooding level both numerically at the bottom of that box and graphically showing in the next box to the right a water level on a cabin with supports at the level they predicted the flooding to be. A trial is composed of the students specifying the factor values, getting the flooding feedback, and then filling in the box at the bottom as to what they now believe about the causal relation between the factors and flooding (to help in this judgment the system also gives the results of the immediately previous trial in a box on the top right-hand corner).

If they followed the variable-isolation rule, then the students would proceed through these trials changing only one factor at a time, but instead they tended to change more than one factor at a time and they tended to stick to their theories about what is causal and what isn't despite the evidence presented by the results of the trials. Gradually, over a several-week period, students' scientific-inquiry skills and understanding of flooding slowly improved a little, but efforts to yield

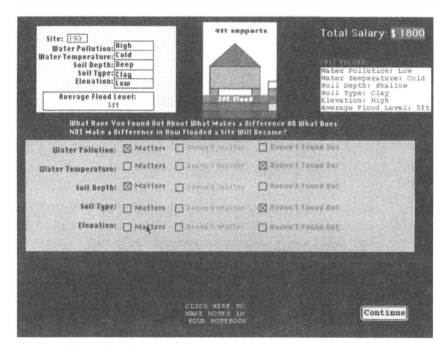

Figure 13–3.   Flooding inquiry simulation.

larger improvement have seldom worked (in this case, we showed them effective and ineffective trial choices by fictitious "other" students but that didn't help).

There are many anecdotes from scientists reporting that they use Imaginary Worlds to conduct "thought experiments" to help them understand and develop theories. This has become an increasingly important ability as the scientific phenomena studied have become more and more removed from everyday experience. A striking example are the wild imaginings of string theorists in modern physics as related by the best-selling book *The Elegant Universe* by Columbia physicist Brian Greene (2000; and the striking graphic visualizations in the accompanying PBS TV show and Web site, www.pbs.org/wgbh/nova/elegant/program.html). Perhaps like these scientists, the participants in scientific reasoning studies are struggling to create Imaginary Worlds integrating a variety of factors rather than looking at factors in isolation. We tested this idea by adding a condition to our earlier experiment where we gave students some information as "hints" that might help them construct an Imaginary World of the causal mechanisms behind the factors (Kaplan & Black, 2003). Figure 13–4 gives an example of one such piece of information.

Students in one condition were given this sort of textual and graphic information that showed that the soil type of sand was more loosely packed and had

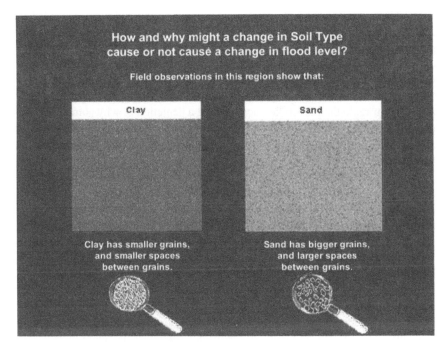

Figure 13–4.   Flooding imaginary world hint.

greater spaces between the particles (and the particles are larger) than did the soil type of clay (with smaller particles). Thus, if they visualize the dynamic Imaginary World using this information, they could potentially see that water will more readily run through sand yielding less flooding than with clay (although, as this visualization could also show, it interacts with bedrock depth). The students who had this kind of Imaginary World component information showed more improvement in their scientific inquiry skills and better understanding of flooding than the students who did not. This suggests that viewing people's scientific reasoning in terms Imaginary Worlds may provide insight into what they are doing and how to improve it.

VIDEO GAMES AND ANIMATED AGENTS

Video games have been proposed by some (e.g., Gee, 2003; Prensky, 2004) as powerful environments for learning the kind of Imaginary World understanding and thinking I have been discussing. I have some sympathy for this position: For example, the flooding simulation described in the last section is like a simple video game. However, I have also argued (Black, 2006) that there is an inherent conflict between commercial entertainment game design and what is needed for effective learning: Specifically, commercial games try to make it as hard as possible for players to figure out why something happened (i.e., to enable the player to fully understand the game's underlying Imaginary World) so that they will play a long time and feel that they got their money's worth in entertainment value. However, for effective learning, games need to be designed so that after a short period of struggle the players/learners can get a depiction of why something happened (according to Schwartz and Bransford's, 1998, results, this should be effective for learning). Commercial entertainment games lack this explanatory transparency.

One system that provides a kind of transparency is the Teachable Agents project being done by Biswas, Schwartz, Bransford, and the Teachable Agents Group at Vanderbilt (2001). In this project, students learn about an ecological system (or potentially anything) by drawing concept maps similar to the system diagram shown in Figure 13–2 (but without the different shapes) to specify what an "agent" depicted as the drawing of a person on the computer screen would know about the topic. The students can then see how good their representation of the knowledge is by how well their agent can answer questions about the topic. An advanced feature of this system is that it can interpret the knowledge diagram drawn and generate the answers from there. Thus the students can learn by "teaching" their agents and then get feedback by whether the agent does well or badly.

We have a related project called the REAL (or REflective Agent Learning environment) in which we are trying to get the computer agents to demonstrate their knowledge by interacting with the environment in addition to answering questions (Bai & Black, 2006) , but the Teachable Agents project is much further along. REAL expands the transparency by adding a representation for procedures to the propositional and function relations in the Teachable Agent. Furthermore, it provides a depiction not only of how the Agent thinks the virtual world works, but also of how the virtual word actually works so that the students can learn from the contrast.

DIRECT-MANIPULATION ANIMATION SIMULATIONS

Some of our most recent research has focused on having students learn and use the functional relations between entities that the research described here and other research I have done with Dan Schwartz (Schwartz & Black, 1996a, 1996b) has seemed to indicate is the crux of being able to effectively construct and reason with dynamic Imaginary Worlds. We have been examining this issue by having middle school students learn physics concepts like conservation of energy (the relation between gravity and kinetic and potential energy) using variations on graphics simulations like the one shown for a roller coaster in Figure 13–5 (created by Maggie Chan). We have found what we call "direct-manipulation animation" to be

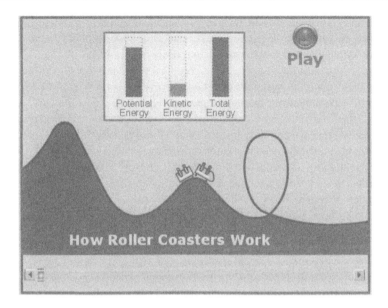

Figure 13–5. Roller coaster simulation.

particularly effective in having students learning these functional relations. Direct-manipulation animation (sometimes also called "user-controlled animation") has students manipulate one variable of interest (here height in the gravity well) by moving a slider, while observing the changes in values of other variables (here potential, kinetic, and total energy of the roller coaster cars).

Students in the direct-manipulation animation condition learned better on a variety of memory and problem-solving measures than did students who were played the animation as a movie (with no control over the cars), shown snapshots of critical points along the path shown as a slide show, or shown just the overall picture with textual explanations (Chan & Black, 2005, 2006a). Like other researchers, we have somewhat surprisingly found that animation is not more effective than the slide show condition, and sometimes worse (Mayer, 2001; Tversky, Morrison, & Betrancourt, 2002), but our direct-manipulation animation condition is better. Thus, graphic simulations that allow learners to directly manipulate entities and observe animations of the resulting changes in other entities is the best way we know so far of having students learn dynamic Imaginary Worlds.

CONSTRUCTING IMAGINARY WORLDS

Though a graphic simulation with direct manipulation animation is an effective way to learn the functional relations of Imaginary Worlds, is it always necessary? As we saw in the in the cathedral study, sometimes learners can construct elaborate mental representations of Imaginary Worlds with fairly minimal input. To investigate this question, Maggie Chan created two more graphic simulations to go along with the Roller Coaster simulation described in the last section—namely, a simple Swing simulation and a more complex Pole Vaulting simulation. Thus, we now have physical-system simulations involving conservation of energy at three levels of complexity: simple (the Swing), medium (the Roller Coaster), and complex (the Pole Vault)—of course, these levels of complexity are relative rather than absolute (one can certainly imagine much more complex systems than a pole vault). We also created two other kinds of learning materials to go along with the graphic simulations: namely, text alone and text plus diagrams. And we tried out these nine kinds of materials-complexity combinations on sixth graders and seventh graders (Chan & Black, 2006b).

For the seventh graders, we found that for the simple system (the Swing) text alone was sufficient (text, text plus diagrams, and simulations yielded similar learning results), but for the medium system (the Roller Coaster) text plus diagrams was needed (the text condition yielded less learning whereas the text-plus-diagrams condition was the same as the simulation), and for the complex system (the Pole Vault) the simulation was needed because it yielded better learning results than the other two conditions. Thus, we have an interaction between presentation type and system complexity. For the sixth graders, there was no interaction: The students with the simulations always learned better regardless of the system complexity, with those with the text plus pictures next best and the text only the worst. We measured learning in this study in several different ways, varying from memory tests to near and far transfer problem solving. The differences were biggest for the problem-solving tasks, but were also there for the other learning tasks.

These results suggest that more capable students (in this case the seventh graders) may be able to construct simple Imaginary Worlds with minimal input (in this case text), but as the Imaginary World to be constructed becomes more complex then more sophisticated kinds of learning materials and activities may be necessary (moving up to text plus pictures and to graphic simulations). However, as in the previous section, it seems you always stand your best chance of constructing an Imaginary World with a graphic simulation using direct manipulation animation—but in some cases simpler materials are sufficient.

SEED IDEAS THAT SPARK THE IMAGINATION

In this chapter, I have described the intellectual journey that I have taken sparked by the ideas seeded by my discussions with Gordon Bower in the later 1970s that are embodied in the paragraph from 1980 quoted at the beginning of this chapter. This seems like a very productive model of education when it can be made to work: namely, that teachers should try to plant seed ideas in their students that with cultivation will spark the imaginations of the students. In fact, this relates to some of the research I have described: Namely, in the graphic simulations described in the last section and the cathedral virtual tour described earlier, students (particularly more capable students) were frequently able to construct Imaginary Worlds based on minimal input. The key, of course, is knowing what minimal seeds need to be planted for what students and how they need to be cultivated in order to enable the Imaginary Worlds to grow.

In my own case described here, the beginning was examining a deeper kind of story understanding where readers would construct an imaginary world of the story that would allow them to consider alternative pathways the story could have taken. From there these ideas expanded into understanding and learning from other media and technologies like multimedia computer programs, simulations, video games, and virtual worlds. The tasks that would show understanding also expanded from remembering and answering questions about stories to solving math and science problems, and conducting scientific inquiry. Gordon Bower is a master at planting and cultivating productive seed ideas. Learning from his example, I try to do the same with my own students.

ACKNOWLEDGMENTS

I would like to thank Steve Kosslyn for valuable comments on an earlier draft of this chapter, and Mark Gluck for keeping us all organized and on schedule.

REFERENCES

Bai, X., & Black, J. B. (2006, May). REAL: An agent-based learning environment. Paper presented at the *Agent-Based Systems for Human Learning Conference,* Hakodate, Japan.

Biswas, G., Schwartz, D. L., Bransford, J. D., & The Teachable Agents Group at Vanderbilt. (2001). Technology support for complex problem solving: From SAD environments to AI. In K. D. Forbus & P. J. Feltovich, (Eds.), *Smart machines in education: The coming revolution in educational technology* (pp. 71–98). Menlo Park, CA: AAAI/MIT Press.

Black, J. B. (2006, March). Games with explanatory transparency for better learning and understanding. Paper presented at the *Game Developers Conference* (Serious Games Summit), San Jose, CA.

Black, J. B., & Bern, H. S. (1981). Causal coherence and memory for events in narratives. *Journal of Verbal Learning and Verbal Behavior, 20,* 267–275.

Black, J. B., Turner, T. J., & Bower, G. H. (1979). Point of view in narrative comprehension, memory and production. *Journal of Verbal Learning and Verbal Behavior, 18,* 187–198

Black, J. B., & Bower, G. H. (1980). Story understanding as problem-solving. *Poetics, 9,* 223–250.

Bower, G. H., & Morrow, D. G. (1990). Mental models in narrative comprehension. *Science, 247,* 44–48.

Chan, M. S., & Black, J. B. (2005). When can animation improve learning? Some implications for human computer interaction and learning. In Proceedings of *EdMedia* (pp. 2725–2732). Norfolk, VA: Association for the Advancement of Computing in Education.

Chan, M. S., & Black, J. B. (2006a). Direct-manipulation animation: Incorporating the haptic channel in the learning process to support middle school students in science learning and mental model acquisition. In *Proceedings of the International Conference of the Learning Sciences* (pp. 64–70). Mahwah, NJ: Lawrence Erlbaum Associates.

Chan, M. S., & Black, J. B. (2006b, April). Learning Newtonian mechanics with an animation game: The role of presentation format on mental model acquisition. Paper presented at the annual meeting of the *American Education Research Association,* San Francisco.

Carnap, R. (1956). *Meaning and necessity* (2nd ed.). Chicago: University of Chicago Press.

Gee, J. P. (2003). *What video games have to teach us about learning and literacy.* New York: Palgrave Macmillan.

Gentner, D. G., & Stevens, A. S. (Eds.). (1983). *Mental models.* Mahwah, NJ: Lawrence Erlbaum Associates.

Goldman, S. R., Graesser, A. C., & van den Broek, P. (Eds.). (1999). *Narrative, comprehension and coherence.* Mahwah, NJ: Lawrence Erlbaum Associates.

Greene, B. (2000). *The elegant universe: Hidden dimensions and the search for the ultimate theory.* New York: Vintage.

Hachey, A. C., Tsuei, L., & Black, J. B. (2001). Fostering mental-model thinking during design. In Proceedings of *EdMedia* (pp. 1713–1718). Norfolk, VA: Association for the Advancement of Computing in Education.

Johnson-Laird, P. N. (1983). *Mental models.* Cambridge, MA: Harvard University Press.

Kaplan, D. E., & Black, J. B. (2003). Mental models and computer-based scientific inquiry learning: Effects of mechanism cues on adolescent representation and reasoning about causal systems. *Journal of Science Education and Technology, 12*(4), 483–493.

Kuhn, D., Black, J. B., Kesselman, A., & Kaplan, D. (2000) The development of cognitive skills to support inquiry learning. *Cognition and Instruction, 18,* 495–523.

Mayer, R. E. (2001). *Multimedia learning.* New York: Cambridge University Press.

Prensky, M. (2004). *Digital game-based learning.* New York: McGraw Hill.

Schwartz, D. L., & Black, J. B. (1996a). Analog imagery in mental model reasoning: Depictive models. *Cognitive Psychology, 30,* 154–219.

Schwartz, D. L., & Black, J. B. (1996b). Shuttling between depictive models and abstract rules. *Cognitive Science, 20,* 457–497.

Schwartz, D. L., & Bransford, J. D. (1998). A time for telling, *Cognition and Instruction, 16*(4), 475–522.

Tsuei, L., & Black, J. B. (2006). Using simulation diagrams to facilitate reasoning about-mechanisms and systems. Manuscript submitted for publication.

Tversky, B., Morrison, J. B., & Betrancourt, M. (2002). Animation: Can it facilitate? *International Journal of Human Computer Studies, 57*(4), 247–262.

van Dijk, T. A., & Kintsch, W. (1983). *Strategies of discourse comprehension.* New York: Academic Press.

van Esselstyn, D., & Black, J. B. (2001). Learning through interactive panoramic imagery. In Proceedings of *EdMedia* (pp. 663–670). Norfolk, VA: Association for the Advancement of Computing in Education.

CHAPTER 14

Continuing Themes in the Study of Human Knowledge: Associations, Imagery, Propositions, and Situations

Lawrence W. Barsalou
Emory University

One of the many remarkable qualities about Gordon Bower is the breadth of his intellectual interests. From a brief perusal of Gordon's contributions, it is readily apparent that he has not worked in one narrow area. Instead, his efforts have produced an unusually broad set of empirical findings across many literatures. Perhaps even more significantly, Gordon has entertained diverse theoretical perspectives in the process. Rather than adhering rigidly to a single position, he has worked with multiple perspectives that exhibit significant tensions between them. Even when it has not been entirely clear how these perspectives might be reconciled, Gordon has entertained them inclusively. Perhaps he believed that there was something inherently correct about each perspective, and that they all could and should be integrated eventually.

I resonate strongly with Gordon in these regards. I share his enthusiasm for diverse empirical areas, and for multiple, sometimes apparently inconsistent, theoretical frameworks. I'm not sure whether I became this way from working with Gordon, or whether I was already like this to some extent and drawn to him for this reason. Regardless, having the unbelievably good fortune to be one of Gordon's students certainly strengthened this aspect of my intellectual orientation, placing it front and center.

I do not attempt to describe all the different research areas and theoretical perspectives that Gordon addressed in his work. Instead, I focus on four themes in our work that we share: association, imagery, propositions, and situation models. I begin by briefly reviewing Gordon's contributions in these areas, and then connect them with my own work. Being exposed to these ideas as a graduate student had tremendous impact on my intellectual framework.

Associationism and Mental Imagery.   As has been well established, Gordon began his career as an associationist, a tradition well-known for its antipathy toward imagery. In the 1960s, when Paivio (1965) reported that the imagability of a word's referent was a strong predictor of its memorability, imagery rose from the dead. Much further work from Paivio's lab followed, summarized in Paivio (1971). A natural expectation would have been that an associationist would have felt deeply suspicious about such findings, and most did. Gordon, however, did not, and resonated to the important role of imagery in cognition as well.

In an empirical style often associated with his work, Gordon attempted to isolate the critical mechanisms that produced imagery benefits in memory, rather than simply demonstrating their presence. Bower (1970), for example, argued that the imagery benefit resulted from increased relational organization rather than from increased stimulus distinctiveness or reliability. Bower and Reitman (1972) further explored the role of imagery in mnemonic strategies, finding that imagining to-be-remembered items in the same scenes facilitated memory, relative to imagining them in different scenes. Gordon summarized his early work on imagery in a chapter that had considerable impact at the time (Bower, 1972a). Notably, the title of this review article was "Mental Imagery and Associative Learning," integrating two theoretical constructs viewed widely at the time as incompatible.

During this period, Gordon was working with Stephen Kosslyn, who went on to make extensive contributions to the study of imagery (summarized in Kosslyn, 1980, 1994). In a joint publication, Kosslyn and Bower (1974) addressed the sources of memory confusions in children versus adults. Of particular interest was whether children confused pictures on the basis of imaginal qualities, conceptual content, or both. They found that children exhibited sensitivity to both, suggesting that children encoded both sources of information. Children, however, showed less sensitivity to conceptual information than adults, suggesting slower development of the conceptual system. Again, this work combined potentially incompatible constructs: imaginal representations and conceptual symbols. As we see in the next section on propositions, conceptual symbols became increasingly central in Gordon's work.

Propositional Representations.   Another major undercurrent of the cognitive revolution was the claim that all knowledge is encoded in propositional representations (i.e., representations that encode knowledge into language-like symbols of the sort found in logic). Many researchers were struck by early studies that showed memory for gist but loss of linguistic surface structure (e.g., Sachs, 1967). These findings were interpreted as indicating the presence of abstract conceptual representations that differed from surface stimuli, lining up with classic arguments about propositions and their bound values (e.g., Pylyshyn, 1973). Rather than simply encoding simple stimuli as in associationist and imagery theories, people appeared to represent perceived stimuli with abstract propositions that described their conceptual properties.

Simultaneously, propositional representations were sweeping across early work in artificial intelligence. Knowledge engineers adapted propositional logic and predicate calculus to create knowledge representations that supported (relatively) intelligent processes in computers (e.g., Schank & Colby, 1973). Psychologists, too, found inspiration in this approach to representation, believing that it captured important properties of human knowledge and cognition (e.g., Norman, Rumelhart, & the LNR Research Group, 1975). Some might think that this approach was inconsistent with associationism, but not Gordon.

Instead, Gordon, taking the lead from another student, John Anderson, developed one of the most ambitious research programs of the time. They argued that memory and knowledge could not be represented in terms of simple associations. Instead, they proposed that more structured, propositional representations are required to capture the rich conceptual structure of knowledge, including predication (e.g., types vs. tokens), conceptual relations (e.g., verbs and prepositions), and recursion (e.g., hierarchical structures).

John and Gordon applied propositional analysis first to recall and then to recognition (Anderson & Bower, 1972, 1974). In one of the most influential books of the modern era, they cast a broad propositional net across cognitive phenomena and implemented it in HAM (i.e., Human Associative Memory; Anderson & Bower, 1973). Through this project, John and Gordon found a way to reconcile what would appear to be a major theoretical incompatibility: combining an associative approach with a propositional approach. What might have appeared to be two irreconcilable frameworks turned out to be complementary theoretical partners.

With many later students, Gordon continued to apply the propositional approach to cognition. Two important directions for later work included applications of the propositional approach to the representation of text meaning (e.g., Bower, 1974, 1976) and scripts (e.g., Bower, Black, & Turner, 1979). As Gordon's interests turned increasingly to language comprehension, he continued to use propositional representations extensively. He also started returning to imagery, following a provocative finding on perspective taking that implicated imagery in comprehension (Black, Turner, & Bower, 1979).

Situation Models.   In an ingenious line of research with Daniel Morrow and Steven Greenspan, imagery returned to Gordon's work full blown (Morrow, Bower, & Greenspan, 1989; Morrow, Greenspan, & Bower, 1987). These experiments demonstrated compellingly that people use spatial representations to represent text meaning. People not only use propositional and associative representations, but use spatial representations as well. Even when a text does not describe an important spatial relationship, people nevertheless compute and use it to answer questions about text content. An article in Science summarized these early studies (Bower & Morrow, 1990).

Much further work with Michael Rinck from 1995 to the current time replicated and developed these initial findings (summarized in Rinck & Bower, 2004). Besides continuing to show that spatial representations affect text processing, Rinck and Bower related them to many other text-processing phenomena, including anaphoric resolution, attentional focus, surface structure, goal relevance, and associative interference. The synthetic character of this work is quintessential Bower, integrating imagery, propositions, and associations. Each is an important part of the story, and the magic of cognition emerges from their synthesis.

These findings on spatial representation in text processing anticipated and contributed to the ascendance of the situation model as one of the most central constructs in discourse analysis (for a review, see Zwaan & Radvansky, 1998). These findings further anticipated the evolution of situation models into a new form, where they are viewed mental simulations that represent text content (e.g., Zwaan & Madden, 2005).

Summary.   The range of theoretical views that Gordon has not only entertained but synthesized in his work is remarkable. I can think of no other researcher who has successfully worked within so many diverse traditions. In the small subset of Gordon's research described here, he applied associative, imaginal, propositional, and situational frameworks. Not only has Gordon's work made major contributions within each framework individually, it has also made significant headway in finding ways to integrate them. Although we are still a long way from having a fully integrated theory, Gordon has pointed the way. He has shown the importance of integrating diverse but fundamental frameworks, and he has demonstrated that this is possible. Given the complexity of cognition, it is unlikely that a single one of these frameworks will be sufficient to explain it. Instead, all of these frameworks and their integration are probably necessary.

GROUNDING CONCEPTUAL PROCESSES IN MODALITY-SPECIFIC SYSTEMS

Prior to becoming one of Gordon's graduate students, my undergraduate training in psychology and cognitive science at the University of California–San Diego, oriented me toward three of the themes that I have described in Gordon's research: associationism, imagery, and propositions. Working on traditional memory research in George Mandler's lab, I was exposed to the associative tradition (which George liked to pit against the Gestalt tradition). I also acquired experimental skills that would be compatible with Gordon's approach to performing laboratory research. My first psych course was Perception, taught by Lynn Cooper, one of Roger Shepard's former students (TAed by Robert Glushko and Arthur Graesser). I acquired a strong appreciation and interest in perception from Lynn's inspired treatment of the topic. Finally, I took several undergraduate and graduate courses from David Rumelhart and Donald Norman, resonating strongly with their emphasis at the time on propositions and structured representations in cognition.

When applying for graduate school, my first choice was to work with Gordon at Stanford because this seemed like the best match with the orientation I had developed as an undergraduate. Although I didn't know what I wanted to study exactly, I knew that it would probably have something to do with propositions and memory. On being accepted to work with Gordon, I felt like I had won the lottery.

Being a student of Gordon's for four years amplified and developed the core themes that structured my initial orientation toward psychology. In particular, associative and propositional structure became particularly central to how I thought about cognitive phenomena. Furthermore, Gordon's interest in the situations that underlie narratives and scripts became a core theme that I had not entertained previously. Although Gordon was not thinking much about imagery at the time, I took courses from Roger Shepard that developed the interest in perception I'd received from Lynn Cooper's course. I also read all of Steve Kosslyn's work and pretty much all of the other work on imagery at the time as well.

Conceptual Processing Is Situated, Dynamic, and Structured

Situations and Ad Hoc Categories.   Some of my first graduate work reflected Gordon's interest in situations. From reading all of Eleanor Rosch's work during James McClelland's cognition lab course at UCSD, I became interested in categorization. From reading Gordon's work on narratives and scripts, I started thinking about how background situations (context) might affect categorization. My work on ad hoc categories developed from trying to resolve this issue (Barsalou, 1983, 1985, 1991). The central theme of this work is that many categories develop to serve goals that agents have in particular situations. The role of situations in cognition has remained central in my work since, and in the work of my students (e.g., Barsalou, 2003b, 2003c, 2005; Chaigneau, Barsalou, & Sloman, 2004; Yeh & Barsalou, 2006).

Another central theme of my graduate work was that categories are dynamic. Rather than there being a fixed set of categories, there is an infinite number. Consistent with the propositional framework, the open-endedness of human categories results from the productive properties of a propositional system. By combining more basic concepts in a productive manner, more complex categories can be constructed dynamically as needed to solve goals in specific situations. Although I didn't think much about the mechanisms that enable this type of productivity during graduate school, I thought a lot about them later. I had the pleasure of eventually publishing an article on the productive bases of ad hoc categories in *Advances in Learning and Motivation,* a series that Gordon was editing at the time (Barsalou, 1991).

Associative Mechanisms in Dynamical Conceptual Processing. Gordon's associative orientation also found its way extensively into my graduate work on categorization. In my work on ad hoc categories, I found that ad hoc categories are less established in memory than taxonomic categories (Barsalou, 1983). I found that the frequency of processing category exemplars affects their typicality (Barsalou, 1985). I found that some properties associated with a category become activated automatically because they are processed frequently, whereas other properties are active only in relevant situations, because they are processed infrequently (Barsalou, 1982). All these findings reflect the underlying assumption that the associative structure of conceptual knowledge is central to its representation and processing. At the time, taking an associative approach to conceptual knowledge was relatively unusual, given that most researchers in the area came from the study of language, and thus had a much stronger propositional orientation, not taking memory into account. Being a student of Gordon's, however, made this approach seem a somewhat naïve and idealized.

After taking my first faculty position at Emory University, the associative underpinnings of knowledge became even more central to my interests. While comparing typicality gradients in ad hoc and taxonomic categories, I discovered that these gradients exhibited considerable instability between and within participants. Different participants exhibited different typicality gradients, and the same participant exhibited different gradients on different occasions 2 weeks apart. After leaving graduate school, my research focused on documenting this instability (Barsalou, 1987, 1989, 1993). In many experiments, I showed that the average correlation between two participants judging typicality in the same category is around .40, and that the average correlation within the same participant over 2 weeks is around .75. Similar instability occurs during feature listing and judgments of category membership (e.g., McCloskey & Glucksberg, 1978). Based on these findings, the representation of a category does not appear to be a fixed prototype or definition. Instead, category representations appear to be constructed online dynamically. Just as the human cognitive system appears capable of creating an infinite number of categories, it also appears capable of creating an infinite number of representations for a single category.

On observing that the representation of a category is dynamic, I became interested in trying to explain this dynamicism. How does the cognitive system produce different representations of a category, and what factors affect this process? The account that I developed assumes that a large body of associative knowledge exists in memory, and that, on a given occasion, a small subset of this knowledge is retrieved to represent the category (Barsalou, 1987, 1989, 1993). On different occasions, different subsets of knowledge are sampled, such that the category's representation varies across time. The subset retrieved is not a random sample but reflects the information currently most accessible in the category's knowledge. Specifically, the information processed most recently and most frequently is likely to be retrieved, as is information associated with the current situation. The core idea of this approach was not all that different from Gordon's stimulus-sampling theory, which had made a significant impression on me as a graduate student (Bower, 1972b). The importance of associative and situational factors in determining the most accessible category knowledge on a given occasion echoes these central themes in Gordon's work.

Frames Organize Underlying Knowledge in Memory.   On adopting this account of dynamic category representation, I became interested in trying to understand the underlying organization of knowledge. What form does a large body of categorical knowledge take? How does it support dynamic sampling? Not surprisingly, I became convinced that categorical knowledge is structured propositionally, following propositional theorists such as Anderson and Bower (1973) and schema theorists such as Rumelhart and Ortony (1978). Like they, I argued that knowledge is organized around conceptual relations, argument-value structure, and recursion (Barsalou, 1992, 1993; Barsalou & Hale, 1993). As people process a category instance, information from the processing episode becomes integrated into this frame structure. Conversely, when people later represent the category, they construct a particular representation dynamically that instantiates this structure. Rather than retrieving all the knowledge in the frame, they retrieve a subset that instantiates it.

Unlike many frame and schema theories, this one assumed that dynamic associative processing is central to category representation. Rather than a fixed frame or schema representing a category on different occasions, this approach assumed that information in a frame is sampled dynamically, such that category representations measured in the laboratory vary widely between and within individuals. I also continued to assume that situations produce powerful context effects on this dynamic representational process. Mirroring Gordon's orientation to the study of knowledge, the integration of associative structure, propositional structure, and situations was central. One important theme of Gordon's work that I had failed to include, however, was the importance of imagery in cognition.

Images in Conceptual Processing

To assess whether frames organize the underlying knowledge for a category, I attempted to measure this knowledge in various ways (e.g., Barsalou, 1991). In particular, I attempted to establish the underlying frame structure for the category of *vacations*. I asked participants to produce knowledge about vacations in feature-listing tasks, and then attempted to organize the content of these protocols into a complex embedded system of frames.

Interestingly, I continually encountered the following two problems. First, there seemed to be no limit to the frame content for *vacation*. Just when I thought that I'd identified all the subframes, relations, and argument structures that constituted knowledge of this concept, participants would produce new ones. Second, any given component of the existing frame structure appeared decomposable into further frame structure. Just when I thought that I'd found the primitive elements of the frame system for *vacations,* one of these primitives would turn out to have additional decomposable structure.

For a couple of years, I believed that these problems reflected inadequate methodology. I thought that the inability to nail down the frame content of *vacations* resulted from using laboratory tasks that were incapable of identifying all the relevant content. I continued to assume that my theoretical approach was correct, namely, that a stable frame structure, represented propositionally in memory, produces infinite category representations via dynamic sampling. It didn't occur to me that the theory might be wrong and that the methodology might be right. Perhaps the continual discovery of new frame structure does not reflect methodological inadequacies but instead reflects a fundamental fact about knowledge. Perhaps no stable frame structure exists in memory for a category. Perhaps the methodology measures category knowledge reliably, indicating that it is not fixed but infinitely open-ended.

I increasingly began to ask myself: What kind of mechanism might produce the open-endedness of knowledge content? Why might there be infinite components of frame structure for a category? Why might a given component of this structure be infinitely decomposable?

One day in 1990 while posing this question to a colleague, imagery came rushing back into my life. It occurred to me that a system examining mental images associated with a category would produce infinite open-ended content about them. Because an image can be described in an infinite number of ways, there should be no limit to the relations, attributes, and values that can be used to describe it. Similarly, because any component of an image can be described in further detail, the descriptions of image content shouldn't decompose into primitives. On entertaining this possible explanation for the open-ended content of knowledge, I was instantly captured by the potential importance of images. Although I was far from convinced that this account was correct, and would not be convinced for several years, I began entertaining it seriously (Barsalou, 1993). I began exploring how images could represent knowledge, and began reading a wide variety of relevant literatures in psychology, cognitive neuroscience, philosophy, cognitive linguistics, and computer science. I had added one more theme from Gordon's worldview to the others that had been structuring my previous work.

Integrating Images and Propositions Theoretically. Although I became increasingly convinced that images are central to knowledge representation, I had a significant worry. I was convinced that propositionalists were correct about the structure of knowledge (e.g., Anderson & Bower, 1973; Rumehart & Ortony, 1978). From their arguments, theory, and data, and from my own data, I had become persuaded that knowledge contains predicates, arguments, values, and recursion. I also believed that the process of interpretation is central to knowledge representation, and that knowledge does not only contain recordings of experience (e.g., Pylyshyn, 1973). I struggled to reconcile these two convictions, much in the spirit of Gordon's tolerance for contradiction. How could images implement the propositional and interpretive qualities of knowledge?

The construct of a *simulator* offered one solution to this problem. According to this construct, propositional representations can be achieved by integrating imagery mechanisms with attentional and memory mechanisms. To see this, assume that selective attention focuses on a particular component of a perceived (or imagined) chair, such as its seat, and that a perceptual memory of this component is established. Further assume that on later occasions, selective attention focuses on other instances of chairs, and that perceptual memories of the same component are integrated with earlier memories. Over time, perceptual information about the component accumulates in memory to establish aggregate knowledge about it.

The developing representational system (what I came to call a *simulator*) functions much like a "type" or "predicate" in classic propositional theories. Accumulated information about instances in the simulator provides a summary representation that has the generic character of a type or predicate. Furthermore, simulators can become bound to perceived (or imagined) instances to interpret them, thereby implementing classic symbolic functions, such as the type–token distinction, conceptual inference, productivity, and propositions. By using selective attention and memory integration to process the components of images (rather than processing entire images holistically), fundamental aspects of the propositional approach emerge. Barsalou (1993), Barsalou et al. (1993), and Barsalou and Prinz (1997) provided preliminary accounts of this view. More developed accounts appear in Barsalou (1999, 2003a, 2005a) and Prinz (2002).

Implementing Classic Symbolic Operations.   According to the theoretical framework developed in these articles, the brain grounds classic symbolic operations in modality-specific systems (although other neural systems are central as well). Consider the symbolic operation of predication. A simulator implements predication when it categorizes, and thereby becomes bound to, a perceived individual. When the bird simulator becomes bound to a perceived bird, for example, the simulator interprets the bird as an instance of the kind of thing in the world that established the simulator's perceptual content in the first place. Binding the simulator to the perceived individual establishes a type–token proposition, where the simulator is the type and the individual is the token. Although such bindings differ considerably in form from classic symbolic propositions, they implement the same basic functionality.

Once a type–token proposition exists, it produces conceptual inferences. A simulator bound to an individual can be run to produce plausible conceptual inferences that go beyond current perceptual information. Once the *bird* simulator becomes bound to a bird sitting in a tree, for example, inferences about the bird could include simulations of it flying away, eating seeds, chirping, and so forth. Furthermore, simulators have the ability to produce compositional simulations, thereby implementing the classic symbolic operations of conceptual combination and productivity. For example, the simulators for *bird* and *purple* could jointly produce a simulation of a *purple bird*. Although a purple bird may have never been seen before, the *purple* simulator could modify the color of a *bird* simulation to create this novel conceptual combination. Similarly, simulators for other colors, such as *red, green,* and *brown,* could be used to systematically vary the color of *bird* simulations productively, thereby producing conceptual combinations for *red bird, green bird,* and *brown bird.* Analogously, simulators for events (e.g., *flying*), mental states (e.g., *frightened*), and locations (e.g., *forest*) could combine with the *bird* simulator to produce compositional simulations that represent *flying bird, frightened bird,* and *forest bird.*

As these examples illustrate, image-based approaches are not necessarily incompatible with symbolic approaches, a fact that philosophers have recognized for some time (e.g., Price, 1953; Russell, 1919). It is possible for knowledge to be grounded in an image-based system, while simultaneously implementing classic symbolic functions. Contrary to what is often assumed, the two views are not mutually exclusive. Indeed, they are probably both essential parts of a complete theory of knowledge and cognition.

Grounding Simulation in Neural Systems.   As I increasingly came to appreciate the importance of grounding cognition in the brain, I realized that the simulation approach makes considerable sense from this perspective. Consider how simulation can be grounded in neural systems. While experiencing the current situation, the brain's modality specific systems become active to represent perception, action, and mental states. Extensive work in neuroscience demonstrates that feature areas throughout the brain represent the content of these modalities.

As feature areas become active to represent experience, selective attention focuses on subsets of them. As a subset is selected, nearby association areas capture it in memory and integrate it with similar subsets stored on previous occasions (Damasio, 1989). Once a modality-specific state becomes stored in memory, it can later be partially reactivated. By activating the associative units that captured the state, the associated features states can be reactivated as well. In this manner, brain states can be triggered that (partially) reenact perceptions, actions, and mental states as simulations.

These simulations result from the same neural process that researchers have been proposing since the 1990s as the basis of mental imagery in working memory (e.g., Farah, 2000; Grezes & Decety, 2001; Jeannerod, 1995; Kosslyn, 1994). Rather than operating only in working memory, however, these simulations are also assumed to underlie conceptual representations that support the spectrum of cognitive tasks (Barsalou, 1999). Furthermore, these simulations may often operate unconsciously, rather than consciously as in mental imagery. Thus, classic mental-imagery mechanisms may play wider roles than previously believed, operating outside working memory unconsciously much of the time. Indeed, such simulations are increasingly viewed as playing central roles, not only in knowledge representation, but also in episodic memory (e.g., Buckner & Wheeler, 2001) and language comprehension (e.g., Zwaan & Madden, 2005).

The simulation process is widely viewed as multimodal. As the brain captures modality-specific content about a category from experience, it stores content on all the relevant modalities. Not only is visual content captured for *chairs,* but motor, somatosensory, auditory, motivational, and emotional content is captured as well by the respective neural systems. As local association areas capture this multimodal content, higher order cross-modal association areas integrate it hierarchically to create a multimodal representation of the category (e.g., Simmons & Barsalou, 2003). Depending on the category, the modalities captured reflect those relevant to interacting with its exemplars (e.g., taste for *foods* vs. audition for *musical instruments;* Cree & McRae, 2003). In general, situated knowledge about categories appears to become established in memory, reflecting all relevant aspects of the situations in which categories are processed (e.g., Barsalou, 2003b, 2005b, 2005c; Barsalou, Niedenthal, Barbey, & Ruppert, 2003).

Empirical Evidence for Simulation in Human Knowledge.   Just because it is possible to develop a theory that integrates simulations and propositions doesn't mean that the brain works this way. Empirical evidence is obviously essential. When my students and I searched for evidence in the literature, we were struck by the fact that very few researchers had explicitly assessed whether knowledge is grounded in simulation. We found much incidental evidence for this view in experiments that addressed other issues (for a partial review, see Barsalou, 2003b). We increasingly believed, however, empirical paradigms needed to be developed that assess the role of simulation in knowledge directly.

Thus, my students and I began designing experiments to test this issue. We began with tasks that were widely believed to measure conceptual knowledge, such as the property generation and property verification. Most theories of knowledge at the time proposed that people generate and verify properties by consulting classic propositional knowledge in the form of feature lists, semantic networks, and frames (e.g., Smith, 1978). Conversely, we wanted to test the hypothesis that people produce and generate properties by simulating category members, and then examining these simulations for the requested properties.

Our initial studies produced surprisingly robust and consistent results (for a preliminary review, see Barsalou, Solomon, & Wu, 1999). Wu and Barsalou (2007) found that occlusion affected property generation and conceptual combination. Solomon and Barsalou (2001, 2004) found that property similarity and property size affect property generation (when a superficial word association strategy is blocked). Kan, Barsalou, Solomon, Minor, and Thompson-Schill (2003) found neural evidence for these conclusions.

Widespread Evidence for Simulation in Cognition

Researchers in many other labs were simultaneously exploring whether cognition is grounded in modality-specific processing. At the time, considerable skepticism existed in the field about this approach. After working with traditional amodal representations for decades, it is not surprising that most researchers found this view implausible. As supporting empirical evidence began to accrue, however, researchers increasingly began to believe that modality-specific processing plays some role in higher cognition (although many still believe that it plays only a peripheral role, with amodal representations lying at the heart of the cognitive system).

Behavioral Research.   Many researchers have played major roles in changing the community's views. One significant source of empirical evidence has come from research on language comprehension. Notably, much of this evidence evolved from work on situation models championed by Bower and Morrow (1990) and by Rinck and Bower (2004). Their seminal work highlighted the importance of spatial representations in language comprehension, driving comprehension researchers increasingly away from classic propositional representations toward situation models.

Increasingly, comprehension researchers began viewing situation models as simulations that reenact modality-specific processing. Gibbs and his colleagues demonstrated the role of embodied metaphors in language comprehension (for a review, see Gibbs, 2005). Glenberg and his colleagues demonstrated the presence of motor, perceptual, and emotional simulation (e.g., Glenberg, Havas, Becker, & Rinck, 2005; Glenberg & Kaschak, 2002; Glenberg & Robertson, 2000). Spivey and his colleagues similarly demonstrated the presence of motor simulation (for a review, see Spivey, Richardson, & Gonzalez-Marques, 2005). Zwaan and his colleagues reported numerous findings demonstrating the presence of visual simulation (for a review, see Zwaan & Madden, 2005). The explosion of findings in this area is transforming the study of language comprehension, and the roots of this transformation can be traced back to Gordon's work on situation models.

Researchers in other behavioral areas also reported lines of work that demonstrated the role of modality-specific processing in cognition. Goldstone (1994, 1995) reported results showing that categories are grounded in perceptual representations (also see Goldstone & Barsalou, 1998). Similarly, Pecher, Zeelenberg, and Barsalou (2003, 2004) found that switching modalities produces a cost during linguistic-property verification, further implicating simulation in this task (for a review, see Barsalou, Pecher, Zeelenberg, Simmons, & Hamann, 2005). Borghi (2005) obtained a variety of findings that implicate visual and motor representations in conceptual processing.

Neural Evidence.   Research in cognitive neuroscience has also played a major role in changing the community's views about the role of modality-specific processing in higher cognition. In the 1980s, Warrington and her colleagues reported that lesions in the brain's modality-specific systems produce deficits in category knowledge (e.g., Warrington & McCarthy, 1987; Warrington & Shallice, 1984). For example, lesions in visual areas compromise categories that rely heavily on visual features (e.g., animals), whereas lesions in motor areas compromise categories that rely heavily on motor features (e.g., tools). Many researchers subsequently reported similar findings, consistent with the view that conceptual knowledge is grounded in perceptual and motor representations (see Martin, 2001, for a review).

Other researchers suggested alternatively that the lesion data implicate other mechanisms, such as statistical and categorical processes (for a broad collection of articles, see Martin & Carramazza, 2003). Nevertheless, considerable evidence exists that category-specific deficits reflect damage to modality-specific systems, at least to some extent (for attempts to integrate multiple mechanisms, see Cree & McRae, 2003; Simmons & Barsalou, 2003).

Still stronger evidence comes from neuroimaging research. Many PET (positron emission tomography), fMRI (functional magnetic resonance imaging), and ERP (event related potential) researchers have measured brain activation as people process conceptual information. Overwhelming support now exists for central roles of modality-specific simulation (for reviews, see Martin, 2001; Thompson-Schill, 2003). For example, Martin and his colleagues found that color-, shape-, motion-, and action-processing areas become active as people process conceptual properties for color, shape, motion, and action. Similarly, Simmons, Martin, and Barsalou (2005) found that the brain's taste-processing areas become active as people view pictures of appetizing foods, suggesting that these simulations represent inferences about taste.

Summary.   Evidence has been accumulating rapidly that cognition is grounded in the brain's modality-specific systems. Much additional evidence in many fields exists that has not been cited here, due to space constraints (for a review, see Barsalou, 2008). Other theoretical views exist as well, also not cited. Nevertheless, all this work suggests that cognition is not a modular system, detached from systems that process perception, action, emotion, and other experiential qualities. Instead, cognition appears grounded in these systems to a significant extent.

Ten years ago, when it seemed unlikely that cognition was grounded in the brain's modality-specific systems, it was important for researchers to demonstrate this grounding. Now that this evidence has become overwhelming, the payoffs of demonstration experiments are likely to decrease. Instead, it will become increasingly important to understand the specific roles of simulation in cognition. To identify these roles, it will become increasingly necessary to develop detailed process models of simulation, and to assess them empirically.

CONCLUSION

I began this chapter by noting major themes in Gordon's work, which might, at first, appear incompatible: associationism, imagery, propositions, and situation models. Over the years, I have increasingly come to believe that Gordon saw the fundamental importance of each theme in human cognition. As far as I know, Gordon never claimed at any point that one and only one of these perspectives is correct. To the contrary, he coexisted comfortably with all of them.

The continuing evolution of research and theory in multiple fields suggests that Gordon had exactly the right instincts. We continue to see strong empirical evidence for the central roles of association, imagery, propositions, and situation models throughout human cognition. We are also beginning to see that they can be integrated.

No one has represented and championed such a diversity of important themes in modern cognitive science as Gordon. His impact on the field and on his students has been tremendous. It has been a privilege and a pleasure to know Gordon and his work. The better I come to understand myself and my work, the more I see the extensive presence of his influence.

ACKNOWLEDGMENTS

This work was supported by National Science Foundation Grants SBR–9421326, SBR–9796200, and BCS–0212134 and by DARPA contracts BICA FA8650–05–C–7256 and FA8650–05–C–7255 to Lawrence W. Barsalou.

REFERENCES

Anderson, J. R., & Bower, G. H. (1972). Recognition and retrieval processes in free recall. *Psychological Review, 79*, 97–123.

Anderson, J. R., & Bower, G. H. (1973). *Human associative memory*. Oxford, England: Winston.

Anderson, J. R., & Bower, G. H. (1974). A propositional theory of recognition memory. *Memory & Cognition, 2*, 406–412.

Barsalou, L. W. (1982). Context-independent and context-dependent information in concepts. *Memory & Cognition, 10*, 82–93.

Barsalou, L. W. (1983). Ad hoc categories. *Memory & Cognition, 11*, 211–227.

Barsalou, L. W. (1985). Ideals, central tendency, and frequency of instantiation as determinants of graded structure in categories. *Journal of Experimental Psychology: Learning, Memory, and Cognition, 11*, 629–654.

Barsalou, L. W. (1987). The instability of graded structure: Implications for the nature of concepts. In U. Neisser (Ed.), *Concepts and conceptual development: Ecological and intellectual factors in categorization* (pp. 101–140). Cambridge, England: Cambridge University Press.

Barsalou, L. W. (1989). Intraconcept similarity and its implications for interconcept similarity. In S. Vosniadou & A. Ortony (Eds.), *Similarity and analogical reasoning* (pp. 76–121). Cambridge, England: Cambridge University Press.

Barsalou, L. W. (1991). Deriving categories to achieve goals. In G. H. Bower (Ed.), *The psychology of learning and motivation: Advances in research and theory* (Vol. 27, pp. 1–64). San Diego, CA: Academic Press.

Barsalou, L. W. (1992). Frames, concepts, and conceptual fields. In E. Kittay & A. Lehrer (Eds.), *Frames, fields, and contrasts: New essays in semantic and lexical organization* (pp. 21–74). Hillsdale, NJ: Lawrence Erlbaum Associates.

Barsalou, L. W. (1993). Flexibility, structure, and linguistic vagary in concepts: Manifestations of a compositional system of perceptual symbols. In A. C. Collins, S. E. Gathercole, & M. A. Conway (Eds.), *Theories of memory* (pp. 29–101). London: Lawrence Erlbaum Associates.

Barsalou, L. W. (1999). Perceptual symbol systems. *Behavioral and Brain Sciences, 22*, 577–609.

Barsalou, L. W. (2003a). Abstraction in perceptual symbol systems. *Philosophical Transactions of the Royal Society of London: Biological Sciences, 358*, 1177–1187.

Barsalou, L. W. (2003b). Situated simulation in the human conceptual system. *Language and Cognitive Processes, 18*, 513–562.

Barsalou, L. W. (2005a). Abstraction as dynamic interpretation in perceptual symbol systems. In L. Gershkoff-Stowe & D. Rakison (Eds.), *Building object categories* (389–431). Carnegie Symposium Series. Mahwah, NJ: Lawrence Erlbaum Associates.

Barsalou, L. W. (2005b). Continuity of the conceptual system across species. *Trends in Cognitive Sciences, 9*, 309–311.

Barsalou, L. W. (2005c). Situated conceptualization. In H. Cohen & C. Lefebvre (Eds.), *Handbook of categorization in cognitive science* (pp. 619–650). St. Louis, MO: Elsevier.

Barsalou, L. W. (2008). Grounded cognition. *Annual Review of Psychology, 59*.

Barsalou, L. W., & Hale, C. R. (1993). Components of conceptual representation: From feature lists to recursive frames. In I. Van Mechelen, J. Hampton, R. Michalski, & P. Theuns (Eds.), *Categories and concepts: Theoretical views and inductive data analysis* (pp. 97–144). San Diego, CA: Academic Press.

Barsalou, L. W., Niedenthal, P. M., Barbey, A., & Ruppert, J. (2003). Social embodiment. In B. Ross (Ed.), *The psychology of learning and motivation* (Vol. 43, pp. 43–92). San Diego, CA: Academic Press.

Barsalou, L. W., Pecher, D., Zeelenberg, R., Simmons, W. K., & Hamann, S. B. (2005). Multi-modal simulation in conceptual processing. In W. Ahn, R. Goldstone, B. Love, A. Markman, & P. Wolff (Eds.), *Categorization inside and outside the lab: Essays in honor of Douglas L. Medin* (pp. 249–270). Washington, DC: American Psychological Association.

Barsalou, L. W., & Prinz, J. J. (1997). Mundane creativity in perceptual symbol systems. In T. B. Ward, S. M. Smith, & J. Vaid (Eds.), *Creative thought: An investigation of conceptual structures and processes* (pp. 267–307). Washington, DC: American Psychological Association.

Barsalou, L. W., Solomon, K. O., & Wu, L. L. (1999). Perceptual simulation in conceptual tasks. In M. K. Hiraga, C. Sinha, & S. Wilcox (Eds.), *Cultural, typological, and psychological perspectives in cognitive linguistics: The proceedings of the 4th conference of the International Cognitive Linguistics Association* (Vol. 3, pp. 209–228). Amsterdam: John Benjamins.

Barsalou, L. W., & Wiemer-Hastings, K. (2005). Situating abstract concepts. In D. Pecher & R. Zwaan (Eds.), *Grounding cognition: The role of perception and action in memory, language, and thought* (pp. 129–163). New York: Cambridge University Press.

Barsalou, L. W., Yeh, W., Luka, B. J., Olseth, K. L., Mix, K. S., & Wu, L. (1993). Concepts and meaning. In K. Beals, G. Cooke, D. Kathman, K. E. McCullough, S. Kita, & D. Testen (Eds.), *Chicago Linguistics Society 29: Papers from the parasession on conceptual representations* (pp. 23–61). Chicago: Chicago Linguistics Society.

Black, J. B., Turner, T. J., & Bower, G. H. (1979). Point of view in narrative comprehension, memory, and production. *Journal of Verbal Learning & Verbal Behavior, 18,* 187–198.

Borghi, A. M. (2005). Object concepts and action. In D. Pecher & R. Zwaan (Eds.), *Grounding cognition* (pp. 8–34). New York: Cambridge University Press.

Bower, G. H. (1970). Imagery as a relational organizer in associative learning. *Journal of Verbal Learning & Verbal Behavior, 9,* 529–533.

Bower, G. H. (1972a). Mental imagery and associative learning. In L. W. Gregg (Ed.), *Cognition in learning and memory* (pp. 51–88). Oxford, England: Wiley.

Bower, G. H. (1972b). Stimulus-sampling theory of encoding variability. In A. W. Melton & E. Martin (Eds.), *Coding processes in human memory* (pp. 85–123). Washington, DC: Winston.

Bower, G. H. (1974). Selective facilitation and interference in retention of prose. *Journal of Educational Psychology, 66,* 1–8.

Bower, G. H. (1976). Experiments on story understanding and recall. *Quarterly Journal of Experimental Psychology, 28,* 511–534.

Bower, G. H., Black, J. B., & Turner, T. J. (1979). Scripts in memory for text. *Cognitive Psychology, 11,* 177–220.

Bower, G. H., & Morrow, D. G. (1990). Mental models in narrative comprehension. *Science, 247,* 44–48.

Bower, G. H., & Reitman, J. S. (1972). Mnemonic elaboration in multilist learning. *Journal of Verbal Learning & Verbal Behavior, 11,* 478–485.

Buckner, R. L., & Wheeler, M. E. (2001). The cognitive neuroscience of remembering. *Nature Reviews Neuroscience, 2,* 624–634.

Cangelosi, A., Greco, A., & Harnad, S. (2000). From robotic toil to symbolic theft: Grounding transfer from entry-level to higher-level categories. *Connection Science, 12,* 143–162.

Cangelosi, A., Coventry, K., Rajapakse, R., Joyce, D., Bacon, A., Richards, L., & Newstead, S. (2005). Grounding language in perception: A connectionist model of spatial terms and vague quantifiers. In A. Cangelosi, G. Bugmann, & R. Borisyuk (Eds.), *Modeling language, cognition and action: Proceedings of the 9th Neural Computation and Psychology Workshop* (pp. 47–56). Singapore: World Scientific.

Cangelosi, A., & Riga, T. (2005). *An epigenetic robotic model for sensorimotor grounding and grounding transfer.* Manuscript under review.

Chaigneau, S. E., Barsalou, L. W., & Sloman, S. (2004). Assessing the causal structure of function. *Journal of Experimental Psychology: General, 133*, 601–625.

Cree, G. S,. & McRae, K. (2003). Analyzing the factors underlying the structure and computation of the meaning of chipmunk, cherry, chisel, cheese, and cello (and many other such concrete nouns). *Journal of Experimental Psychology: General, 132*, 163–201.

Damasio, A. R. (1989). Time-locked multiregional retroactivation: A systems-level proposal for the neural substrates of recall and recognition. *Cognition, 33*, 25–62.

Farah, M. J. (2000). The neural bases of mental imagery. In M. S. Gazzaniga (Ed), *The cognitive neurosciences* (2nd ed., pp. 965–974). Cambridge, MA: MIT Press.

Gibbs, R. W., Jr. (2005). Embodiment in metaphorical imagination. In D. Pecher & R. Zwaan (Eds.), *Grounding cognition* (pp. 65–92). New York: Cambridge University Press.

Glaser, W. R. (1992). Picture naming. *Cognition, 42*, 61–105.

Glenberg, A. M., Havas, D., Becker, R., & Rinck, M. (2005). Grounding language in bodily states: The case for emotion. In D. Pecher & R. Zwaan (Eds.), *The grounding of cognition* (pp. 115–128). New York: Cambridge University Press.

Glenberg, A. M., & Kaschak, M. P. (2002). Grounding language in action. *Psychonomic Bulletin & Review, 9*, 558–569.

Glenberg, A. M., & Robertson, D. A. (2000). Symbol grounding and meaning: A comparison of high-dimensional and embodied theories of meaning. *Journal of Memory and Language, 43*, 379–401.

Goldstone, R. (1994). Influences of categorization on perceptual discrimination. *Journal of Experimental Psychology: General, 123*, 178–200.

Goldstone, R. L. (1995). Effects of categorization on color perception. *Psychological Science, 6*, 298–30

Goldstone, R., & Barsalou, L. W. (1998). Reuniting cognition and perception: The perceptual bases of rules *and* similarity. *Cognition, 65*, 231–262.

Grezes, J., & Decety, J. (2001). Functional anatomy of execution, mental simulation, observation, and verb generation of actions: A meta-analysis. *Human Brain Mapping, 12*, 1–19.

Jeannerod, M. (1995). Mental imagery in the motor context. *Neuropsychologia, 33*, 1419–1432.

Joyce, D., Richards, L., Cangelosi, A., & Coventry, K. R. (2003). On the foundations of perceptual symbol systems: Specifying embodied representations via connectionism. In F. Detje, D. Dörner, & H. Schaub (Eds.), *The logic of cognitive systems. Proceedings of the Fifth International Conference on Cognitive Modeling* (pp. 147–152). Bamberg, Germany: Universitätsverlag Bamberg.

Kan, I. P., Barsalou, L. W., Solomon, K. O., Minor, J. K., & Thompson-Schill, S. L. (2003). Role of mental imagery in a property verification task: fMRI evidence for perceptual representations of conceptual knowledge. *Cognitive Neuropsychology, 20*, 525–540.

Kosslyn, S. M. (1980). *Image and mind.* Cambridge, MA: Harvard University Press.

Kosslyn, S. M. (1994). *Image and brain.* Cambridge, MA: MIT Press.

Kosslyn, S. M., & Bower, G. H. (1974). The role of imagery in sentence memory: A developmental study. *Child Development, 45*, 30–38.

Langacker, R. W. (1987). *Foundations of cognitive grammar: Vol. 1. Theoretical prerequisites.* Stanford, CA: Stanford University Press.

Martin, A. (2001). Functional neuroimaging of semantic memory. In. R. Cabeza & A. Kingstone (Eds.), *Handbook of functional neuroimaging of cognition* (pp. 153–186). Cambridge, MA: MIT Press.

Martin, A., & Caramazza, A. (Eds.). (2003). *The organisation of conceptual knowledge in the brain: Neuropsychological and neuroimaging perspectives.* East Sussex, England: Psychology Press.

McCloskey, M., & Glucksberg, S. (1978). Natural categories: Well-defined or fuzzy sets? *Memory & Cognition, 6,* 462–472.

Morrow, D. G., Bower, G. H., & Greenspan, S. L. (1989). Updating situation models during narrative comprehension. *Journal of Memory and Language, 28,* 292–312.

Morrow, D. G., Greenspan, S. L., & Bower, G. H. (1987). Accessibility and situation models in narrative comprehension. *Journal of Memory and Language, 26,* 165–187.

Norman, D. A., Rumelhart, D. E., & the LNR Research Group. (1975). *Explorations in cognition.* New York: Freeman.

O'Reilly, R. C. (1998). Six principles for biologically-based computational models of cortical cognition. *Trends in Cognitive Sciences, 2,* 455–462.

Paivio, A. (1965). Abstractness, imagery, and meaningfulness in paired-associate learning. *Journal of Verbal Learning & Verbal Behavior, 4,* 32–38.

Paivio, A. (1971). *Imagery and verbal processes.* New York: Holt, Rinehart & Winston.

Pecher, D., Zeelenberg, R., & Barsalou, L. W. (2003). Verifying properties from different modalities for concepts produces switching costs. *Psychological Science, 14,* 119–124.

Pecher, D., Zeelenberg, R., & Barsalou, L. W. (2004). Sensorimotor simulations underlie conceptual representations: Modality-specific effects of prior activation. *Psychonomic Bulletin & Review, 11,* 164–167.

Price, H. H. (1953). *Thinking and experience.* London: Hutchinson's Universal Library.

Prinz, J. (2002). *Furnishing the mind: Concepts and their perceptual basis.* Cambridge, MA: MIT Press.

Pylyshyn, Z. W. (1973). What the mind's eye tells the mind's brain: A critique of mental imagery. *Psychological Bulletin, 80,* 1–24.

Rinck, M., & Bower, G. H. (2004). Goal-based accessibility of entities within situation models. In B. H. Ross (Ed.), *The psychology of learning and motivation: Advances in research and theory* (Vol. 44, pp. 1–33). New York: Elsevier Science.

Roy, D. (2005). Grounding words in perception and action: Insights from computational models. *Trends in Cognitive Science, 9,* 389–396.

Rumelhart, D. E., & Ortony, A. (1978). The representation of knowledge in memory. In R. C. Anderson, R. J. Spiro, & W. E. Montague (Eds.), *Schooling and the acquisition of knowledge* (pp. 99–135). Hillsdale, NJ: Lawrence Erlbaum Associates.

Russell, B. (1919). On propositions: What they are and how they mean. *Aristotelean Society Supplementary, 2,* 1–43. (Reprinted in *The collected papers of Bertrand Russell, Volume 8: The philosophy of logical atomism and other essays, 1914–19,* pp. 276–306, by J. G. Slater, Ed., 1986, London: Allen & Unwin)

Sachs, J. D. S. (1967). Recognition memory for syntactic and semantic aspects of connected discourse. *Perception & Psychophysics, 2,* 437–442.

Schank, R. C., & Colby, K. M. (Eds.). (1973) *Computer models of thought and language.* San Francisco: Freeman.

Simmons, W. K., & Barsalou, L. W. (2003). The similarity-in-topography principle: Reconciling theories of conceptual deficits. *Cognitive Neuropsychology, 20,* 451–486.

Simmons, W. K., Hamann, S. B., & Harenski, C. L., & Barsalou, L. W. (2006). *Word association and situated simulation in conceptual processing.* Manuscript under review.

Simmons, W. K., Martin, A., & Barsalou, L. W. (2005). Pictures of appetizing foods activate gustatory cortices for taste and reward. *Cerebral Cortex, 15,* 1602–1608.

Smith, E. E. (1978). Theories of semantic memory. In W. K. Estes (Ed.), *Handbook of learning and cognitive processes* (Vol. 6, pp. 1–56). Hillsdale, NJ: Lawrence Erlbaum Associates.

Solomon, K. O., & Barsalou, L. W. (2001). Representing properties locally. *Cognitive Psychology, 43,* 129–169.

Solomon, K. O., & Barsalou, L. W. (2004). Perceptual simulation in property verification. *Memory & Cognition, 32,* 244–259.

Spivey, M. J., Richardson, D. C., & Gonzalez-Marques, M. (2005). On the perceptual-motor and image-schematic infrastructure of language. In D. Pecher & R. Zwaan (Eds.), *Grounding cognition* (pp. 246–281). New York: Cambridge University Press.

Thompson-Schill, S. L. (2003), Neuroimaging studies of semantic memory: Inferring "how" from "where." *Neurosychologia, 41,* 280–292.

Warrington, E. K., & McCarthy, R. A. (1987). Categories of knowledge: Further fractionations and an attempted integration. *Brain, 110,* 1273–1296.

Warrington, E. K., & Shallice, T. (1984). Category specific semantic impairments. *Brain, 107,* 829–854.

Wu, L., & Barsalou, L. W. (2007). *Perceptual simulation in property generation.* Manuscript under review.

Yeh, W., & Barsalou, L. W. (2006). The situated nature of concepts. *American Journal of Psychology, 119*(3), 349–384.

Zwaan, R. A., & Madden, C. J. (2005). Embodied sentence comprehension. In D. Pecher & R. Zwaan (Eds.), *Grounding cognition* (pp. 224–245). New York: Cambridge University Press.

Zwaan, R. A., & Radvansky, G. A. (1998). Situation models in language comprehension and memory. *Psychological Bulletin, 123,* 162–185.

15

Category Learning: Learning to Access and Use Relevant Knowledge

Brian H. Ross
University of Illinois

Gordon H. Bower has had a major influence on psychology, particularly on his many students, including me (PhD, 1982). I am honored to write a chapter discussing that influence and my current work. To best present the information, the chapter is divided into two sections. The first discusses some of Gordon's work that most affected me, along with some evidence of that impact. The second section jumps ahead several (well, more than several) years and outlines part of my current work in which some influence is still obvious.

GORDON'S INFLUENCE

It is an interesting (if humbling) exercise after a number of years into one's career to think back to the intellectual influences from much earlier, especially when the impact is large. Before providing specifics, I mention two general aspects of

Gordon's influence. First, he is a broad thinker, "keeping his eye on" the big picture. I realize he is known for many of his classic experiments, but if you are around Gordon for long, you come to appreciate his broad view of cognition. Second, he believes strongly that one should understand what one is talking about—do the work to make sure you know what is going on. So, it is really not so difficult—think broadly and work hard.

Gordon and Me.   My direct research involvement with Gordon was focused on one project begun in my 1st year of graduate study at Stanford on associative models of recall (Ross & Bower, 1981). It was an education to have him outline the issues and discuss the possibilities with me (though in retrospect I suspect he already knew the approach he wanted to take and presented it in such a way that I would help "find" it).

As an adviser, Gordon H. Bower was a force to be reckoned with. I do not detail our many adviser–advisee interactions, but rather summarize my relationship by saying that his rules were simple: You can work on whatever you want, but it better be good and there better be a lot of it. As I look back, I am much more appreciative of his adviser and mentoring skills after having tried to do this for many years with my own students—it is a lot harder than it looks to (positively) influence so many students. (Much like one comes to appreciate one's own parents more after having children.) He continues to play a role. I don't think I have given a talk at Psychonomics without Gordon in the audience, near the front, and asking a question. In fact, at one talk he asked a tough question, which I reminded him he had asked me when I first began the work, almost 10 years before. He then suggested I should have an answer by now (no shrinking violet is he). I did because I had conducted a line of research to address that question.

His presence in the Cognitive group and the department was strong and pervasive. He would stop by offices, ask students what they were doing, and make suggestions. He would bring visitors by, introduce us, and "help" our careers. (For example, I remember one very eminent psychologist who he told that I had done this person's experiments "the right way." Ouch.). He would always be prepared for classes he taught and seminars he sat in on. At talks, he always had questions (and answers when the speaker faltered). He took time to help the students get ready for our annual Stanford–Berkeley graduate student talks, including listening to our presentations until we (and he) were happy with them. Stanford ex-students have a common bond with the telling of Gordon stories, and some may even be true. I am too circumspect to repeat any here.

When I was a student at Stanford, Gordon was involved in two main projects, neither of which I ended up working on, but both of which have had an indirect but strong influence on my thinking about cognition and on my career: mood and scripts.

Mood and Memory.   Gordon was conducting much research on mood and memory, extending the idea of state-dependent learning to moods, working closely with two students, Stephen Gilligan and Kenneth Monteiro. The main issue at the time was a focus on mood dependency effects—those words learned under one mood would be better recalled under the same mood (e.g., Bower, 1981). This research had a big impact in various psychological areas and continues to be well cited, though the research story became more complicated (see chap. 16, this volume). Three aspects of this research impressed and affected me greatly as a student. One, the power of contextual effects is much greater than one might intuit. It is not that the effects are so large and easy to obtain, but that so many types of context can influence so much cognitive processing and memory. I have used this contextual idea often in my research after hearing about it in his lab meetings. Two, think widely about independent and dependent variables. Many people who have worked with Gordon probably can remember his incredible ability to take an issue and construct a list of independent variables to consider ("What if you varied frequency? What about recency? What if you varied ... ?"). I was amazed at how often the first few independent-variable suggestions would lead to an interesting new experiment. Although he often examined explicit memory for some newly learned material, he had a broad view of how to examine memory or what other cognitive event would be interesting to examine. Three, Gordon takes a very liberal view as to what cognitive psychologists should/can study. As a corollary, which Gordon made explicit in his plenary Psychonomics address in 2004, one should expect to change research interests periodically.

Scripts and Understanding.   In addition to the work on mood and memory, Gordon was continuing work on scripts that he had started with John Black (see chap. 13, this volume). The work focused on how comprehension of situations/narratives was aided by taking into account the goals of the protagonists and the prior knowledge that underlies many common situations (e.g., Bower, 1976; Bower, Black, & Turner, 1979). This research was part of a change in the field for understanding comprehension and memory. It showed how a system could bring to bear relevant knowledge without an inference explosion, it argued that causal networks were a critical part of understanding, and it helped to bridge the work in artificial intelligence and psychology. Two aspects of this work had a large impact on my research and thinking about cognition. One, the experimental research provided strong evidence that so much of the cognitive processing depends on the goals the person has rather than just the stimulus or situation presented. Many of the experiments had short, mundane (boring) vignettes, yet the reader could make dozens of inferences based on applying prior knowledge. Two, the interest was not on memory per se but how people used their knowledge to understand. One can (and I do) think about this work as how people access and apply relevant knowledge to understand.

Thesis.   My thesis was conducted while I was also an intern at the Applied Information Processing Department at Xerox PARC (Palo Alto Research Center), a connection that Gordon was instrumental in establishing. At the time, many cognitive psychology PhDs were joining the industrial workforce and PARC's group was on the forefront of applying cognitive psychology to human–computer interaction (with Thomas Moran and Stuart Card). I began my work at PARC with the idea of working on a mathematical model of learning of complex cognitive skills that would focus on the development of knowledge in more complex domains. I videotaped a number of people learning a new cognitive skill, learning to use a computer word processor (in the early 1980s, many people did not know how). In reviewing the videotapes, a common occurrence was that people referred to earlier word-processing episodes and used them to help figure out what to do in the current case. "How do I move a paragraph? Oh, the last time I had to move a paragraph ... ." My thesis topic changed to then focus on these remindings, unintentional retrievals of earlier episodes, and their influence in the learning of complex cognitive skills such as word processing and probability theory (Ross, 1984).

I hope the connection back to the Gordon's influence is clear, but let me make it explicit. Although I used real-world domains and examined people learning to accomplish complex goals, this thesis was largely about memory. I manipulated *contextual factors* that I hypothesized would influence remindings (e.g., the content of the text, such as whether it was a restaurant review or a shopping list, or the story line of a mathematical word problem) and showed an influence of the reminding. The dependent variable was not memory, but performance on the task, with a focus on the *goals* that people brought to bear. I thought about this work in much the way that I thought about Gordon's examination of scripts—the *access and use of relevant knowledge* to accomplish some goal. A main reason for turning to problem-oriented domains was so that the goals would be an intrinsic part of the task (editing the text, solving the problem) and the influence of memory could be measured more indirectly.

Besides the background Gordon helped me obtain on memory, learning, and experimentation, two other influences were less direct. First, he taught students how to go from ideas to experiments. I already mentioned his ability to generate a host of relevant independent variables to consider. Although I have never mastered his high hit rate, it is a useful idea-generating tool. The point is not to know the best way to look the problem right away, but a means of trying out a variety of ideas until one seems a good way to look at it. Second, he encouraged considering the issues and finding good ways to test them, only later worrying about the paradigm or materials. Many researchers try to stay within a paradigm or two that they understand well so that experiments are easier to generate and execute. Gordon certainly has that practical side as well, but he also encouraged trying out new ideas in new ways. His work on mood was an excellent example for his own work, but looking at the wide variety of research conducted by his students while they were students also makes clear that he promoted this approach in students. As he said, it is useful to change areas every once in a while and this was a change for me from mathematical models of memory to a consideration of memory in use.

I end this section by noting that Gordon was not always the easiest adviser to have. He had (has) strong opinions, a powerful voice, and a more powerful mind. Arguing for one's point was not for the timid, but it made going out on job interviews and talks seem easy. He was a driving force behind making Stanford an exciting place to be and to learn.

CURRENT WORK

For the rest of the chapter, I discuss my more recent work on the goal-oriented use of categories and its influence on category learning and representation. Rather than focus on how people learn to classify, I examine category learning from the perspective of how people use categories to accomplish their goals.

Although Gordon's work has not focused on categories, he has conducted some research in this area (as in most cognitive areas), especially with John Clapper and Mark Gluck, and has had several other students who have conducted work on categories (e.g., John Anderson, Larry Barsalou, Arnold Glass, Evan Heit, Keith Holyoak, and Steve Sloman, just to choose some authors in this volume). Gordon affected my research on categories in at least three ways. First, the focus on goals was partly due to the script work (plus see some discussion later of the script categories in foods) as well as the work of Larry Barsalou, also a student of Gordon's. Second, the general idea that the type of processing of information influences the representation was a common theme during this time in Gordon's lab. Third, and perhaps most important, Gordon set an example and made explicit that areas of research were not rigid. His work on mood and memory, as well as his widespread publications, made it easier to consider connections across areas.

Categories are critical for much intelligent behavior. When we know an item is in a particular category, we can use knowledge of that category to access relevant information that can be useful in many ways. Category information about an object often allows us to make a prediction about an unobserved property or explain its behavior. We can use knowledge of the type of situation to understand the events that are occurring. We can use problem category knowledge to decide how best to solve a problem. Categories can be thought of as memories about classes, and the use of category information for accomplishing our goals is a means by which we use memory to access and retrieve relevant knowledge.

Given the importance of category information for many cognitive (and non-cognitive) activities, one would guess that category-learning research would have a huge influence across many areas in psychology, especially higher level cognition. There certainly has been some impact on other areas, such as the research on whether representations of a category take the form of prototypes versus exemplars (e.g., Brooks, 1978; Medin & Schaffer, 1978; Nosofsky, 1986; Posner & Keele, 1968; Rosch, 1978) and the influence of prior knowledge (e.g., Murphy

& Medin, 1985). However, many of these core ideas are at least 20 years old and there has been a great deal of research in category learning in the last 20 years that has been very specific to issues in category learning. I realize everyone will not agree with this assessment and I don't mean to suggest that there have not been advances. Even so, I think most researchers believe it would be useful to make stronger connections from category learning to other areas in which categories are so critical. I begin with a quick examination of why the influence has been less than ideal, not to assess blame, but to offer a partial solution.

At least part of the problem, I think, has been the emphasis of category learning research on classification learning, how we assign new items to prespecified categories. Category-learning theories have heavily focused on the particular configurations of features and relations that can be used to tell whether an item is in one of (usually) two experimenter-defined categories. Classification is a critical function of categories—if we did not know what category an item was in, we could not access relevant categorical knowledge about it. The idea is that by understanding how people learn these simple classifications, we would have insight to how people learn categories in more complex situations. The usual classification-learning task is:

An item is presented.

Subject responds with the category.

Feedback is given.

The next item is presented.

In these experiments, people continue until they meet some criterion by which they are said to have learned the category. As a generalization, diagnostic features, those predictive of the category, are attended to and nondiagnostic features are not, even if they are common in the category.

Although classification is a critical function of categories, there are at least three reasons why the focus on classification learning has been a problem. First, it is not enough. Learning to classify items into a category is not the same as learning a category, knowing what category members are like. I can classify items as cars or motorcycles by the number of wheels, but learning the category of car would entail much more than that. I would need to know at least what it is used for and probably some idea of the interiors, how to drive, and so on. Second, even if it were enough, it does not match our real category learning. It seems likely that we learn categories in many ways beyond classification. At the very least, we spend much time interacting with items and pick up additional category knowledge once an item has been classified. Thus, other category-related activities are influencing what we learn about categories. If so, then an understanding of category learning requires encompassing these other means of category learning. A nearly-exclusive focus on classification learning leads to a very restricted view. Third, classification is often not a goal. That is, although classification is critical, it is critical because it allows us to access relevant knowledge to help us accomplish the goal. If we want to understand a person's behavior or what is happening in a particular situation, it is very useful to figure out the type of person or situation, but the goal is the understanding not the classification. If we want to solve a problem, the goal is the problem solution not the classification of the problem, though that classification may be a critical part of solving the problem. (Also, see chap. 19, this volume.)

CATEGORY USE

My research has been exploring the influence of various types of goal-oriented category learning on category representations. Motivated partly by the work of another of Bower's students, Larry Barsalou (1983, 1991), I have been considering classification not as a goal in itself but as part of a larger goal-oriented task. For example, in problem solving, the task is to solve the problem, but the classification is an important part. We can think about this as classification learning *plus* some use made of the category. I refer to this as the *category use* paradigm (e.g., Ross, 1997) and it includes classification learning plus use (the use is italicized in the following list):

An item is presented.

Subject responds with the category.

Feedback is given.

Subject uses the category to do something (make a prediction, solve a problem).

Feedback is given on this use.

The next item is presented.

The results of this category use paradigm are easy to summarize: It affects a variety of category-related judgments. The use of the category often influences the representation, even including knowledge used for classification. That is, if one takes the standard classification paradigm to study category learning and embeds it in a larger task, then the category representation can be changed in ways that influence later classifications.

Let's start with a simple example, using a common classification-learning paradigm, in which each item is a patient consisting of a set of symptoms and the task is to learn to classify patients as having one of two diseases, A or B (Ross, 1997). So, the symptom set {*fever, headaches, nausea*} might be given and the person responds Disease A and is told that is correct. With the category use paradigm, the category is used to go beyond classification. In this situation, the learner is given two possible drug treatments for Disease A, say Treatments A1 and A2, and has to respond with which treatment is more likely to be helpful for a patient with these symptoms and this disease. (In the experiments, more interesting names are given for diseases and treatments.) The learner responds A2, is told no it is A1, and then the next patient's symptoms are presented. Suppose that in this design, two of the symptoms, *fever* and *headaches,* are equally predictive of Disease A, but that only *fever* is also predictive of the treatment. After reaching some criterion on the classification (disease) and use (treatment), the person is given a variety of tests. Let's examine a simple classification test: A single symptom is given and the person is asked what disease a patient is likely to have if this is all that is known. People are good at classifying on the basis of *headaches,* the symptom that is predictive of the classification but not predictive of any treatment, with 80% accuracy. However, for *fever,* which is predictive of both the disease and treatment, performance is near perfect, 96%. Both symptoms are equally predictive of the disease and occurred equally often during the learning, so there is no classification-based reason why one would be viewed as a better predictor of the disease classification. However, *fever* is predictive of the treatment and *headaches* is not. This use (deciding which treatment for a disease should be used for a patient with these symptoms) leads *fever* to being viewed not only as a better predictor of treatment, which it is, but also as a better predictor of disease, which it is not. A variety of other findings support this result—for example, when people are asked to generate symptoms for a disease, *fever* is generated earlier and with greater probability than *headaches,* plus is judged to have occurred more frequently during the experiment. The use is influencing the category representation of the disease, which in turn is influencing a variety of category-related judgments, including classification. Similar findings have been obtained with other materials and even with 5-year-old children (Ross, Gelman, & Rosengren, 2005).

Two objections have been raised about possible limitations of these findings. One possibility, pointed out to me by Gordon Bower (and reviewers), is that the use task here can be viewed as another type of classification, so maybe that is why the use-relevant symptoms are better predictors. For instance, people may be learning subcategories (Disease A symptoms treated by Treatment A1), so symptoms predictive of both disease and treatment get a boost relative to ones predictive of only the disease. This explanation does not deny the influence of the use but suggests it might be specific to classification-like use tasks. However, this finding of a use influence on later category-related judgments, including classification, has been found with a number of nonclassification uses, such as problem-solving tasks with mathematical categories (Ross, 1997, Experiment 6) and a spy code paradigm (Ross, 1997, Eperiment 7; Ross & Warren, 2002).

A second possible limitation is that the use effect is restricted to cases in which the classification and the use are learned in an interleaved way. Because the task requires classification and use responses on each trial, people's knowledge of the classification may get influenced by factors relevant to the use as well, perhaps more of a confusion between tasks than an influence of use on classification. Again, this explanation does not deny the finding but suggests it is limited to these interleaved cases. Although I think one could argue that these interleaved cases are quite common, the effect of use on later classification judgments does not require this interleaving. Using the disease paradigm, the disease classifications can be learned to criterion before the treatment possibilities are even introduced and one still finds the effect. That is, imagine an experiment with two study phases before classification tests. First, people learn to classify patients, just like in the usual classification test, so *fever* and *headaches* are both equally predictive of the disease. Second, after reaching criterion on the disease classification, people then learn to decide which treatment the patient should get, learning the use of the category. Even with this *postclassification* learning of the use, those symptoms predictive of the treatment (e.g., *fever*) are better classified (Ross, 1999). The same postclassification effect is found with 5-year-olds (Ross et al., 2005) and with problem-solving tasks (Ross, 2000).

Implications.   Classification is influenced by the use made of the category. Classification is determined by the diagnosticity of the features but also their importance for the use. The results of these studies argue for thinking about category learning as consisting of more than classification. In some cases (with other cases discussed shortly), people learn categories by a combination of learning to classify and learning to use. When they do, the category representation is influenced by both the classification and the use. Even if one is only interested in classification performance, one needs to consider other ways in which the category is used because they may affect classification. Classification is not an isolated process, with changes in classification-relevant category knowledge influenced only by classification learning. Rather, it is useful to think of classification as embedded in a larger, goal-related task and to ask what category knowledge supports what category-related activities.

One complaint raised by a classification researcher at a talk I gave was "We don't even know how classification works and now you have complicated the question." Ignoring the blame for this complication, I think considering use may simplify the question rather than complicate it. In the laboratory, if the goal is to learn to classify items with three binary features that the subject is told about, then learning the classification scheme may be made more complicated by adding a use. However, if one is learning to classify complex real-world items with hundreds of features and relations that are potentially relevant, how does one decide what is relevant and what is not? Salience and knowledge influences may be helpful, but salient features are not always predictive of the category and the knowledge may not be available or sufficient to help determine the relevant differences. The use may provide a good, simple heuristic for getting a handle on some of the relevant features and relations—if it is relevant to how an item is used, it may be relevant to the classification as well. It is a heuristic, so is not guaranteed to work, but it provides some help in situations that otherwise may be quite difficult. Even in the relatively simple disease classification task, it may have led the use-relevant symptoms (e.g., *fever*) to be considered as a better predictor of the category than the use-irrelevant symptoms (e.g., *headaches*) that were equally good predictors.

The final implication concerns how to study category learning. I have argued for thinking about category learning as including both classification and use. If one thinks of category learning as simply classification learning, there are not many variations on how to examine it. If however, one considers category learning more broadly, there are a large number of variations: how the classification is learned, how the use is learned, and how they interrelate. The next subsection considers two of these variations that do not require the person to learn to classify. I was influenced much by Gordon's consideration of goals and his encouragement to consider the tasks more broadly.

BROADENING THE STUDY OF CATEGORY LEARNING: LEARNING WITHOUT CLASSIFICATION LEARNING

What do categories do for us? J. R. Anderson (1991) has suggested that category representations are optimized for making predictions. I have discussed how much of the earlier research considered classification alone, then introduced a classification plus use paradigm. Now we look at cases in which the learners have the goal of making a predictive inference, but do not get any practice classifying; either the classification is given (*inference learning*) or there is no information about categories presented (*indirect learning*).

How we learn influences what we learn, so how we learn categories might well influence the category representation. Transfer-appropriate processing (Morris, Bransford, & Franks, 1977) suggests that what people remember about an item is a function of how they interacted with it, as well as how their knowledge is tested. Art Markman and I (Markman & Ross, 2003) have extended this idea to category learning, combining it with the assumptions that learning is conservative and that people rarely do more than is necessary to complete the task. Thus, the information necessary to complete a category-learning task is most, if not all, of what is learned about a category. To the extent that different category-learning tasks require processing of different information, one would predict that they would lead to different category representations. In addition, this view predicts that one cannot understand category learning by examining only the category structures but must also take into account the type of category learning. If it is true that classification is not usually the category-learning goal, then we clearly need to examine a wider range of tasks to understand how category representations are formed that can support the rich variety of functions for which categories are used. In this subsection, we consider two other category-learning tasks and contrast them with classification.

Inference Learning.   Consider a task that has many similarities to classification, but instead of being given the features of an item and having to respond with the category label, the learner is given the label and many of the features and has to respond with the value of a missing feature. In classification learning, one might see features {1a, 2a, and 3a} and be asked what category the item is in, A or B, whereas in inference learning one might see {Category A, 1a, 2a} and be asked whether the third feature is 3a or 3b. Amending the classification procedure with italics for the changed parts:

An item is presented *with the category label but without one of the features.*

Subject responds with the *missing feature value.*

Feedback is given.

The next item is presented.

Why examine inference learning among the possible ways of category learning? It provides a clear comparison to classification in terms of both task similarity and hypothesized differences in the representations formed. These, and additional, arguments are laid out in more detail in Markman and Ross (2003), but let me focus on the main point, the possible differences in the representations.

The transfer-appropriate processing approach suggests that differences in processing may result in differences in representation that can be observed by various test tasks. In classification learning, the processing is done with the goal of distinguishing the categories—is this item in Category A or B? Under this task, the focus is on those features that are predictive of category membership, diagnostic features. Although the representations used to make these decisions can vary across different theories (including prototypes, exemplars, rules, or some combinations), they all focus on the diagnostic features precisely because these are the features that predict category membership (i.e., classify).

In inference learning, however, classification is not the goal. The item is presented with its category label and the goal is to predict a missing feature value. A major difference from classification is that any search for representations for which to make the decision is likely to include mainly (only) information from the specified category, not what the other categories are like. That is, because one knows the category, one can focus on the single category to make the inference. To do so, the learners have to place special importance on the category label, not treating it as another feature, and there is ample evidence that they do (see Markman & Ross, 2003, for a detailing of the arguments). Why is this so important for the representation? The hypothesis is that because the learners are focused on the single category provided, the task is one of learning what the members of this particular category are like. So, rather than focus on diagnostic features, they focus on features (and relations among features) that are prototypical of the category. Some prototypical features will be diagnostic as well (ear shape for dogs vs. cats) but some will not (number of ears for dogs vs. cats).

So the hypothesis is that inference learning will tend to focus people on learning the prototypical features and the internal structure of the category, whereas classification learning will tend to focus on learning the diagnostic features (Yamauchi & Markman, 1998). Markman and Ross (2003) review a variety of evidence consistent with this hypothesis, but I mention two illustrative findings here. First, to the extent that inference learning leads to learning of the prototypical feature values for each category, one might predict that it should lead to high performance on classifying a single feature, whereas classification learners would presumably do better on full classification tests given that is what they were trained on. We (A. L. Anderson, Ross, & Chin-Parker, 2002, Experiment 1) found this predicted interaction with inference learners better able to classify single features (.84 vs. .72), but less able to classify full items (.62 vs. .84). Chin-Parker and Ross (2004) show that the typicality ratings of classification learners are determined exclusively by diagnostic features, whereas the performance of inference learners is also affected by the prototypical features, even ones that are not diagnostic.

A second piece of evidence for the difference in what is learned in the two tasks examines within-category correlations. Within-category correlations do not add to the diagnosticity, but do indicate structure within the category in terms of what feature values tend to co-occur. For example, bicycles have different types of handlebars and different types of bike tires, all of which are highly predictive of bicycles. Some handlebars tend to be found correlated with some tires, often indicating subcategories, such as mountain bikes. Although one could successfully classify something as a bicycle without this correlation, this correlation does provide important information for understanding aspects of bicycles and how they are used, and for predicting missing feature values. Thus, one would predict that classification learners would not be sensitive to these within-category correlations whereas inferences learners would, and that is exactly what Chin-Parker and Ross (2002) found. When faced with a test that presented the value on one feature and asked to choose from one of two feature values on the other feature of the correlation (e.g., equivalent to being given straight handlebars and being asked whether a bike with these handlebars was likely to have knobby or slick bike tires), the classification learners were at chance, whereas the inference learners were correct about 75% of the time.

The importance of the classification–inference distinction is even greater when one considers more complex categories in which the features are interrelated in a coherent way. Most of our categories are not defined by simple features or co-occurrences of features, but by underlying relations that provide a coherence to the category (e.g., Murphy & Medin, 1985). We know little about how such categories are learned, but one hypothesis is that the difference between learning by classification and inference might lead to large differences in learning such categories. Rehder and Ross (2001) presented *abstract coherent categories* that were defined by interconnecting systems of relations, although the feature values were not diagnostic. For example, pollution-cleaning devices (though the learners were simply told they were Morkels) might have interconnecting locations, pollutants, and instruments for removing the pollution (e.g., sponges for removing spilled oil from the ocean), though the features would vary across category members. How might these be learned by classification and inference? When focusing on the classification, it may be difficult to learn the underlying coherence of the category (how the location, pollutant, and instrument interrelate). It is difficult because the same feature values are used across categories, so learners need to pick out what feature pairs or triplets predict a category. However, inference learning focuses the learner on what each category is like, so items within categories may be compared and commonalities of internal structure perhaps noticed. Consistent with this analysis, when tested on novel devices (with new feature values not seen before in the experiment), classification learners were unable to tell which were Morkels (coherent, with performance of .52 for chance of .50), whereas inference learners were able to tell (.68; Erickson, Chin-Parker, & Ross, 2005).

Category learning by inferences does lead to a different category representation than by classification. Classification focuses the learner on the diagnostic features, whereas inference leads to better learning of the internal structure of each category, including co-occurring features and underlying interrelations among the features. The point is that some of the problems with classification relative to other category-learning means may become more apparent as we move away from categories defined by observable features and simple relations to consider more complex interconnected concepts.

Indirect Learning.   I briefly mention one other type of nonclassification category learning. Some categories are not explicitly pointed out to us by a helpful teacher who gives us a category label for each item. There may not even be any mention that there are categories. Rather, as we accomplish goals we may begin to "discover" the categories, in that some items are treated similarly to accomplish our goals and some are not. One can think of this as a type of unsupervised category learning, but rather than focusing on memory for the items (e.g., Clapper & Bower, 1994, 2002), the focus here is on accomplishing some goal, such as a prediction. Revising the classification paradigm procedure:

An item is presented.

Subject responds *to the item to accomplish some goal.*

Feedback *(on the goal)* is given.

The next item is presented.

The hypothesis is that the processing of items to accomplish this goal will lead to a representation that highlights the item-to-goal relation, rather than distinguishing which items are in which category.

Paul Minda and I (Minda & Ross, 2004) provided a preliminary investigation of this type of category learning using a simple prediction paradigm in which learners are presented with fictitious alien animals and have to decide how many pounds of food each animal should eat. We contrasted two groups of learners, a classification and prediction group versus a prediction-only group. The classification and prediction group classified each item (Category A or B), received feedback, made a prediction of the food amount, and received feedback. The prediction-only group made a prediction of the food amount and received feedback. The category was helpful in determining the food amount—one can think of the categories as light and heavy eaters. The category structures were such that there was a strong family resemblance among the items in each category (most features occurred predominantly in one category), but also a redundant defining feature (which appeared in every item in the category and never appeared in the other category). At test, we presented conflict trials that allowed us to determine whether learners were using the family resemblance or defining feature to make a prediction of food amount. We expected that the classification and prediction group would rely on the defining feature, because it is a more diagnostic feature than any of the features involved in the family resemblance. The main issue was whether the prediction-only group would be more likely to rely on the family resemblance because they are focused on the item to goal relations, not on the diagnosticity per se. Although even this group used the defining feature more than half the time, they were much more likely to use the family resemblance than the classification and prediction group. In addition, a model-based analysis of the attention weights showed that the prediction-only learners were much more likely to consider a wider range of features than the classification and prediction learners.

Clearly much remains to be done to understand what is learned from this indirect learning. The main point, though, is that one can learn category-related information from this indirect learning and it is not the same knowledge one gets learning to classify and use. This paradigm may provide an interesting contrast to a more classify and use view of learning, especially in informal domains where there is unlikely to be someone (or something) to organize the area and provide feedback on your intermediate decisions. People are still able to learn and use categories, as they get feedback from the consequences of their decisions. (As an aside, the alert reader might note that the classification and prediction group is the category use group from earlier in the chapter. Correct. One sign of progress is that my earlier experimental condition is now the control group.)

IMPLICATIONS

In this final section, I consider some implications of this work along two lines: for examining categories in more real-world settings and for our theories of category learning. The main point I wish to make, as in the introduction, is that considering the goals is critical to understanding category learning and representation.

Real-World Categories. What does this perspective suggest about real-world categories? If there is some consistent use made of a category, then one would expect to see an effect of that use on the category representation. Gregory Murphy and I examined people's representation of food categories (Ross & Murphy, 1999) and found such influences. People know a lot about food, think about it often, and use it every day. Although people clearly have taxonomic categories (e.g., fruits, vegetables) that provide rich sources of inductive inferences, they also have categories defined by human activity, uses, such as the circumstances under which they eat foods (e.g., breakfast foods, snack foods), which we called *script categories*. Our results indicate that these categories are not simply some fact people know about the foods, but also provide rich sources of inductive inference (with strong confidence) and show up in the residuals of people's sorting by taxonomic categories.

In addition to providing some evidence for the lasting effects of uses on representations, these categories force us to consider other ways in which categories might be used. It seems unlikely that script categories are primarily for classification—one usually classifies an item as an apple or fruit, not as a snack food. Of course, under context one might see these items as examples of particular script categories, but it may also be that the uses of script categories are more for activities such as planning than classifying. Category-related tasks do not require us to be driven by a proximal stimulus, such as an apple, but can make use of our mental representations in accomplishing a variety of goals. If we wake up and want to decide what to eat, we can search the kitchen cabinets or we can stay in our warm beds and think about what foods we might want for breakfast (which could include meats, fruits, beverages, grains).

This perspective on categories has led to two sets of issues when considering real-world categories. First, there is evidence for long-term use influences in these categories. An interesting avenue would be to better understand the representation and how knowledge about cross-classified items is accessed and used in different situations. Second, a consideration of goal-oriented categories has led to questions about the circumstances under which these categories might be used. This suggests a further broadening of the investigation of category use to move away from only cases in which items are presented and people respond to them, to include situations in which people's goals involve uses of categories without category members present (Barsalou, 1983, 1991).

Category-Learning Theories. Category-learning theories need to address a broader range of tasks, category structures, and category types. First, they need to address far more than classification. I do not mean to imply that there have not been any such views (e.g., J. R. Anderson, 1991) or that new ones are not being proposed (e.g., J. R. Anderson & Betz, 2001; Love, Medin, & Guerkis, 2004). However, it is important to realize the restriction of focusing on classification and to consider a variety of other ways in which categories might be learned. The inclusion of additional tasks also provides further constraints on the theories, as the same representation must accomplish multiple goals. The specific effects of different category-learning tasks are not yet clear, but it is clear that we need to know much more about how the tasks influence the representations. Second, we need to beyond simple features and feature co-occurrences to address structures that more like ones we face in learning real-world categories. Most categories are much more complex than the simple ones in the laboratory and the means of learning them may be quite different. Third, we need to broaden our examination beyond objects to consider the many other types of things that are routinely categorized, such as people, situations, and problems. These other types of categories will further encourage consideration of different means of learning and more complex structures, as well as being interesting in their own right.

CONCLUSIONS

Research on category learning needs to consider a wider variety of ways in which categories are learned as well as more complex categories. How one learns a category may greatly influence its representation, so an understanding of category learning will need to take into account how the items are processed during learning as well as the structure of the category. In addition, because the richness of the category structure interacts with the learning, we need to consider more complex, coherent categories and examine how the types of category learning facilitate (or not) the learning of these categories with more realistic structures. Broadening the study of category learning in these ways will help to make connections to the many areas of psychology in which categories are so important.

I want to end with thanks to Gordon for his many years of mentorship, encouragement, and constructive criticism. At my presentations, I sometimes imagine him listening, asking tough questions, providing positive feedback, and then suggesting, "What if you varied frequency? What about ... ?"

REFERENCES

Anderson, A. L., Ross, B.H., & Chin-Parker, S. (2002). A further investigation of category learning by inference. *Memory & Cognition, 30,* 119–128.

Anderson, J. R. (1991). The adaptive nature of human categorization. *Psychological Review, 98,* 409–429.

Anderson, J. R., & Betz, J. (2001). A hybrid model of categorization. *Psychonomic Bulletin & Review, 8,* 629–647.

Barsalou, L. W. (1983). Ad hoc categories. *Memory & Cognition, 11,* 211–217.

Barsalou, L. W. (1991). Deriving categories to achieve goals. In G. H. Bower (Ed.), *The psychology of learning and motivation* (Vol. 27, pp. 1–64). San Diego, CA,: Academic Press.

Bower, G. H. (1976). Experiments on story understanding and recall. *Quarterly Journal of Experimental Psychology, 28,* 511–534.

Bower, G. H. (1981). Mood and memory. *American Psychologist, 36,* 129–148.

Bower, G. H., Black, J., & Turner, T. (1979). Scripts in memory for text. *Cognitive Psychology, 11,* 177–220.

Brooks, L. (1978) Nonanalytic concept formation and memory for instances. In E. Rosch & B. B. Lloyd (Eds.), *Cognition and categorization* (pp. 169–215) Hillsdale, NJ: Lawrence Erlbaum Associates.

Chin-Parker, S., & Ross, B. H. (2002). The effect of category learning on sensitivity to within-category correlations. *Memory & Cognition, 30,* 353–362.

Chin-Parker, S., & Ross, B. H. (2004). Diagnosticity and prototypicality in category learning: A comparison of inference learning and classification learning. *Journal of Experimental Psychology: Learning, Memory, and Cognition, 30,* 216–226.

Clapper, J. P., & Bower, G. H. (1994). Category invention in unsupervised learning. *Journal of Experimental Psychology: Learning, Memory, and Cognition, 20,* 443–460.

Clapper, J. P., & Bower, G. H. (2002). Adaptive categorization in unsupervised learning. *Journal of Experimental Psychology: Learning, Memory, and Cognition, 28,* 908–923.

Erickson, J. E., Chin-Parker, S., & Ross, B. H. (2005). Inference and classification learning of abstract coherent categories. *Journal of Experimental Psychology: Learning, Memory, and Cognition, 31,* 86–99.

Love, B. C., Medin, D. L., & Gureckis, T. M. (2004). SUSTAIN: A network model of category learning. *Psychological Review, 111,* 309–332.

Markman, A. B., & Ross, B. H. (2003). Category use and category learning. *Psychological Bulletin, 129,* 592–613.

Medin, D. L., & Schaffer, M. M. (1978). Context theory of classification learning. *Psychological Review, 85,* 207–238.

Minda, J. P., & Ross, B. H. (2004). Learning categories by making predictions: An investigation of indirect category learning. *Memory & Cognition, 32,* 1355–1368.

Morris, C. D., Bransford, J. D., & Franks, J. J. (1977). Levels of processing versus transfer appropriate processing. *Journal of Verbal Learning and Verbal Behavior, 16,* 519–533.

Murphy, G. L., & Medin, D. L. (1985). The role of theories in conceptual coherence. *Psychological Review, 92,* 289–316.

Nosofsky, R. M. (1986). Attention, similarity and the identification–categorization relationship. *Journal of Experimental Psychology: General, 115,* 39–57.

Posner, M. I. & Keele, S. W. (1968). On the genesis of abstract ideas. *Journal of Experimental Psychology, 77,* 353–363.

Rehder, B., & Ross, B. H. (2001). Abstract coherent categories. *Journal of Experimental Psychology: Learning, Memory, and Cognition, 27,* 1261–1275.

Rosch, E. (1978). Principles of categorization. In E. Rosch & B. B. Lloyd (Eds.), *Cognition and categorization* (pp. 27–48). Hillsdale, NJ: Lawrence Erlbaum Associates.

Ross, B. H. (1984). Remindings and their effects in learning a cognitive skill. *Cognitive Psychology, 16,* 371–416.

Ross, B. H. (1997). The use of categories affects classification. *Journal of Memory and Language, 37,* 240–267.

Ross, B. H. (1999). Post-classification category use: The effects of learning to use categories after learning to classify. *Journal of Experimental Psychology: Learning, Memory, and Cognition, 25,* 743–757.

Ross, B. H. (2000). The effects of category use on learned categories. *Memory & Cognition, 28,* 51–63.

Ross, B. H., & Bower, G. H. (1981). Comparisons of models of associative recall. *Memory & Cognition, 9,* 1–16.

Ross, B. H., Gelman, S. A., & Rosengren, K. S. (2005). Children's category-based inferences affect classification. *British Journal of Developmental Psychology, 23,* 1–24.

Ross, B. H., & Murphy, G. L. (1999). Food for thought: Cross-classification and category organization in a complex real-world domain. *Cognitive Psychology, 38,* 495–553.

Ross, B. H., & Warren, J. L. (2002). Learning abstract relations from using categories. *Memory & Cognition, 30,* 657–665.

Yamauchi, T., & Markman, A. B. (1998). Category learning by inference and classification. *Journal of Memory and Language, 3,* 124–148.

CHAPTER
16

Mood and Memory at 26: Revisiting the Idea of Mood Mediation in Drug-Dependent and Place-Dependent Memory

Eric Eich
University of British Columbia

Recent decades have seen a surge of scientific interest in issues long considered central to understanding human action, intention, and experience, but that once seemed beyond the reach of rigorous research methods. Consciousness is arguably the best example, with unconsciousness—especially in the guise of implicit learning and memory—placing a close second.

A third revitalized issue involves the interplay between affect and cognition. Philosophers, politicians, and playwrights alike have recognized for centuries the ability of affective states—short-lived emotions as well as longer-lasting moods— to color the way people remember the past, experience the present, and forecast the future. Psychologists, however, were relatively late to acknowledge this reality, despite a number of promising early leads (e.g., Rapaport, 1942/1961; Razran, 1940). Even the forward-looking cognitive revolutionaries of the early 1960s had no truck with affective states, dismissing them as nagging sources of hot noise in an otherwise coolly rational system of information processing. Indeed, it is only within the last quarter-century that empirical studies of the impact of affect on cognition, and vice versa, have appeared with regularity in mainstream psychology and neuroscience journals.

No single publication did more to jump-start modern research on affect–cognition interactions than Gordon Bower's article titled "Mood and Memory" (M&M), which appeared in the February 1981 issue of the *American Psychologist*. In M&M, Bower called attention to two phenomena that quickly captured, and still hold, the interest of researchers in cognitive, clinical, and social psychology.

One phenomenon, *mood congruence,* refers to the observation that people tend to think about themselves, and the world around them, in a manner that is congruent with their current mood. Thus, in comparison with their sad-mood counterparts, happy subjects tend to produce more positive than negative free associations to neutral words and to identify more strongly with the upbeat than with the downcast character in a fictional narrative. Analogously, angry individuals are prone to tell hostile stories, find fault with others, and interpret ambiguous social situations in a negative light.

The second phenomenon of interest, *mood dependence,* implies that what has been learned in a certain state of affect or mood is best remembered in that mood. Drawing on his own work and that of other investigators, Bower surmised that mood-dependent memory occurs in conjunction with exogenous (experimentally induced) affects, such as hypnotically induced states of happiness or sadness, as well as with endogenous (naturally occurring) states, such as episodes of mania or depression experienced by individuals with bipolar disorder. Bower also maintained that mood dependence could be demonstrated using a variety of cognitive tasks, including the recall of word lists, childhood experiences, and personal incidents recorded in a daily diary.

In addition to reviewing the nascent literatures on mood congruence and mood dependence, Bower (1981, p.129) proposed an associative network theory to explain both effects. On this account,

> An emotion serves as a memory unit that can enter into associations with coincidental events. Activation of this emotion unit aids retrieval of events associated with it; it also primes emotional themata for use in free associations, fantasies, and perceptual categorization.

Derived from HAM, Anderson and Bower's (1973) influential model of human associative memory, the network theory described in M&M was later developed in detail by Bower and Cohen (1982) and it continues to play a prominent role in contemporary accounts of affect priming (see Bower & Forgas, 2000; Fiedler, 1991; Forgas, 1995).

M&M's theoretical insights, coupled with its novel experimental approach, made it an instant hit and secured its permanent standing as a publication classic. In fact, by the time Bower's Festschrift took place at Stanford (September 2005), M&M had been cited 747 times, making it the first true jumbo jet of the modern affect/cognition era.

Most of the major issues raised by Bower have been reexamined repeatedly over the past 25 years, by him and many others. These issues include mood congruence (see Blaney, 1986; chap. 17, this volume), mood dependence (see Bower, 1992; Eich, 1995b), and the network theory of affect (see Ellis & Moore, 1999; Singer & Salovey, 1988). To move the discussion in a new direction, this chapter deals with an intriguing—but long overlooked—idea that Bower introduced near the end of his 1981 essay.

The point of departure for this discussion concerns the phenomenon of *drug-dependent memory:* the observation that events encoded in a particular pharmacological state (such as alcohol intoxication) are more retrievable in the same state than in a different one (such as sobriety). Under the heading of "Speculative Extensions," Bower (1981) remarked that:

> It is an interesting fact that most of the drugs that produce state-dependent effects also produce radical shifts in emotional mood (see Weingartner, 1978). The successful state-dependent drugs are marijuana, amphetamine, Thorazine, alcohol, and barbiturates like Demerol, all of which are frequently abused mood-altering drugs. Thus, one might conjecture that these drugs achieve their state-dependent effects by virtue of their impact on moods. (p. 146)

Unlike much else in M&M, this conjecture captured little research interest, either immediately or over the long term. Nonetheless, the idea that drug-dependent memory represents a special, and rather subtle, form of mood-dependent memory remains both plausible and promising from a theoretical standpoint.

Discussion soon turns to why Bower's mood mediation idea did not—indeed, could not—catch on, what makes the idea a potentially important innovation, and how this potential could be realized through new research. But first let us look closely at *place-dependent memory*—a phenomenon to which the concept of mood mediation has already been applied with some success.

MOODS AND PLACES

Place-dependent memory (PDM) and mood-dependent memory (MDM) have much in common. Both phenomena relate to the enduring issue of how changing contexts—or "altered stimulating conditions," in McGeogh's (1942) words— affect learning and remembering. Both are operationally defined as an interaction between encoding and retrieval contexts, where contexts refer to either two different physical environments or two different affective states. Place dependence, like mood dependence, is more apt to occur when target events are retrieved in the absence than in the presence of observable reminders or cues (see Eich, 1980; Smith, 1988). And as subjects of scientific inquiry, both phenomena have had patchy histories, with the mostly positive results reported in the 1970s (e.g., Smith, Glenberg, & Bjork, 1978) giving way to mostly negative results in the 1980s (e.g., Saufley, Otaka, & Bavaresco, 1985), leaving theorists in the 1990s to wonder whether either PDM or MDM even exists (see Bjork & Richarson-Klavehn, 1989).

Yet another point of commonality is suggested by a study of mine (Eich, 1995a, Experiment 2). During the encoding session, subjects were asked to recollect or generate specific events, from any time in their past, that were called to mind by neutral-noun probes such as *ship* and *street*. Every participant recollected as many as 16 different events, each evoked by a different probe. After recounting the details a given event (what happened, who was involved, etc.), subjects rated it along several dimensions (including emotional valence and personal significance). This task of *autobiographical-event generation* has been used successfully in several studies of mood dependence (Eich, Macaulay, & Lam, 1997; Eich, Macaulay, & Ryan, 1994) and it seems to work by ensuring that the to-be-remembered or target events become closely connected to, or deeply colored by, the subject's current mood.

During the retrieval session, held 2 days after encoding, subjects were asked to recall, in any order and without benefit of any observable reminders or cues, the gist of as many of their previously generated events as possible, preferably by recalling their precise corresponding probes. This task of *autobiographical-event recall* has also been shown to be sensitive to the detection of mood-dependent effects (Eich et al., 1994, 1997).

Superimposed on these procedures was a 2 × 2 design, where one factor was the physical environment—Inside (I) or Outside (O)—in which subjects completed the task of autobiographical-event generation, and the other factor was the locale—again, I or O—in which they were later tested for autobiographical-event recall. Subjects (N = 48 undergraduates) were assigned at random, and in equal numbers, to each of the four conditions of the design: two denoting matched encoding/retrieval environments (I/I and O/O) and two signifying mismatched environments (I/I and O/I).

The Inside environment was a small, windowless office that was sparsely furnished, dimly lit, and austere in overall appearance. In contrast, the Outside environment was a stunningly scenic and secluded section of a nearby Japanese garden. All testing took place on warm and sunny summer days.

Table 16–1 shows the mean percentage of autobiographical events that were recalled in each of the four conditions. Performance was better when encoding and retrieval environments matched (mean = 46%) than when they mismatched (mean = 36%). On first impression, these results provide unequivocal evidence of environmental-context or place-dependent memory.

Table 16-1
Autobiographical-Event Recall and Subjective-Similarity Ratings as a
Function of Encoding/Retrieval Environments

Encoding/Retrieval Environment	All-Event Recall	Subjective-Similarity Rating
Inside/Inside	40%	5.83
Inside/Outside	34%	3.50
Outside/Inside	38%	3.25
Outside/Outside	52%	6.08

Source: Eich (1995b, Experiment 2).

On further analysis, however, the interpretation becomes more intricate, and more interesting. Not only did the Inside and Outside environments *look* different, they also *felt* different. Analysis of mood ratings taken just before the event-generation and event-recall tasks revealed that, on average, subjects experienced significantly higher levels of both pleasure and arousal—in other words, they were happier—while in the garden than in the office. Accordingly, had subjects been asked to rate how similar they felt during event recall, relative to how they felt during event generation, their rating probably would have been higher had they been in the same environment (Inside or Outside) on both occasions.

This was so. Next to the recall data in Table 16-1 are the mean ratings of *subjective similarity* that participants made, shortly after recall, on an 11-point scale ranging from *not at all similar* (0) through *moderately similar* (5) to *extremely similar* (10). Subjects claimed that they felt more similar when they completed the generation and recall tasks in the same setting (mean rating = 5.96) than in different places (mean = 3.38).Given that event recall covaried with subjective similarity, the question arises: Was it the confluence of feelings or, instead, the equivalence of environments that contributed to the advantage in recall of matched over mismatched conditions?

Data depicted in Figure 16-1 provide a tentative answer. The gray bars in the figure represent subjects who, at the time of event recall, felt *moderately* to *extremely similar* to the way they felt at the time of event generation (i.e., subjective similarity scores between 5 and 10). Unsurprisingly, most of these subjects with *high subjective similarity* had been tested under matched rather than mismatched environmental conditions (Ns = 16 and 3, respectively). Subjects with *low subjective similarity* (i.e., scores ranging from 0 to 4) are represented by the black bars: All but 8 of these 29 participants came from either of the two mismatched conditions.

Comparison of the two outermost bars of Figure 16–1 offers a clear view of place-dependent memory, with event recall averaging 50% under matched conditions and 35% under mismatched. Note, however, that this comparison involves subjects whose ratings of subjective similarity were typical of their condition—that is, high if matched and low if mismatched. Subjects with atypical scores showed no sign of place dependence. Indeed, as the two innermost bars indicate, subjects who experienced similar feelings in different environments fared somewhat better in recall than did those who experienced different feelings in the same environment. These results provide indirect, correlational support for the idea that PDM represents a special, and rather subtle, form of MDM.

To see whether this hypothesis would hold up under direct test, another study was run (Eich, 1995a, Experiment 3). All participants ($N = 48$ undergraduates) generated autobiographical events while in the outside environment (the Japanese garden)—a setting that was expected to engender a moderately happy mood in most subjects. This expectation was confirmed through subsequent analysis of the subjects' pleasure and arousal ratings.

Two days later, subjects were tested for autobiographical-event recall in one of four conditions, defined by the factorial combination of (a) same versus different environment and (b) same versus different mood. Thus, in one condition, subjects returned to the garden for testing and were administered a "portable" version of the musical mood-induction technique described in Eich, Ng, Macaulay, Percy, and Grebneva (in press). Before beginning recall, these subjects were asked to spend several minutes thinking pleasant thoughts while listening to lively music,

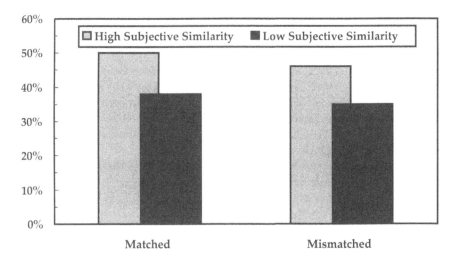

Figure 16–1. Autobiographical-event recall as a function of encoding/retrieval environment and subjective similarity. From Eich (1995b, Experiment 2). Copyright 1995 by American Psychological Association. Adapted by permission.

so as to instill a moderately happy mood similar to the one they had experienced in the same (Outside) environment 2 days earlier. In a second condition, recall in the garden was preceded by a period in which subjects pondered depressing thoughts and listened to languorous music. The intent here was to induce a moderately sad mood that would feel very different from the way these subjects felt "naturally" when last in the garden. In the other two conditions, subjects were tested for recall in the Inside environment (the windowless office). Whereas some of these subjects first received the happy-mood induction just mentioned, others received the sad-mood induction.

The reasoning behind the experiment was as follows. If memory is truly and simply place dependent, then recall should be higher when tested in the original (Outside) than in the alternative (Inside) setting, irrespective of testing mood (happy or sad). If what really matters, instead, is how similar subjects feel at event generation and event recall, rather than how similar the task environments look, then recall should be higher when tested in a happy than in a sad mood, irrespective of the retrieval environment (Inside or Outside). Yet a third possibility is that the helpful effects of similar physical settings are offset by the harmful effects of dissimilar affective states, or vice versa.

As can be seen in Table 16–2, it made no difference to memory performance whether subjects were tested for recall in the same (Outside) environment in which they had generated the target autobiographical events or in the contrasting (Inside) context (mean event recall = 48% and 52% under matched and mismatched environmental conditions, respectively). What did matter was whether subjects were tested in a happy or sad mood, with recall being higher in the former case (mean = 55%) than in the latter (mean = 45%). This was true regardless of setting.

What accounts for the advantage in recall of happy over sad moods? One straightforward answer is that the former affect is generally more conducive to

Table 16–2
Autobiographical-Event Recall and Subjective-Similarity Ratings as a Function of Encoding/Retrieval Environments and Induced Mood at Retrieval

Encoding/Retrieval Similarity Environment	Retrieval Mood	All-Event Recall	Subject Rating
Outside/Outside	Happy	52%	5.75
Outside/Outside	Sad	44%	4.00
Outside/Inside	Happy	59%	6.33
Outside/Inside	Sad	46%	3.42

Source: Eich (1995b, Experiment 3).

recall than is the latter. On this view, the advantage in recall of happy over sad moods is precisely what is appears to be—a simple main effect (see Smith, 1996). Despite its intuitive appeal, this account cannot accommodate the absence of a reliable main effect of recall environment in the earlier study (Eich, 1995a, Experiment 2), even though the mood-rating data had shown that subjects were in a better mood when tested in the garden than in the office. In addition, the "main effect" argument has other, more serious problems that are discussed in detail in the original article (see Eich, 1995a, pp. 304–305).

An alternative answer is that the advantage in recall of happiness over sadness reflects a form of mood-dependent memory: Putting people into a happy mood increased the correspondence between their event generation and event recall states, which in turn increased the likelihood of recall. Consistent with this interpretation, data presented in Table 16–2 show that, like event recall, postexperimental ratings of subjective similarity were affected solely by the subjects' mood at recall.

Considered collectively, the results reviewed in this section suggest that how well information transfers from one environment to another depends on how similar the environments feel, not on how similar they look. Even when target events are generated and recalled in the same physical setting, memory performance suffers if the attending affective states differ. Conversely, a change in environment produces no appreciable deficit if, whether by chance or by design (Experiment 2 vs. Experiment 3 in Eich, 1995a), the mood at encoding matches the mood at retrieval. These results imply that place-dependent effects are mediated by alterations in affect or mood, and that data that appear on the surface to demonstrate *place*-dependent memory may, at a deeper level, denote the presence of *mood*-dependent memory.

MOODS AND DRUGS

Perhaps the same applies to *drug*-dependent memory (DDM). Though this is precisely what Bower proposed many years ago in "Mood and Memory," the possibility has never been taken seriously, for reasons that are reviewed shortly. In essence, the idea is that memory performance depends not on the objective similarity between encoding and retrieval states—that is, on whether or not the experimenter administers to subjects the same dose of the same drug on both occasions—but instead on the subjective similarity between these states—that is, on whether or not subjects experience the same emotional feelings at retrieval that they experienced at encoding.

Timing is everything and this is especially so for the mood mediation hypothesis. It originated during a period (the early 1980s) when Bower and other researchers were taking their first shots at demonstrating mood-dependent memory—and almost always hitting the mark. By that same time, a strikingly—but inexplicably—inconsistent literature had developed around drug-dependent memory, with positive and negative reported in roughly equal numbers (see Eich, 1980; Overton, 1984). Thus, at the start of the 1980s, it seemed plausible, even probable, that MDM could hold the key to understanding the apparent capriciousness of DDM.

By the end of the decade, however, this idea seemed absurd. After all, though it would have been fair to say, at the time, that *drug-dependent memory* is "an unreliable, chance event" (Bower & Mayer, 1989, p. 145) with "the properties of a will-o'-the-wisp" (Kihlstrom, 1989, p. 26) that "presents more problems than solutions" (Ellis & Hunt, 1989, p. 280), these statements actually had been made about *mood*-dependent memory—and for good reason. Mirroring the mercurial history of research on DDM, clear and convincing demonstrations of DDM, which were commonplace in the 1970s, became a scarce commodity in the 1980s (for reviews, see Bower, 1987; Ucros, 1989). This is why the statements just cited were made, and this is also why the possible connection between MDM and DDM—the crux of Bower's (1981) conjecture—was never pursued. Most important, this is why it is of immediate interest to ask: How can one seemingly precarious phenomenon possibly provide insight into another?

The answer comprises three points. First, mood dependence is not the erratic effect it was widely believed to be some 15 years ago. To the contrary, recent research suggests that clear and consistent evidence of MDM can be obtained, provided that subjects (a) take responsibility for generating the target events by engaging in constructive, open-ended cognitive processing, (b) also assume responsibility for generating the cues required for target retrieval, and (c) experience strong, stable, and sincere affective states in the course of both event encoding and event retrieval (Eich, 1995b; Eich & Forgas, 2004).

Second, as discussed in the last section, the mood mediation hypothesis has already been successfully applied to yet another phenomenon that, like DDM and MDM, has a long history of mixed results—namely, PDM or place-dependent memory: the observation that events encoded in a particular physical environment (e.g., a sunlit garden) are more retrievable in the same environment than in a different one (e.g., a windowless office). The studies summarized earlier (Eich, 1995a, Experiments 2 & 3) showed that how well information transfers from one physical environment to another one depends not on how similar these places look, but rather on how similar they feel. One need only substitute "drugs" for "places" to see the analogy between our prior analysis of place-dependent memory and our present interest in drug-dependent memory.

Third, if DDM really is a special case of MDM, then one would expect that the factors or variables that regulate one phenomenon should also regulate the other. Comparison of the two literatures reveals several respects in which this seems to be so.

Nature of the Retrieval Task.   Earlier we remarked that mood-dependent memory is more apt to obtain when target events are retrieved in the absence than in the presence of observable, experimenter-provided cues. The same applies to drug-dependent memory: Of the 50 studies of DDM surveyed by Eich (1980), 26 involved uncued tests of retention (such as free or serial-order recall) and 24 involved cued procedures (including paired-associates learning and old/new recognition). Whereas 88% (23/26) of the uncued experiments evinced drug-dependent memory, only 13% (3/24) of their cued counterparts did likewise.

Nature of the Encoding Task.   Recall from prior discussion that just as the odds of demonstrating mood-dependent memory are improved by having subjects generate their own cues for retrieval, so too are these prospects improved by having subjects generate the target events themselves. Is this also true of drug-dependent memory?

Though the existing DDM does not provide a definitive answer, it does contain some informative clues. Consider a study by Goodwin, Powell, Bremer, Hoine, and Stern (1969). After consuming a nonalcoholic beverage or a strong vodka/tonic cocktail, medical students (a) memorized a list of sentences that varied in meaningfulness, (b) viewed photographs of dressed or undressed fashion models ("neutral" vs. "emotional" pictures), and (c) generated free associations to common words. One day later, the students tried to (a) recall the sentences, (b) reproduce their original free associations, and (c) decide whether or not a given picture had been seen before (i.e., old/new recognition). Half of the subjects performed these tasks in the same state (sobriety or intoxication) they had experienced the day before; the other half did so in the contrasting drug condition.

The results showed (a) no sign of drug-dependent memory in the recognition of either type of picture (no surprise there), (b) marginally significant DDM in sentence recall, and (c) robust DDM in word association recall. On average, subjects who switched from sobriety to intoxication, or vice versa, made nearly twice as many errors of word association recall (mean = 3.42) than did subjects whose state stayed the same (mean = 1.87). Accordingly, Goodwin et al. (1969) concluded that "Our data suggest that the word-association task, measuring single-trial, 'self-generated' learning, may be particularly useful in studying [DDM]" (p. 1359). Results that are broadly consistent with this conclusion have been found in other studies of drug-dependent memory (see Weingartner, Adefris, Eich, & Murphy, 1976; Weingartner, Eich, & Allen, 1973) and as we have already seen, the same inference applies to mood-dependent memory as well.

Nature of the Encoding and Retrieval States.   Even if one were to carry out a study of mood-dependent memory in which subjects generate both the target events and the cues required for their retrieval, the chances of finding the phenomenon would be slim in the absence of strong, stable, and sincere moods. In connection with the first of these characteristics, Bower (1992) claimed that:

> Unless the moods are fairly intense and the two mood conditions are rather different from one another, then MDR [mood-dependent retrieval] is not likely to occur. This follows, of course, from the premise that MDR reflects a failure of items learned in one condition (mood) to generalize to the other, and generalization is more likely to fail the more dissimilar the two conditions are. (p. 23)

An analogous proviso applies to drug-dependent memory. During the heyday of DDM research (mid-1960s through early 1980s), many studies sought to demonstrate the phenomenon using a variety of centrally acting agents, including sedatives, stimulants, anxiolytics, volatile anesthetics, and cholinesterase inhibitors (see Colpaert, 1991; Eich, 1980; Overton, 1984). No matter which drug was administered, DDM occurred only at doses high enough to produce either (a) obvious signs of intoxication (e.g., blurred vision; slurred speech), (b) a marked increase or decrease in either or both the pleasure and arousal dimensions of mood, or (c) a significant drug-produced improvement or impairment of acquisition or learning (as indicated, e.g., by a reliable main effect of drug—either facilitative or inhibitory—on the rate at which a list of words is learned to criterion). Thus, for example, shifting from a mildly intoxicated state at encoding to a sober state at retrieval is no more likely to impair memory performance than is a shift from feeling, say, "slightly happy" to "slightly sad." More generally, sizable drug doses are as critical to the occurrence of DDM as strong moods are vital to the appearance of DDM.

CONCLUDING COMMENTS

We have seen that several of the factors that figure prominently in mood-dependent memory also play important roles in drug-dependent memory. Though this is consistent with Bower's (1981) mood mediation hypothesis, as it relates to DDM, it is hardly conclusive. More direct empirical evidence is called for.

The search for such evidence could take several paths; here are three examples:

• One could start by decoding the affective "signature" of a given drug—that is, how different doses of the agent affect a person's sense of pleasure and arousal. The next step would be to develop a technique for inducing these same feelings by purely psychological means—perhaps through a combination of mood-appropriate music and ideation, as alluded to earlier. Though shifting from a drug-present state at encoding to a drug-absent state at retrieval would normally be expected to impair memory performance, this deficit may disappear if participants are able to recapture, via music and ideation, the feelings of pleasure and arousal that the drug had infused in them before.

- Alternatively, one could conceivably capitalize on the power of placebo or expectancy effects so as to lead participants to believe that they received, say, a mild sedative when in fact they had been given no drug at all. In this situation, subjects experiencing a *subjective* state of sedation may perform surprisingly well when asked to retrieve events they had earlier encoded in an *objective* state of sedation—for instance, following the administration of a small dose of lorazepam or other benzodiazepine.

- The premise underlying the third example is that even though two drugs may differ *pharmacologically* in their mode of action, they nevertheless may be similar *affectively* in their impact on mood. For instance, research by Curran (1991; Curran, Poovibunsuk, Dalton, & Lader, 1998) indicates that the dosage of lorazepam—a benzodiazepine that acts at specific receptors to facilitate the release of GABA, the brain's major inhibitory neurotransmitter—can be titrated to produce feelings of sedation similar to those instilled by diphenhydramine—an H1 (hystamine) receptor antagonist. It follows from the mood mediation hypothesis that information should transfer freely between lorazepam and diphenhydramine states, provided they are affectively attuned (in terms of level of sedation), though pharmacologically distinct (in terms of mode of action).

Though any or all of these paths could prove to be blind alleys, their potential payoff is big. As noted elsewhere (Eich, in press), memory theorists have been struggling for decades with the problem of how extrinsic or global contexts—pharmacological conditions, physical environments, emotional states, and the like—affect learning and remembering (Davies & Thompson, 1988; Roediger & Guynn, 1996). Were it possible to show that three seemingly distinct phenomena—drug-dependent, place-dependent, and mood-dependent memory—can be reduced to just one (MDM), then the problem would immediately become more manageable, and ultimately more solvable.

ACKNOWLEDGMENTS

Preparation of this chapter was aided by grants from the (Canadian) Natural Sciences and Engineering Research Council (37335) and the (American) National Institute of Mental Health (MH59636). Sincere thanks to a wonderful group of colleagues and students: Andrea Bull, Kirsten Campbell, Susan Carsky, Irina Grebneva, Meagan Hasek-Watt, Adam Margesson, Andrea Nelson, Joycelin Ng, Jim Russell, Lee Ryan, and Reiko West. The advice and assistance provided by the late, great Sherry Eich are also deeply appreciated and will always be remembered.

REFERENCES

Anderson, J. R., & Bower, G. H. (1973). *Human associative memory.* Washington, DC: Winston.

Bjork, R. A., & Richardson-Klavehn, A. (1989). On the puzzling relationship between environmental content and human memory. In C. Izawa (Ed.), *Current issues in cognitive processes: The Tulane Flowerree Symposium on cognition* (pp. 313–344). Hillsdale, NJ: Lawrence Erlbaum Associates.

Blaney, P. H. (1986). Affect and memory: A review. *Psychological Bulletin, 99,* 229–246.

Bower, G. H. (1981). Mood and memory. *American Psychologist, 36,* 129–148.

Bower, G. H. (1987). Commentary on mood and memory. *Behavior Research and Therapy, 25,* 443–455.

Bower, G. H. (1992). How might emotions affect learning? In S.-A. Christianson (Ed.), *Handbook of emotion and memory* (pp. 3–31). Hillsdale, NJ: Lawrence Erlbaum Associates.

Bower, G. H., & Cohen, P. R. (1982). Emotional influences in memory and thinking: Data and theory. In M. S. Clark & S. T. Fiske (Eds.), *Affect and cognition: The seventeenth annual Carnegie symposium on cognition* (pp. 291–331). Hillsdale, NJ: Lawrence Erlbaum Associates.

Bower, G. H., & Forgas, J. P. (2000). Affect, memory, and social cognition. In E. Eich, J. F. Kihlstrom, G. H. Bower, J. P. Forgas, & P. M. Niedenthal, *Cognition and emotion* (pp. 87–168). New York: Oxford University Press.

Bower, G. H., & Mayer, J. D. (1989). In search of mood-dependent retrieval. *Journal of Social Behavior and Personality, 4,* 121–156.

Colpaert, F. C. (1991). State dependency as a mechanism of central nervous system drug action. *NIDA Research Monograph, 116,* 245–66.

Curran, H. V. (1991). Benzodiazepines, memory and mood: A review. *Psychopharmacology, 105,* 1–8.

Curran, H. V., Poovibunsuk, P., Dalton, J., & Lader, M. H. (1998). Differentiating the effects of centrally acting drugs on arousal and memory: An event-related potential study of scopolamine, lorazepam and diphenhydramine. *Psychopharmacology, 135,* 27–36.

Davies, G. M., & Thomson, D. M. (Eds.). (1988). *Memory in context: Context in memory.* Chichester, England: Wiley.

Eich, E. (1980). The cue-dependent nature of state-dependent retrieval. *Memory & Cognition, 8,* 157–173.

Eich, E. (1995a). Mood as a mediator of place dependent memory. *Journal of Experimental Psychology: General, 124,* 293–308.

Eich, E. (1995b). Searching for mood dependent memory. *Psychological Science, 6,* 67–75.

Eich, E. (in press). Mood, memory, and the concept of context. In H. L. Roediger, Y. Dudai, & S. Fitzpatrick (Eds.), *Science of memory.* New York: Oxford University Press.

Eich, E., & Forgas, J. P. (2003). Mood, cognition, and memory. In A. F. Healy & R. W. Proctor (Eds.), *Handbook of Psychology: Vol. 4. Experimental psychology* (pp. 61–83). New York: Wiley.

Eich, E., Macaulay, D., & Lam, R. W. (1997). Mania, depression, and mood dependent memory. *Cognition and Emotion, 11,* 607–618.

Eich, E., Macaulay, D., & Ryan, L. (1994). Mood dependent memory for events of the personal past. *Journal of Experimental Psychology: General, 123,* 201–215.

Eich, E., Ng, J. T. W., Macaulay, D., Percy, A. D., & Grebneva, I. (in press). Combining music with thought to change mood. In J. A. Coan & J. B. Allen (Eds.), *The handbook of emotion elicitation and assessment.* New York: Oxford University Press.

Ellis, H. C., & Hunt, R. R. (1989). *Fundamentals of human memory and cognition* (4th ed.). Dubuque, IA: Brown.

Ellis, H. C., & Moore, B. A. (1999). Mood and memory. In T. Dalgleish & M. J. Power (Eds.), *Handbook of cognition and emotion* (pp.193–210). Chichester, England: Wiley.

Fiedler, K. (1991). On the task, the measures and the mood in research on affect and social cognition. In J. P. Forgas (Ed.), *Emotion and social judgments* (pp. 83–104). Oxford, England: Pergamon.

Forgas, J. P. (1995). Mood and judgment: The affect infusion model (AIM). *Psychological Bulletin, 117,* 39–66.

Goodwin, D. W., Powell, B., Bremer, D., Hoine, H., & Stern, J. (1969). Alcohol and recall: State-dependent effects in man. *Science, 163,* 1358–1360.

Kihlstrom, J. F. (1989). On what does mood-dependent memory depend? *Journal of Social Behavior and Personality, 4,* 23–32.

McGeogh, J. A. (1942). *The psychology of human learning.* New York: Longmans, Green.

Overton, D. A. (1984). State dependent learning and drug discriminations. In L. L. Iverson, S. D. Iverson, & S. H. Snyder (Eds.), *Handbook of psychopharmacology* (Vol. 18, pp. 59–127). New York: Plenum.

Rapaport, D. (1961). *Emotions and memory.* New York: Science Editions. (Original work published in 1942)

Razran, G. H. S. (1940). Conditioned response changes in rating and appraising socio-political slogans. *Psychological Bulletin, 37,* 481–493.

Roediger, H. L., & Guynn, M. J. (1996). Retrieval processes. In E. L. Bjork & R. A. Bjork (Eds.), *Memory: Vol. 10. Handbook of perception and cognition* (pp. 197–236). New York: Academic Press.

Saufley, W. H., Otaka, S. R., & Bavaresco, J. L. (1985). Context effects: Classroom tests and context independence. *Memory & Cognition, 13,* 522–528.

Singer, J. A., & Salovey, P. (1988). Mood and memory: Evaluating the network theory of affect. *Clinical Psychology Review, 8,* 211–251.

Smith, S. M. (1988). Environmental context-dependent memory. In G. M. Davies & D. M. Thomson (Eds.), *Memory in context: Context in memory* (pp. 13–33). Chichester, England: Wiley.

Smith, S. M. (1995). Mood is a component of mental context: Comment on Eich (1995). *Journal of Experimental Psychology: General, 124,* 309–310.

Smith, S. M., Glenberg, A., & Bjork, R. A. (1978). Environmental context and human memory. *Memory & Cognition, 6,* 342–353.

Ucros, C. G. (1989). Mood state-dependent memory: A meta-analysis. *Cognition & Emotion, 3,* 139–167.

Weingartner, H., Adefris, W., Eich, E., & Murphy, D. L. (1976). Encoding-imagery specificity in alcohol state-dependent learning. *Journal of Experimental Psychology: Human Learning and Memory, 2,* 83–87.

Weingartner, H., Eich, E., & Allen, R. (1973). Alcohol state-dependent associative processes. *Proceedings of the 81st Annual Convention of the American Psychological Association, 8,* 1009–1010.

CHAPTER 17

Affect, Cognition, and Social Behavior: The Effects of Mood on Memory, Social Judgments, and Social Interaction

Joseph P. Forgas
University of New South Wales

The role of serendipity is much underestimated in science. Thinking back on my 25 years of friendship and collaboration with Gordon Bower, I am struck by the accidental nature of our first encounter, and how easily we may not have met at all. In 1980 I was a young academic, just 3 years after finishing my doctorate at Oxford. I was already planning my first sabbatical leave, thanks to the generous provisions of my university in Sydney. I decided to go to Stanford, even though I had no personal contacts or a sponsor there. My request for sabbatical facilities was handled by one Gordon Bower, who just happened to be chair of the Stanford department. After several exchanges that revealed no marked enthusiasm by Stanford social psychologists to sponsor me, Gordon wrote back a characteristically generous and to-the-point letter, to the effect that "well, hell, why don't you just come and work with my group?"

Such were the accidental beginnings of two and a half decades of fun, friendship, collaboration, and much more that have profoundly affected me, my career, and my research. My arrival at Stanford was similarly memorable—I loved the place at first sight, and the all-pervasive aroma of eucalyptus trees made me feel immediately at home. My first face-to-face encounter with Gordon was somewhat intimidating. When I turned up in his office, he was not visibly pleased to see me, with a huge pile of papers on his desk, and his secretary and several students hovering in the background hoping catch a few minutes with him. After I introduced myself, he said something like this in his best John Wayne intonation: "Oh hell, well, frogshit, so its you—I guess we'd better make a time to meet ..." (Frogshit was the "bon mot" of the time; over the years I came to realize that Gordon regularly takes a shine to particular and usually unconventional words, and uses them with relish and to inimitable effect, while they last. A few years later, during a subsequent visit, he was in his "dealburger" phase, and most conversations would feature "dealburger" somewhere).

After this serendipitous beginning, our friendship and collaboration flowered in the course of numerous return visits to Stanford, and trips by Gordon and Sharon to Sydney. Our meeting was well-timed in other respects as well. The Zeitgeist was ripe for a serious empirical attempt to explore the links between affect and cognition, social judgments, and behavior. Within social psychology, Robert Zajonc (1980) had just published his influential paper arguing for the independence and indeed primacy of affect in many social phenomena. Within cognitive psychology Neisser (1982) had done much to rekindle interest in real, everyday "hot" cognitive phenomena as distinct from the kind of de-contextualized and sterile "cold" cognitive tasks typically studied in the cognitive laboratory. And Ernest Hilgard, with whom I had the good fortune to have several memorable discussions while at Stanford, had just published a historical review paper exploring why affect had remained the most neglected aspect of the "trilogy of mind"—cognition, conation, and effect—despite enduring fascination with the role of affect in human affairs by philosophers and writers since time immemorial (Hilgard, 1980).

The main objective of this chapter is to provide a brief overview of our collaboration, and the subsequent research that flowed from it. The first half of the chapter reviews the origins of our joint work based on Bower's (1981) associative network model of mood and memory and the experiments that followed. The second half of the chapter discusses subsequent research, including an outline of a revised theory, the affect infusion model (AIM; Forgas, 1995a, 2002), which attempts to locate network explanations within an integrated theory of affect and cognition.

THE ORIGINS: MOOD, MEMORY, AND SOCIAL JUDGMENT

When I first met Gordon, I was mostly interested in the cognitive processes involved in interpersonal behavior. In the 3 years since completing my DPhil, I published a bunch of papers and a book summarizing a research program analyzing people's cognitive representations of their everyday social interaction episodes (Forgas, 1976, 1979, 1982). These studies showed that affective reactions—how people *feel* rather than *think* about their interpersonal encounters—dominate mental representations. Interest in the social functions of affect was already on my mind, and my arrival at Stanford fortunately coincided with Gordon's groundbreaking work on affective phenomena. He had just received the Distinguished Scientific Contribution Award from the American Psychological Association, and his paper on affect and memory in the *American Psychologist* (Bower, 1981) was making waves in cognitive, social, and clinical psychology. His associative network model offered a parsimonious and influential explanation for mood congruence and mood state dependency and was already supported by a range of ingenious experiments. According to this view, the experience of an affective state spreads activation throughout a network of cognitive associations linked to that emotion (Bower, 1981, 1983; Bower & Cohen, 1982). As a result, affectively primed material is more likely to be activated, recalled, and used in various constructive cognitive tasks, leading to a marked mood congruency in memory, associations, evaluations, and judgments.

As social judgments are necessarily constructive (Heider, 1958) and so require the selective activation and use of primed information from memory, it should follow that mood ought to have a mood-congruent impact on the outcome of such judgments. In other words, in terms of Bower's (1981) model, affect is an inseparable part of how we see and represent the world around us, and the way we select, store, and retrieve information, and use stored knowledge in various cognitive and social tasks. As the network model suggests:

> [Affective states have a] specific node or unit in memory that ... is also linked with propositions describing events from one's life during which that emotion was aroused. ... Activation of an emotion node also spreads activation throughout the memory structures to which it is connected. (Bower, 1981, p. 135)

Several important consequences followed from this basic principle (Forgas & Bower, 1988).

The Basic Effects

Most evidence for affect-priming effects comes from experiments involving two separate stages. After inducing an affective state, aspects of cognitive performance (memories, associations, judgments, attention) are assessed in what subjects believe is a separate, unrelated experiment (Bower, 1981, 1991; Forgas, 1992, 1995a, 2002). Naturally occurring moods after attendance at movies, sports events, and the like can also be used to study mood effects on cognitive and social performance (Forgas & Moylan, 1987; Mayer, Gaschke, Braverman, & Evans, 1992). *Mood-state dependent retrieval* occurs when retrieval mood matches the original encoding mood, consistent with the encoding specificity principle proposed by Tulving (1983). For example, memory for word lists is better when recall mood matches encoding mood, and people also seem to be better at remembering autobiographical memories that match their prevailing mood (Bower, 1981; Bower & Forgas, 2001; Eich et al., 2001).

A second effect, *mood-congruent retrieval,* occurs when affective state facilitates the recall of affectively congruent material from memory. Thus, depressed subjects are faster to retrieve unpleasant rather than pleasant memories (Teasdale & Fogarty, 1979), and implicit memory tasks also show that depressed people tend to complete word stems to produce negative rather than positive words (Ruiz-Caballero & Gonzalez, 1994). Affect can also influence *selective attention* (Niedenthal & Setterlund, 1994) as people tend to spend longer reading affect congruent information, linking it into a richer network of primed associations and are better able to remember such information (Bower, 1981; Forgas, 1992; Forgas & Bower, 1987, 1988). These effects occur because "concepts, words, themes, and rules of inference that are associated with that emotion will become primed and highly available for use [in] top-down or expectation-driven processing [acting] as interpretive filters of reality" (Bower, 1983, p. 395).

Many cognitive tasks require people to "go beyond the information given," and mood may also influence the use of *associations and inferences* to construct a judgment or a decision (Heider, 1958). This occurs because the greater availability of mood-consistent associations can influence the top-down, constructive processing of complex or ambiguous social stimuli (Bower, 1981, 1991). For example, in word associations to an ambiguous word like *life,* happy subjects generate more positive associations (love, freedom), whereas sad subjects produce words like *struggle* or *death* (Bower, 1981), and emotional subjects make up more mood-congruent stories about fictional characters on the Thematic Apperception Test (Bower, 1981).

Affect and Behavior Interpretation

Combining Gordon's interest in mood and memory, and my interest in social cognition, within a week or so after our first encounter we were already designing our first experiment, intended to explore affective influences on social impressions (Forgas, Bower, & Krantz, 1984). A stringent test of mood effects on social judgments requires that we demonstrate mood effects on a relatively simple and direct kind of social judgment, such as the way people interpret their own, and others' ongoing social behaviors. As the meaning of social actions is often inherently ambiguous (Heider, 1958), affect priming may well influence the way people interpret others' and their own behaviors. To test this prediction, in our first experiment we asked participants induced into happy or sad moods (using a hypnotic procedure) to watch and make judgments of their own social interactions with a partner from the previous day as recoded on a videotape (Forgas et al., 1984). As predicted, we found significant affective distortions: Happy people identified more positive, skilled and fewer negative, unskilled behaviors both in themselves and in their partners than did sad subjects. In contrast, observers who received no mood manipulation saw no such differences. These effects were entirely consistent with affect-priming effects on the kinds of inferences that people make as they interpret intrinsically complex and indeterminate social behaviors. We also found that negative affect had a markedly greater influence on the way people evaluated themselves than others; such a selective self-bias is also commonly observed in clinical populations, suggesting that our experimental study tapped into the same kinds of mental processes that also operate in depressed cognition.

These results confirm that affect influences the way observed social behaviors are evaluated even when objective, videotaped evidence is available. It seems that the same gesture or smile that may be seen as "friendly" in a good mood could just as easily be interpreted as "awkward" or "condescending" when the observer experiences negative affect. Later we found that these affect infusion effects persevere even when people form attitudes and make judgments about familiar and well-known others, such as their intimate partners (Forgas, 1994).

Follow-up experiments confirmed that it is indeed affect priming and memory mechanisms that seem largely responsible for affect infusion. Using reaction time data and recall measures in an impression formation task (Forgas & Bower, 1987), we found that people spend longer reading and thinking about affect-congruent information when forming impressions, but are faster in producing an affect-congruent judgment. These processing differences are consistent with affect-priming theories. When *learning* new information, affect priming produces a richer activated knowledge base, and thus increases the time it takes to learn and link new information to this more elaborate memory structure. In contrast, the *production* of affect-congruent judgments takes less time because the relevant response is already primed by the affective state. Thus, affect appears to have a clear influence on what we notice, what we learn, what we remember, and ultimately, the kinds of judgments we make.

Affect and Attributions

Later we found that these effects are even more pronounced when judgments are not based on simple and directly observable videotaped behaviors, but require more elaborate inferences about the causes of behavior. In several studies, participants who were feeling happy, sad, or neutral made attributions about success or failure in typical life situations (job performance, financial success, etc.) (Forgas, Bower & Moylan, 1990). Our results showed that happy persons made significantly more lenient, positive attributions, crediting success to themselves, and selectively blaming failure on external causes (Fig. 17–1). Sad participants in turn used a more negative, self-blaming attributional strategy, and were more likely to emphasize their own responsibility for negative outcomes, while failing to take due credit for positive results (Forgas et al., 1990, Experiment 1; Forgas & Locke, 2005).These effects prevailed even when students were explaining their real-life good or bad performance on a recent exam (Forgas et al., 1990). An additional series of experiments investigated mood effects on how people interpret personal problems within their current real-life initimate relationships (Forgas, Levinger, & Moylan, 1994). Happy people felt more content and satisfied with their relationships and partners, but sad people felt more dissatisfied with this critical domain of their lives (Forgas et al., 1994).

When More Thinking Increases Affect Infusion: The Paradoxical Effects of Task Complexity

However, by the mid-1980s there was growing evidence suggesting that affect priming is not a universal and context-independent phenomenon (Bower & Mayer,

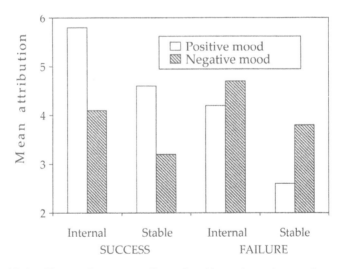

Figure 17–1. The mood congruent effects of positive and negative mood on attributions for success and failure to (a) internal, and (b) stable causes in an exam. Happy people claim credit for success (make more attributions to internal, and stable causes) but reject blame for failure (make more attributions to external, and unstable causes). People in negative mood in turn take less credit for success, and blame themselves more for failing. (Data are based on Forgas, Bower, & Moylan, 1990.)

1985). The pattern of results reported in the literature suggested a new and interesting question: Why do we get strong affect congruence in some situations, and not in others? One hunch I had was that affect congruence should be significantly greater when people need to engage in more extensive and elaborate thinking that increases the opportunity for using primed memory-based information. This of course is precisely what network theories should also imply.

This prediction was tested in several experiments when people formed judgments about more or less complex, typical or familiar targets in order to manipulate the degree of constructive processing required. One idea for these studies came from a real-life experience in a restaurant, when I noticed a very attractive, vivacious young woman and a rather unattractive older man who were obviously engaged in a close romantic relationship. I realized that this unusual sight caused me to engage in more extensive, elaborate, and constructive processing as I thought about this unusual couple and tried to figure out the nature of their relationship. It occurred to me that it is precisely this kind of constructive and elaborate thinking that should amplify affect-priming influences. To test this, in one experiment we basically replicated that restaurant scene under controlled conditions. We first made participants feel happy or sad after showing them standard mood induction films, and then presented them with images of couples who were well-matched or badly matched in terms of physical attractiveness. As expected, all judgments showed significant affect infusion. However, when the couples were unusual and badly matched, and so required more lengthy processing, affect had a much greater effect on judgments than it did for couples that were typical and well-matched (Forgas, 1993, 1995b).

This pattern has been confirmed in a number of other studies (Forgas & Moylan, 1991). For example, affect also had a markedly greater influence on judgments about unusual, mixed-race rather than same-race couples. In other studies, we manipulated *both* the physical attractiveness and the racial match of observed couples, and so created well-matched (same race, same attractiveness), partly matched (either race, or physical attractiveness matched), and mismatched, unusual couples (different race, different attractiveness). Affect had the greatest influence on judgments about completely mismatched couples, had a weaker effect when they were partly matched, and had the smallest effect when they were well-matched (Forgas, 1995b). Other studies looking at how impressions about people are formed showed that affect is far more likely to infuse judgments about people who possess atypical, unusual rather than typical personality characteristics (Forgas, 1992). Other researchers confirmed the same effect when people make judgments about themselves: affect has a greater influence when people are judging less familiar, peripheral aspects of the self, but these effects are reduced when central, familiar features are judged (Sedikides, 1995).

Interestingly, this paradoxical pattern holds even when people are thinking about intimate and well-known others, such as their intimate partners. When we asked happy or sad people to think about their own intimate relationships, mood effects were consistently greater when more extensive thinking was required to deal with more complex and serious rather than simple, everyday interpersonal issues (Forgas, 1994). In a way, it seems that the more we know about a person or an issue, the richer and more extensive the number of relevant memories we can call upon, and the more likely that affect will have a selective influence on what comes to mind when more extensive processing is required.

This might explain why there is so much affective fluctuation in the way people evaluate their intimate relationships. When feeling good, memories about happy, positive events are more accessible and the relationship seems fabulous. When in a negative mood, all that comes to mind is problems and difficulties, and the same relationship seems hardly worth having (Forgas, et al., 1994). Such affective biases in relationship judgments can be magnified even further when we are forced to think elaborately about complex, difficult issues. In fact, we found that more complex targets actually receive longer processing, and it is this difference in processing latency that mediates the mood effects observed (Forgas, 1993, 1995b). Longer processing producing greater affect congruence is consistent with the predicted memory-based priming effects originally outlined by Bower (1981). However, these experiments seem inconsistent with alternative theories of affect congruence, such as the affect-as-information model that assumes that mood congruence occurs because people use their prevailing mood states as simple heuristic cues when producing a response (Clore, Schwarz, & Conway, 1994).

BEYOND AFFECT PRIMING

Although Bower's (1981) network model generated a great deal of interest and numerous experiments confirmed its predictions, there was also accumulating empirical evidence by the mid-1980s suggesting that the model does not apply universally. Some of the predicted memory effects, such as lexical priming and mood-state-dependent recall appeared less robust than expected (Blaney, 1986; Bower & Mayer, 1985; Eich et al., 2001). The difficulty of obtaining reliable mood-state-dependent memory effects was variously explained as due to the lack of sufficiently *intense* mood manipulations (Bower & Mayer, 1985), the lack of *causal belonging* between mood induction and the experimental task (Bower, 1991), and the fact that mood priming may be difficult to obtain in conditions that are "antithetical to self-referencing" (Blaney, 1986, p. 232). Gordon, as a cognitive psychologist seeking universal and robust effects that manifest invariable properties of the human mind, found such failures to replicate troubling. In contrast, given my background as a social psychologist, long accustomed to situational influences on almost every phenomenon we study, I found these findings intriguing and even stimulating, and certainly not unexpected.

Interestingly, the problems of replicating mood-congruent effects seemed to be confined to standard memory tasks, where people try to learn and recall relatively meaningless word lists. In studies using more realistic stimuli, such as people or events, mood-state-dependent retrieval remained a robust and reliable phenomenon (cf. Bower, 1991; Eich, 1995; Forgas, 1991, 1992; Forgas & Bower, 1987, 1988; Mayer et al., 1992). These tasks provide people with a richer and more elaborate set of encoding and retrieval cues, and thus allow affect to more readily function as a differentiating context (Bower, 1981). Somewhat similar conclusions were reached by Eich (1995), suggesting that mood-dependent retrieval is a robust effect that best appears when the moods induced are strong, when free recall rather than recognition is called for, and when the memories are self-generated rather than externally imposed.

On balance, Bower's (1981) associative network model remains a robust, parsimonious, and well-supported explanation for a wide variety of the mood congruity effects reported. However, these effects—not surprisingly—are most likely to occur in circumstances that call for open, constructive information processing that promotes the generative use of previously stored and affectively primed information in computing a response (Fiedler, 1991). The network model thus needs to be supplemented by a more careful specification of the processing conditions under which it is or is not likely to apply; this was the objective of the affect infusion model, described next.

THE AFFECT INFUSION MODEL (AIM)

The affect infusion model (AIM; Forgas, 1995a, 2002) has been developed to integrate existing affect cognition theories, and to specify the conditions under which affect priming is more or less likely to occur. *Affect infusion* can be defined as the process whereby affectively primed information becomes incorporated into people's constructive processing, selectively influencing their learning, memory, attention, and associative processes, and eventually coloring the outcome of their deliberations in an affect-congruent direction (Forgas, 1995a, p. 39). However, similar effects can also occur when people directly use affect as information in circumstances that call for simple, heuristic processing (Clore et al., 1994). Within the AIM, these two mechanisms of affect congruence—affect priming, and affect as a heuristic cue—can be integrated as complementary rather than competing accounts, both capable of explaining mood congruity effects, albeit under different processing conditions.

In order to achieve these objectives, the AIM predicts that the nature and extent of mood effects should depend on the kind of processing strategy employed to deal with a given task. Most information-processing models—such as the network model—are "single process" theories, postulating robust, universal, and context-insensitive cognitive mechanisms. As evidence accumulates, the "boundary conditions" for the theory become obvious. This is indeed what happened as the network theory has been extended to deal with an increasingly broad and heterogeneous set of phenomena (Forgas & Bower, 1988). The AIM seeks to systematize the boundary conditions of mood congruity effects, by identifying four different processing strategies, representing the factorial combination of two underlying processing characteristics: the degree of processing *effort* (low vs. high), and the kind of information *search strategy* used (open vs. directed). According to the model, only open, unbiased information search should produce affect congruence. Such open-search strategies can be either low effort (*heuristic* processing) or high effort (*substantive* processing). Both heuristic and substantive processing can produce affect infusion, due to either the affect priming mechanism (substantive processing) or the affect-as-information mechanism (heuristic processing). In contrast, strategies that involve relatively closed and directed information search processes (such as *direct access* and *motivated* processing) should limit the opportunity for the incidental affect infusion.

Direct access is the simplest processing strategy based on the strongly cued retrieval of preexisting, stored responses from the rich repertoire of crystallized, precomputed reactions and evaluations we all possess. Direct access is most likely when the task is familiar, there is little personal involvement, and there are no other motivational, cognitive, affective, or situational forces mandating more elaborate processing. This is by definition a robust, low-effort, and directed process that resists affect infusion, as little constructive thinking is required. *Motivated processing* occurs when responses are guided by a strong, preexisting objective, and thus little constructive open-ended processing occurs, reducing the likelihood of affect infusion. Motivated processing is most likely when a specific outcome is desired, and a highly selective, targeted information search strategy is used. Affect can also trigger such motivated processing, directed at achieving mood repair or mood maintenance (Clark & Isen, 1982). Such processing strategies are again impervious to affect infusion.

Heuristic processing occurs when people employ readily available shortcuts to produce a response with the least amount of effort, using whatever shortcuts are available to them. This style is likely when the task is simple or typical, personal relevance is low, motivational objectives are absent, cognitive capacity is limited, and the situation does not demand accuracy or substantive processing. During heuristic processing reactions may be based on irrelevant associations with environmental variables (Griffitt, 1970), and may also be informed by one's prevailing mood according to the affect-as-information model (Clore et al., 1994).

Finally, *substantive processing* is the most constructive and generative strategy that promotes affect infusion due to affect-priming mechanisms. The likelihood of substantive processing is greater when the task is complex or atypical, when it is personally relevant, when people have adequate processing capacity, and when they have no specific motivational goal guiding them. It is during substantive processing that memory mechanisms such as affect priming are most likely to produce affect infusion (Bower, 1991; Forgas, 1995a). In terms of the AIM, affect infusion is more likely when more extensive processing is required to compute a more complex judgment, a counterintuitive prediction that has been supported in several experiments considered earlier (Fiedler, 1991; Forgas, 1992, 1993, 1995a; Sedikides, 1995). The AIM also specifies a range of antecedent variables associated with the task, the person, and the situation that determine processing choices, including such factors as task complexity, personal relevance, motivation, processing capacity, and affective state (for details, see Forgas, 1995a, 2002).

Thus, in terms of the AIM, both heuristic and substantive processing can produce affect-congruent outcomes, through either the affect-as-information or the affect-priming mechanism. Whether heuristic or substantive processing was used can be empirically distinguished in terms of processing measures, such as memory and latency data, making the processing predictions of the AIM empirically testable (Forgas & Bower, 1987). The evidence suggests that affect priming typically occurs in the course of substantive, elaborate processing, and disappears when other (heuristic, direct access, or motivated) processing strategies are used (Forgas, 1994, 1995a, 1995b). In several studies, happy or sad subjects encoded, and later recalled and evaluated more or less typical others (Forgas, 1992), formed impressions about more or less well-matched couples (Forgas, 1993, 1995b; Forgas & Moylan, 1991), and explained more or less serious relationship conflicts (Forgas, 1994). In all cases, affect priming was observed but only in circumstances conducive to substantive processing according to the AIM. Thus, the AIM provides a parsimonious and general framework within which network theories can be located, suggesting that affect priming effects are most likely in conditions conducive to substantive, elaborate processing strategies (Fiedler, 1991; Forgas, 1995a).

EXTENSIONS AND APPLICATIONS

In recent years, the work we started with Gordon Bower in the 1980s developed in a number of new and exciting directions. Following our initial experiments demonstrating mood effects on social judgments and decisions, and the subsequent development of the affect infusion model, we continued to explore affective influences on a variety of real-life social behaviors. Only a brief overview of these directions is possible here.

Affect Infusion and Social Behavior

As social interaction necessarily involves many open-ended, rapid, and subconscious cognitive decisions about alternative actions, affect is likely to influence how people behave in social situations. All things being equal, we may expect that people in a positive mood should behave in a more confident, friendly, skilled, and constructive way than do those in a negative mood, as they are more likely to form positive, optimistic inferences about the complex social situations they face. Of course, as we have seen previously, this prediction should hold only if the situation facilitates open, constructive processing. As face-to-face interaction is an intrinsically open-ended task, affect infusion could reasonably be expected to occur. This prediction was confirmed when we asked female undergraduates to interact with a confederate immediately after they were made to feel good or bad as a result of watching a mood induction film (Forgas, 2002). Happy students communicated more and did so more effectively, used more engaging nonverbal signals, were more talkative, and disclosed more about themselves. Yet when asked, the students did not realize that their behavior was in any way influenced by their moods.

Several studies also show that affect has a specific influence on the way people communicate in social situations. For example, in a number of experiments we investigated the possibility that affect influences specific verbal moves, such as request strategies. The greater availability of positive thoughts in a happy mood produces a more optimistic assessment of the felicity conditions of a request, and so leads to a more confident, direct requesting style. In several studies, we showed that happy people indeed interpreted request situations in a more confident, optimistic way, and consequently used more direct, less elaborate, and less hedging request strategies. Sad people used more cautious, less direct, more elaborate, and more hedging request forms (Fig. 17–2). Furthermore, these mood effects on requesting were much stronger when the request situation was more demanding and difficult, and so required more extensive thinking (Forgas, 1998a, 1999b). These effects also occur in real-life situations. In one study, we recorded the requests made by subjects who were asked to get a file from a neighboring

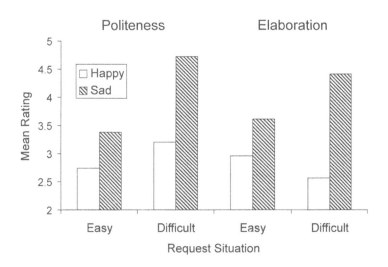

Figure 17–2.   The effects of happy, and sad mood on (a) the level of politeness, and (b) degree of elaboration of requests used in easy or difficult interpersonal situations. Positive mood produces more direct, less polite, and less elaborate requests, and these mood effects are significantly greater when the situation is difficult and requires more extensive processing. (Data are based on Forgas, 1999a.)

office after receiving a mood induction (Forgas, 1999a, Experiment 2). Even in this "real" situation, negative mood produced more polite, cautious, and hedging requests than did positive mood.

Another difficult but common communication task found to be affect sensitive is *self-disclosure.* We found that people who were induced to feel good were more willing to disclose intimate information about themselves and did so sooner than did people experiencing temporary negative affect. This mood effect was even stronger when the partner reciprocated with matching levels of disclosure (Forgas, 2006b). In a way, it seems that by selectively priming positive thoughts, positive affect creates a more optimistic evaluation of indeterminate social situations, and produces a sense of confidence and well-being that leads people to adopt more direct, open, and confident interpersonal strategies.

One example of strategic interaction that may well be affect sensitive is bargaining and negotiation. In several experiments, we found that when induced into a happy mood, people set themselves higher and more ambitious negotiating goals, expected to succeed more, and made plans and used strategies that were more optimistic and cooperative than did people in a neutral, or negative mood (Forgas, 1998c; see Fig. 17–3). Interestingly, we also found that people experiencing positive mood were actually more successful and achieved better outcomes than did sad participants. However, these mood effects were reduced for individuals who scored high on personality measures such as social desirability and machiavellism, features that are likely to produce more motivated and less open processing strategies. In addition to studying instances of affect congruence

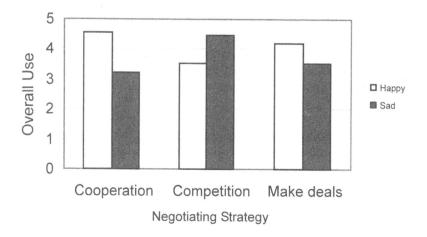

Figure 17–3. Mood-congruent influences on planned and actual negotiating strategies: Happy people plan, use more cooperative and less competitive bargaining strategies, and are more likely to make and honor deals than do negotiators experiencing negative affect. (Data are based on Forgas, 1998a.)

in the *content* of thinking and behavior, in a complementary series of recent studies we also explored affective influences on the *processing strategies.*

Affective Influences on Thinking Styles

Positive and negative affect can influence not only *what* people think (the content of cognition), but also *how* people think (the process of cognition). Evidence for mood effects on thinking style is broadly consistent with evolutionary ideas that suggest that affect functions as an automatic signal recruiting appropriate ways of responding to different situations. Positive affect functions like a cue informing us that the situation is familiar and benign and that we can rely on our existing knowledge in responding. Negative affect is more like an alarm signal, alerting us that the environment is potentially dangerous and that we need to pay close attention to new, external information. Research exploring the subtle processing consequences of positive and negative affect is a rapidly developing field. It is often assumed in everyday life that being in a good mood has universally desirable consequences. Yet in several experiments we found that the kind of careful, vigilant, and systematic attention to stimulus details typically recruited by negative moods can also be of considerable benefit in certain situations.

For example, mild negative moods may help individuals to avoid certain judgmental mistakes, such as the *fundamental attribution error* (FAE), a common tendency to infer intention and internal causation even when observed behavior is due to external, situational pressures (Forgas, 1998b). In a series of experiments, we asked people in induced good or bad moods to infer the attitudes of people based on essays they have written that were either freely chosen, or assigned to the writers. People in a positive mood were far more likely to commit the FAE, and infer the writers' attitude from the essays, even when the topic was clearly assigned and so uninformative. In contrast, negative affect reduced this common judgmental mistake: Those in a bad mood were more likely to realize that the topics were assigned, and so cannot be informative about underlying attitudes (Forgas, 1998b).

In another series of recent experiments, we also evaluated mood effects on eyewitness accuracy (Forgas, Vargas, & Laham, 2005). We first allowed people to witness complex real-life or videotaped social events. Some time later, good or bad mood was induced before they received questions that either included, or did not include "planted," misleading information about the scenes. When eyewitness accuracy was subsequently tested, those in a negative mood were more resistant to incorporating "false," misleading details into their memory. In contrast, those in a positive mood reported far more "false alarms," and remembered the misleading details as part of the original scene (Fig. 17–4).

If mild everyday mood states can influence how well people think in strategic social situations, these mood effects should also influence the quality and efficacy of their interpersonal strategies. In a recent series of studies, we asked people in

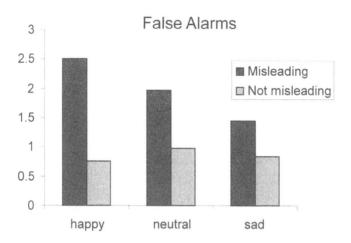

Figure 17–4.   The effects of mood on eyewitness accuracy: People in a negative mood are less likely to incorporate misleading information received after the event into their eyewitness memories (false-alarm rates are greater when misleading information is received in positive rather than negative mood; after Forgas, Vargas, & Laham, 2005).

positive or negative moods to produce persuasive arguments to convince an acquaintance of various topical issues. People in a negative mood produced higher quality and more effective persuasive arguments on issues such as (a) student fees should be increased, and (b) nuclear testing should be banned (Forgas, 2006a). Better argument quality was due to the use of more concrete and specific information in the persuasive arguments produced in negative mood, consistent with the more detailed and accommodative processing style associated with negative affect (Fiedler, 1991). Furthermore, naïve participants were more persuaded by, and showed more attitude change after reading arguments written in a negative rather than a positive mood. These experiments confirm that affective states can color both the content, and the process of how people deal with complex social information, and may ultimately also impact on the quality and efficacy of social interaction strategies (see Fig. 17–5).

SUMMARY AND CONCLUSIONS

Looking back, meeting Gordon Bower in 1980 was one of those chance events that profoundly affected my interests and research, decidedly for the better. I had a great deal of fun, learned much, and gained a charming, generous, kind, and supportive friend. Our collaboration represented a fortuitous merging of cognitive

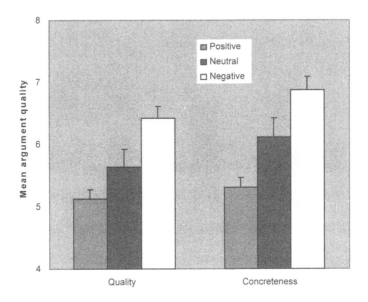

Figure 17–5. Mood effects on the quality and concreteness of the persuasive messages produced by happy, neutral, and negative-mood participants: Those in a negative mood produce more concrete and specific arguments, which are also of higher quality, more persuasive, and more effective (after Forgas, 2006b).

and social psychological interests, and led not only to a number of empirical articles, but also a theoretical reformulation of the original network model we started from. The affect-priming model provided a robust and universal conceptual framework for understanding the mechanisms that link affect and cognition, and has stimulated an impressive amount of research during the last few decades (Bower, 1981, 1991). The first part of this chapter reviewed the major implications of this theory, and considered some of the empirical evidence supporting it. In the second half of the chapter, a broader, multiprocess theory linking affect and cognition was outlined, the affect infusion model (Forgas, 1995a), defining some important boundary conditions for the network theories, and a range of experiments stimulated by that model were reviewed.

Some interesting counterintuitive results show that more extensive, substantive processing enhances mood congruity, providing strong support for the AIM, and network models (Forgas, 1992, 1994, 1995b, 2002). The implications of network theories apply not only in the laboratory, but also in many real-life situations. Numerous studies found affective influences on a variety of social judgments and interpersonal behaviors. These effects can even influence such involved and complex tasks as seeking an explanation for difficult relationship conflicts (Forgas, 1994), remembering witnessed events (Forgas et al., 2005), and producing persuasive arguments (Forgas, 2006b). To conclude, without Gordon Bower's crucial influence, and our serendipitous encounter more than 25 years ago, much of the work reported here would not have been done. Gordon's ideas, friendship, and support over the years had a major influence on my work and ideas, and I consider myself extremely fortunate to have had the opportunity to be one of his many collaborators.

ACKNOWLEDGMENTS

Support from the Australian Research Council and the Alexander von Humboldt Foundation, Germany, are gratefully acknowledged.

REFERENCES

Blaney, P. H. (1986). Affect and memory: A review. *Psychological Bulletin, 99,* 229–246.

Bower, G. H. (1981). Mood and memory. *American Psychologist, 36,* 129–148.

Bower, G. H. (1983). Affect and cognition. *Philosophical Transactions of the Royal Society of London B, 302,* 387–402.

Bower, G. H. (1991). Mood congruity of social judgments. In J. P. Forgas (Ed.), *Emotion and social judgments* (pp. 31–53). Oxford, England: Pergamon.

Bower, G. H., & Cohen, P. R. (1982). Emotional influences in memory and thinking: Data and theory. In M. S. Clark & S. T. Fiske (Eds.), *Affect and cognition* (pp. 291–332). Hillsdale, NJ: Lawrence Erlbaum Associates.

Bower, G. H., & Forgas, J. P. (2001). Mood and social memory. In J. P. Forgas (Ed.), *Handbook of affect and social cognition* (pp. 95–120). Mahwah, NJ: Lawrence Erlbaum Associates.

Bower, G. H., & Mayer, J. D. (1985). Failure to replicate mood-dependent retrieval. *Bulletin of the Psychonomic Society, 23,* 39–42.

Clark, M. S., & Isen, A. M. (1982). Towards understanding the relationship between feeling states and social behavior. In A. H. Hastorf & A. M. Isen (Eds.), *Cognitive social psychology* (pp. 73–108). New York: Elsevier-North Holland,.

Clore, G. L., Schwarz, N., & Conway, M. (1994). Affective causes and consequences of social information processing. In R. S. Wyer & T. K. Srull (Eds.) *Handbook of social cognition* (2nd ed.). Hillsdale, NJ: Lawrence Erlbaum Associates.

Eich, E. (1995). Searching for mood dependent memory. *Psychological Science, 6,* 67–75.

Eich, E. E., Kihlstrom, J. F., Bower, G,. H., Forgas, J. P., & Niedenthal, P. (2000). *Cognition and emotion.* New York: Oxford University Press.

Fiedler, K. (1991). On the task, the measures and the mood in research on affect and social cognition. In J. P. Forgas (Ed.), *Emotion and social judgments* (pp. 83–104). Oxford, England: Pergamon.

Forgas, J. P. (1976). The perception of social episodes: Categorical and dimensional representations in two different social milieus. *Journal of Personality and Social Psychology, 34,* 199–209.

Forgas, J. P. (1979). *Social episodes: The study of interaction routines.* London: Academic Press.

Forgas, J. P. (1982). Episode cognition: internal representations of interaction routines. In L. Berkowitz (Ed.), *Advances in experimental social psychology* (pp. 59–104), New York: Academic Press.

Forgas, J. P. (1991). Mood effects on partner choice: Role of affect in social decisions. *Journal of Personality and Social Psychology, 61,* 708–720.

Forgas, J. P. (1992). On bad mood and peculiar people: Affect and person typicality in impression formation. *Journal of Personality and Social Psychology, 62,* 863–875.

Forgas, J. P. (1993). On making sense of odd couples: Mood effects on the perception of mismatched relationships. *Personality and Social Psychology Bulletin, 19,* 59–71.

Forgas, J. P. (1994). Sad and guilty? Affective influences on the explanation of conflict episodes. *Journal of Personality and Social Psychology, 66,* 56–68.

Forgas, J. P. (1995a). Mood and judgment: The affect infusion model (AIM). *Psychological Bulletin, 117,* 1–28.

Forgas, J. P. (1995b). Strange couples: Mood effects on judgments about prototypical and atypical targets. *Personality and Social Psychology Bulletin, 21,* 747–765.

Forgas, J. P. (1998a). Asking nicely? Mood effects on responding to more or less polite requests. *Personality and Social Psychology Bulletin, 24,* 173–185.

Forgas, J. P. (1998b). Happy and mistaken? Mood effects on the fundamental attribution error. *Journal of Personality and Social Psychology, 75,* 318–331.

Forgas, J. P. (1998c). On feeling good and getting your way: Mood effects on negotiation strategies and outcomes. *Journal of Personality and Social Psychology, 74,* 565–577.

Forgas, J. P. (1999a). Feeling and speaking: Mood effects on verbal communication strategies. *Personality and Social Psychology Bulletin, 25,* 850–863.

Forgas, J. P. (1999b). On feeling good and being rude: Affective influences on language use and request formulations. *Journal of Personality and Social Psychology, 76,* 928–939.

Forgas, J. P. (2002). Feeling and doing: Affective influences on interpersonal behavior. *Psychological Inquiry, 13*(1), 1–28.

Forgas, J. P. (2006a). *Mood effects on persuasive message production.* Manuscript under review.

Forgas, J. P. (2006b). *Mood effects on self disclosure.* Unpublished manuscript, University of South Wales, Sydney, Australia.

Forgas, J. P., & Bower, G. H. (1987). Mood effects on person perception judgements. *Journal of Personality and Social Psychology, 53,* 53–60

Forgas, J. P., & Bower, G. H. (1988a). Affect in social judgements. *Australian Journal of Psychology, 40,* 125–145.

Forgas, J. P., & Bower, G. H. (1988b). Affect in social and personal judgments. In K. Fiedler & J. P. Forgas (Eds.), *Affect, cognition and social behaviour* (pp. 183–208). Toronto, Ontario, Canada: Hogrefe International.

Forgas, J. P., Bower, G. H., & Krantz, S. (1984). The influence of mood on perceptions of social interactions. *Journal of Experimental Social Psychology, 20,* 497–513.

Forgas, J. P., Bower, G. H., & Moylan, S. J. (1990). Praise or blame? Affective influences on attributions for achievement . *Journal of Personality and Social Psychology, 59,* 809–818.

Forgas, J. P., Levinger, G., & Moylan, S. (1994). Feeling good and feeling close: Mood effects on the perception of intimate relationships. *Personal Relationships, 2,* 165–184.

Forgas, J. P., & Locke, J. (2005). Affective influences on causal inferences: The effects of mood on attributions for positive and negative interpersonal episodes. *Cognition and Emotion, 19,* 1071–1081.

Forgas, J. P., & Moylan, S. J. (1987). After the movies: The effects of transient mood states on social judgments. *Personality and Social Psychology Bulletin, 13,* 478–489.

Forgas, J. P., & Moylan, S. J. (1991). Affective influences on stereotype judgments. *Cognition and Emotion, 5,* 379–397.

Forgas, J. P., Vargas, P., & Laham, S. (2005). Mood effects on eyewitness memory: Affective influences on susceptibility to misinformation. *Journal of Experimental Social Psychology, 41,* 574–588.

Griffitt, W. (1970). Environmental effects on interpersonal behavior: Ambient effective temperature and attraction. *Journal of Personality and Social Psychology, 15,* 240–244.

Heider, F. (1958). *The psychology of interpersonal relations.* New York: Wiley.

Hilgard, E. R. (1980). The trilogy of mind: Cognition, affection, and conation. *Journal of the History of the Behavioral Sciences, 16,* 107–117.

Mayer, J. D., Gaschke, Y. N., Braverman, D. L., & Evans, T. W. (1992). Mood congruent judgment is a general effect. *Journal of Personality and Social Psychology, 63,* 119–132.

Neisser, U. (1982). Memory: What are the important questions? In U. Neisser (Ed.) *Memory observed* (pp. 3–24). San Francisco: Freeman.

Niedenthal, P. M., & Setterlund, M. B. (1994). Emotion congruence in perception. *Personality and Social Psychology Bulletin, 20*(4), 401–411.

Ruiz Caballero, J. A., & Gonzalez, P. (1994). Implicit and explicit memory bias in depressed and non-depressed subjects. *Cognition and Emotion, 8,* 555–570.

Sedikides, C. (1995). Central and peripheral self-conceptions are differentially influenced by mood: Tests of the differential sensitivity hypothesis. *Journal of Personality and Social Psychology, 69*(4), 759–777.

Teasdale, J. D., & Fogarty, S. J. (1979). Differential effects on induced mood on retrieval of pleasant and unpleasant events from episodic memory. *Journal of Abnormal Psychology, 88,* 248–257.

Tulving, E. (1983). *Elements of episodic memory.* Oxford, England: Oxford University Press.

Zajonc, R. B. (1980). Feeling and thinking: Preferences need no inferences. *American Psychologist, 35,* 151–175.

Behavioral and Neural Correlates of Error Correction in Classical Conditioning and Human Category Learning

Mark A. Gluck
Rutgers University–Newark

To what extent are the processes of human learning analogous to the more elementary learning processes studied in animal-conditioning experiments? This question, and the broader goal of integrating mathematical models of animal and human learning, was the focus of my collaborative research at Stanford with Gordon Bower in the mid-1980s as well as my doctoral dissertation, which he supervised (Gluck & Bower, 1988a, 1988b, 1990). While working with Gordon, I also began a parallel line of research with another faculty member at Stanford, Richard Thompson. This research had the same conceptual starting point as the cognitive studies with Gordon, mathematical models of animal learning, but asked a different question: How are these learning principles embodied by neural circuits for various forms of classical conditioning (Gluck & Thompson, 1987; Thompson & Gluck, 1989, 1991).

In the late 1980s, these two research projects—one with Bower and the other with Thompson—shared only a common conceptual starting point. They were otherwise completely independent: The neuroscience research with Thompson made no direct links to cognition and the cognitive work with Bower made no direct links to neuroscience. These parallel projects continued throughout my graduate years at Stanford (1982–1987) as well as during several years of post-doctoral research at Stanford prior to my moving to Rutgers University–Newark in 1991. In the subsequent 15 years, my research has built upon the foundations of these two earlier research projects, extending them to create more direct bridges from neuroscience to human cognition. This newer cognitive neuroscience research fills in the gaps left by the earlier work with Bower and Thompson, showing how experimental and computational studies of the neural circuits for classical conditioning in animals has direct relevance for understanding the anatomy, physiology, neuropharmacology, and genetics of human learning, especially probabilistic category learning.

The remainder of this chapter is divided into four sections. In the first, I review the concept of error correction, and discuss how this learning principle has been a building block for models of both animal and human learning. Then, I turn to the neural substrates of error correction learning in classical conditioning, discussing the functional roles of three brain regions: the cerebellum, the basal ganglia, and the hippocampus. In the third section, I show how past bridges between animal and human learning (specifically my earlier doctoral dissertation research with Bower), provides a behavioral bridge for using models and data on the neural substrates of classical conditioning to inform our understanding of the cognitive neuroscience of human learning, especially probabilistic category learning. This research combines two methodologies, functional brain imaging and neuropsychological studies of patients with localized brain damage. In the fourth and final section, I briefly review the status of our understanding of the cognitive neuroscience of category learning, and some exciting new research directions that lie ahead.

ERROR CORRECTION IN LEARNING AND BEHAVIOR

For most of the first half of the 20th century, psychologists believed that as long as a cue (the conditioned stimulus, or CS) and an outcome (the unconditioned stimulus, or US) occurred closely together in time and nearby in space, an association would develop between them. However, in the late 1960s several psychological studies showed that pairing a CS and a US is not sufficient for conditioning to occur. Rather, for a CS to become associated with a US, it must provide valuable new information that helps an animal predict the future. Moreover, even if a given cue is predictive of a US, it may not become associated with that US if its usefulness has been preempted ("blocked") by another co-occurring cue that has a longer history of predicting the US. For example, if a rat is first trained that a light predicts a shock, and later is trained that a compound stimulus of a light and tone together also predicts the shock, the rat will learn very little about the tone because the tone does not add any predictive information for the animal. This phenomenon, first described in animal conditioning by Leon Kamin, is known as blocking (Kamin, 1969). It demonstrates that classical conditioning occurs only when a cue is both a useful and a nonredundant predictor of the future.

The blocking effect challenged early theories of classical conditioning because it suggested that cues do not evoke conditioned responses based solely on their individual relationships with the US. Rather, blocking and other related experimental studies done in the late 1960s and early 1970s led to a new view of classical conditioning in which (a) cues that co-occur compete with each other to predict the US, and (b) a cue must impart reliable and nonredundant information about the expected occurrence of the US to produce effective conditioning. Apparently "simple" Pavlovian conditioning is not as simple as psychologists once thought it was. Even rats and rabbits act like sophisticated statisticians, sensitive to the relative informational value of cues in their environment.

Rescorla and Wagner's (1972) Error Correction Model of Classical Conditioning

In the early 1970s, two psychologists working at Yale University developed an elegant learning model to explain how animals might learn about the informational value of cues (Rescorla & Wagner, 1972). Rescorla and Wagner's key idea was that the changes in association between a CS and a US are driven by a prediction error, that is, the difference between whether or not the animal expects the US (i.e., the Expected US), and whether or not the US actually occurs (i.e., the Actual US). Rescorla and Wagner argued that if the occurrence of the US is unexpected, learning should occur proportional to the degree to which the US is surprising, where the surprise, that is the prediction error, is calculated as the difference between the Expected US and the Actual US. Key to their formulation was their assumption that an animal's expectation of the US is based on the sum of the strengths of all the CSs that are present on a trial. This allowed the model to account for many learning phenomena in which training to one cue can affect what is learned about other cues that are present in the same trials. In contrast, prior learning theories had assumed that each CS–US relationship is learned independently and were, thus, not able to address such cue–cue interactions during learning.

The Rescorla–Wagner model implied that a US that is totally unexpected given all the cues that are present (high error) should cause lots of learning whereas a US that is only partially expected (medium error) should result in less learning. The learning rule in the Rescorla–Wagner model is called an error correction rule because, over many trials of learning, it reduces—that is, "corrects"—the prediction error.

More than a quarter century after its publication, the Rescorla–Wagner model is generally acknowledged as the most powerful and influential formal model of learning ever produced by psychology. The model gained broad acceptance because it is simple, elegant, and explains a wide range of previously puzzling empirical results. It revealed an underlying order among a series of results that initially seem unrelated or even contradictory. The model also made novel and surprising predictions about how animals will behave in new experimental procedures, and experimenters rushed to test these predictions.

By virtue of its simplicity, the Rescorla–Wagner model does not account for all kinds of learning. Many researchers devoted themselves to showing how one or another addition to the model allows it to account for a wider range of phenomena—but with too many additions, the model loses some of its simplicity and appeal. Within its domain, the Rescorla–Wagner model combines explanatory power with mathematical simplicity. It takes an intuitively reasonable idea— classical conditioning is driven by a prediction error—and then pares away all but the most essential details, and uses this as a tool to explore implications of this idea that were not obvious before. The Rescorla–Wagner model is also a starting point from which many subsequent models were built, including the category-learning model of Gluck and Bower (1988) described next.

Gluck and Bower's (1988) Error Correction Model of Category Learning

To what extent are the processes of human learning analogous to the more elementary learning processes studied in animal-conditioning experiments? One consequence of the lack of communication between animal and human researchers in the 1960s is the fact that few, if any, animal researchers were aware that Gordon Bower and Tom Trabasso had demonstrated a form of blocking in human learning several years before the Kamin study (Trabbasso & Bower, 1964). During late 1960s and into the 1970s animal learning remained primarily concerned with elementary associative learning, whereas human-learning studies began to focus more on memory abilities, characterized in terms of information processing and rule-based symbol manipulation, approaches borrowed from the emerging field of artificial intelligence. Ironically, this historical schism between animal and human researchers occurred just as animal-learning theory was being invigorated by the Rescorla–Wagner model in the early 1970s.

Interest in relating human cognition to elementary associative learning was revived in the late 1980s by the expanding impact of computational "neural network" (or "connectionist") models of human learning. These models showed that many human abilities—including speech recognition, motor control, and category learning—emerge from configurations of elementary associations similar to those studied in conditioning paradigms (Rumelhart, McClelland, & the PDP Research Group, 1986).

One example of a connectionist model in cognition from that era is a simple neural network that Gordon Bower and I developed to model how people learn complex probabilistic categories (Gluck & Bower, 1988a). The study of category learning has been a central paradigm within cognitive psychology for more than 50 years. Category learning has aspects of both elementary associative learning as well as higher order cognition. On one hand, category learning can be viewed as a "cognitive skill" that shares many behavioral properties, and possibly some neural substrates, with motor-skill learning and conditioning. On the other hand, categorization underlies many higher order cognitive abilities. When a connoisseur distinguishes a cabernet from a merlot, or a doctor diagnoses a disease based on a pattern of symptoms, they are performing categorization. It is this dual nature—part elementary skill, part higher cognition—that makes category learning a valuable paradigm for studying fundamental aspects of human learning, at both the behavioral and neural levels of analysis.

The Gluck and Bower (1988) model of category learning was based on applying the Rescorla–Wagner model of animal conditioning to human learning. In our study, college students were asked to learn how to diagnose patients, according to which of two fictitious diseases they had, Midosis or Burlosis. The students reviewed medical records of fictitious patients, each of whom was suffering from one or more of the following symptoms: bloody nose, stomach cramps, puffy eyes, or discolored gums. During the study, subjects reviewed several hundred such medical charts, tried to diagnose each patient, and were then told the correct diagnosis. Initially, of course, the students had to guess; but with practice, they were able to diagnose the fictitious patients rather accurately. What helped them guess was that the different symptoms were differentially diagnostic of the two diseases. Thus, bloody noses were very common in Burlosis patients (but rare in Midosis) whereas discolored gums were common in Midosis patients (but rare in Burlosis). The other two symptoms, stomach cramps and puffy eyes, were only moderately diagnostic of either disease.

This kind of learning can be modeled using the network in Figure 18–1. The four symptoms are represented by four input nodes at the bottom of the network and the two diseases correspond to the two output nodes at the top of the network. The weights between the symptoms and the diseases are updated according to the learning rule from the Rescorla–Wagner model, much as if the symptoms were CSs and the diseases were alternate USs.

Learning and performance in the model works as follows: If on a particular trial, the symptoms "Bloody Nose" and "Stomach Cramp" are presented, then this is modeled by turning "on" the corresponding input nodes (solid black nodes in Fig. 18–1). These act like two CSs present on a conditioning trial. In contrast to the classical conditioning paradigms described earlier, where there is one US (e.g., a shock), here there are two possible outcomes, the diseases Burlosis and Midosis. For each outcome category, there is a teaching node that provides error-correcting feedback with the correct (actual) category for each input training pattern. In Figure 18–1, the correct category is Burlosis. Thus, activating two features

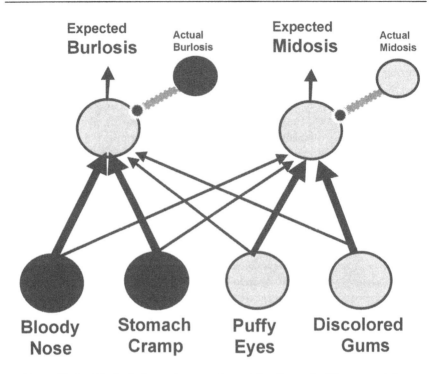

Figure 18–1. Medical diagnosis network applying Rescorla–Wagner model to human category learning (after Gluck & Bower, 1988a). The Model. The weights from bloody nose to Burlosis and from discolored gums to Midosis are thick indicating highly diagnostic relationships. The other cues are of only moderate diagnosticity. The input nodes for bloody nose and stomach cramp are shown activated by the dark fill. For each outcome category there is a teaching node that provides error-correcting feedback with the correct (actual) category for each input training pattern. In this case, the correct category is Burlosis.

(two input nodes) causes activity to travel up four weights, two to Burlosis and two to Midosis as shown in Figure 18–1.

By analogy with the Rescorla–Wagner model, the output node activations are equivalent to the network's expectation of one disease versus another, and the correct answer (the disease name given by the experimenter) was then used to modify the weights to reduce the error between the expected disease and the actual disease category outcome, according to Rescorla–Wagner's error correction learning rule. The network model shown in Figure 18–1 incorporates nothing more than the learning principle of the 1972 Rescorla–Wagner conditioning model. Nevertheless, this "animal-conditioning" model of human cognition accounts for many aspects of how people in our experiments classified different patients.

With four possible symptoms, there are 16 possible patient charts that can be constructed depending on whether each of the four symptoms is present or absent. We actually used only 14 of these, eliminating the charts with no symptoms (all absent) or all four symptoms (all present). After subjects had completed a long series of training trials, we asked if the model could predict the proportion of times that each of the 14 patterns was classified as Burlosis versus Midosis by their subjects. To generate this prediction, we looked at two output nodes, *Expected-Burlosis* and *Expected-Midosis,* for each of the 14 patterns. If, for a particular symptom pattern, such as "Bloody Nose & Stomach Cramp," the output values were *Expected-Burlosis* = 80 and *Expected-Midosis* = 20, then, we argued, the subjects should likely classify this pattern as Burlosis 80% of the time and as Midosis 20% of the time. In this way, we calculated a predicted proportion of "Burlosis" responses for each of these 14 patterns based on their model and compared this to the actual proportion of subjects who responded "Burlosis" to these patterns during the final 50 trials of the experiments (Gluck & Bower, 1988a).

The results of this analysis are shown in Figure 18–2, where each of the 14 patterns is represented by a dot. The location of each dot corresponds (on the horizontal axis) to the model's predicted proportion (ranging from 0 to 1), whereas its location on the vertical axis corresponds to the actual experimental data. Thus, the "Bloody Nose & Stomach Cramp" patient from Figure 18–1 who has a predicted proportion of 80% Burlosis categorization would be located as a dot at 0.8 on the horizontal axis. If, indeed, the subjects in this experiment did label this pattern as Burlosis on 80% of the trials, then the dot for "Bloody Nose & Stomach Cramp" would be found at the point (0.8,0.8) in this graph. Thus, the better the fit of the model the more likely that each of the 14 patterns (dots) would lie on the straight line from (0,0) through (1,1). As you can see from Figure 18–1, the fit is excellent.

In addition to these fits, the model was applied to many other types of data from these and other experiments. It was able to account for the relative differences in difficulty among many different tasks (i.e., why some tasks are harder than others and take longer to solve) and it predicted some surprising generalization behaviors when people, following category learning, were later asked to predict the marginal probabilities of different categories given the presence of individual features (Gluck & Bower, 1988a, 1988b). For learning more complex discrimination rules in which sensitivity to the relationships between stimulus features was necessary, we borrowed again from Rescorla and Wagner, adopting their convention of including configural nodes that represented the unique configuration of various pairs of features (e.g., bloody nose and stomach cramps both being present); again, this approach showed a remarkable ability to explain a wide range of human category-learning behaviors (Gluck & Bower, 1988b; Gluck, Bower, & Hee, 1989).

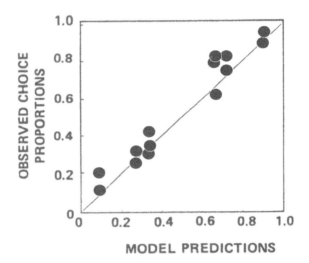

Figure 18–2.   Fits of the Rescorla–Wagner network model for pattern classification of 14 items (from Gluck & Bower, 1988a). Each pattern is represented by a dot whose location is determined by the model predictions (x-axis) and the actual pattern classification proportions (y-axis). The fact that the 14 dots lie very close to the diagonal line indicates a very close fit of model to data.

THE NEURAL SUBSTRATES OF ERROR CORRECTION LEARNING IN CLASSICAL CONDITIONING

The behavioral studies described in the previous section demonstrate that error correction learning is common to both animal conditioning and human category learning. But how is error correction computed in the brain? In this section, I briefly review what is known about the neural substrates of error correction in animal studies of classical conditioning, including the work of Richard Thompson and myself on the cerebellum and aversive conditioning of motor reflexes, as well as the work of Wolfram Shultz and colleagues on the basal ganglia and midbrain dopamine neurons and their role in appetitive conditioning. This leads into discussing the role of the hippocampus in modulating both forms of learning. The following section then builds on this discussion to address what is known so far about the neural substrates of error correction in human learning.

THE CEREBELLUM AND ERROR CORRECTION IN AVERSIVE CONDITIONING OF MOTOR REFLEXES

In the early 1980s, Richard Thompson and his coworkers discovered that small lesions in the cerebellum of rabbits permanently and completely prevented the acquisition of new classically conditioned eyeblink responses and abolished retention of previously learned responses (Thompson, 1986). As shown in Figure 18–3, the cerebellum has two main layers. The top surface of the cerebellum is the cerebellar cortex (which includes the Purkinje cells). Below the cerebellar cortex lies the interpositus nucleus, one of the cerebellar deep nuclei.

To follow the pathways in and out of the cerebellum, we begin with the CSs that project first to an area in the brain stem called the pontine nuclei. The pontine nuclei include different subregions for each kind of sensory stimulation. Thus, a tone CS would project to one area of the pontine nuclei and a light CS to another. This CS information then travels up to the deep nuclei of the cerebellum along mossy fibers, which branch in two directions. First, they make contact in the deep nuclei with the interpositus nucleus. Second, they project up to the cerebellar cortex (via a few other cells not shown) and then connect to the Purkinje cells in the cerebellar cortex. The second sensory input pathway is the US pathway. An air puff to the eye, the US, activates the inferior olive, a structure that activates the interpositus in the deep nucleus of the cerebellum. In addition, a second pathway from the inferior olive projects up to the cerebellar cortex via climb-

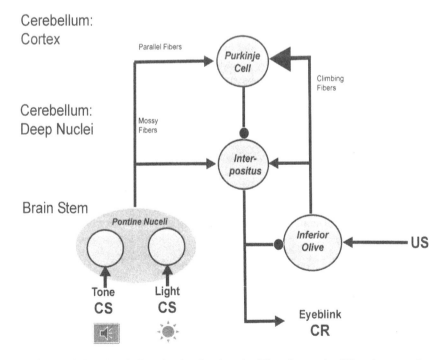

Figure 18–3.   Cerebellar circuits showing the CS pathway, the US pathway, and the CR pathway, projecting up from the sensory cues into the cerebellar cortex and deep nuclei. Excitatory synapses are shown as arrows and inhibitory synapses terminate with a filled circle.

ing fibers. Complementing these two input pathways is a single-output pathway for the CR (conditioned response), which originates with the Purkinje cells. The Purkinje cells project down from the cerebellar cortex into the deep nuclei where they form an inhibitory synapse with the interpositus. The interpositus is the only output from the cerebellum; activity in the interpositus projects to the motor cortex which, in turn, projects to the muscles in the eye to generate the eyeblink CR.

There are two sites in the cerebellum where CS and US information converge and, thus, where information about the CS–US association might be stored: (a) the Purkinje cells in the cerebellar cortex and (b) the interpositus nucleus. These two sites of convergence are intimately interconnected through an output pathway; the Purkinje cells project down to the interpositus nucleus with strong inhibitory synapses, as shown in Figure 18–3.

Note that there is also an additional pathway within the cerebellum that we have not yet discussed. This inhibitory feedback pathway projects from the interpositus nucleus to the inferior olive. Thus, in a well-trained animal that makes a CR and activates the interpositus nucleus, this activity will, in turn, inhibit the inferior olive carrying US information (Sears & Steinmetz, 1991). Thus, activity in the inferior olive will reflect the *Actual-US* less (due to inhibition) the *Expected-US,* where the *Expected-US* is measured by the interpositus activity, which drives the CR. *Actual-US—Expected-US.* Note that this is the same difference (*Actual-US—Expected-US*) that the Rescorla–Wagner model uses to calculate the error on a trial, and which is then used to determine how much learning should accrue to the CS association weights. In several papers, Richard Thompson and I developed computational models that showed how these circuits could implement the essential error correction principle of the Rescorla–Wagner model, along with various other aspects of timing and response behaviors (Donegan, Gluck, & Thompson, 1989; Gluck, Allen, Myers, & Thompson, 2001; Thompson & Gluck, 1991).

Our interpretation for how the cerebellum computes the Rescorla–Wagner model's error correction procedure implies that Kamin's blocking effect (the clearest experimental evidence for error correction learning) should depend on that inhibitory pathway from the interpositus to the inferior olive. This prediction was experimentally confirmed in a later study by Thompson and colleagues, who disabled this inhibitory pathway and, in doing so, showed that they could *block* blocking (Kim, Krupa, & Thompson, 1998). More generally, our computational modeling, along with various other experimental studies, argues that the cerebellum acts as a predictive system that learns through error correction principles to make anticipatory adjustments in timing-sensitive behaviors.

The Basal Ganglia and Error Correction in Appetitive Conditioning

The previous section showed that the inferior olive in the cerebellum codes for the prediction error during eyeblink conditioning, much as described by the Rescorla–Wagner model. The inferior olive activity is high when the air puff US is unexpected, drops down to baseline when the US is predicted, and shows below-baseline firing rates when an expected US does not occur (i.e., when the error term is negative). These cerebellar circuits, however, are not responsible for all forms of classical conditioning, but only for conditioning of discrete well-timed motor reflexes like the eyeblink response. What about other forms of classical conditioning, especially those where the US is a positive reward, such as food or drink?

A series of electrophysiological recording studies in monkeys led researchers to suggest that dopamine neurons in the midbrain play a critical role in reward-related learning (for a review, see Schultz, 1998; Schultz, Dayan, & Montague, 1997). Specifically, these dopamine neurons respond with strong bursts of activity to unexpected rewards (but not to expected rewards), and show a decrease in firing when an expected reward fails to occur. Thus, these dopamine neurons appear to behave in appetitive conditioning (where the US is a positive rewarding stimulus) very much like the inferior olive cells do during motor-reflex conditioning to an aversive US: They code for the prediction error. More generally, work by Schultz and others has confirmed that dopamine neurons in the midbrain (both in substantia nigra compacta and in the ventral tegmental area) play a role in implementing the error-correcting principles of the Rescorla–Wagner model in certain appetitive forms of classical conditioning, in ways broadly analogous to the role of the cerebellum in aversive conditioning of motor-reflex responses.

What Does the Hippocampus Do in Classical Conditioning?

If the cerebellum is essential for aversive conditioning of well-timed motor reflexes and midbrain dopamine neurons are key for conditioning of appetitive reward prediction tasks, what, if any, role does the hippocampus play in these forms of classical conditioning? For half a century, it has been appreciated that the hippocampal region plays a critical role in acquisition of new memories, particularly rapidly acquired memories for autobiographical events, sometimes collectively called episodic memory (e.g., Squire, 1987). More recently, data from human and animal studies have documented that the hippocampal region is also involved in many kinds of incrementally acquired learning, including simple associative learning such as conditioning and category learning. What does the hippocampus contribute to classical conditioning, above and beyond the functions subserved by the cerebellum and basal ganglia?

After moving to Rutgers–Newark in 1991, I began a new program of hippocampal modeling with my (then) postdoctoral fellow, Catherine Myers. Together, we developed a neural network model of cortico-hippocampal processing to account for data from studies of classical conditioning in animals with lesions to their hippocampal region (Gluck & Myers, 1993, 2001; Myers & Gluck, 1994). The model conceptualizes the brain as a series of interacting modules, each implementing the information-processing function subserved by a particular brain region, but without regard for whether that function is implemented in a biologically plausible way.

As described earlier, the cerebellum is the substrate for storage and expression of learned CS–US associations in motor-reflex conditioning (Thompson, 1986). We adapted our earlier Thompson–Gluck cerebellar model of Figure 18–3 into a simpler connectionist network model shown in the left of Figure 18–4 (Gluck, Myers, & Thompson, 1994). This network learns to map from inputs specifying the presence of CSs and contextual cues, to a pattern of activation in an internal layer of nodes via a layer of weighted connections. This internal activation pattern constitutes a remapping or rerepresentation of the input, which is then mapped to output driving the behavioral CR via a second layer of weighted connections. On each trial, the system "error" is the difference between the actual response (CR) and the desired response (US). An error correction learning rule (analogous to the Rescorla–Wagner model) was used to modify the weights between the internal-layer and output-layer nodes, proportional to this error. However, no such error measure is defined for the internal-layer nodes, and so this error correction rule cannot be used to modify the lower layer of weights. As a result, no learning takes place in the lower layer and thus, the "internal representation" of stimuli at the intermediate layer of nodes is fixed if the hippocampal region model is missing (i.e., lesioned). Nevertheless, for many simple problems,

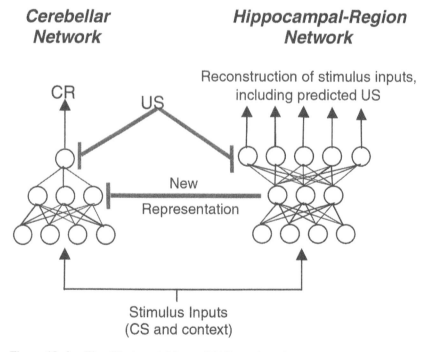

Cerebellar Network

Hippocampal-Region Network

Figure 18–4.   The Gluck and Myers (1993) cortico-hippocampal model. The hippocampal region forms new representations that compress redundancy while differentiating predictive information; these new representations can be adopted by long-term memory sites such as the cerebellum.

this system can learn appropriate CS–US association and produce a behavioral CR similar to empirical learning curves (Gluck et al., 1994). The abstract connectionist model of the cerebellar contributions to classical conditioning, shown on the left of Figure 18–4, can be directly related to the same information-processing capabilities of the more physiologically detailed and biologically realistic model in Figure 18–3: Both alter CS–US associations according to the error-correcting principle of the Rescorla–Wagner model.

With this simplified cerebellar model of conditioning, we were now able to ask: What does the hippocampus do? Catherine Myers and I proposed that the hippocampal region contributes to this cerebellar learning by developing new representations that encode stimulus–stimulus regularities (Gluck & Myers, 1993). In particular, if two stimuli reliably co-occur or are otherwise redundant, their representations become compressed, or more similar. Conversely, if two stimuli predict different future events, their representations become differentiated, or less similar.

We implemented this theory in a connectionist network model as shown in the full network model of Figure 18–4 (Gluck & Myers, 1993, 2001). Hippocampal-region processing is implemented via a network that learns to map CS inputs, through an internal node layer, to outputs that reconstruct those inputs and also predict the US. This network, unlike the cerebellar network, is able to modify both layers of weighted connections through a learning algorithm such as error back-propagation (Rumelhart et al., 1986). In the process, internal-layer nodes form a representation of the input that tends to compress redundant information while differentiating information that predicts the US, just as required by our theory.

A random recoding of the hippocampal-region network's internal-layer activations becomes the "desired output" for each node in the internal layer of the cerebellar network, and each node's error is the difference between this desired output and its own actual output. The cerebellar network then uses the error-correcting rule to adapt its lower-layer weights, just as it uses simple error correction learning to adapt its upper-layer weights. Over time, representations develop in the internal-layer nodes of the cerebellar network that are linear recombinations of the new representations developed by the hippocampal region network. Within this model framework, broad hippocampal-region damage is simulated by disabling the hippocampal-region network, leading to a network model in which the cerebellum alone processes information without modulating input from the hippocampal region. In this lesioned model, the error-correcting cerebellar network cannot adopt any new representations, although it can still learn to map from its existing representations to new behavioral responses by modifying its upper layer of weights.

Our model of hippocampal-region function correctly accounted for data showing that hippocampal-region damage does not impair simple delay conditioning but does impair more complex behaviors including contextual sensitivity and sensory preconditioning (Gluck & Myers, 1993, 2001; Myers & Gluck, 1994). It also made several novel predictions. For example, it predicted that learned irrelevance (slower CS–US learning following uncorrelated CS–US exposure) should be disrupted following hippocampal-region damage; we confirmed this in our lab at Rutgers in studies with rabbit eyeblink conditioning (Allen, Chelius, & Gluck,

2002) as well as humans (Myers et al., 2000). Similarly, our model expected that acquired equivalence (transfer of associations between objects previously associated with similar consequences) should be disrupted following hippocampal-region damage; this has also been confirmed in animals (Coutureau et al., 2002) and in studies we did in humans (Myers et al., 2003). In all these tasks, the common theme, as predicted by the model, is that the hippocampal region is not required for simple stimulus–response learning, but is required for learning about contextual or stimulus–stimulus regularities that support subsequent transfer generalization, phenomena that are not predicted by the error correction learning principle of the Rescorla–Wagner model.

As noted previously, many behavioral phenomena that cannot be explained by the Rescorla–Wagner model are not found in animals that have lesions to the hippocampal region. This suggests that the Rescorla–Wagner model may be better described as a model of the cerebellar contributions to motor-reflex conditioning in hippocampal-lesioned animals than as a model of conditioning in healthy, intact animals. Thus, the limitations of the Rescorla–Wagner model might now be reinterpreted as symptoms that this mathematical model of learning from the 1970s isn't really dead, just "brain damaged." That is to say, the model applies to the brain regions responsible for error correction learning such as the cerebellum, but does not explain the additional contributions of the hippocampal region.

Within its limited domain, the early Gluck and Myers model was reasonably successful at providing an account of the role of the hippocampal region in associative learning. However, it was implemented without particular regard for the anatomical or physiological details of the brain substrate. In part, this reflected the state of the empirical literature at the time: Most data on hippocampal-region function were based on lesion studies using techniques like ablation that were not sufficiently selective to allow complete destruction of a specific brain structure without conjoint damage to other nearby structures and to fibers of passage. Newer lesion techniques (such as neurotoxic lesions using ibotenic acid; see also Jarrard, 2002) have since allowed the accumulation of a large body of data contrasting, for example, the selective effects of entorhinal versus hippocampal damage, and electrophysiological recording studies have provided additional insights and constraints. As a result, there is now a sufficient body of empirical data to constrain a model differentiating these structures; this is the focus of current modeling efforts at Rutgers, including collaborative work with a former postdoctoral fellow in my lab, Martijn Meeter, who is now at the Free University in Amsterdam.

THE COGNITIVE NEUROSCIENCE OF ERROR CORRECTION IN PROBABILISTIC CATEGORY LEARNING

To summarize the results discussed so far: The cerebellum and basal ganglia can be understood as implementing the error correction mechanisms for learning described by the Rescorla–Wagner model for two forms of classical conditioning whereas the hippocampus operates during all forms of conditioning to create novel stimulus representations that reflect stimulus–stimulus regularities in the environment. What do these results imply about the neural bases of human learning? One avenue for seeking linkages between animal conditioning and human learning is to look at studies of classical conditioning in humans. Indeed, there exists an extensive literature on classical conditioning of the human eyeblink response, including those that used functional brain imaging in healthy normal people and studies of behavior in clinical populations. The conclusion that can be drawn from this is that the neural substrates for motor-reflex conditioning appear to be identical in humans and other animals (Daum et al., 1993; Gabrieli et al., 1995; Logan & Grafton, 1995).

Another avenue for seeking linkages between animal research and human learning is by using more cognitive tasks that employ analogous error correction principles of learning. This is where the earlier work that Gordon and I did in the late 1980s becomes relevant once again. Given our prior results showing that people learn probabilistic categories using *behavioral* principles of error correction analogous to those seen in classical conditioning, we can now ask: Are there also analogous *neural* mechanisms involved in human category learning that are similar or identical to those involved in classical conditioning? This leads to two specific questions: First, in human category learning, what are the neural mechanisms for error correction based on cognitive feedback? Second, does the hippocampal region play an analogous role in category learning as it does in classical conditioning creating novel stimulus representations? These two questions have driven my lab's more recent research on the cognitive neuroscience of category learning.

Probabilistic Category Learning

Beginning with the Gluck and Bower (1988a) studies reviewed earlier, category-learning research in my lab has focused primarily on learning probabilistic categories. These are categories in which there is no clear-cut rule for membership. Rather, various features are more, or less, probabilistically associated with one category or another. For example, "red sky at night" is a feature that is partially correlated with the category of "good weather tomorrow" but this feature is not a perfect rule for predicting the weather—only a useful heuristic. The weather might be better predicted, on average, by employing evidence from several such features, although even then, it might be impossible to predict the upcoming weather with 100% accuracy.

In the mid-1990s, we developed at Rutgers several novel probabilistic category-learning tasks based on variations of the earlier studies by Gluck and Bower (Gluck & Bower, 1988a, 1988b). The most well-known—and widely adopted—of our new category-learning tasks is often referred to as the "weather prediction" task (Gluck, Shohamy, & Myers, 2002; Knowlton, Squire, & Gluck, 1994; Poldrack et al., 2001). It uses four cards with geometric patterns as stimulus features, as shown in Figure 18–5A. On each trial, a subject sees one or more of these cards and is asked to predict whether the next day's weather will be rain or sunshine, as illustrated in Figure 18–5B.

The actual weather outcome is determined by a probabilistic rule based on the cards: Each card predicts rain or sunshine with a fixed probability as shown in Figure 18–5A, based on the same categories used in Gluck and Bower (1988a). Thus, the card with squares (S1) is strongly predictive of rain whereas the card with triangles (S4) is strongly predictive of sunshine. The other two cards have more intermediate statistical relationship with the two outcome categories. The actual outcome is based on the cumulative probabilities associated with all cards present on a trial. The probabilistic relationships between cues and outcomes ensures that it is impossible for subjects to learn the categorization with complete certainty, although it is possible to achieve significant learning by inducing how diagnostic each card is for each category.

In an early study of this task, we collaborated with Larry Squire and Barbara Knowlton using amnesic patients from the San Diego area who presented with a variety of etiologies including those with Korsakoff's syndrome, unknown lesions, as well as more focal medial temporal lobe damage. These amnesic patients learned the weather prediction task at about the same rate as control subjects, improving from chance performance (50% correct) to approximately 65% correct over the first 50 trials (Knowlton et al., 1994). With extended training, however, control subjects outperformed amnesic patients. In a more recent study, however, we used a group of patients with more localized hippocampal-region damage all of whom had a common etiology for their amnesia: hypoxia, the loss of oxygen to the brain (Hopkins et al., 2004). We found that these amnesics were uniformly impaired at two forms of probabilistic category learning, both early and late in training, in

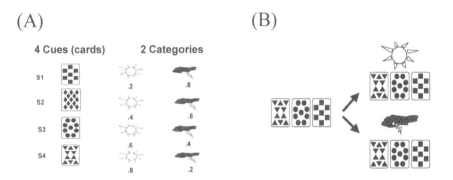

Figure 18–5.   (a) Four cards with geometric patterns are each related probabilistically to two different outcome categories, good weather and bad weather. (b) On each trial, a subject sees one or more of these cards (shown on the left) and is asked to predict whether the next day's weather will be sunshine (top right) or rain (bottom right).

contrast to the previous report by Knowlton et al., which had found deficits only later in training.

Together these results suggest that the weather prediction task, using the category structures from Knowlton et al. (1994) and Gluck and Bower (1988a), requires considerable hippocampal mediation. The Gluck and Myers (1993) model would argue that this reflects the many stimulus–stimulus relationships that can be used by an intact hippocampal region to support learning in this category structure, even if the task, being linearly separable, could, in principle, be learned without recourse to configural cues. This does not, however, imply that all forms of category learning, probabilistic or otherwise, will depend on an intact hippocampal region. Rather, simpler forms of category learning without significant stimulus–stimulus correlations are expected by our model to be largely independent of the hippocampal region. Consistent with this prediction, we have more recently shown that hypoxic amnesic patients are able to acquire a simpler category learning tasks at about the same rate as healthy controls (Shohamy, Myers, Geghman, Sage, & Gluck, 2006).

Functional Brain Imaging of Probabilistic Category Learning

Our prior computational models of hippocampal-region function (Gluck & Myers, 1993, 2001) suggest that hippocampal region develops new stimulus representations that are eventually acquired by other brain regions. In the last few years, support for the applicability of our model of hippocampal-region function to human learning has come from studies using functional brain imaging. Our model predicts that the hippocampal region should be very active early in category learning tasks when participants are learning about stimulus–stimulus regularities and evolving new stimulus representations, but that the hippocampal region should be less active later in training when other brain regions (e.g., cerebellum or basal ganglia) are using these representations to perform the behavioral response. In collaboration with Russ Poldrack at UCLA, we conducted a functional neuroimaging (fMRI) study of normal humans learning the weather prediction task. As expected by our model, we found that activity in the hippocampal region was high early in training and then tapered off; in contrast, basal ganglia activity was low at first and increased during training (Poldrack et al., 2001).

In Poldrack et al. (2001), we also examined whether activity in the basal ganglia and MTL was modulated by task demands. In particular, we compared two versions of the weather prediction task: the standard feedback-based version of the task, and an observational learning version in which subjects simply viewed stimulus–outcome pairs on each trial, and were later tested on these associations. Although learning on these two versions was equivalent in terms of percent optimal responding during a final testing phase, basal ganglia activation and MTL deactivation were significantly stronger during the feedback-based version of the task compared to the observational version of the task. This is consistent with the view that the basal ganglia (but not the MTL) are key for learning based on error-correcting feedback, but not during observational learning in which no response and no feedback is involved.

More recently, in collaboration with Daniel Weinberger and colleagues at NIMH, we have shown that probabilistic category learning engages neural circuitry that includes both the prefrontal cortex and the caudate nucleus of the basal ganglia, two regions that show prominent changes with normal aging (Fera et al., 2005). When trained on the weather prediction task, young and older adults displayed equivalent learning curves, used similar strategies, and activated analogous brain regions as seen using fMRI. However, the extent of caudate and prefrontal activation was less, and parietal activation was greater, in older participants. This suggests that some brain regions, such as the parietal cortices, may provide compensatory mechanisms for healthy older adults in the context of deficient prefrontal cortex and caudate nuclei responses. Further research will be required to better understand these age-related changes, but the initial study points to the promise of using probabilistic category learning tasks as a means to understand changes in neural function over the life span.

The Basal Ganglia and Category Learning in Parkinson's Disease

If the basal ganglia are key for error correction learning that is based on feedback, we should expect people with damage to the basal ganglia to show impairments on probabilistic category learning. One such population is patients with Parkinson's disease (PD) who have a profound loss of dopamine containing neurons in the substantia nigra pars compacta (SNc), leading to dopamine depletion in the basal ganglia. These are among the dopamine cells that Wolfram Schultz and colleagues have identified with error correction computations in reward prediction conditioning, as described earlier.

The loss of dopamine in PD leads most prominently to a loss of motor control. However, recent studies have shown that the loss of dopamine that occurs in PD also leads to a variety of cognitive deficits, especially tasks that involve incremental learning of associations between cues and outcomes based on error-correcting feedback (Knowlton, Mangels, & Squire, 1996; Myers, Shohamy et al., 2003a, 2003b; Shohamy, Myers, Grossman, et al., 2004; Shohamy, Myers, Onlaor, & Gluck, 2004). These findings suggest that midbrain dopamine may be particularly important for learning that involves the incremental acquisition of stimulus–outcome associations via error-correcting feedback. This is consistent with converging evidence from the functional imaging studies described earlier (Poldrack et al., 2001).

To explore this issue further, Daphna Shohamy, who was then a graduate student in my laboratory, initiated a series of studies of category learning in Parkinson's patients. In the first study, we looked at how Parkinson's patients learn the weather prediction task over 3 days of extensive training. As shown in Figure 18–6, the

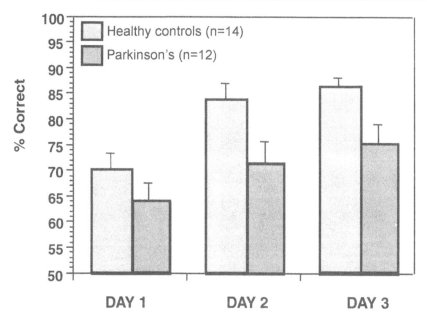

Figure 18–6.   Parkinson's patients are slower to learn the weather prediction task over three days of training. Data from Shohamy, Myers, Onlaor, and Gluck (2004).

patients were significantly impaired relative to matched controls over the course of learning (Shohamy, Myers, Onlaor, & Gluck, 2004). Additional analyses showed differences in the learning strategies used by these two groups. Healthy controls all began to solve the task by using single features and then shifted over the course of 3 days of training to using more complex rules that integrated information from multiple cues. In contrast, the Parkinson's patients continued throughout the study to use the less accurate simpler single-cue rules.

More recently, Shohamy, Myers, and I have followed up on this study with further analyses of probabilistic category learning, using a variant on the weather prediction task in which the stimuli are digital photographs of Mr. Potato Head figures that have one or more facial features (e.g., moustache, hat, glasses, and bowtie) that can each be present or absent (Fig. 18–7). Rather than predicting the weather, the subjects are asked to predict which flavor of ice cream (vanilla or chocolate) Mr. Potato Head prefers. Each facial feature is probabilistically associated with each outcome, just as in the weather prediction experiment.

In several recent studies , we have used this as a cover story for probabilistic category learning, using category structures analogous to those in the weather prediction task and the earlier Gluck and Bower studies. We found that subjects find the Mr. Potato Head task more engaging and appealing. It also allows for a wider range of possible features and task demands, because of the large number of facial features available.

Figure 18–7. Examples of stimuli used in Shohamy, Myers, Grossman, et al. (2004) including Mr. Potato Head figures with different features (hat and moustache) and different category membership feedback (vanilla and chocolate ice cream).

Using this Mr. Potato Head task, we began a series of studies to examine how manipulations of training procedures would affect learning performance in Parkinson's patients (Shohamy, Myers, Grossman, et al., 2004). In one study, we trained participants using standard "feedback" training. On each trial, subjects saw the stimulus, responded with a guess as to the outcome, and then received feedback as to whether that response was correct (Fig. 18–8A). In a second, "observational" version, subjects saw the same stimuli, but are shown the correct outcome (Fig. 18–8B). To assess learning in the "observational" group, subjects were then given test trials in which they see the stimulus and must respond with the outcome information—but no feedback is provided. Thus, we can compare learning under observation or feedback by comparing the last block of the feedback training (last 50 trials) with the 50 test trials following observation training.

Based on the proposed role of the dopamine signals in reward feedback processing by the basal ganglia and the aforementioned imaging data with Poldrack, we predicted that PD patients would be impaired at the feedback-based version (during both training and transfer testing) but would perform as well as controls on the observational version on the transfer test phase.

As shown in Figure 18–9, performance was impaired in the PD patients who had been trained in the feedback condition, but not in those trained in the obser-

A.

B.

Figure 18–8.   (a) Standard feedback training in which subjects first see the stimulus alone, make a categorization response (*vanilla* or *chocolate*), and then get feedback. (b) Observational training in which subjects are exposed to the stimuli with their correct category and are not required to make a categorization response, nor get any feedback.

vational condition. Thus, as predicted by our hypothesis, the PD patients are impaired at learning that involves incremental feedback, but are not impaired at learning cue–outcome associations if those are presented in a nonfeedback manner.

These results provide behavioral evidence that the basal ganglia are necessary for feedback-based learning in a cognitive task. The results provide a direct confirmation of a prediction inspired by our previous neuroimaging results with healthy humans (Poldrack et al., 2001), which had demonstrated differences in engagement of basal ganglia and midbrain dopaminergic regions between feedback-based and observational learning.

More recent studies in our laboratory, using novel forced-choice and concurrent discrimination tasks developed by Catherine Myers, have also demonstrated a double dissociation between MTL and basal ganglia contributions to learning within single associative-learning tasks (Myers, Shohamy, et al., 2003; Shohamy et al., 2006). We found that PD patients were slow to acquire a discrimination

% correct

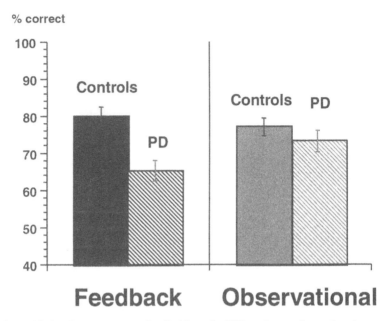

Figure 18–9.   Percent correct for Parkinson's (PD) and controls on the observational task (right) and the test phase of the feedback-based task (left). Parkinson's patients are impaired at probabilistic category learning in feedback training but show no deficit when trained using observational training. Data from Shohamy, Myers, Onlaor, & Gluck (2004).

task, but were unimpaired when subsequently challenged to transfer what they had learned to a novel set of stimuli. The opposite pattern was found among individuals with hippocampal-region damage—spared initial learning, but impaired transfer. This suggests that PD patients do not have a general memory or cognitive deficit; rather, their deficit appears specific to the acquisition of cognitive skills through error-correcting feedback over many trials.

GENERAL DISCUSSION

In the late 1980s, Gordon Bower and I showed that there were common error correction principles for associative learning in both classical conditioning and probabilistic category learning, which allowed us to map the Rescorla–Wagner model of classical conditioning up to a larger-scale connectionist network model of human learning (Gluck & Bower, 1988a). In the intervening years, there has been significant progress in understanding the neural substrates of classical conditioning, implicating the cerebellum for error correction learning in aversive conditioning of motor reflexes, the basal ganglia for error correction learning for appetitive conditioning of reward-predicting stimuli, and the hippocampal region for supporting both forms of learning through modulation of the representations of stimuli that enter into these forms of learning. Integrating across both traditions, Catherine Myers, Daphna Shohamy, and I at Rutgers University-Newark (along with numerous collaborators at various other institutions) have shown in recent years that there are also common neural mechanisms for classical conditioning and human category learning, drawing on multiple methodologies in cognitive neuroscience, including neuropsychological studies of clinical populations and functional brain imaging. This provides a foundation for ongoing and future studies that seek further understanding of the cognitive neuroscience of human learning and memory, along with clinically relevant insights into neurological and psychiatric disorders that affect the basal ganglia (e.g., Parkinson's disease, Huntington's disease, and dystonia) and the hippocampal region (e.g., amnesia and Alzheimer's disease). The two strands of research begun at Stanford 20 years ago as independent avenues of inquiry into, first, human learning behavior and, second, the neural substrates of learning are now deeply intertwined into a single line of cognitive neuroscience research.

REFERENCES

Allen, M. T., Chelius, L., & Gluck, M. A. (2002) Selective entorhinal lesions and non-selective cortical-hippocampal region lesions, but not selective hippocampal lesions, disrupt learned irrelevance in rabbit eyeblink conditioning. *Cognitive Affective and Behavioral Neuroscience, 2,* 214–226.

Coutureau, E., Killcross, A., Good, M., Marshall, V., Ward-Robinson, J., & Honey, R. (2002). Acquired equivalence and distinctiveness of cues: II. Neural manipulations and their implications. *Journal of Experimental Psychology: Animal Behavior Processes, 28*(4), 388–396.

Daum, I., Schugens, M. M., Ackermann, H., Lutzenberger, W., Dichgans, J., & Birbaumer, N. (1993). Classical conditioning after cerebellar lesions in humans. *Behavioral Neuroscience, 107*(5), 748–56.

Donegan, N. H., Gluck, M. A., & Thompson, R. F. (1989). Integrating behavioral and biological models of classical conditioning. In R. D. Hawkins & G. H. Bower (Eds.), *Psychology of learning and motivation* (Vol. 23, pp. 109–156). New York: Academic Press.

Fera, F., Weickert, T. W., Goldberg, T. E., Tessitore, A., Hariri, A., Das, S., Lee, B., Zoltick, B., Meeter, M., Myers, C. E., Gluck, M. A., Weinberger, D. R., & Mattay, V. S. (2005). Neural mechanisms underlying probabilistic category learning in normal aging. *The Journal of Neuroscience, 24*(49), 11340–11348.

Gabrieli, J. D. E., McGlinchey-Berroth, R., Carrillo, M. C., Gluck, M. A., Cermak, L. S., & Disterhoft, J. F. (1995). Intact delay-eyeblink classical conditioning in amnesia. *Behavioral Neuroscience, 109*(5). 819–827.

Gluck, M. A., Allen, M. T., Myers, C. E., & Thompson, R. F. (2001). Cerebellar substrates for error-correction in motor-reflex conditioning. *Neurobiology of Learning and Memory, 76,* 314–341.

Gluck, M. A., & Bower, G. H. (1988a). Evaluating an adaptive network model of human learning. *Journal of Memory and Language, 27,* 166–195.

Gluck, M. A., & Bower, G. H. (1988b). From conditioning to category learning: An adaptive network model. *Journal of Experimental Psychology: General, 117*(3), 227–247.

Gluck, M. A., & Bower, G. H. (1990). Component and pattern information in adaptive networks. *Journal of Experimental Psychology: General, 119*(1), 105–109.

Gluck, M. A., Bower, G. H., & Hee, M. (1989). A configural-cue network model of animal and human associative learning. In *Proceedings of the 11th Annual Conference of the Cognitive Science Society*, Ann Arbor, MI (pp. 323–332). Hillsdale, NJ: Lawrence Earlbaum Associates.

Gluck, M. A., & Myers, C. (1993). Hippocampal mediation of stimulus representation: A computational theory. *Hippocampus, 3*(4), 491–516

Gluck, M. A., & Myers, C. E. (2001). *Gateway to memory: An introduction to neural network models of the hippocampus and learning.* Cambridge, MA: MIT Press.

Gluck, M. A., Myers, C. E., & Thompson, R. F. (1994). A computational model of the cerebellum and motor-reflex learning. In S. Zournetzer, J. Davis, T. McKenna, & C. Lau (Eds.), *An introduction to neural and electronic networks* (2nd ed., pp. 91–80). San Diego: Academic Press.

Gluck, M. A., Oliver, L. M., & Myers, C. E. (1996). Late training amnesic deficits in probabilistic category learning: a neurocomputational analysis. *Learning and Memory, 3,* 326–340.

Gluck, M. A., Shohamy, D., & Myers, C. E. (2002). How do people solve the "weather prediction" task?: Individual variability in strategies for probabilistic category learning. *Learning and Memory, 9,* 408–418.

Gluck, M. A., & Thompson, R. F. (1987). Modeling the neural substrates of associative learning and memory: A computational approach, *Psychological Review, 94*(2), 176–191.

Hopkins, R. O., Myers, C. E, Shohamy, D., Grossman, S., & Gluck, M. A. (2004). Impaired probabilistic category learning in hypoxic subjects with hippocampal damage. *Neuropsychologia, 42,* 524–535.

Jarrard, L. E. (2002). Use of excitotoxins to lesion the hippocampus: Update. *Hippocampus, 12*(3), 405–414.

Kamin, L. (1969). Predictability, surprise, attention and conditioning. In B. Campbell & R. Church (Eds.), *Punishment and aversive behavior* (pp. 279–296). New York: Appleton-Century-Crofts.

Kim, J., Krupa, D., & Thompson, R. F. (1998). Inhibitory cerebello-olivary projections and blocking effect in classical conditioning. *Science, 279,* 570–573.

Knowlton, B. J., Mangels, J. A., & Squire, L. R. (1996). A neostriatal habit learning system in humans. *Science, 273,* 1399–1402.

Knowlton, B. J., Squire, L. R., & Gluck, M. A. (1994). Probabilistic classification learning in amnesia. *Learning and Memory, 1,* 106–120.

Logan, C. G., & Grafton, S. T. (1995). Functional anatomy of human eyeblink conditioning determined with regional cerebral glucose metabolism and positron-emission tomography. *Proceedings of the National Academy of Sciences of the United States of America, 92*(16), 7500–7504.

Myers, C. E., & Gluck, M. A. (1994). Context, conditioning and hippocampal re-representation. *Behavioral Neuroscience, 108*(5), 835–847.

Myers, C., McGlinchey-Berroth, R., Warren, S., Monti, L., Brawn, C. M., & Gluck, M. A. (2000). Latent learning in medial temporal amnesia: Evidence for disrupted representational but preserved attentional processes. *Neuropsychology, 14*(1), 3–15.

Myers, C., Shohamy, D., Gluck, M., Grossman, S., Kluger, A., Ferris, S., Golomb, J., Schnirman, G., & Schwartz, R. (2003). Dissociating hippocampal versus basal ganglia contributions to learning and transfer. *Journal of Cognitive Neuroscience, 15*(2), 185–193.

Poldrack, R. A., Clark, J., Pare-Blagoev, E. J., Shohamy, D., Creso-Moyano, J., Myers, C. E., & Gluck, M. A. (2001). Interactive memory systems in the brain. *Nature, 414,* 546–550.

Rescorla, R., & Wagner, A. (1972). A theory of Pavlovian conditioning: Variations in the effectiveness of reinforcement and non-reinforcement. In A. Black & W. Prokasy (Eds.), *Classical conditioning II: Current research and theory* (pp. 64–99). New York: Appleton-Century-Crofts.

Rumelhart, D., McClelland, J., & the PDP Research Group. (1986). *Parallel distributed processing: Explorations in the microstructure of cognition* (2 vols.). Cambridge, MA: MIT Press.

Schultz, W. (1998). Predictive reward signal of dopamine neurons. *Journal of Neurophysiology, 80,* 1–27.

Schultz, W., Dayan, P., & Montague, P. R. (1997) A neural substrate of prediction and reward. *Science, 275,* 1593–1599.

Sears, L., & Steinmetz, J. (1991). Dorsal accessory olive activity diminishes during acquisition of the rabbit classically conditioned eyelid response. *Brain Research, 545*(1–2), 114–122.

Shohamy, D., Myers, C. E., Geghman, K. D., Sage, J., & Gluck, M. A. (2006). L-Dopa impairs learning, but not generalization, in Parkinson's disease. *Neuropsychologia, 44*(5), 774–84.

Shohamy, D., Myers, C., Grossman, S., Sage, J., Gluck, M., & Poldrack, R. (2004b). Cortico-striatal contributions to feedback-based learning: Converging data from neuroimaging and neuropsychology. *Brain, 127*(4), 851–859.

Shohamy, D., Myers, C. E., Onlaor, S., & Gluck, M. A. (2004a). The role of the basal ganglia in category learning: How do patients with Parkinson's disease learn? *Behavioral Neuroscience, 118*(4), 676–686.

Squire, L. (1987). *Memory and brain.* New York: Oxford University Press.

Thompson, R. F. (1986). The neurobiology of learning and memory. *Science, 233,* 941–947.

Thompson, R. F., & Gluck, M. A. (1989). A biological neural-network analysis of learning and memory. In S. Zournetzer, J. Davis, & C. Lau (Eds.), *An introduction to neural and electronic networks* (pp. 91–107). New York: Academic Press.

Thompson, R. F., & Gluck, M. A., (1991). Brain substrates of basic associative learning and memory. In H. J. Weingartner & R. F. Lister (Eds.), *Cognitive neuroscience* (pp. 24–45). New York: Oxford University Press.

Trabasso, T., & Bower, G. (1964). Concept identification. In R. C. Atkinson (Ed.), *Studies in mathematical psychology* (pp. 32–93). Stanford, CA: Stanford University Press.

Category Learning as Schema Induction

John P. Clapper
California State University–San Bernardino

Categories are essential for practically all aspects of human cognition, and an enormous amount of research has been devoted to understanding how they are learned and represented in memory (see, e.g., Murphy, 2002; Smith & Medin, 1981). In this chapter, I describe a program of research on category learning that Gordon Bower and I began a number of years ago, when I was a graduate student in his laboratory at Stanford University, and which I have continued to extend and develop over the succeeding years. This research began by investigating how people use category knowledge (schemas) to guide attention and organize memory, and later focused on the basic mechanisms by which such categories are discovered and learned. Although category learning has been a traditional focus of research within cognitive psychology, we have taken a rather non-traditional approach in our own investigations of this area. My primary goal in this chapter (besides paying tribute to Gordon) will be to convince readers of the value of this non-traditional approach.

It is important to note that most category learning research has been carried out within a standard conceptual framework or *paradigm* that describes what categories are, what they are for, and the kinds of situations in which they are normally acquired. Within this paradigm, category learning typically is regarded as a form of *discrimination learning* and is investigated using standard discrimination-learning procedures (e.g., Kling & Riggs, 1971). In a discrimination-learning task, the participant is presented with a series of stimuli and is taught (using corrective feedback) to respond differently to different classes of stimuli (e.g., Bruner, Goodnow, & Austin, 1956; Medin & Schaffer, 1978; Posner & Keele, 1968, 1970). Within the category-learning literature, this task is usually called classification learning or *supervised* learning (Michalski & Stepp, 1983); the latter term refers to the fact that discrimination feedback is provided by an external "supervisor."

Although the discrimination-learning paradigm has proved itself useful over many years of research, I will argue that it has also led to a somewhat limited and misleading view of categories and category learning (see Markman & Ross, 2003 for related arguments). Perhaps the most fundamental limitations of this paradigm are due to the way that categories are defined in discrimination-learning tasks. In this type of task, a category is simply an equivalence class defined by a common label or response, and "knowing" a category means nothing more than being able to assign instances to that category—in other words, being able to discriminate examples of that category from examples of the other category or categories currently being shown. Because members of a category need have nothing more in common than a shared label, categories can be defined arbitrarily, that is, any arbitrary collection of stimuli may be defined as a valid category simply by assigning them all the same label. And because categories are defined only in terms of discriminative responding, one need learn only the minimum features required for correct discrimination to be regarded as knowing a category (Markman & Ross, 2003), even if that means *not* learning most of the consistent structure within that category (e.g., even diagnostic features need not be learned if they are redundant with other diagnostic features).

This is a rather odd definition relative to our everyday way of thinking about categories, in which knowing a category means knowing what members of that category are *like,* not just the ability to distinguish category members from members of a specific contrast category (Chin-Parker & Ross, 2004). As we see later, this definition leads to a tendency to ignore a number of important issues relating to how categories are learned, represented, and used. In addition to defining category learning in this narrow way, the discrimination-learning task also includes such artificial features as explicit instructions to classify each stimulus, a convenient set of predefined category labels to choose among, and corrective feedback on every trial. One might reasonably ask whether these features are really necessary for people to learn categories, and if not, whether a simpler task might not provide a more appropriate model learning situation.

In principle, the *minimal* category-learning task would be one in which the participant simply receives a series of training instances that are *potentially* divisible into separate categories, with no instructions to search for categories and no predefined category labels or trial-by-trial feedback. As they examine each stimulus, the person's current knowledge state would presumably be altered in some way by that experience. If it were possible to track those changes unobtrusively over time, it might be possible to find out whether they discovered the categories on their own and to trace the course of this learning over trials. Any learning in this kind of task would obviously be *unsupervised,* because no category-level feedback is provided, as well as *incidental,* because the person is not asked to search for categories and would therefore have to notice and learn any categories on their own initiative.

In this chapter, I refer to this as a "schema induction" task; I also refer to the particular approach that goes along with it as the schema induction framework or paradigm. As I explain in greater detail later, this task differs from a discrimination-learning task in several ways; most important is the fact that learning is defined in terms of knowing as many features as possible within a given category, not merely being able to tell members of different categories apart. One benefit of this re-framing is that it facilitates the investigation of interesting questions that either do not arise or are difficult to study within the standard discrimination-learning approach.

EARLY RESEARCH ON SCHEMA APPLICATION

The original impetus for this approach came not from traditional studies of supervised categorization, but rather from studies of memory for text and other forms of discourse, and the role that organized knowledge or *schemas* play in this kind of memory (e.g., Bartlett, 1932; Minksy, 1975; Rumelhart & Ortony, 1977; Schank & Abelson, 1977). Here, the term *schema* is used to refer to an internal model or representation that contains knowledge about a specific category. In theory, research on schema-based memory is directly relevant to understanding categories because it investigates how general, category-level knowledge is used to remember specific instances or situations. However, such issues are outside the purview of standard discrimination-learning procedures, in which people are only asked to classify the stimuli rather than using category knowledge to predict or reconstruct their features.

Part of our interest in these issues stemmed from Gordon's prior research on the role of schemas in memory for text (e.g., Bower, Black, & Turner, 1979; Belleza & Bower, 1981). Historically, most proposals about schemas and memory have been variations of the "schema-plus-corrections" (S + C) theory put forward several decades ago (e.g., Attneave, 1954; Oldfield, 1954). This theory begins by noting that many of an object's features are predictable from its schema, which specifies the structure common to the category as a whole. Therefore, the most economical way to represent an object in memory is to include only features that are not inferable from the general schema, while referring to the schema itself for those that are. Economy of storage is thus gained by eliminating unnecessary redundancy from the memory trace. This framework featured prominently in early research on memory for meaningful text. One of the main findings of this research is that people are likely to falsely recall or recognize events from a script-based story that were in the underlying script (event schema; see Schank & Abelson, 1977) but were not actually stated in the text (e.g., Bower, Black, & Turner, 1979). Graesser and coworkers (e.g., Graessar, 1981; Graesser, Woll, Kowalski, & Smith, 1980) showed that people's ability to discriminate whether or not an event had been explicitly stated in a text declined as a function of the typicality of that event within the script or schema, such that highly typical events showed nearly zero memory discrimination following a 30-minute retention interval. To explain these findings, Graesser proposed a "schema-pointer-plus-tags" (SP + T) model of memory. The SP + T model proposed that schema-based texts were encoded by (a) creating a "pointer" to the general script or schema referred to in the text and (b) encoding specific traces or "tags" for any events that were not highly typical or expected within that schema. Bower, Black, and Turner proposed a similar model that assumed that readers create a partial memory trace of the story and rely on their script-based knowledge to fill in missing details. Both models were closely related to the original S + C framework in relying on a general schema to reconstruct the typical or expected features of a given instance.

Whereas these theories emphasized the storage and retrieval aspects of schemas, another theory, the attention-elaboration hypothesis (e.g., Belleza & Bower, 1981; Bobrow & Norman, 1975) argued that at least some of the advantage in memory discrimination for atypical or deviant events may have been due to differences in the amount of attention they received at the time of encoding. For example, Belleza and Bower showed that people spend more time reading atypical compared to typical statements during a prose comprehension task.

Gordon and I later proposed a theory that combined the S + C theory and the attention-elaboration hypothesis within a single framework (Clapper & Bower, 1991; Fig. 19–1). The theory assumes that people attempt to categorize each stim-

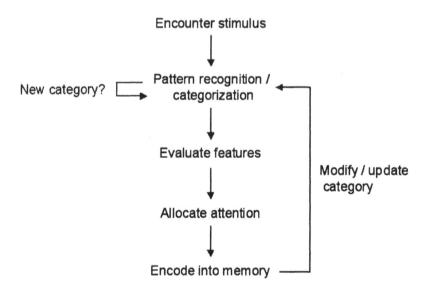

Figure 19–1.   Instance- and category-learning model based on Clapper and Bower (1991).

ulus they encounter as part of their normal pattern recognition process. Features that are expected or typical within that category are considered uninformative because they are redundant with the general schema; therefore they should receive little attention during encoding. Unpredictable or surprising features are considered highly informative and should receive a much greater share of the learner's attention. The result of these attentional/encoding biases is that the distinctive features of an instance should tend to be associated directly with that instance in memory, whereas features typical of the general category should tend to be associated mainly with the schema and only weakly, if at all, with the individual instance (Fig. 19–2).

This kind of memory organization has important implications for memory retrieval. A large number of experiments on the so-called "fan effect" (e.g., J. R. Anderson, 1976, 1983; J. R. Anderson & Bower, 1974) have shown that the more items that are associated with a given concept in memory, the slower people are to retrieve any of those items. This suggests that the more features that a person has directly associated with an instance in memory, the longer it should take them to verify any of these features for a speeded recognition task. However, if category-typical features are not associated directly with the instance, but rather with the category schema (as in Fig. 19–2), then the situation becomes more complex. In this case, the number of category-typical features should have no effect on the time to verify distinctive features of an instance, because the category features are not directly associated with that instance in memory. The opposite, however,

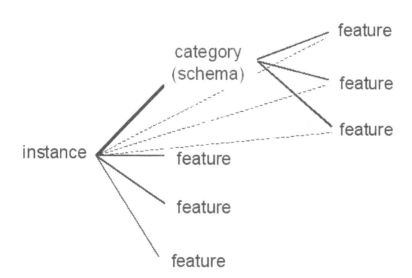

Figure 19–2.   Schema-plus-corrections memory organization resulting from the attentional assumptions of the Clapper and Bower (1991) model.

would not be true; if we think of category membership as a feature of an instance, then the more distinctive features associated that that instance the longer it should take to retrieve its category membership and the typical features associated with that category.

An experiment that we conducted to test these ideas consisted of three phases (see Clapper & Bower, 1991, for a more complete description). In the first phase, people learned several different categories, each presented in the form of a verbal feature list (the categories were types of astronomical stars and the features were their chemical constituents). In the second phase, they learned several instances of each category. Each instance contained all the elements possessed by its parent category, as well as one or more additional elements distinctive to that particular instance. The number of features (fan) associated with each category of stars (2, 3, or 4) and the number of distinctive features associated with each individual star (1 or 3) were varied orthogonally. In the third phase, participants were given a speeded recognition task in which they had to verify whether or not particular instances possessed particular features or belonged to a specific category.

The results were strongly consistent with our hypothesis that people were storing category information separately from information about specific instances. The more distinctive features possessed by a given instance, the longer it took people to verify either distinctive or category features of that instance. By contrast, the number of category features had no effect on verification times, suggesting that these features were stored separately in memory, in accordance with our modified S + C model.

LATER RESEARCH ON SCHEMA ACQUISITION

In the experiment just described, people were directly taught several categories prior to encountering specific instances of those categories. As a next step, we wanted to extend our findings to situations in which people learned categories inductively, via exposure to individual instances. In addition, we wanted more direct evidence for our assumption that the S + C memory organization detected in the last experiment was actually a side effect of events that occurred at encoding.

Schema induction tasks.   We developed two new tasks that proved especially useful in pursuing these goals. Both are good examples of the type of schema induction task described at the beginning of this chapter. The first (Clapper & Bower 1991, 1994) was an "attribute-listing" task that involved presenting a series of instances from one or more categories and asking participants to list some of the features of those instances. (The stimuli were pictures of fictitious insects that varied along several dimensions; see Fig. 19–3). They were asked to include only those features that they believed would be useful for identifying that specific instance while omitting redundant features that provided no identifying information. The stimulus sets were designed so that members of a given category shared

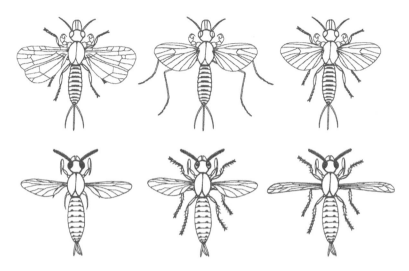

Figure 19-3. Insect stimuli similar to those used in the attribute-listing experiments of Clapper and Bower (1991, 1994). Instances of one category are shown on the top row and instances of another category are shown on the bottom row.

a large proportion of their features, while also varying along several dimensions (Fig. 19–4). Learning was indicated by a decrease in the listing of consistent values, as these were redundant with the instances' category memberships and thus were uninformative for picking out specific instances. At the same time, listing of variable dimensions increased because these were informative for distinguishing among different instances within a category. Listings of variable dimensions minus those of consistent dimensions could be plotted to reveal "learning curves" for the presented categories (Fig. 19–5).

Our second schema induction task employed an immediate-memory procedure. In this task, participants were again presented with a series of training instances from one or more different categories. This time, the stimuli were verbal feature lists describing, for example, fictitious trees, insects, or people (Fig. 19–6). The features in each list were masked by a string of Xs (Fig. 19–6a), and the participant could uncover and view only one feature at a time (by pressing a designated "up" or "down" key). The computer recorded the amount of time the person spent studying each feature in the list. The list remained on the screen for a preset period of time (say, 24 sec), after which it disappeared and was followed by a series of forced-choice recognition tests (Figs. 19–6b and 19–6c; later versions of this task have also employed cued-recall tests). Following these tests, another instance list would appear and the process would repeat, until all the training stimuli had been shown.

There are two measures of learning in this task. As people learn the categories, they should learn to spend less time attending to the consistent features of each

Dimensions

	Example	Shape	Markings	Jaws	Forelimbs	Tails	Antennae	Legs	Wings	Eyes
Category A	A1	1	1	1	1	1	1	1	1	2
	A2	1	1	1	1	1	1	1	2	1
	A3	1	1	1	1	1	1	2	1	2
	A4	1	1	1	1	1	1	2	2	1
	etc.	1	1	1	1	1	1	X	X	X
Category B	B1	2	2	2	2	2	2	3	3	3
	B2	2	2	2	2	2	2	3	3	4
	B3	2	2	2	2	2	2	4	4	3
	B4	2	2	2	2	2	2	4	4	4
	etc.	2	2	2	2	2	2	Y	Y	Y

Figure 19–4.   The design of the stimulus sets in the attribute listing experiments of Clapper and Bower (1991, 1994). Notice that each category has six dimensions with consistent values and three dimensions with variable values.

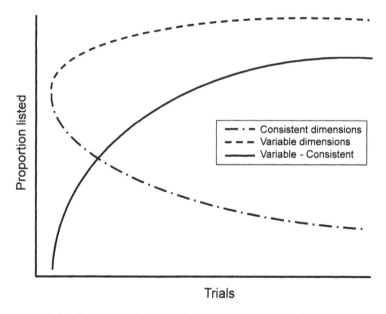

Figure 19–5.   Indicators of category learning in the attribute-listing task. The proportion of consistent dimensions listed should decline with trials, whereas the proportion of variable dimensions should increase over trials. When the former is subtracted from the latter, the resulting difference score provides an overall index of feature learning.

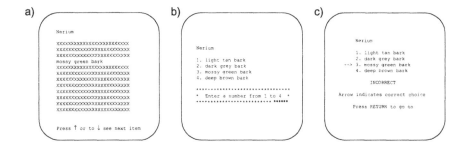

Figure 19–6.   Exemplar-memory test procedure (structure of a single trial). Each trial involves presenting a study list and several recognition tests. The experiments discussed in this chapter used 30 to 60 trials. (a) Training instance presented on a single trial of the study–test procedure. (b) Example of a multiple choice recognition test for the training instance shown to the left (several such tests were given per trial). (c) The participant has entered a response to the recognition test, and the correct answer is shown. (Adapted from Clapper & Bower, 2002).

instance (because these are redundant with category membership) and more time attending to their variable features. Subtracting the mean study time for consistent features from that of variable features yields a difference score that can be plotted to reveal learning curves for each category, similar to the difference score used in the attribute listing measure (Fig. 19–7). The memory tests following each instance provide a second measure. As people learn the consistent features of the categories, their memory for these features should improve (Fig. 19–7). Thus, memory performance can also be used to trace learning curves for the categories over trials.

These tasks differ from a discrimination learning task in several ways. Most important, they define (measure) category learning *indirectly,* as a function of how well the person learns the individual features within the category, rather than directly by having them sort or classify the stimuli. This indirect measurement permits *incidental* learning: Participants need not be informed about the categories they are expected to learn, because their memory, study times, or attribute listings will automatically indicate whether they notice such categories on their own. Learning is also assessed *continuously* in these tasks; that is, the output measures provide what amounts to a trial-by-trial record of changes in the learner's knowledge state.

One of the main advantages of these tasks is that they allow us to investigate how people discover categories for themselves, without labels, feedback, or other forms of external guidance. The problem of discovering new categories, and the learnability issues that it raises, do not arise in studies of conventional discrimination learning.

Testing theories of learning.   In our initial experiments using these tasks (Clapper & Bower, 1991), people performed well when shown instances from a single category; that is, they quickly learned which dimensions had consistent

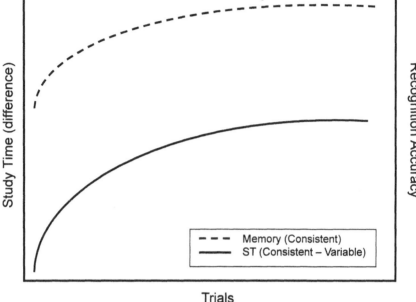

Figure 19–7.   Indicators of category learning in the exemplar memory task. As people shift their attention from consistent to variable dimensions, the difference in the amount of study time they receive should gradually increase. Memory for consistent dimensions should also increase over trials.

values within that category, and which were variable. However, when instances of two different categories were shown together in random order, people showed much poorer learning (Clapper, 2006; Clapper & Bower, 1994, 2002). This lack of learning was surprising given the very strong predictive structure that defined the categories in these experiments; most theories would predict that these kinds of categories should be learned very easily.

The simplest model of how people might learn categories in these tasks relies on simple feature association. In such a model, co-occurring features become strongly associated over time and separate feature clusters gradually emerge as the basis for distinct categories. This notion of auto-associative concept learning goes back at least to the mid-18th century (e.g., Bain, 1855/1968; Hume, 1739/2000) and still forms the basis of many learning algorithms today, for example, McClelland and Rumelhart (1985), J. A. Anderson (1977; Anderson, Silverstein, Ritz, & Jones, 1977), Davis (1985), Zeaman and House (1963), and Billman and Heit (1988). Given such a learning process, the kinds of categories used in our tasks should have been very easy for people to learn, contrary to our actual data.

Further research has clarified the conditions under which people will learn categories in these tasks. One factor that has turned out to be very important is the particular order in which examples of different categories are shown. As already noted, when instances of two categories are presented in a randomly intermixed sequence, relatively little learning of either category is observed. However, when the sequence is arranged so that one category (call it "A") is well-learned prior to the introduction of the second category ("B"), then people will learn both categories easily. Thus, categories A and B will both be learned much better in a "contrast-enhancing" sequence like A A A A A A A A A A A A B A B B B A B A A A B, and so forth, than in a "mixed" sequence like A B A B B A B A A B B A B A B B A B A A A B, and so on. The only difference between these two sequences is the fact that the first six Bs in the second (mixed) sequence are absent and replaced by the same number of As in the first (contrast) sequence. Thus, simply reducing the number of B instances (by eliminating all of them from the first 12 trials of the training sequence) leads to a dramatic improvement in B learning (Clapper & Bower, 1994, 2002). This "negative exposure effect" is a violation of the monotonic (mutually increasing) relationship between exposure and learning normally expected in experiments on human and animal learning.

Interestingly, this effect is incompatible with simple feature association models, all of which are strongly committed to the assumption that additional exposure will lead monotonically to an increase (or at least not a decease) in learning. However, it is easily accommodated within a different type of model, one based on the notion that categories are generated by a discrete, nonincremental "category invention" process (Clapper, 2006; Clapper & Bower, 1994, 2002). This model assumes that people create new categories in response to a specific environmental "trigger" such as a novel or unusual stimulus that fails to match any of a person's existing categories. This kind of learning process implements a "failure-driven" (Schank, 1982) or "win-stay-lose-shift" strategy in which new categories are created only in response to the direct failure of existing categories.

The negative exposure effects described previously are easily accommodated within the category invention framework. To explain poor learning in the mixed condition, it need only be assumed that the first A and B instances appear similar enough for many learners to lump them together into a single category at the start of training. Once this has occurred, they will tend to remain "stuck" in this aggregated state because further A and B instances will continue to fit the combined category; hence, there is never any "surprise event" to trigger the invention of separate categories. By contrast, when people receive a sequence like A A A A A A A A A A A B A B B A B A A A B, and so on, they have time to learn category A before seeing any examples of category B. As a result, the first B will be seen as contrasting sharply with previous As, and the learner will invent a new category to accommodate this obvious mismatch. The upshot is that is it easier to add a new category to an already-learned category than to learn two categories at the same time, due to the potential for aggregation in the latter situation.

An interesting characteristic of category invention models is that they posit a dichotomous-state conception of learning: A learner generates separate cate-

a) Opposite Themes	b) Neutral (No Themes)	c) Same Theme
Category A favorite drink: **sherry** favorite activity: **yachting** enjoys watching: **the opera** drives: **a Mercedes** clothes by: <u>variable</u> lives in: Sacramento employed as: **a lawyer** TV show: <u>variable</u> favorite food: steak last vacation: New Orleans favorite music <u>variable</u> graduated: **Harvard**	**Category A** favorite drink: coffee favorite activity: soccer enjoys watching: basketball drives: a Honda clothes by: <u>variable</u> lives in: Sacramento employed as: an accountant TV show: <u>variable</u> favorite food: steak last vacation: New Orleans favorite music by: <u>variable</u> graduated: community college	**Category A** favorite drink: **sherry** favorite activity: **yachting** enjoys watching: **the opera** drives: **a Mercedes** clothes by: <u>variable</u> lives in: Sacramento employed as: **a lawyer** TV show: <u>variable</u> favorite food: steak last vacation: New Orleans favorite music <u>variable</u> graduated: **Harvard**
Category B favorite drink: **beer** favorite activity: **bowling** enjoys watching: **pro wrestling** drives: **an old Pickup** clothes by: <u>variable</u> lives in: Tucson employed as: **is unemployed** TV show: <u>variable</u> favorite food: fish last vacation: San Francisco favorite music by: <u>variable</u> graduated: **high school**	**Category B** favorite drink: cola favorite activity: softball enjoys watching: movies drives: a Toyota clothes by: <u>variable</u> lives in: Tucson employed as: a technician TV show: <u>variable</u> favorite food: fish last vacation: San Francisco favorite music by: <u>variable</u> graduated : state university	**Category B** favorite drink: **fine wine** favorite activity: **polo** enjoys watching: **the symphony** drives: **a Lamborghini** clothes by: <u>variable</u> lives in: Tucson employed as: **a plastic surgeon** TV show: <u>variable</u> favorite food: fish last vacation: San Francisco favorite music by: <u>variable</u> graduated: **Princeton**

Figure 19–8. Sample categories used in experiments on prior knowledge and schema induction. Thematic consistent values within each category are indicated by boldface type, neutral values by plain type, and variable values are underlined (all were shown in plain type in the actual experiments).

gories for different subsets of stimuli, whereas a nonlearner fails to do so and aggregates all the stimuli into a single category. In principle, this overaggregated state should be very stable over time. Clapper (2006) provides an example in which initial aggregation prevents people from later acquiring separate categories from a sequence in which they otherwise would easily do so. In this experiment, categories A and B were learned more poorly in sequence **A B A B B A A B** A A A A A A A A A A A A B A B B A B A A A B, and so on, than in A A A A A A A A A A A A B A B B A B A A A B, and so on. However, the only difference between these sequences is that several instances of both categories have been added to the beginning of the second sequence in order to create the first sequence. Thus, simply adding a few instances of both categories to an already "good" training sequence had the paradoxical effect of turning it into a "bad" sequence, a dramatic violation of monotonicity. Once the categories became aggregated during the early mixed trials, people were apparently unable to "de-aggregate" them during the trials that followed. (Additional experiments have shown that if the interval of all-A trials is made longer, say, 24 instead of 12 instances, people are able to de-aggregate and learn the two separate categories.)

Optimality issues.   While these otherwise paradoxical results make sense within the category invention framework, they also seem to contradict commonsense intuitions about rational design: The insensitivity to category structure and extreme order sensitivity demonstrated in these experiments seem to suggest a highly nonoptimal learning process. Surprisingly, this turns out not to be the case: A normatively optimal category invention algorithm *can* produce the same patterns of sequence sensitivity observed in our experiments, given certain reasonable assumptions about memory and learning biases.

Our explorations of this issue (Clapper, 2006; Clapper & Bower, 2002) have been carried out using a Bayesian ideal-observer model proposed by J. R. Anderson (1990, 1991). This model, known as the rational model of categorization, provides an example of a formally specified computational theory that fits our qualitative category invention framework. In its usual mode of application, the model assumes perfect memory for each training instance. In this mode, it is highly sensitive to the correlational structure of the input stimuli regardless of training sequence—which means that it cannot simulate the results described earlier. However, if the model is "weakened" by reducing memory for individual training instances and by assuming a low a priori estimate of the likelihood of new categories, very different results can be obtained. Under these conditions, the model becomes highly sensitive to training sequence and can reproduce the non-monotonic sequence effects (negative exposure effects) described previously.

What makes this supposedly optimal algorithm so sensitive to training sequence under certain parameter settings? The answer to this question lies partly in the structure of the model itself, and partly in human processing limitations that can be simulated within a specific region of the model's parameter space. The rational model is a dichotomous-state model that implements a win-stay-lose-shift learning procedure. If it happens to assign the first B in a mixed sequence to the same category as the previous A(s), then it will find itself in an aggregated state from which it will usually be unable to recover. This will not occur if a long sequence of A's is presented before any B's, or if only one or two A's have been shown but the model remembers them accurately enough to avoid lumping them with later B's.

Of course, poor memory would have completely different effects on a different type of learning process. For example, in a feature association model poor memory might translate into a lower-than-usual learning rate, but this would not alter the fundamentally monotonic nature of the model itself—more instances would still result in better learning, all else being equal.

CURRENT DIRECTIONS

Knowledge effects.   The previous experiments investigated how people use observed training instances to generate and learn new categories. But empirical observation is not the only foundation on which categories are built; a large body of research shows that prior knowledge and intuitive theories also play an important role (e.g., Heit & Bott, 2000; Murphy, 2002; Murphy & Medin, 1985).

I have carried out several experiments (Clapper, 2005, in press) on these issues using the exemplar memory task and categories related to familiar themes (i.e., personality stereotypes such as highbrows vs. lowbrows, young vs. old, male vs. female). It is clear that prior knowledge (thematic relatedness) helps people discover separate categories in this task. Thus, people were much more likely to notice that the training instances could be divided into two categories if those categories were related to different themes, e.g., highbrows vs. lowbrows (Fig. 19–8a) as opposed to "average" or "normal" individuals (Fig. 19–8b). The themes also helped people learn the features within each category. In particular, features that were related to the themes (e.g., enjoys watching the opera vs. pro wrestling for the highbrow/lowbrow themes) were learned more quickly than "neutral" features that were unrelated to the themes (e.g., lives in Sacramento vs. Tucson; note the two different types of consistent features within the thematic categories in Figures 19–8a and 19–8c).

It is possible to test hypotheses concerning exactly *how* knowledge facilitates the learning of thematic features in this task. One possibility is a *within*-category effect in which knowledge binds and integrates the features within a category, thereby making them easier to learn and remember. Another possibility is a *between*-category effect in which knowledge reduces the amount of confusion and interference that would otherwise occur between the features of related categories. A within-category effect should be detectable whether a category is presented alone or with another category; also, in a two-category task, it should not matter whether the categories are related to the same theme or different themes, just so long as they are related to *some* theme that can help bind their features together. A between-category effect, by contrast, cannot occur unless more than one category is present and only when those categories are related to different themes (so that the themes can provide a basis for telling their features apart). Several experiments (described in Clapper, 2005, in press) have provided clear evidence for between-category effects—in other words, less interference between the features of related categories when those categories are related to contrasting themes, e.g., highbrows vs. lowbrows. However, these experiments showed no evidence for within-category effects—in other words, no benefit of thematic relatedness in a single-category task, and no benefit in a two-category task when both categories were related to the same theme (as in Fig. 19–8c). These results are especially interesting because previous research has tended to stress the importance of knowledge in promoting within-category coherence (e.g., Kaplan & Murphy, 1999; Murphy & Kaplan, 2000; Spalding & Murphy, 1996), whereas the possibility of between-category knowledge effects has been almost completely ignored.

The structural basis of categories.   The idea of interference across category boundaries raises some interesting questions about how category schemas are actually represented in memory. It is often convenient to think of schemas as though they are isolated, independent data structures, each existing separately from the larger web of knowledge. But that cannot be correct. In fact, what I am calling "schemas" may not exist as unitary, precomputed structures at all, but might actually consist of many smaller components distributed throughout memory, with each component shared by many categories (Rogers & McClelland, 2004). At a minimum, schemas must interact with other schemas in order to capture the generative capacity of human reasoning (McClelland, Rumelhart, & Hinton, 1986). In general, it seems reasonable to assume that schemas representing related categories might contain overlapping representational structure, and that the properties of one schema might affect the learning or the stability of other schemas. If so, then one way to learn more about how schemas are represented might be to investigate how they affect (e.g., interfere with) other schemas.

One way to study interference effects is to manipulate the degree of structural overlap between different categories and observe the effects on learning within each category. The stimulus sets used in the experiments described so far—and in the vast majority of category-learning experiments ever conducted—contained stimuli that all varied along the same attribute dimensions, with categories defined in terms of specific values or clusters of values along these shared dimensions. In the terminology of Garner (1974), stimuli within these sets shared a common *dimensional* structure whereas different categories were defined in terms of *correlational* structure. In the experiments discussed next, people's learning of categories based on correlational structure was directly compared with that of categories based on dimensional structure (Fig. 19–9); that is, categories that varied along the *same* dimensions (Fig. 19–9a) were compared to categories that varied along *different* dimensions (Fig. 19–9b). In the language of structure-mapping theory (e.g., Gentner, 1983; Gentner & Markman, 1997), this is a contrast between categories with *alignable* dimensions vs. categories with *non-alignable* dimensions.

The main result of this research is that correlation-based categories suffer considerable interference along their shared dimensions (Clapper, 2004). I have already described how people have difficulty discovering separate categories in these kinds of stimulus sets. Further experiments have shown evidence of feature-level interference even after it is clear that separate categories have already been recognized. For example, even if people have already learned two categories in the exemplar memory task, presenting a third category has a strongly negative effect; not only is the third category learned poorly compared to the previous two, but levels of learning for the previous categories also decline following the introduction of the third category (Clapper, 2004). However, such interference is observed only when the third category has the same dimensional structure as the first two. In general, when the categories in a set are distinguished at the level of dimensional structure, people perform as though they were learning each category in isolation (i.e., in a one-category task). They immediately partition the set into separate categories, show no interference in learning the features within each category, and learning of each category is unaffected by how many other categories are present.

Research on interference and other schema-level interactions may provide useful information about how category knowledge is represented in memory; it may

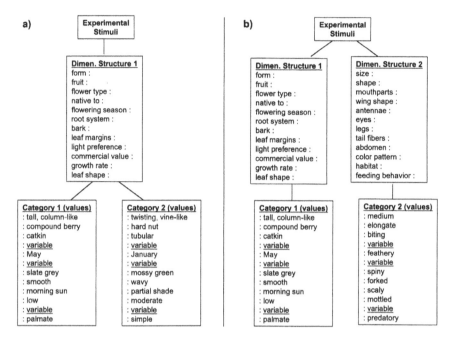

Figure 19–9.   Sample categories defined by (a) correlational vs. (b) dimensional structure. Note that both categories in (a) vary along the same dimensions, while the two categories in (b) vary along different dimensions.

also serve as an antidote for the simplifying tendency to think of schemas as isolated, encapsulated "boxes in the head." In fact, the current paradigm may provide a context in which many hypotheses related to schema structure and schema-level interactions can usefully be tested.

SUMMARY AND CONCLUSIONS

This chapter began by discussing the contrast between discrimination learning and schema induction as frameworks or "paradigms" for the investigation of category learning. I argued that discrimination learning fails to capture some important aspects of category learning and that a number of issues that have been poorly articulated or difficult to study within the discrimination-learning framework happen to be much more approachable within a schema induction framework.

One of these issues concerns how category knowledge affects instance processing and memory organization when instance learning, rather than categorization, is the proximal task goal (as assumed by schema induction). This issue is of major importance to researchers who study the role of schemas in problem solving, reasoning, language comprehension, and other higher level cognitive abilities. However, for the most part they have studied this issue using naturally occurring schemas acquired outside the laboratory, and that research has had little direct connection with studies of artificial category learning. The first experiment described earlier (and several others described in Clapper & Bower, 1991) attempts to bridge the gap between research on artificial category learning and studies of schema application. The greater control enabled by synthesizing knowledge structures to our own specifications allowed us to test hypotheses about memory organization that would have been difficult or impossible to test with natural materials.

A second issue concerns what might be called the "discovery problem" in category learning—namely, the issue of how people detect the existence of separate new categories without externally provided labels or corrective feedback to guide them. Obviously, this issue does not arise in supervised classification tasks. Several experiments (Clapper, 2006; Clapper & Bower, 1994, 2002) were described that provided strong evidence that this process conforms to a category invention framework first described in Clapper and Bower (1991) and elaborated in Clapper and Bower (1994, 2002) and Clapper (2006).

More recent experiments have focused on the role of prior knowledge in category learning, specifically how prior knowledge is used to help people discover new categories and the role of such knowledge in helping to reduce feature-level interference between closely related categories. Further experiments have focused on those between-category interference effects and have shown that they depend critically on the existence of shared dimensional structure between the categories, along with specific assumptions about memory and task biases. All of these experiments deal with issues that have received little attention by researchers working within the standard discrimination-learning paradigm.

I'd like to conclude this chapter with a word of thanks to Gordon, who was there from the beginning and who has supported and contributed to this research in so many ways. Gordon always had a knack for encouraging creative thinking and new approaches among his students and co-workers, while at the same time adhering to the highest standards of rigor and excellence. I hope this research has proved worthy of those high standards, and that it will continue to generate new findings and new surprises in the years ahead.

REFERENCES

Anderson, J. A. (1977). Neural models with cognitive implications. In D. LaBerge & S. J. Samuels (Eds.), *Basic processes in reading: Perception and comprehension* (pp. 27–90). Hillsdale, NJ: Lawrence Erlbaum Associates.

Anderson, J. A., Silverstein, J. W., Ritz, S. A., & Jones, R. S. (1977). Distinctive features, categorical perception, and probability learning: Some applications of a neural model. *Psychological Review, 84,* 413–451.

Anderson, J. R. (1976). *Language, memory, and thought.* Hillsdale, NJ: Lawrence Erlbaum Associates.

Anderson, J. R. (1983). A spreading activation theory of memory. *Journal of Verbal Learning and Verbal Behavior, 22,* 261–295.

Anderson, J. R. (1990). *The adaptive character of thought.* Hillsdale, NJ: Lawrence Erlbaum Associates.

Anderson, J. R. (1991). The adaptive nature of human categorization. *Psychological Review, 98,* 409–429.

Anderson, J. R., & Bower, G. H. (1974). Interference in memory for multiple contexts. *Memory & Cognition, 2,* 509–514.

Attneave, F. (1954). Some informational aspects of visual perception. *Psychological Review, 61,* 183–193.

Bain, J. (1868). *The senses and the intellect.* New York: Appleton. (Original work published 1855).

Bartlett, F. C. (1932). *Remembering: A study in social psychology.* Cambridge, England: Cambridge University Press.

Bellezza, F. S., & Bower, G. H. (1981). The representation and processing characteristics of scripts. *Bulletin of the Psychonomic Society, 18,* 1–4.

Billman, D., & Heit, E. (1988). Observational learning from internal feedback: A simulation of an adaptive learning method. *Cognitive Science, 12,* 587–625.

Bobrow, D. G., & Norman, D. A. (1975). Some principles of memory schemata. In D. G. Bobrow & A. Collins (Eds.), *Representation and understanding.* New York: Academic Press.

Bower, G. H., Black, J. B., & Turner, T. J. (1979). Scripts in memory for text. *Cognitive Psychology, 11,* 177–220.

Bruner, J. S., Goodnow, J. J., & Austin, G. A. (1956). *A study of thinking.* New York: Wiley.

Chin-Parker, S., & Ross, B. H. (2004). Diagnosticity and prototypicality in category learning: A comparison of inference learning and classification learning. *Journal of Experimental Psychology: Learning, Memory, and Cognition, 30,* 216–226.

Clapper, J. P. (2004, November). *Dimensional structure, alignability, and unsupervised learning.* Poster presented at the annual convention of the Psychonomic Society, Minneapolis, MN.

Clapper, J. P. (2005, November). *Within- vs. between-category knowledge effects in observational learning.* Poster presented at the Annual Convention of the Psychonomic Society, Toronto, Ontario, Canada.

Clapper, J. P. (in press). Prior knowledge and correlational structure in unsupervised learning. *Canadian Journal of Experimental Psychology.*

Clapper, J. P. (2006). When more is less: Negative exposure effects in unsupervised learning. *Memory & Cognition, 34,* 890–902.

Clapper, J. P., & Bower, G. H. (1991). Learning and applying category knowledge in unsupervised domains. In G. H. Bower (Ed.), *The psychology of learning and motivation* (Vol. 27, pp. 65–108). New York: Academic Press.

Clapper, J. P., & Bower, G. H. (1994). Category invention in unsupervised learning. *Journal of Experimental Psychology: Learning, Memory, and Cognition, 20,* 443–460.

Clapper, J. P., & Bower, G. H. (2002). Adaptive categorization in unsupervised learning. *Journal of Experimental Psychology: Learning, Memory, and Cognition, 28,* 908–923.

Davis, B. R. (1985). An associative hierarchical self-organizing system. *IEEE Transactions on Systems, Man, and Cybernetics, SMC–15,* 570–579.

Garner, W. R. (1974). *The processing of information and structure.* New York: Lawrence Erlbaum Associates.

Gentner, D. (1983). Structure-mapping: A theoretical framework for analogy. *Cognitive Science, 7,* 155–170.

Gentner, D. & Markman, A. B. (1997). Structure mapping in analogy and similarity. *American Psychologist, 52*, 45–56.

Graesser, A. C., (1981). *Prose comprehension beyond the word*. New York: Springer-Verlag.

Graesser, A. C., Woll, S. B., Kowalski, D. J., & Smith, D. A. (1980). Memory for typical and atypical actions in scripted activities. *Journal of Experimental Psychology: Human Learning and Memory, 6*, 503–513.

Heit, E., & Bott, L. (2000). Knowledge selection in category learning. In D. L. Medin (Ed.), *The psychology of learning and motivation* (Vol. 39, pp. 163–199). San Diego, CA: Academic Press.

Hume, D. A. (2000). *A treatise of human nature*. New York: Oxford University Press (Original work published 1739).

Kaplan, A. S., & Murphy, G. L. (1999). The acquisition of category structure in unsupervised learning. *Memory & Cognition, 27*, 699–712.

Kling, J. W., & Riggs, L. A. (1971). *Experimental psychology* (3rd ed.). New York: Holt, Rinehart & Winston.

Markman, A. B., & Ross, B. H. (2003). Category use and category use and category learning. *Psychological Bulletin, 129*, 592–613.

McClelland, J. L., & Rumelhart, D. E. (1985). Distributed memory and the representation of general and specific information. *Journal of Experimental Psychology: General, 114*, 159–188.

McClelland, J. L., Rumelhart, D. E., & Hinton, G. E. (1986). The appeal of parallel distributed processing. In D. E. Rumelhart & J. L. McClelland (Eds.), *Parallel distributed processing: Explorations in the microstructure of cognition* (Vol. 1, pp. 3–44). Cambridge, MA: MIT Press.

Medin, D. L., & Schaffer, M. M. (1978). A context theory of classification learning. *Psychological Review, 85*, 207–238.

Michalski, R. S., & Stepp, R. E. (1983). Learning from observation: Conceptual clustering. In R. S. Michalski, J. G. Carbonell, & T. M. Mitchell (Eds.), *Machine learning: An artificial intelligence approach* (pp. 331–364). Palo Alto, CA: Tioga.

Minsky, M. (1975). A framework for representing knowledge. In P. H. Winston (Ed.), *The psychology of computer vision* (pp. 211–277). New York: McGraw-Hill.

Murphy, G. L. (2002). *The big book of concepts*. Cambridge, MA: MIT Press.

Murphy, G. L., & Kaplan, A. S. (2000). Feature distribution and background knowledge in category learning. *The Quarterly Journal of Experimental Psychology, 53A*, 962–982.

Murphy, G. L., & Medin, D. L. (1985). The role of theories in conceptual coherence. *Psychological Review, 92*, 289–316.

Oldfield, R. C. (1954). Memory mechanisms and the theory of schemata. *British Journal of Psychology, 45*, 14–23.

Posner, M. I., & Keele, S. W. (1968). On the genesis of abstract ideas. *Journal of Experimental Psychology, 77*, 353–363.

Posner, M. I., & Keele, S. W. (1970). Retention of abstract ideas. *Journal of Experimental Psychology, 83*, 304–308.

Rogers, T. T., & McClelland, J. L. (2004). *Semantic cognition: A parallel distributed processing approach*. Cambridge, MA: MIT Press.

Rumelhart, D. E., & Ortony, A. (1977). The representation of knowledge in memory. In R. C. Anderson, R. J. Spiro, & W. E. Montague (Eds.), *Schooling and the acquisition of knowledge* (pp. 99–135). Hillsdale, NJ: Lawrence Erlbaum Associates.

Schank, R. C. (1982). *Dynamic memory*. Cambridge, England: Cambridge University Press.

Schank, R. C., & Abelson, R. P. (1977). *Scripts, plans, goals, and understanding: An inquiry into human knowledge structures*. Hillsdale, NJ: Lawrence Erlbaum Associates.

Smith, E. E., & Medin, D. L. (1981). *Categories and concepts.* Cambridge, MA: Harvard University Press.

Spalding, T. L., & Murphy, G. L. (1996). Effects of background knowledge on category construction. *Journal of Experimental Psychology: Learning, Memory, and Cognition, 22,* 525–538.

Trabasso, T., & Bower, G. H. (1968). *Attention in learning: Theory and research.* New York: Wiley.

Zeaman, D., & House, B. J. (1963). The role of attention in retardate discrimination learning. In N. R. Ellis (Ed.), *Handbook of mental deficiency* (pp. 159–223). New York: McGraw-Hill.

CHAPTER 20

Categorization, Recognition, and Unsupervised Learning

Evan Heit
University of California–Merced

Noellie Brockdorff
University of Malta, Msida, Malta

Koen Lamberts
University of Warwick, Coventry, England

In this chapter, we review several strands of research that share one common theme: the close conceptual and empirical links between categorization and recognition memory. We demonstrate that these links are strong, and often surprising. We explore the relation between recognition and unsupervised learning, and we investigate how perceptual processes can provide a unifying link between categorization and recognition.

In Gordon Bower's laboratory in the late 1980s and early 1990s, unsupervised learning was in the air. Several of his students were working on categorization as well as memory, and it appeared that dominant ideas in categorization research were being overturned. In particular, the traditional supervised-learning paradigm of category learning (e.g., Bruner, Goodnow, & Austin, 1956; Medin & Schaffer, 1978) was being challenged. In this paradigm, which was closely connected to paired-associate learning in the study of cued-recall memory (e.g., Bower, 1961), subjects would learn to link stimuli with category labels. On a learning trial, a subject would categorize a stimulus as, say, an A or a B, then receive corrective feedback. Although some work in the Bower lab during this period did use the supervised-learning paradigm (e.g., Gluck & Bower, 1988), his students were also asking what could be learned without feedback.

Intuitively speaking, although it is readily possible for people to be explicitly trained to associate stimuli with category labels, by no means is this procedure necessary. People can observe different kinds of houses, different kinds of landscapes, or different kinds of social interactions, and sort them into categories, even without having to label them and wait for corrective feedback from some external tutor. Experimental evidence supported the idea that people could learn categories without feedback. For example, Fried and Holyoak's (1984) subjects were able to learn to distinguish between categories of geometric designs even when category labels were not provided and in fact no information was given about the number of categories to be learned (see also Homa & Cultice, 1984). Lewicki (1986) presented a number of surprising results on the topic of nonconscious social information processing, for example, that subjects could observe personality descriptions of a set of people and successfully make predictions about additional persons, without being able to report the rules relating different personality traits.

Around this time, several models were proposed that could learn without feedback. The array model of Estes (1986) and the Minerva 2 model of Hintzman (1986) described category learning as simply storing memory traces, with or without presented labels or feedback. Connectionist models such as auto-associators (McClelland & Rumelhart, 1985) were being developed. These models learned the internal structure of stimuli without any training signal needed. Likewise, Billman and Heit (1988) presented an associationist model that generated its own internal feedback, making an external signal unnecessary. Anderson (1990) proposed a rational model of categorization, making the explicit claim that the most important function of categories is not to facilitate labeling but to enable any kind of prediction among stimulus features. During this period, two of Gordon Bower's graduate students conducted research on unsupervised learning. In experiments by John Clapper (Clapper & Bower, 1991, 1994), subjects learned about fictitious categories of insects by simply observing a series of pictures. Their sensitivity to implicit categorical structure was shown in an attribute-listing task. Over the course of learning, subjects were less likely to list attributes that correlated with each other and were predictable based on category structure, and more likely to list uncorrelated features that helped identify individual items. In experiments by Evan Heit (Heit, 1992), subjects observed featural descriptions of people and were able to make predictions about missing features for transfer items, with no category labels presented at all. These predictions were fairly elaborate, involving transitive inferences across chains of observed descriptions. Heit modified Medin and Schaffer's (1978) exemplar model of categorization to account for this unsupervised learning.

Over the past two decades, it has been increasingly accepted that category learning is not just a matter of learning from corrective feedback about explicit category labels, and the role of unsupervised learning is now emphasized (e.g., Love, Medin, & Gureckis, 2004; Markman & Ross, 2003). In general, categorization research has shown that people are able to learn about the detailed structure of what they observe, even without explicit tutoring, labeling, or feedback. Unsupervised learning allows people to adapt to complex and dynamic environments, without explicit feedback. Unsupervised learning can therefore be expected to play a role in numerous tasks that have been used in psychological studies, and accounting for this role can improve our understanding of a wide range of cognitive processes. In this chapter, we illustrate this point in the context of memory research, more specifically in terms of recognition memory.

Unsupervised Learning of Recognition List Structure

What can people learn implicitly about the structure of what they observe, when they try to remember the items they come across? Is recognition memory mainly passive storage and retrieval, or is there active, unsupervised adaptation to the structure of the information and the context in which it occurs? There is great intuitive appeal to the idea that people's response strategies can adapt to the structure of the stimulus environment. After leaving Stanford, Evan Heit dallied in the American Midwest for several years before moving to the Midlands of England, where he found colleagues Noellie Brockdorff and Koen Lamberts at the University of Warwick. As part of a larger project on categorization and recognition, they studied the issue of whether people can adapt strategically to the proportion of new versus old items on a recognition memory test. It seems logical that if the test list contains mostly new items, then people should maintain a conservative criterion for saying "old," because responding "new" will be correct most of the time. Furthermore, given the success of subjects in learning the finer details of stimulus structure in unsupervised category-learning tasks, it would seem straightforward to simply respond in accord with the proportion of new test items on a recognition test. Yet despite the inherent plausibility, there has been little empirical evidence that people can actually adapt their response criteria to the proportions of old and new items in a recognition test. As reviewed by Estes and Maddox (1995, p 1076), few recognition experiments have addressed this issue systematically. Ratcliff, Sheu, and Gronlund (1992) reported significant effects of test list composition, using a study–test recognition procedure and word stimuli. However, subjects were informed in advance of the proportion of new items before each test list, so it is not clear whether they were actually influenced by the content of the test list. Indeed, other studies have found that subjects are sensitive to misinformation about the content of test lists (Hirshman & Henzler, 1998; Strack & Foster, 1995), which implied a lack of sensitivity to list composition itself. In contrast, Estes and Maddox varied the test list without informing subjects about the proportion of new items. They used a continuous recognition procedure, with digits, letters, and words as stimuli. Surprisingly, for words, Estes and Maddox did not report significant effects of proportion of new test items (33% or 67%) on a measure of response bias, c. For digits and letters, proportion of new test items had an effect only when trial-by-trial feedback was provided. In the absence of this detailed feedback, subjects showed no sensitivity to composition of the test list. Therefore, previous research presents a fairly pessimistic picture of the extent to which people can adapt their responses strategically according to what is on the test list.

Although our focus here is just on adaptation to proportion of new test items, the question of whether people can vary their response criterion strategically is quite general in memory research. For example, Gillund and Shiffrin (1984) suggested that subjects have different biases for high-frequency versus low-frequency words on recognition tests, allowing them to take account that lure items that are high-frequency words might still seem quite familiar. This issue has also come up in interpreting results from the false-recognition paradigm (e.g., Gallo, Roediger, & McDermott, 2001; Miller & Wolford, 1999; Wixted & Stretch, 2000) in which people show a high false-alarm rate to nonpresented lure items that are semantically associated to a set of studied words. Here, again, the question is whether people's response biases are implicitly responding to the structure of test stimuli.

We now present two previously unpublished experiments directly addressing the issue of how people can vary their response criterion strategically, as a result of unsupervised learning in a recognition memory experiment. In Experiment 1, as in Ratcliff et al. (1992), we used a study–test recognition procedure. We varied, between groups of subjects, the proportion of new items on the test list, but we did not inform subjects in advance about the composition of the test list. We compared two kinds of stimuli, words (for which Estes and Maddox, 1995, did not find an effect of test list composition) and pictures (which we expected would lead to better overall performance). Unlike Estes and Maddox, we did not provide trial-by-trial feedback. It is possible that the continuous recognition procedure, employed by Estes and Maddox, made it particularly difficult for subjects to track the proportion of new items on the test list, because in this procedure the same test item can be both new and old depending on how many times it is tested. Therefore we predicted that even without detailed feedback, subjects' response criteria would be influenced by the composition of the test list, when using a study–test procedure. In our Experiment 2, we examined whether individual subjects could vary response criterion strategically within a test list. Other research (Hintzman, Caulton, & Curran, 1994; Rotello & Heit, 1999) has come to conflicting conclusions about whether response criterion varies within a list, particularly when the response signal technique is used, requiring subjects to respond to different stimuli at different time lags.

EXPERIMENT 1

Method

Two stimulus sets were used, pictures and words. Picture stimuli consisted of 360 color photographs, showing a variety of outdoor scenes, and looking much like postcards. Word stimuli consisted of 360 common English nouns, between five and seven letters in length.

Each subject attended one session, consisting of two old–new recognition memory tests. In each study phase, 90 stimuli were presented on the computer screen, 1 stimulus at a time, at a rate of 4 s per stimulus. Immediately following the study phase, a recognition test was given on 135 stimuli. Overall feedback about accuracy was given at the end of each test block.

The 80 subjects were randomly assigned to four different conditions, with 20 subjects in each condition. The four conditions used were: picture stimuli with 33% new test stimuli (45 new stimuli, 90 old stimuli), picture stimuli with 67% new test stimuli (90 new stimuli, 45 old stimuli), word stimuli with 33% new test stimuli (ratios same as for pictures), and word stimuli with 67% new test stimuli. The study phase in all four conditions was the same, aside from using pictures or words.

Results

The main results from Experiment 1, in terms of sensitivity (d') and bias (c), are shown in Figures 20–1 and 20–2. Note that higher values of d' indicate greater sensitivity, and higher values of c indicate more conservatism, that is, greater tendency to say "new." Visual inspection of Figure 20–1 suggests that accuracy was high for both picture and word stimuli, with better performance for pictures. There does not seem to be much of a systematic effect of proportion of new items or list number on performance. An analysis of variance (ANOVA) supported these observations. There was a main effect of stimulus type, $F(1,76) = 12.60$, $p < .001$, $MSE = 15.53$. Most important, there was no significant effect of proportion of new items, $F(1,76) = 0.01$, $MSE = 0.01$, suggesting that overall sensitivity was comparable in the 33% new and 67% new conditions. (In general, results not meeting a .05 criterion of statistical significance are not reported.)

Next, turning to the response bias results in Figure 20–2, there are clear, systematic differences between the first and second lists. The first list does not seem to show an effect of proportion of new items. In contrast, on the second list there is a consistent pattern for pictures and words. It appears that subjects were more

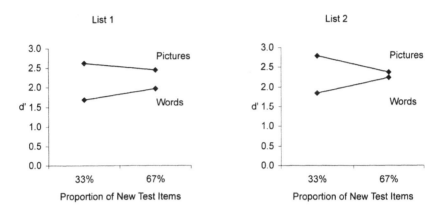

Figure 20–1. Sensitivity (d') for test lists containing 33% and 67% new words, Experiment 1.

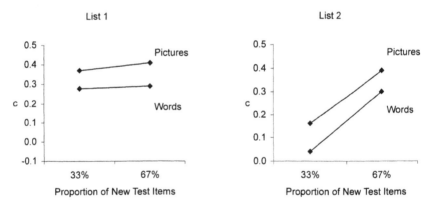

Figure 20–2. Bias (c) for test lists containing 33% and 67% new words, Experiment 1.

conservative in the 67% new conditions compared to the 33% new conditions. In an ANOVA, this was reflected by a significant list by proportion new interaction, $F(1,76) = 17.09, p < .001$, MSE = 0.50. However, the overall main effect of proportion new did not reach the level of significance. The effect of list number was significant, $F(1,76) = 18.48, p < .001$, MSE = 0.54, reflecting somewhat lower conservatism overall in the second list.

To clarify the interaction between list and proportion of new items, we conducted an additional ANOVA on response bias for just the second list. Here we found a significant main effect of proportion of new items, $F(1,76) = 9.20, p < .01, MSE = 1.20$, such that subjects were more conservative in the 67% new conditions compared to the 33% new conditions.

Discussion

In this experiment, it was clear that by the time of the second block, subjects had become sensitive to the proportion of new items on the test list, showing a more conservative response bias when there were more new items on the test list. We found these results consistently for both kinds of stimuli. These findings contrast with those of Estes and Maddox (1995) who, using a continuous recognition procedure and the same measure c of response bias, reported no effects of test list composition for words, and for other stimuli reported that the effect depended on the presence of detailed feedback.

Following the success of subjects in Experiment 1 in varying response criteria strategically in response to proportion of new items on a test list, we turned to a more challenging test of this ability. In particular, we looked at whether people could adopt different response criteria for different test items within a list. This is related to the issue raised by Miller and Wolford (1999), who claimed that people had different criteria for lure items versus studied items. In contrast, results by Stretch and Wixted (1998) suggested that subjects did not adopt varying criteria within a test list, for high- versus low-linguistic frequency words that were marked with different colors.

Furthermore, Rotello and Heit (1999) have raised the issue of varying response criteria in a different context, with respect to the response signal technique. With this technique, the subject is interrupted at various points in time while making a recognition judgment. The subject is instructed to respond quickly after an interrupting signal, making a judgment based on whatever assessment has been completed up until that point. The response signal comes at some point from, say, 100 ms to 2,000 ms from stimulus onset, determined randomly for each judgment trial.

Rotello and Heit (1999) reported some significant changes in response bias, as a function of time of response signal, for a subset of conditions in their own experiments and those of Hintzman and Curran (1994). The general finding in Rotello and Heit's experiments was a more conservative response bias at later times, when more information would be available to the subject. Therefore, Rotello and Heit argued that for response signal experiments, raw scores need to be interpreted with caution, because changes in false-alarm rate could reflect mere changes in response bias. Still, the empirical picture is unclear, because most other studies using this procedure have not reported bias measures. One exception was Hintzman et al. (1994), which reported no significant changes in response bias as a function of time to process test stimuli, for three experiments.

Still, null results such as those in Hintzman et al. (1994) could be due to averaging responses from subjects who each took their own strategic approaches to varying response bias. (Indeed, Hintzman et al. reported that individual subjects' response biases were correlated from one response signal to another, fitting the idea that there were systematic individual differences.) Therefore in Experiment 2, we manipulated the pattern of test stimuli to encourage different patterns of response bias in different conditions, to document people's ability to vary response bias for items tested at early time signals versus items tested at late test signals.

In Experiment 2, we compared two main configurations in which the proportion of new items tested varied as a function of processing time. In the *rising* configuration, the proportion of new items tested was low at early response signals but this proportion increased at later signals. In the *falling* configuration, the proportion of new items tested was high at early response signals, falling at later response signals. We predicted that subjects in the two groups would show different patterns of response bias over processing time, reflecting different strategies based on the distribution of old and new test items at different signals. For comparison, we also included a third configuration in which the proportion of new test items was *constant* across response signals. The test phase was organized in terms of two series of blocks, and the test proportions shifted from the first series to the second series. Therefore we investigated whether subjects could quickly adopt one response bias strategy for the first series, then take on a different strategy for the second series. (See Heit, Brockdorff, & Lamberts, 2003, for a related experiment in which there was only a single series of test blocks.)

There were four conditions in Experiment 2. In the rising/falling condition, subjects were first tested on a series of rising test blocks. For the rising test blocks, there was a low proportion of new items at early response signals and a high proportion of new items at late response signals. Then subjects in the rising/falling condition were tested on a series of falling test blocks, that is, with a high proportion of new items at early response signals and a low proportion of test items at late test signals. The second condition was rising/constant, in which a rising test series was followed by a series in which the proportion of new items was constant at different test lags. One purpose of the rising/constant condition was to see whether a response bias strategy acquired in the first series would carry over to the second series that had a more neutral character, or would subjects take a probability-matching strategy in the second, constant test series. The remaining two conditions were falling/rising and falling/constant.

EXPERIMENT 2

Method

This experiment used picture stimuli only. For each subject, the 360 stimuli were randomly assigned to six study–test blocks. Each study list consisted of 30 experimental pictures. In each study phase the pictures were presented, one at a time, at a rate of 3 s per picture. Immediately following the study phase, a recognition test was given on 30 old and 30 new pictures, using the response signal procedure. On each test trial, a cue (a cross) was shown at the center of the screen for 500 ms. The screen went blank for 100 ms and then a picture appeared. At variable time lags after the stimulus appeared on screen (100, 250, 500, or 1,250 ms) a tone sounded and the stimulus was replaced by a mask made up of small multicolored squares. Subjects were instructed to make a recognition judgment immediately after they heard the tone, and to respond as accurately as possible. If no response was made within 300 ms of the onset of the tone, or if a response was made before the onset of the tone, an appropriate error message was displayed. In addition, summary feedback about accuracy and proportion within time was given at the end of each test block.

The 32 subjects were assigned to four different conditions, with 8 subjects in each condition: rising/falling, rising/constant, falling/rising, falling/constant. The study phases in the four conditions were identical, but the four conditions differed in the test phase. Each test block in all four conditions consisted of 60 trials. In a falling test block, for the two earliest time lags the ratio of new stimuli to old stimuli was 10 new:2 old, in the middle time lag the ratio was 6 new:6 old, and in the last two time lags the ratio was 2 new:10 old. In a rising test block, for the two earliest time lags the ratio of new stimuli to old stimuli was 2 new:10 old, in the middle time lag the ratio was 6 new:6 old, and in the last two time lags the ratio was 10 new:2 old. In a constant test block, 6 new stimuli and 6 old stimuli were assigned to each response signal. Depending on the condition, each subject had three test blocks of one type followed by three test blocks of another type. For example, in the falling/rising condition, subjects faced a series of three falling test blocks followed by a series of three rising test blocks. See Table 20–1 for a summary of the conditions in this experiment.

Table 20–1
Ratio of New to Old Test Stimuli Across Time Lags And Blocks in the Four Conditions of Experiment 2

Condition	Series I (Blocks 1 to 3)					Series II (Blocks 4 to 6)				
	Time lag (ms)					Time lag (ms)				
	100	250	500	900	1,500	100	250	500	900	1,500
Falling/Rising	10:2	10:2	6:6	2:10	2:10	2:10	2:10	6:6	10:2	10:2
Falling/Constant	10:2	10:2	6:6	2:10	2:10	6:6	6:6	6:6	6:6	6:6
Rising/Falling	2:10	2:10	6:6	10:2	10:2	10:2	10:2	6:6	2:10	2:10
Rising/Constant	2:10	2:10	6:6	10:2	10:2	6:6	6:6	6:6	6:6	6:6

RESULTS

The data were trimmed to remove responses in which subjects either failed to respond within 350 ms of a response signal (8%), or made anticipatory responses, earlier than 100 ms after the response signal (2%).

The mean accuracy in each condition, in terms of d', is shown in Figure 20–3. The clear results are that d' increased over the time course of judgment, reaching a high level of performance, and that d' did not vary as a function of condition (rising/falling, rising/constant, falling/rising, and falling/constant). The conclusions were supported by an ANOVA. There was only a significant main effect of time of response signal, $F(4,28) = 360.16, p < .001, MSE = .24$.

To improve the power of our response bias analyses, and more important, to improve their interpretability, we pooled the response bias scores, combining results from the first and second test signals, and the fourth and fifth test signals, for each subject. Within each of these pairs of response signals, a subject saw the same proportion of new versus old items. For example, a subject in the falling/rising condition saw ⅚ new items at response signals 1 and 2 in the first series, and saw ⅙ new items at response signals 4 and 5. We dropped the data from the third test signal, for which every subject always saw 50% new items.

The pooled bias results are presented in Figure 20–4. At the left are the response bias patterns for the first series, for all four conditions. Clearly, the falling/rising and falling/constant conditions showed falling patterns in the first series, whereas the rising/falling and rising/constant conditions showed rising patterns. Next, turning to the panels at the right, for the second series, it is clear that there is strong influence of the test configuration observed during this second series of test blocks. Subjects in the falling/rising condition showed a rising pattern in the second series, whereas subjects in the falling/constant condition continued to show a falling pattern (perhaps attenuated). In the rising/falling

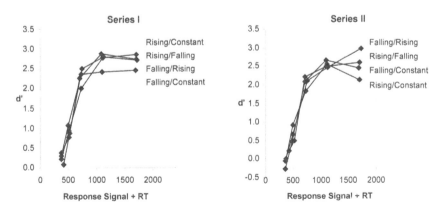

Figure 20–3.   Sensitivity (d') at varying response signals, Experiment 2.

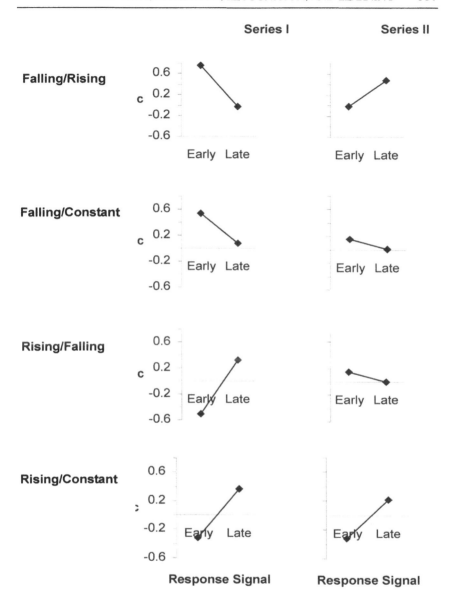

Figure 20–4.   Bias (c) at varying response signals, Experiment 2.

condition, subjects showed a falling pattern in the second series. Finally, in the rising/constant condition, subjects continued to show a robust rising pattern in the second series.

Our analyses of the pooled response bias results targeted specific aspects of the data. We looked at each condition separately, to see when subjects truly changed their response bias patterns from the first series to the second series. That is, we were looking for series by response signal interactions. In the falling/rising condition, the interaction between series and response signal was significant, $F(1,7) = 46.80$, $p < .001$, $MSE = .07$. Likewise in the rising/falling condition, the interaction between series and response signal was significant, $F(1,7) = 28.46$, $p < .001$, $MSE = .07$. In comparison, for the falling/constant and rising/constant conditions, the interactions were not significant. Therefore, there was substantial evidence that subjects changed their pattern of response biases when the test configuration reversed from the first series to the second series, either rising to falling or falling to rising. However, there was no evidence that subjects changed their response patterns when the test configuration was constant (50% new at each time signal) in the second series, as if subjects in the falling/constant and rising/constant conditions carried over their response strategies from the first series to the second series.

Discussion

It was clear that in Experiment 2, people could not only adopt a response bias strategy quickly, in just the first three test blocks, but they could also change their strategy quickly, for the next three test blocks. Just as this experiment showed dramatic changes in the pattern of response biases from the first series to the second series in the rising/falling and falling/rising conditions, it is also notable that no significant changes were found in the rising/constant and falling/constant conditions. There was no statistical evidence that subjects in either condition changed their response strategies for the second series, even though the test configuration had changed from the first series. If subjects had simply tried to match the test configuration, then they should have shown a constant response bias pattern for the second series. Instead they showed a rising pattern in the rising/constant condition and a falling pattern in the falling/constant condition. Putting together the results from all four conditions, it appears that subjects quickly adopted a strategy for varying response bias over time, and carried on with this strategy unless it was greatly discrepant with the test configuration in the second series.

It is also interesting to compare the results on the second series for the rising/constant and falling/constant conditions. Subjects in both conditions saw the same test configuration, with a constant proportion of new items at different response signals. This configuration is also comparable to past studies using the response signal technique, in which the proportion of new test items was not manipulated across response signals. Despite seeing the same configuration of test items, subjects in the rising/constant and falling/constant conditions showed completely opposite patterns of response bias on the second series. The reason for this dramatic difference is that the two groups of subjects brought different expectations to this neutral situation, leading them to take different strategies.

These experiments demonstrate the importance of unsupervised learning in a recognition memory task. The subjects in the experiments showed exquisite sensitivity to statistical properties of the task environment, and adapted their response criterion rapidly to these properties without ever receiving explicit feedback on the outcome of these adaptive processes. The results thus provide a powerful demonstration of the ubiquity of unsupervised learning processes. Moreover, they demonstrate that a full understanding of recognition performance can be achieved only if unsupervised adaptation is taken into account.

GENERAL DISCUSSION

Strategic Changes in Response Criterion

In related research conducted at about the same time at the University of Warwick (Heit et al., 2004), we examined people's ability to vary response criterion strategically as a result of explicit instruction. Ratcliff et al. (1992) had found that response criterion had varied with explicit information about test list composition. However, more generally in recognition memory research, particularly in the false-recognition memory paradigm, there was an unanswered question of what happens when people are warned about a memory illusion—can they avoid it? For example, after studying the words *pillow, rest, slumber, nap,* and *rest,* people are likely to falsely recognize the lure item *sleep.* In the extreme, people will respond at the same level to nonpresented lures as to words that had actually been presented. But what if they are forewarned about this illusion, namely that there will be a central word, closely related to presented words but not actually studied, and that they should avoid saying that this word had been presented? Can this kind of memory error be prevented?

We answered this question using the response signal technique and word lists from previous research (Stadler, Roediger, & McDermott, 1999). The main comparison was between a standard condition, with standard instructions for a recognition memory experiment, and a forewarning condition, in which people were told about the illusion and instructed to avoid it. By using the response signal technique, we were able to pinpoint not only what effect the forewarning instructions had, but at what point in time the instructions had an effect. We assumed that responses to earlier signals, say within 500 msec of test item presentation, would reflect mainly automatic processing, and that responses to later signals increasingly would reflect strategic processing. The analyses in Heit et al. (2004) were very similar to the analyses of Experiments 1 and 2 in this chapter. We assessed sensitivity, in this case using a d' measure of whether people responded different to lure items versus presented items. And we assessed response bias, using the c measure.

The standard condition on its own revealed some interesting points about the false-memory illusion. At the earliest response signals (200 msec and 400 msec), the illusion was at its strongest, in that people were insensitive to the difference between lure items versus presented items. At later response signals (600 msec and 1,100 msec), the illusion was reduced, in that people responded differently to the two kinds of items, correctly recognizing presented items with a lower rate of falsely recognizing lure items. Just based on the standard condition, we concluded that the false-memory illusion arises due to automatic processes and is reduced somewhat as strategic processes become available.

Next, we compared the standard condition to the forewarning condition. The surprising result was that the forewarning instructions had no effect at all on the extent of the false-memory illusion! That is, forewarning did not increase sensitivity to the distinction between presented items and lures. However, forewarning did have a substantial effect on response criterion, at all response signals. In particular, people became more conservative overall—they were less likely to recognize any item as having been studied. Although the false-memory illusion was reduced in absolute terms—that is, people were less likely to say they recognized lure items—this was accompanied by a reduction in correctly recognizing presented items. Hence there was a change only in response criterion and not in sensitivity to the distinction between lure items and presented items.

Although there are some notable differences between Heit et al. (2004) and Experiments 1 and 2 in this chapter, especially in regard to whether results were due to explicit instruction or unsupervised learning, both lines of work do highlight the adaptability of response criterion and the importance of considering it when interpreting recognition performance.

Perceptual Processes in Recognition and Categorization

A central theme in our research project at the University of Warwick was the relation between perceptual processes in categorization and in recognition memory. This relation was made explicit in the FESTHER (FEature-Sampling THEory of Recognition) model proposed by Brockdorff and Lamberts (2000), derived from previous modeling work in perceptual categorization (Lamberts, 2000; Nosofsky & Palmeri, 1997). A key assumption in the FESTHER model of recognition is that recognition performance depends on the perceptual information that is available. To inform a recognition judgment, stimulus information must be perceived, which takes time. FESTHER indicates how the characteristics of feature perception affect the time course of recognition judgments.

A testable prediction from the model is that information about the time course of perception can be used in the prediction of the time course of recognition judgments. If we know how long it takes to perceive specific stimulus features, and if we understand the relation between features and recognition decisions, we can predict recognition judgments at different response latencies. Lamberts, Brockdorff, and Heit (2002) carried out four experiments, in which they first measured perceptual processing times of various features, and then used these estimates to predict old–new recognition performance with the same stimuli. The stimuli in the four experiments were drawings of various objects and scenes. Some of the stimuli had been obtained by modifying a single feature in one of the other stimuli, such that there were pairs of highly similar stimuli in the set.

The first three experiments were designed to measure the perceptual processing rates of the features that distinguished the stimuli in these similar pairs. In the first experiment, the participants carried out a perceptual same–different matching task. Two stimuli were presented simultaneously on each trial, and the participants were instructed to judge their identity as quickly as possible. Response times for "different" judgments on trials with similar stimulus pairs were taken as an index of the perception time of the critical feature that distinguished the members of the pair. In Experiments 2 and 3, the response signal technique was used with perceptual matching tasks to obtain further measurements of the processing rates of the critical features. In Experiment 4, the participants carried out an old–new recognition task using the response signal technique, with the same stimuli as in the matching experiments. The accuracy results for the different stimulus types showed strong effects of response signal interval. Most important, it proved possible to account for the data from the recognition experiment using the perceptual processing rates estimated from the matching experiments. Therefore, the results demonstrated that it was possible to predict speeded recognition performance from performance in perceptual matching, by adapting a categorization model to the recognition task.

The relation between the time course of categorization and recognition memory was also studied in another project by the same authors (Lamberts, Brockdorff, & Heit, 2003). The three experiments in this study used a new method for collecting and analyzing response times in recognition experiments. The usual tradition in categorization research is to examine performance on individual items. In contrast, in most studies of recognition, the data are obtained by averaging across stimuli. The reason for aggregation across stimuli is that each test stimulus in a recognition experiment can be presented only once to each subject (to avoid interference). However, averaging data, including response times, across items is potentially misleading, and response times to individual items can provide critical information about the underlying processes. In three experiments, Lamberts et al. used a technique that offered a compromise between the need for repeated observations for modeling and analysis, and the need to avoid interference due to repetition of individual test stimuli. Instead of repeating individual stimuli, they tested recognition using classes of structurally equivalent stimuli. The subjects repeatedly carried out a study–test procedure with pseudowords as the stimuli. All the lists used in an experiment were generated from a template that constrained the structure of the stimuli. The lists were created by mapping the template onto different sets of characters. As a result, the study and test lists in an experiment had a different appearance, but at the same time represented exactly the same underlying structure. The common structure across the lists allowed us to treat the different instantiations of a template item as repetitions of a single stimulus. There were robust and systematic differences in response times between items. Most important, these differences were in agreement with the predictions from process models of recognition memory that were derived from process models of perceptual categorization.

CONCLUSION

In the most general, and perhaps most important sense, all of our results point to the close conceptual and empirical links that exist between memory and category learning. Whereas few modern researchers would dispute the fundamental connections between processes of memory and category learning, we believe that the research areas of memory and category learning are still treated too much as separate topics; for example, there are memory phenomena and categorization phenomena, memory models and categorization models, memory workshops and categorization workshops, memory chapters in textbooks and categorization chapters in textbooks. Still, there are many positive examples of modeling memory and categorization together (e.g., Estes, 1994; Heit & Hayes, 2005; Lamberts et al., 2003; Nosofsky, 1988). In Gordon Bower's own work on category learning, models were developed that embodied learning principles that were so universal that they applied in a wide range of settings. For instance, Gluck and Bower's (1988) associative model of category learning uses learning principles, based on error correction in response to feedback, that are universal, covering a wide range of tasks and processes that involve explicit feedback. Similarly, the principles of unsupervised learning proposed by Clapper and Bower (1991, 1994) should apply to all contexts in which structured information is presented, but in which no explicit feedback is available. Indeed, unsupervised learning of detailed stimulus structure is a powerful phenomenon illustrating the importance of studying the relations between memory and category learning.

REFERENCES

Billman, D., & Heit, E. (1988). Observational learning without feedback: A simulation of an adaptive method. *Cognitive Science, 12,* 587–625.

Bower, G. H. (1961). Application of a model to paired-associate learning. *Psychometrika, 26,* 255–280.

Brockdorff, N., & Lamberts, K. (2000). A feature-sampling account of the time course of old–new recognition judgments. *Journal of Experimental Psychology: Learning, Memory, and Cognition, 26,* 77–102.

Bruner, J. S., Goodnow, J. J., & Austin, G. A. (1956). *A study of thinking.* New York: Wiley.

Clapper, J. P., & Bower, G. H. (1991). Learning and applying category knowledge in unsupervised domains. In G. H. Bower (Ed.), *The psychology of learning and motivation* (Vol. 27, pp. 65–108). San Diego, CA: Academic Press.

Clapper, J. P., & Bower, G. H. (1994). Category invention in unsupervised learning. *Journal of Experimental Psychology: Learning, Memory, and Cognition, 20,* 443–460.

Estes, W. K. (1986). Array models for category learning. *Cognitive Psychology, 18,* 500–549.

Estes, W. K. (1994). *Classification and cognition.* New York: Oxford University Press.

Estes, W. K., & Maddox, W. T. (1995). Interactions of stimulus attributes, base rates, and feedback in recognition. *Journal of Experimental Psychology: Learning, Memory, and Cognition, 21,* 1075–1095.

Fried, L. S., & Holyoak, K. J. (1984). Induction of category distributions: A framework for classification learning. *Journal of Experimental Psychology: Learning, Memory and Cognition, 10,* 234–257.

Gallo, D. A., Roediger, H. L., & McDermott, K. B. (2001). Associative false recognition occurs without strategic criterion shifts. *Psychonomic Bulletin & Review, 8,* 579–586.

Gillund, G., & Shiffrin, R. M. (1984). A retrieval model for both recognition and recall. *Psychological Review, 91,* 1–67.

Gluck, M. A., & Bower, G. H. (1988). From conditioning to category learning: An adaptive network model. *Journal of Experimental Psychology: General, 117,* 227–247.

Heit, E. (1992). Categorization using chains of examples. *Cognitive Psychology, 24,* 341–380.

Heit, E., Brockdorff, N., & Lamberts, K. (2003). Adaptive changes of response criterion in recognition memory. *Psychonomic Bulletin & Review, 10,* 718–723.

Heit, E., & Hayes, B. (2005). Relations among categorization, induction, recognition, and similarity. *Journal of Experimental Psychology: General, 134,* 596–605.

Hintzman, D. (1986). Schema abstraction' in a multiple-trace memory model. *Psychological Review, 93,* 411–428.

Hintzman, D. L., Caulton, D. A., & Curran, T. (1994). Retrieval constraints and the mirror effect. *Journal of Experimental Psychology: Learning, Memory, and Cognition, 20,* 275–289.

Hirshman, E., & Henzler, A. (1998). The role of decision processes in conscious recollection. *Psychological Science, 8,* 61–65.

Homa, D., & Cultice, J. (1984). Role of feedback, category size, and stimulus distortion on acquisition and utilization of ill-defined categories. *Journal of Experimental Psychology: Learning, Memory and Cognition, 8,* 37–50.

Lamberts, K. (2000). Information-accumulation theory of speeded categorization. *Psychological Review, 107,* 227–260.

Lamberts, K., Brockdorff, N., &. Heit, E. (2002). Perceptual processes in matching and recognition of complex pictures. *Journal of Experimental Psychology: Human Perception and Performance, 28,* 1176–1191.

Lamberts, K., Brockdorff, N., & Heit, E. (2003). Feature-sampling and random-walk models of individual stimulus recognition. *Journal of Experimental Psychology: General, 132,* 351–378.

Lewicki, P. (1986). *Nonconscious social information processing.* New York: Academic Press.

Love, B. C., Medin, D. L., & Gureckis, T. M. (2004). SUSTAIN: A network model of category learning. *Psychological Review, 111,* 309–332.

Markman, A. B., & Ross, B. H. (2003). Category use and category learning. *Psychological Bulletin, 129,* 592–613.

McClelland, J. L., & Rumelhart, D. E. (1985). Distributed memory and the representation of general and specific information. *Journal of Experimental Psychology: General, 114,* 159–197.

Medin, D. L., & Schaffer, M. M. (1978). Context theory of classification learning. *Psychological Review, 85,* 207–238.

Miller, M. B., & Wolford, G. L. (1999). The role of criterion shift in false memory. *Psychological Review, 106,* 398–405.

Nosofsky, R. M. (1988). Exemplar-based accounts of relations between classification, recognition, and typicality. *Journal of Experimental Psychology: Learning, Memory, and Cognition, 14,* 700–708.

Nosofsky, R. M., & Palmeri, T. J. (1997). An exemplar-based random walk model of speeded classification. *Psychological Review, 104,* 266–300.

Ratcliff, R., Sheu, C.-F., & Gronlund, S. D. (1992). Testing global memory models using ROC curves. *Psychological Review, 99,* 518–535.

Rotello, C. M., & Heit, E. (1999). Two-process models of recognition memory: Evidence for recall-to-reject? *Journal of Memory and Language, 40,* 432–453.

Stadler, M. A., Roediger, H. L., & McDermott, K. B. (1999). Norms for word lists that create false memories. *Memory & Cognition, 27,* 494–500.

Strack, F., & Forster, J. (1995). Reporting recollective experience: Direct access to memory systems? *Psychological Science, 6,* 352–358.

Stretch, V., & Wixted, J. T. (1998). On the difference between strength based and frequency-based mirror effects in recognition memory. *Journal of Experimental Psychology: Learning, Memory, and Cognition, 24,* 137–196.

Wixted, J. T., & Stretch, V. (2000). The case against a criterion-shift account of false memory. *Psychological Review, 107,* 368–376.

Updating Beliefs With Causal Models: Violations of Screening Off

Clare Walsh
University of Plymouth, England

Steven Sloman
Brown University

Upon encountering a line of research in cognitive psychology, it is rare to find that it does not trace back in one way or another to Gordon Bower. Gordon is like the taproot of cognitive psychology, stouter than other cognitive psychologists and tending to develop along straight lines.

Gordon is not only an experimentalist's experimentalist and the granddaddy of computational models of cognition, he is also a patriarch of mathematical psychology. Gordon was developing Markov models of memory processes before the field was old enough to say "rehearsal buffer." Indeed, as a new student of Gordon's, the second author remembers vividly sitting in Gordon's office discussing a methodological issue. Gordon said, "Oh yeah, we worked that out about 25 years ago," took out a pad of paper and quickly proceeded through three pages of mathematical analysis to prove to the young upstart that aggregate and individual performance could not be distinguished (or some topic like that. Gordon remembers detailed proofs; the second author only vaguely remembers discourse topics.)

At one point, Gordon suggested to the second author that he do something worthwhile and rigorous for his dissertation, like develop a probabilistic model of his idea. At the time, Gordon's idea was rejected as old-fashioned. Fifteen years later, the second author's research has turned to probability models, a topic he wishes he had studied more thoroughly as a younger man.

In the early 1960s, Markov models were all the rage at Stanford, models that are explicit about how much of an individual's history is required to determine the mental state of a cognizer. One basic idea of such models is that we can model the probability of some mental state by considering only a finite set of prior mental states, often only one. Call that set of relevant states R. Then mental states prior to the critical states R are rendered independent of the current mental state by knowledge of R. This is a form of what is these days called "screening off": Once you know R, events prior to R cannot tell you anything about events subsequent to R. States in R are able to screen off prior states from the current state. Like all ideas that interest Gordon, this is not only a nice general property that, if true, would reveal a lot about the nature of cognition, it is also highly testable as it asserts a clear prediction about human behavior. In Gordon's field of memory, the prediction in the simplest case is that what people remember at time t should be a function of what they know about events at time $t-1$. Once a person's knowledge at time $t-1$ is specified, events before that should provide no further information about what people will say at time t. Events at $t-1$ screen off events at time t from events prior to $t-1$. Screening off is a property that holds of a large class of graphical probability models, models that attempt to represent human knowledge and cognitive processes using nodes and links in a way that relates them intimately to probability distributions. For instance, screening off holds not only of Markov models, but of Bayes's nets (Glymour, 2001; Sloman, 2005).

BELIEF UPDATING

In this chapter, we examine the validity of screening off as a descriptor of how people revise their beliefs about simple events that they have causal knowledge of. How do people update their beliefs in the face of new information? Imagine for example that four students move into the apartment above you. You imagine that their apartment may be quite untidy. You may also worry that they may play music late in the evening and so on. Imagine they then have a party during their first weekend there. When people encounter information that is consistent with their expectations, then that information may reinforce their existing views.

However, sometimes people encounter information that is inconsistent with what they expected. Imagine that during the first weekend after the students move in you don't hear a sound. In some cases, people may choose to discredit this information (Lord, Ross, & Lepper, 1979). For example, they may still expect the students to be noisy. However, if they accept that their new neighbors are genuinely quiet, then they will need to change some of their existing beliefs. But what beliefs will they change? For example, will they also revise their belief that the students' apartment is untidy?

The question of how people update their beliefs when they encounter unexpected information has been addressed by psychologists (e.g., McKenzie, 2004), philosophers (e.g., Harman, 1986), and artificial-intelligence researchers (e.g., Gardenfors, 1988). The predominant view is that people accommodate new information by making the minimal possible change to their existing beliefs. When they discover that a cause occurs but its usual effect does not, one option is to adjust belief in the strength of the relation between these two events. For example, if we know there was heavy rain but the tennis match wasn't canceled, we may revise our belief that rain causes these matches to be canceled and we may lower our expectation that the match will be canceled next time it rains. However, when people encounter an unexpected outcome, they tend to construct explanations for it. These explanations often describe disabling conditions (i.e., factors that prevent a cause from producing its usual effect; Byrne & Walsh, 2002; Walsh & Johnson-Laird, 2007). For example, they may suggest that this tennis match was played under cover. We propose that these explanations may determine how people update their beliefs.

In the current experiments, we constructed pairs of causal statements that shared a cause. Bayes's nets provide an excellent medium for representing this kind of causal knowledge. According to Bayes's net theory, when two events have a common cause, they tend to be correlated. The reason for this is that they both tend to be present when their cause is present and absent when their cause is absent. However, in cases in which we know whether or not the cause has occurred, this correlation disappears. Hence, we can no longer infer anything about the likelihood of one effect from the knowledge that the other event did or did not happen. In this case, the cause screens off judgments about one event from information about the other (see Fig. 21–1). Based on this principle, if a cause occurs (e.g., it rains) and one effect does not (e.g., the tennis match is not canceled), people's strength of belief that the second event will occur (e.g., umbrellas are sold) should be left unchanged. However if people construct explanations for why the effect didn't occur, they may use these explanations to revise their expectations. Along with examining whether people's judgments are consistent with the screening-off principle, our studies were designed to examine whether explanations play a role in belief updating.

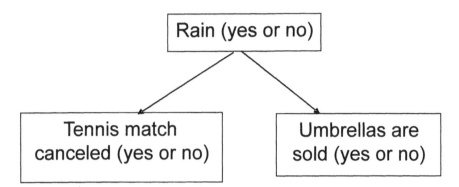

Figure 21–1.   Screening off in a common cause model. On a particular day, if we know whether it has rained or not, there's nothing more we can learn about whether umbrellas are sold from knowledge about whether the tennis match was canceled. For instance: P(Umbrellas are sold | It rained) = P(Umbrellas are sold | It rained, Tennis match not canceled).

UPDATING BELIEFS

In our first experiment, we presented 23 Brown University undergraduates with pairs of causal statements (methodological details are reported in Walsh & Sloman, 2004). In each case, the two statements shared the same cause but had different effects. Hence, they described a common cause model. An example is:

Following this diet causes you to have a good supply of iron.

Following this diet causes you to lose weight.

After presenting participants with these statements, we then asked them two questions. First, we measured their initial belief in one of the statements by asking them to judge the probability of the effect given that the cause occurred. For example:

John followed this diet. What is the probability that he lost weight?

We then presented participants with new information. Specifically, we told them that the second effect (i.e., the one that we had not previously asked about) did not occur. Our goal was to see how people revise their judgments in the light of this new information. Participants judged again the probability of the same effect, this time given that the cause occurred and the second effect did not. For example:

Tom followed this diet but he did not have a good supply of iron. What is the probability that he lost weight?

If probability judgments are compatible with the screening-off principle, then judgments before and after the new information should be the same. Once it is known that the cause occurred (Tom followed the diet), any correlation between the two effects (supply of iron and weight loss) will disappear. Hence, knowing that one was absent should have no effect on the likelihood of the second. However, if people do not abide by the screening-off principle, then their judgments may change.

The results showed that participants lowered their judgments in the second question on 56% of trials (means are presented in Table 21–1). Twenty-one out of 23 participants lowered their judgments in at least one problem and the remaining 2 showed no change in any problem. There was no difference in the change in probability across the different problem contents. We also gave participants two control problems that contained no unexpected information. For example:

Tom followed this diet and he did have a good supply of iron. What is the probability that he lost weight?

In this case, there was no significant change in judgments after reading the new information (see Table 21–1). When events were consistent with causal expectations, people did screen off.

Table 21–1
Mean Judged Probability of Event B Under Various Conditionalizations for Experimental and Control Problems in Experiment 1

Abstract problem format	
If A then B	If A then C
Experimental Problems	
Given A	77
Given A and not C	59
Control Problems	
Given A	81
Given A and C	82

The results show that when events were inconsistent with causal constraints, judgments were not consistent with the screening-off principle. One explanation for this result is that people do not understand this principle. They may not realize that once a cause is known to have occurred, then any effects of that cause are no longer correlated; people continue to believe that knowing whether one effect occurred provides information about other possible effects. However, an alternative possibility is that when people encounter unexpected outcomes they construct explanations for why they occur. These explanations often refer to disabling conditions; they may conclude that this diet affects only some people. As a result, explanations may lead people to add new factors to their causal models and to update their beliefs on the basis of this new model. When two effects share a common cause, then disabling conditions for one outcome may often disable the second outcome also and as a result people may adjust their judgments regarding the likelihood of a second outcome, that everyone will lose weight on this diet. The aim of our second experiment was to test this hypothesis. We compare it to an alternative account of our result, that contradictory information simply reduces confidence in all related judgments.

UPDATING BELIEFS AND EXPLANATIONS

In this experiment, our aim was to test the role of explanations in belief change. We did so by explicitly asking participants to generate explanations when we gave them the unexpected information that one of the effects did not occur. The study addressed two main questions. First, we wanted to know whether causal judgments depend on the explanation that was generated for the contradiction and on that explanation alone. If their probability judgments depend on their explanations, then their judgments should be predictable from their explanation regardless of the contradicted fact. In contrast, if a contradiction just reduces confidence, then their probability judgments should vary with contradiction, and not with the explanation. We tested this by explicitly asking participants to generate an explanation for the contradiction before making a causal judgment, for example:

Jogging regularly causes a person to increase their fitness level.

Jogging regularly causes a person to lose weight.

(Q2) Anne jogged regularly but she didn't lose weight.

Why?

What is the probability that her fitness level increased?

We then asked participants to use this explanation to make another causal judgment. For example, if a participant gave the explanation that Anne's appetite increased, then we asked them the following question:

(Q5) John jogged regularly and his appetite increased.

What is the probability that his fitness level increased?

The full sequence of questions is illustrated in Table 21–2. If people use their stated explanation (and not the contradicted fact) to make the causal judgment in Question 2 and they don't consider any other hypotheses, then we expect the probability judgments in Questions 2 and 5 to be equal. Previous research has shown that people frequently neglect alternative hypotheses (e.g., Klayman & Ha, 1987). However, if reasoners do consider other explanations or if their causal judgments are reduced merely because they have less confidence in what they have been told, then we expect these judgments to differ.

The second question that we addressed in this study was whether people draw on information that already exists in their causal model to generate an explanation for a contradiction or whether resolving a contradiction leads people to revise the causal model itself. We did this by asking participants two further questions. Before reading the contradiction we asked them the following:

(Q1) Tom jogged regularly.

What is the probability that his fitness level increased?

And after reading the contradiction and generating the explanation, we asked them the following:

(Q3) Mary jogged regularly and you don't know if her appetite increased.

What is the probability that her fitness level increased?

If a reasoner's causal model already contains information about the relation between appetite and fitness level and they use this information in answering Question 1, then we expect their responses to Questions 1 and 3 to be equal. But if they change their causal model when resolving the contradiction, we expect their answer to these two questions to be different.

The results of this study replicated the results of the previous study (see Table 21–2). The probability of the second effect was rated as significantly higher in Question 1 before reading the new information ($M = 85\%$) than in Question 2 after reading the new information ($M = 63\%$).

Our second finding was that responses to Question 2 and Question 5 ($M = 62\%$) did not differ significantly and this pattern occurred for all six types of problem content. For problems in which the contradiction reduced the judged probability of B (response to Question 2 was lower than to Question 1), participants gave the same answer to Questions 2 and 5 for 53% of problems. We would expect greater variety if participants were considering multiple hypotheses. Hence the results are consistent with the view that in many cases people consider just the one hypothesis given in their explanation and they fail to consider other possibilities. They allow this hypothesis to mediate their later causal judgments without considering the possibility that they are wrong (see also Shaklee & Fischhoff, 1982).

Table 21–2
The Format of the Problems Used in Experiment 2.

Worrying causes difficulty in concentrating.

Worrying causes insomnia.

	Mean
1. Mark was worried. What is the probability that he had difficulty concentrating?	85%
2. Kevin was worried but he didn't have insomnia. Why?	63%
What is the probability that he had difficulty concentrating?	
3. Frank was worried but *you don't know if the explanation holds.*	71%
What is the probability that he had difficulty concentrating?	
4. Helen was worried and *you know that the explanation does not hold.*	85%
What is the probability that she had difficulty concentrating?	
5. Evelyn was worried and *you know that the explanation does hold.*	62%
What is the probability that she had difficulty concentrating?	

Note.   In question 2 participants provide an explanation and this is used in questions 3, 4 and 5. Mean judgments for questions of each type are reported.

Finally, our results suggest that people resolve contradictions by making a change to their causal model. Ratings for Question 1 were significantly higher than for Question 3 when the explanation was unknown ($M = 71\%$). People do not merely change their causal judgments about the specific case in which the contradiction occurred. They extend these changes to new situations. Responses to Question 1 did not differ significantly from responses to Question 4 ($M = 85\%$ for both). People do not generally resolve contradictions by drawing on events that they have already represented in their causal model.

We also examined the nature of explanations given for the inconsistency. The most common explanation was to introduce a disabling condition that would prevent the cause from producing its usual effect. Seventy-four percent of responses were of this type. In many cases, the conditions disabled the cause from both consequences. For example, the fact that worry did not lead to insomnia may be explained by the fact that the person did relaxation exercises. This in turn may reduce the probability that worry will lead to a difficulty in concentrating. The next most common type of response was to suggest that the level or amount of the cause was not sufficient to produce the effect; for example, the person was not very worried. Eighteen percent of responses were of this type. In both cases, the pattern of responses and significance ratings for the probability of B were the same as for the overall ratings. We return to this question in our next experiment.

TYPES OF EXPLANATIONS

In our third experiment, we examined different types of explanations and their influence on belief revision. This time we provided people with explanations for why an unexpected outcome didn't occur and we examined the effect of these explanations on belief change.

Once again in this study we presented people with pairs of causal statements such as the following:

Playing loud music in Paul's apartment causes the neighbors on his left to complain.

Playing loud music in Paul's apartment causes the neighbors on his right to increase the volume on their TV.

As in the previous studies, we compared people's judgments about the likelihood of an outcome given that the cause occurred:

Last Friday night, Paul was having a party and he played loud music. What is the probability that the neighbors on the left complained?

to the likelihood of the same outcome given that the cause occurred and the second effect did not. However in this study, we provided people with one of three types of explanation for why the second effect did not occur and we predicted that these explanations would have different effects on belief change:

This Friday night, Paul was having a party and he played loud music but the neighbors on the right don't turn up the volume on their TV. [Explanation provided or generated here.] What is the probability that the neighbors on the left complained?

The first type of explanation described an additional condition that would prevent both effects from occurring, for example:

You discover that Paul invited all of his neighbors to the party.

This condition would provide a reason for why the neighbors on the right did not turn up the volume on their TV but it would also reduce the likelihood that the neighbors on the left would complain. They may have been at the party. For this reason, we expected that the probability of the first effect would be judged to be lower after learning that the second effect didn't occur.

The second type of explanation that we gave people described an additional condition that would prevent only one effect from occurring, for example:

You discover that they are out.

This condition again provides a reason for why the neighbors on the right did not turn up the volume on their TV. But, the influence of this on judgments of the first effect is less clear. If judgments are based on these new facts alone, then the probability of the first effect should not change. We might expect that the probability of the neighbors on the left complaining would be the same given that Paul had a party as it would be given that Paul had a party and the neighbors on the right are out. However, an alternative possibility is that this explanation might bring possible disabling conditions to mind. In this case, people may judge the second question to ask the probability that the neighbors on the left will complain given that Paul had a party and it is not known whether the neighbors on the left were at home. If in their earlier judgment, people made the default assumption that the neighbors were at home, then they may change their judgment now as they did in Experiment 2.

Finally, the third type of explanation that we gave also prevented only one of the effects, for example:

You discover that they are not watching TV.

Again this provides a reason for why the neighbors on the right did not turn up the volume on their TV, but we would not expect these facts to influence the likelihood that the neighbors on the left would complain. This explanation differs from the previous one in that it doesn't provide a plausible disabling condition for the first effect. In other words, we might expect that the probability of the neighbors on the left complaining given that Paul was playing loud music to be the same as they would be given that Paul was playing loud music and it is not known whether or not the neighbors on the left are watching TV. If people are basing their judgments on the explanations that we provided, then we expected the probability of the first effect to be the same for both questions.

We presented 20 participants with a series of scenarios and provided them with one of these three explanations or we asked them to generate their own.

Our results appear in Table 21–3. After reading the first type of explanation, which disabled both effects, participants changed their judgment of the probability of the outcome from 89% to 34%. After reading the second type of explanation, which prevented the first effect only but provided a plausible disabling condition for the second, participants also changed their judgment of the probability of the outcome significantly from 84% to 72%. This result supports the view that people begin by making default assumptions that the necessary background conditions are present but explanations can remind them of these conditions and lead them to question their earlier assumptions. Finally, after reading the third type of explanation, participants also changed their judgments significantly from 84% to 76%, $p < .02$. The results show that even giving people explanations that are not relevant to a particular judgment can lead to changes in those judgments. One possible reason for this outcome is that explanations may have the more general effect of reminding people that things may not go as expected and that their default assumptions may be wrong. For example, people may make a new judgment about the probability that the neighbors on the left will complain given that Paul played loud music and it is not known if other background conditions are met. When participants were asked to provide their own explanation, they generated each of the three different types and accordingly, they changed their judgments significantly from 89% to 67%.

Table 21–3

Mean Judged Conditional Probability of Effect B for Baseline Condition and After Different Explanations of the Non-Occurrence of Effect A in Experiment 3

Explanation Type	Before told A did not occur	After told A did not occur and explanation
Both effects disabled	89%	34%
Plausible application to B	84%	72%
Implausible application to B	84%	76%
Generate Own	89%	67%

SUMMARY AND CONCLUSIONS

In three experiments, we have provided support for the view that explanations play an important role in belief updating. In the first study, we demonstrated that when people encounter an unexpected outcome, they often fail to follow the screening-off principle and they diminish their expectation that other outcomes of the same cause will occur. One explanation for this is that people seek to explain outcomes and these explanations lead them to add new elements to their causal models. Our second study tested this hypothesis by asking people to make judgments after generating an explanation and then to make the same judgment assuming that the explanation held. The majority of responses were the same in both cases, lending support to the view that their explanations underlie their change in judgment. Finally, in our third experiment we presented people with explanations and we showed that the extent to which people change their judgments is influenced by the nature of these explanations. This suggests that explanations may change judgments through three different effects. One way is by suggesting other relevant facts that change the likelihood of an outcome. The second is by reminding people of specific conditions that could be relevant. Finally, explanations may remind people more generally that there could be conditions that are not met. In each of these ways, explanations may have an impact on the judgments that people make.

Like so many studies of human reasoning, these data undermine the old idea that human reasoning can be understood using systems of monotonic logic (see Evans, 2002). Some form of nonmonotonic inference—such as probabilistic reasoning—is necessary to describe how people think.

Can human reasoning be described using graphical representations of probability? If so, then it is important that judgments satisfy screening off, one of the most basic inferential principles of many such models. Our data indicate that they don't. The question remains whether people will obey the screening-off principle in situations in which their causal expectations are not so starkly contradicted. Some other evidence suggests that they won't. In studies examining people's causal models of category knowledge, both Chaigneau, Barsalou, and Sloman (2004) and Rehder and Burnett (2005) found small violations of screening-off. Chaigneau et al.'s violations involved causal chains. Rehder and Burnett's, like ours, concerned common cause models. Rehder and Burnett's response to these violations, again like ours, is to suggest that people are reasoning in terms of a different causal model than the experimenters initially attributed to them. All of these studies test adults who enter the laboratory with a lot of causal knowledge. That fact, combined with people's sophisticated ability to generate explanations, means that pinning down the causal model that people are actually reasoning with in any given situation is far from trivial. Subsequent tests of screening off need to study models consisting of causal beliefs that are uncontroversial and not easily revisable.

Although the flexibility of people's causal models makes testing the psychological reality of screening off harder, it doesn't make screening off immune to empirical validation. Any principle that's consistently violated in the laboratory cannot serve as a useful description of human cognition. We feel confident that Gordon Bower would agree. And that's good enough for us.

ACKNOWLEDGMENTS

This research was supported by NASA Grant NCC2–1217 to Steven Sloman. Experiments 1 and 2 were reported at the 2004 meeting of the Cognitive Science Society and the 2004 International Conference on Thinking.

REFERENCES

Byrne, R. M. J., & Walsh C. R. (2002). Contradictions and counterfactuals: Generating belief revisions in conditional inference. In W. Gray & C. Schunn (Eds.), *Proceedings of the 24th Annual Conference of the Cognitive Science Society* (pp. 160–165). Mahwah, NJ: Lawrence Erlbaum Associates.

Chaigneau, S. E., Barsalou, L. W., & Sloman, S. (2004). Assessing the causal structure of function. *Journal of Experimental Psychology: General, 133,* 601–625.

Evans, J. S. B. T. (2002). Logic and human reasoning: An assessment of the deduction paradigm. *Psychological Bulletin, 128,* 978–996.

Gardenfors, P. (1988). *Knowledge in flux.* Cambridge, MA: MIT Press.

Glymour, C. (2001). *The mind's arrows: Bayes nets and graphical causal models in psychology.* Cambridge, MA: MIT Press.

Harman, G. (1986). *Change in view.* Cambridge, MA: MIT Press.

Klayman, J., & Ha, Y. (1987). Confirmation, disconfirmation and information in hypothesis testing. *Psychological Review, 94,* 211–228.

Lord, C. G., Ross, L., & Lepper, M. R. (1979). Biased assimilation and attitude polarization: The effects of prior theories on subsequently considered evidence. *Journal of Personality and Social Psychology, 37,* 2098–2109.

McKenzie, C. R. M. (2004). Hypothesis testing and evaluation. In D. J. Koehler & N. Harvey (Eds.), *Blackwell handbook of judgment and decision making* (pp. 200–219). Oxford, England: Blackwell.

Rehder, B., & Burnett, R. (2005). Feature inference and the causal structure of categories. *Cognitive Psychology, 50,* 264–314.

Shaklee, H., & Fischhoff, B. (1982). Strategies in information search in causal analysis. *Memory & Cognition, 10,* 520–530.

Sloman, S.A. (2005). *Causal models: How people think about the world and its alternatives.* New York: Oxford University Press.

Walsh, C. R., & Johnson-Laird, P. N. (2005). *Changing your mind.* Manuscript submitted for publication.

Walsh, C. R., & Sloman, S. A. (2004). Revising causal beliefs. In K. Forbus, D. Gentner, & T. Regier (Eds.), *Proceedings of the 26th Annual Conference of the Cognitive Science Society* (pp. 1423–1427). Mahwah, NJ: Lawrence Erlbaum Associates.

Spatial Situation Models and Narrative Comprehension

Mike Rinck

Radboud University, Nijmegen, the Netherlands

In this chapter, I review more than 10 years of work on the role of spatial situation models in text comprehension. Gordon Bower's influence on this work is quite obvious because almost all of my studies reviewed here were conducted in collaboration with him. Our collaboration started when I came to Stanford University as a postdoc in 1991, ready to work with Gordon Bower on models of memory retrieval. However, it turned out immediately that he had more exciting things in stock, and I quickly got infected by his interest in a topic that he had begun investigating earlier, together with Daniel Morrow and Steven Greenspan. Unknown to me at that time, this infection should last for many years to come, resulting in a decade of cross-Atlantic collaboration.

TEXT COMPREHENSION AND SITUATION MODELS

In the late 1980s and early 1990s, Gordon Bower was very interested in understanding the comprehension of text and discourse. The consensus view of theories in this field was and is that different processes go on in parallel as people read a text or listen to somebody telling them about events. According to these theories of text comprehension, readers build multilevel representations during the comprehension process (e.g., Gernsbacher, 1990; Johnson-Laird, 1983; Kintsch, 1988, 1998; Van Dijk & Kintsch, 1983; Zwaan, Langston, & Graesser, 1995; Zwaan & Radvansky, 1998). First readers take in the *surface structure* of what they read. Second, they extract a propositional *text base,* which contains the logical relations between the concepts and the predicates and the arguments being made. Third, they construct a referential representation, a *mental model* or a *situation model,* which is what the text is about.

A situation model is constructed by connecting the concepts that are in the text to the real-world or imaginary-world referents. The situation model sets the parameters of space and time that are going to pervade the activities during the whole story. The model is used for deriving inferences, for interpreting the text, for filling out what the whole text is describing, for evaluating statements, as well as for updating the story. The situation model of a text is also largely what people remember about it. They remember not what the author wrote or said, but what he or she talked about—the gist of the story. This definition is based on the contents of the representational level called *situation model,* not on its representational format. It should be noted, however, that there is considerable debate over the representational format of situation models, in particular, whether they are analog or symbolic in nature (see Rinck, 2005).

These differences notwithstanding, there is consensus that many different aspects of a situation are represented in situation models, for instance, spatial, temporal, and causal relations as well as the protagonists' goals and emotions (Zwaan et al., 1995). Thus, situation models are multidimensional by definition. Nevertheless, most experimental studies have addressed single dimensions, and among these, spatial relations have been most prominent. The work reviewed here also concentrates on the *spatial situation model* of the physical situation in which a story takes place. This model includes the spatial layout of objects described in the story as well as the changing locations of the main characters (called protagonists).

THE SPATIAL DISTANCE EFFECT

Situational models can be studied in several ways. One approach studies how people construct a model online as they read or hear it line by line. Another approach examines what readers do with the model once they have constructed it, and how they update it on the basis of new information given in the text. This is the approach we followed in many experiments. In these experiments, we have examined a phenomenon called foregrounding or focusing of attention, showing that spatial situation models guide readers' allocation of attention during text comprehension. In general, readers focus attention on the protagonist and on his or her location and movements, yielding a narrative "Here and Now" point centered around the protagonist (see Morrow, 1994).

One consequence of the reader's focusing of attention around the Here-and-Now of the protagonist is an effect of spatial distance on accessibility: Known objects spatially close to the protagonist become more primed and more accessible in memory than spatially distant objects. This effect has been referred to as the *spatial gradient of accessibility* or *spatial distance effect*. The spatial distance effect was extensively investigated in a number of studies using an experimental paradigm that was introduced by Daniel Morrow and his colleagues (Morrow, Bower, & Greenspan, 1989; Morrow, Greenspan, & Bower, 1987) and later modified by Gordon Bower and myself (Rinck & Bower, 1995). In the following, I refer to this paradigm as the *map-and-narrative task*.

In experiments employing the map-and-narrative task, participants first memorize the layout of a building with many rooms, each containing a number of critical objects. A sample layout taken from Rinck and Bower (1995) is depicted in Figure 21–1. This procedure serves to supply participants with the prior knowledge necessary to create spatial situation models during the second part of the experiment. In this part, participants read a series of brief narratives, each one describing a new protagonist's activities in that building. The narratives contain critical *motion sentences* describing how the protagonist moves from one room (the *source room*) through an unmentioned *path room* into another room (the *location room*); for instance, "*Wilbur walked from the laboratory into the washroom*" (see Fig. 22–1).

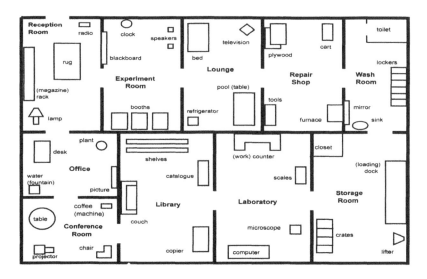

Figure 22–1.   A sample layout. From Rinck and Bower (1995). Copyright 1995 by Academic Press. Reprinted by permission.

Accessibility of objects in readers' memory may be measured online in one of two ways directly after reading of the motion sentence. In the studies by Morrow et al. (1987, 1989), reading was interrupted and a test probe was presented instead of the next sentence. The test probes consisted of the names of two previously studied objects. For each of these object pairs, subjects had to decide whether the two objects were located in the same room or in different rooms. The observed decision times revealed the spatial distance effect: Accessibility of objects was higher, if spatial distance between the objects and the subjects' current focus of attention was shorter. Usually, attention was focused on the current location of the protagonist of the narrative. Object pairs located in the same room as the protagonist (e.g., in this case lockers-mirror) were easier to access than object pairs from the unmentioned "path" room (e.g., closet-crates) that the protagonist had just passed through. These path room objects were in turn more accessible than objects in the source room from which the protagonist had commenced his or her movement (e.g., scales-microscope), or objects in some other room not recently visited in the building (e.g., clock-booths).

Morrow et al. (1989) also asked whether the physical location of the main character or his or her mental location is more important in determining the focus of attention. Does it matter where the protagonist is actually located or where he or she is thinking about? To answer this question, they had participants read stories containing sentences of the type *"The protagonist was in Room A thinking about [doing something] in Room B."* The "something being done" mentioned only neutral topics (e.g., cleaning the floor, painting the walls) and never mentioned a specific object memorized in that room. Following such a sentence, the accessibility of objects in Room A and in Room B was probed. Morrow et al. (1989) found that participants were faster to retrieve information about objects in the room where the protagonist's mental focus was (Room B) than in the room where he or she was physically located (Room A). This indicates a very flexible spatial focus of attention: It moves to what the main character is thinking about; that is, readers are in some sense simulating his or her thoughts.

One could object to the map-and-narrative task employed by Morrow and his colleagues because it involves interrupting participants as they read a story and asking them about the current location of the protagonist and various objects. Such a task might make readers concentrate unduly on the locations of things. Therefore, we devised a different technique to measure the accessibility of objects represented in the spatial situation model (Rinck & Bower, 1995). This task is unobtrusive and consists solely of having participants read the text at their own rate. With this technique, people also learn a spatial layout (see Fig. 22–1), and then read narratives containing motion sentences such as the one mentioned earlier: *"Wilbur walked from the laboratory into the washroom."*. After each motion sentence, a critical "think about" sentence is inserted, which contains an anaphoric noun phrase referring to one of the objects learned previously. An example of these anaphoric target sentences would read *"He thought that the toilet in the washroom still looked like an awful mess"* (see Fig. 22–1). In this case, the anaphoric noun phrase refers to an object in the location room, that is, the room the protagonist is located in right now. Slightly different versions of the anaphoric target sentences referred to objects in the path room, the source room, or some other room.

With this method, we found a spatial gradient in the reading times of these sentences (see Fig. 22–2): Anaphora resolution, and therefore reading of the anaphoric sentence, was faster if the sentence referred to an object in the location room, next fastest for an object in the path room, next fastest for an object in the source room, and slowest for an object in some other room in the building (Rinck & Bower, 1995). These anaphor resolution times closely resembled the test probe reaction times observed in earlier experiments by Morrow and his colleagues (1987, 1989). The close resemblance suggests that access to situation model entities involves the same processes, no matter whether it occurs in order to recall the objects' spatial location or to understand an anaphoric reference to them.

STUDIES OF THE SPATIAL DISTANCE EFFECT

Subsequent research has shown that this spatial gradient of accessibility is a surprisingly robust phenomenon. It was observed repeatedly, in studies in which participants learned a building layout before reading the narratives (e.g., Bower &

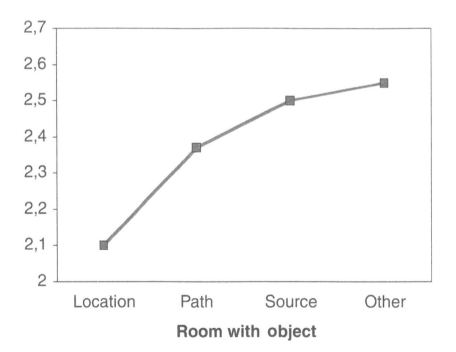

Figure 22–2. A prototypical spatial gradient of accessibility (see text for explanations).

Rinck, 2001; Dutke & Rinck, in press; Haenggi, Gernsbacher, & Bolliger, 1994; Haenggi, Kintsch, & Gernsbacher, 1995; Morrow et al., 1987, 1989; Morrow, Leirer, Altieri, & Fitzsimmons, 1994; Morrow, Stine-Morrow, Leirer, Andrassy, & Kahn, 1997; Rinck & Bower, 1995, 2000, 2004; Rinck, Hähnel, Bower, & Glowalla, 1997; Wilson, Rinck, McNamara, Bower, & Morrow, 1993), as well as in studies in which the layout was learned from a verbal description (Rinck, Williams, Bower, & Becker, 1996, Experiment 1), or when there was no prior learning procedure as in the experiment by Traill and Bower described later. Moreover, in one study (Rinck et al., 1996), we systematically varied a number of factors that might influence the spatial gradient: the way the relevant spatial information was acquired (studying a text vs. a layout), the spatial scenario (a research center vs. a day-care center), the direction of spatial distance (backward vs. forward on the protagonist's route), the language used (English vs. German), the manner in which the accessibility of objects was probed (object pair test probes vs. anaphoric sentences), the existence of prior knowledge about the objects (objects learned as part of the scenario vs. unknown objects), and the participants' task (reading narratives vs. imagining their own movements). Despite these variations, we observed a spatial gradient in all three experiments, indicating that the effects of spatial situation models may be generalized to a variety of experimental paradigms and cognitive tasks.

Control experiments also ruled out a number of alternative explanations of the spatial distance effect. First, one might object that higher accessibility of objects in the location room compared to objects in the source room is due to recency of mention rather than spatial distance in the situation model. In motion sentences of the type *"The protagonist went from the source room into the location room,"* the location room is mentioned more recently (closer to the probe test) than the source room. However, the same pattern of results was observed when the order of mention was reversed using motion sentences such as *"The protagonist went into the location room from the source room"* (Morrow et al., 1987, Experiment 2). In fact, the spatial gradient of accessibility appears even if the location room is not mentioned at all. In one experiment, we observed similar distance effects when access was probed after motion sentences such as *"Then he walked into the next room"* (Rinck, Bower, & Wolf, 1998). So not even mentioning the location room, just implying it in the situation model yielded exactly the same differences in accessibility. Second, differences in accessibility observed in these experiments could not be explained by surprising anaphoric references or by the order in which the rooms of the building were studied during the learning phase of the experiments (Rinck & Bower, 1995).

Another objection that is often raised against the map-and-narrative task is that the results may be due to the rather artificial map-learning procedure. People usually learn about spatial environments by experiencing them directly rather than by memorizing a map. The objection seems unjustified, however. First, the same distance effects occurred after people learned about the relevant spatial information from studying a text describing the building (Rinck et al., 1996). These distance effects also arose when the texts and questions referred to a well-known spatial environment that people did not have to memorize at all. In an unpublished study by Saskia Traill and Gordon Bower, participants read stories about salespeople who traveled to various cities around the United States. For instance, a sentence in one story described how the main character drove his car from Miami to New York City. Following such motion sentences, participants read anaphoric sentences designed to measure the accessibility of the source city (Miami), the location city (New York), or an unmentioned intermediate path city (Baltimore). As before, a spatial gradient of accessibility occurred in reading times, indicating that the location city was more available than the path city which in turn was more available than the source city.

The latter result highlights one of the most impressive aspects of the spatial gradient of accessibility: Objects from the unmentioned path location may be more accessible than objects from the source location, even though only the source location is being explicitly mentioned in the motion sentence directly before accessibility is probed (see Fig. 22–2). This result suggests that spatial distance in situation models may be a more important cause of accessibility than surface characteristics of the text such as explicit mentioning. In fact, the spatial gradient of accessibility may be used as an index of situation model updating during narrative comprehension: If it is not observed, for instance when objects in the source room are more accessible than objects in the path room, there is reason to assume that readers did not create and update a spatial situation model during reading.

THE METRICS OF SPATIAL SITUATION MODELS

After establishing the reliability and validity of the spatial gradient of accessibility, we conducted more studies to better understand the nature of the effect. One question we asked early on was how "distance" is to be measured in this effect. Is it metric, Euclidean distance as a crow flies, or is it categorical distance based on the number of rooms? Is an object's accessibility determined by the size of the rooms located between the object and the protagonist, or by the number of discrete rooms between them? The earlier experiments had always confounded categorical and metric distance. But maps can be constructed in which these types of distance are unconfounded. In the experiments by Rinck et al. (1997), these maps contained paths leading through single path rooms that were either short or long, and paths through two path rooms that were either short or long. In this way, Euclidean distance (size of the path rooms) and categorical distance (number of path rooms) of different paths were varied orthogonally in the map. As before, after memorizing the map, participants read stories containing motion sentences implying that the protagonist walked through a path room (or rooms) of one of these four kinds.

A first surprising finding of these experiments was that reading times of motion sentences were longer when the implied path led through two rooms compared to one room. The size of the intermediate room (or rooms), that is, Euclidean distance traveled by the protagonist, had no effect on reading times at all. Furthermore, after each motion sentence, people read an anaphoric sentence that referred to an object in the part of the path room that was near or far from the protagonist. As noted, categorical distance between the protagonist and the object referred to was either one or two rooms, and Euclidean distance was either short or long. Reading times of these anaphoric sentences yielded the same surprising finding. Metric distance between the object referred to and the protagonist had no effect whatsoever on anaphor reading times. Rather, reading times varied solely with categorical distance: References to an object that was one room away from the protagonist were understood more readily than reference to an object that was two rooms away, regardless of the Euclidean distances involved.

In summary, reading times were determined by categorical segments of space (i.e., rooms), not Euclidean metric distance. Paradoxically, in this situation people had in memory all the knowledge about metric information necessary to draw (after the experiment) a correctly scaled map of the building. However, they seemed not to use this metric knowledge during reading, presumably because it was not necessary for the task at hand. In this respect, situation models created during narrative comprehension seem to differ markedly from mental images created in a mental imagery task.

In experiments conducted by Rinck and Denis (2004), spatial layouts were used that had exactly the same spatial properties as the ones used by Rinck et al. (1997). However, participants in the experiments by Rinck and Denis did not read narratives about protagonists moving through the building. Instead, they were asked to create mental images of the described building and the objects in it, and to imagine that they themselves walked around in the building. Despite this difference, comparable mental motion instructions and object test probes were used. Despite this equivalence in terms of spatial information, the results observed by Rinck and Denis differed clearly from the ones reported by Rinck et al.: Both mental motion instructions and test probe reaction times revealed effects of Euclidean distance as well as categorical distance. Thus, it seems that mental images represent spatial distance at the more detailed level of Euclidean distance. For situation models created during narrative comprehension, in contrast, a rough, categorical representations of spatial distance will often suffice.

SPACE AND OTHER DIMENSIONS OF SITUATION MODELS

As mentioned previously, situation models created from narratives will not be purely spatial. In addition to spatial relations, other important aspects of the situation will be represented in the model, such as causal and temporal relations, people and objects, and the protagonists' goals and emotions. This multidimensionality of situation models has been addressed both theoretically and empirically (e.g., Friedman & Miyake, 2000; Haenggi et al., 1994; Zwaan et al., 1995; Zwaan & Radvansky, 1998). In our own studies, we again employed the map-and-narrative task to investigate how the spatial dimension of situation models is related to other dimensions.

In one study (Rinck et al., 1998), we varied spatial distance in the situation model independently of surface distance. The latter was varied by probing the accessibility of objects in rooms that the protagonist had or had not visited earlier. The clear result of these studies was that situation model distance, but not surface distance affected accessibility. We (Rinck & Bower, 2000) also pitted spatial distance in the situation model against two types of temporal distance, namely story time distance and discourse time distance. Discourse time refers to real time passing "outside" a narrative during text comprehension, whereas story time refers to fictitious time passing (by description) "inside" the narrative. Story time was varied by describing that intervening episodes lasted only for a few minutes versus for 1 or 2 hours. Discourse time was varied by describing the episodes in a single sentence versus in several sentences. These experiments revealed that accessibility of situation model entities depended on both spatial distance and story time distance, but was unaffected by discourse time distance.

In another study (Bower & Rinck, 2001), we combined the spatial gradient of accessibility with the fan effect (e.g., Anderson & Reder, 1987, 1999) to find out how the spatial dimension of situation models interacts with the representation of single and multiple objects. In these experiments, we varied the number of objects located in each room independently of spatial distance between a probed object and the protagonist. In these experiments, reading was word-by-word and self-paced. Accessibility was measured by readers' time to understand anaphoric target sentences containing a definite noun phrase referring to an object in its room. Spatial distance between the probed object and the current focus of attention consistently affected reading times of the object name, the room name, and final sentence wrap-up time, replicating the spatial gradient of accessibility shown previously. Multiplicity of objects affected reading time only if multiple examples of a target object type were scattered across different rooms. Accessibility of the target object was unaffected by multiple examples located in the same room and by the number of additional objects in the target room. To interpret this complex pattern of results, we developed an associative model of memory retrieval during text comprehension (Bower & Rinck, 2001).

Finally, we (Rinck & Bower, 2004) varied spatial distance independently of goal relevance by probing the accessibility of objects that were either close to or far from the protagonist, and either relevant or irrelevant to the protagonist's current goal. These experiments showed that spatial proximity of objects to the current location of the protagonist as well as the relevance of these objects to the protagonist's current goal increased the objects' accessibility in memory, so that close, relevant objects were most accessible whereas distant, irrelevant objects were least accessible.

Surprisingly, almost all of the studies mentioned in the previous paragraphs have one curious result in common: Most of them yielded additive effects of the spatial variable and the other variables. Spatial distance in the situation model hardly ever interacted with emotional, temporal, goal-related, causal, or other types of information represented in the situation model. Thus, it seems that the spatial dimension of situation models is rather independent of other dimensions.

CONCLUSIONS

To summarize, this chapter has described how we have studied the consequences of shifting the focus of attention in situation models. During narrative reading, access to information about objects close to the focus is particularly fast; this spatial priming effect follows a spatial gradient; intermediate priming occurs on objects and places along the path of the protagonist; the focus moves to where the protagonist's thoughts are, not where he or she is located at the moment; distance effects are categorical rather than Euclidean; distance effects can be observed after learning of fictitious environments from texts as well as maps, and as well with familiar natural environments; and finally, the accessibility of objects is affected in an additive fashion by their spatial proximity and by other factors such as goal relevance or temporal distance.

In my review of these findings, I have limited myself almost exclusively to studies conducted by Gordon Bower, myself, and some close collaborators. Obviously, this implies that a lot of important work done by other people was left out. However, the purpose of this chapter was not to give a comprehensive review of the literature on spatial situation models and their role in text comprehension (for that purpose, see Rinck, 2005). Instead, the chapter was meant to illustrate— in a personal and subjective way—how Gordon affected my own research agenda for about a decade. During this time, we obtained the findings described herein with different variations of the map-and-narrative task, leading to a fairly long and comprehensive series of experiments.

My own conclusion from the studies reviewed in this chapter is that a good research paradigm can last a surprisingly long time, and employing it systematically took us a long way from where we started in 1991. Doing this research together with Gordon Bower has always been very gratifying for me. This was true for the early times when we could see each other almost daily, and just as well for the many years in which we met once or twice a year, at Stanford or in Dresden, in order to discuss finished experiments and design new ones. Naturally, I consider myself honored by Gordon's friendship, by his long-lasting interest in my work, and by his willingness to collaborate with me. I am also grateful for all of his suggestions, encouragements, and critical remarks. The latter is true even for the remarks that showed to me that some of my seemingly new and brilliant ideas had been developed, tested, and proven wrong by him years ago. Most of all, however, working with him has been a whole lot of fun, and that may be the most important reason for our long-lasting collaboration.

ACKNOWLEDGMENTS

This chapter is based in part on the chapter "Spatial Situation Models," published in a book edited by Shah and Miyake (2005).

REFERENCES

Anderson, J. R., & Reder, L. M. (1987). Effects of number of facts studied on recognition versus sensibility judgments. *Journal of Experimental Psychology: Learning, Memory, and Cognition, 13,* 355–367.

Anderson, J. R., & Reder, L. M. (1999). The fan effect: New results and new theories. *Journal of Experimental Psychology: General, 128,* 186–197.

Bower, G. H., & Rinck, M. (2001). Selecting one among many referents in spatial situation models. *Journal of Experimental Psychology: Learning, Memory, and Cognition, 27,* 81–98.

Dutke, S., & Rinck, M. (in press). Predictability of locomotion: Effects on updating of spatial situation models during narrative comprehension. *Memory & Cognition.*

Friedman, N. P., & Miyake, A. (2000). Differential roles for visuospatial and verbal working memory in situation model construction. *Journal of Experimental Psychology: General, 129,* 61–83.

Gernsbacher, M. A. (1990). *Language comprehension as structure building.* Hillsdale, NJ: Lawrence Erlbaum Associates.

Haenggi, D., Gernsbacher, M. A., & Bolliger, C. A. (1994). Individual differences in situation-based inferencing during narrative text comprehension. In H. van Oostendorp & R. A. Zwaan (Eds.), *Naturalistic text comprehension* (pp. 79–96). Norwood, NJ: Ablex.

Haenggi, D., Kintsch, W., Gernsbacher, M. A. (1995). Spatial situation models and text comprehension. *Discourse Processes, 19,* 173–199.

Johnson-Laird, P. N. (1983). *Mental models.* Cambridge, England: Cambridge University Press.

Kintsch, W. (1988). The role of knowledge in discourse comprehension: A construction-integration model. *Psychological Review, 95,* 163–182.

Kintsch, W. (1998). *Comprehension.* New York: Cambridge University Press.

Morrow, D. G. (1994). Spatial models created from text. In H. van Oostendorp & R. A. Zwaan (Eds.), *Naturalistic text comprehension* (pp. 57–78). Norwood, NJ: Ablex.

Morrow, D. G., Bower, G. H., & Greenspan, S. L. (1989). Updating situation models during narrative comprehension. *Journal of Memory and Language, 28,* 292–312.

Morrow, D. G., Greenspan, S. L., & Bower, G. H. (1987). Accessibility and situation models in narrative comprehension. *Journal of Memory and Language, 26,* 165–187.

Morrow, D. G., Leirer, V. O., Altieri, P., & Fitzsimmons, C. (1994). Age differences in creating spatial models from narratives. *Language and Cognitive Processes, 9,* 203–220.

Morrow, D. G., Stine-Morrow, E. A. L., Leirer, V. O., Andrassy, J. M., & Kahn, J. (1997). The role of reader age and focus of attention in creating situation models from narratives. *Journal of Gerontology: Psychological Sciences, 52B,* 73–80.

Rinck, M. (2005). Spatial situation models. In P. Shah & A. Mijake (Eds.), *The Cambridge handbook of visuospatial thinking* (pp. 334–382). Cambridge, England: Cambridge University Press.

Rinck, M., & Bower, G. H. (1995). Anaphora resolution and the focus of attention in situation models. *Journal of Memory and Language, 34,* 110–131.

Rinck, M., & Bower, G. H. (2000). Temporal and spatial distance in situation models. *Memory & Cognition, 28,* 1310–1320.

Rinck, M., & Bower, G. H. (2004). Goal-based accessibility of entities within situation models. In B. Ross (Ed.), *The psychology of learning and motivation* (Vol. 44, pp. 1–33). San Diego, CA: Elsevier.

Rinck, M., Bower, G. H., & Wolf, K. (1998). Distance effects in surface structures and situation models. *Scientific Studies of Reading, 2,* 221–246.

Rinck, M., & Denis, M. (2004). The metrics of spatial distance traversed during mental imagery. *Journal of Experimental Psychology: Learning, Memory, and Cognition, 30,* 1211–1218.

Rinck, M., Hähnel, A., Bower, G. H., & Glowalla, U. (1997). The metrics of spatial situation models. *Journal of Experimental Psychology: Learning, Memory, and Cognition, 23,* 622–637.

Rinck, M., Williams, P., Bower, G. H., & Becker, E. S. (1996). Spatial situation models and narrative understanding: Some generalizations and extensions. *Discourse Processes, 21,* 23–55.

van Dijk, T. A., & Kintsch, W. (1983). *Strategies of discourse comprehension.* New York: Academic Press.

Wilson, S. G., Rinck, M., McNamara, T. P., Bower, G. H., & Morrow, D. G. (1993). Mental models and narrative comprehension: Some qualifications. *Journal of Memory and Language, 32,* 141–154.

Zwaan, R. A., Langston, M. C., & Graesser, A. C. (1995). The construction of situation models in narrative comprehension: An event-indexing model. *Psychological Science, 6,* 292–297.

Zwaan, R. A., & Radvansky, G. A. (1998). Situation models in language comprehension and memory. *Psychological Bulletin, 123,* 162–185.

Author Index

Page numbers in *italics* refer to the reference lists at the end of chapter.
Page references followed by *f* indicate figure.
Page references followed by *t* indicate table.
Page references followed by *n* indicate footnote.

Subject Index